impressum

Träger des internationalen literaturfestivals berlin
Peter-Weiss-Stiftung für Kunst und Politik e.V.

Herausgeber
Ulrich Schreiber

Redaktion
Jana Thiele

Biographien
s. Anhang

Fotorechte
Andre Lottmann

Lektorat
Beatrice Faßbender
Anouschka Urrejola

Übersetzung der Biographien ins Englische
Katy Derbyshire
Cathy Lara
Kathleen Noreisch

Korrektorat
Bettina Baer
Tom Bantock
Katy Derbyshire
Reinald Gußmann
David Wilby

Gestaltung
Veruschka Goetz mit Anika Grebe

Satz
Anika Grebe

Titelgestaltung
Veruschka Goetz

Titelfoto
»Poema«, Ersi Sotiropoulos

Titelzitat unter Verwendung des Gedichts
»Letter to John Fuller« von James Fenton

Verlag
Vorwerk 8
www.verlag-vorwerk8.de

Druck
druckhaus köthen

Papier
Holzfreies Salzer-Werkdruck, 1,5-faches Volumen, 100g/qm, bläulich-weiß, gefertigt von Salzer Papier GmbH, St. Pölten, geliefert durch Geese Papier GmbH, Hamburg

Bindung
Kunst- und Verlagsbuchbinderei Leipzig

Wir danken Salzer Papier und Geese Papier für ihre großzügige Unterstützung.

SALZER PAPIER GMBH

Geese Papier

ISBN 3-930916-64-9

3. internationales literaturfestival berlin

inhaltsverzeichnis
Content

literaturen der welt | 010

kaleidoskop | 078

internationale kinder- und jugendliteratur | 156

fokus griechenland | 188

gäste des DAAD berlin | 210

scritture giovani | 226

reflections | 230

vorwort
Ulrich Schreiber

Willkommen

zum 3. internationalen literaturfestival berlin !

Nach den Jahren des Aufbaus unseres Projekts und den ersten beiden Realisationen können wir nun das Programm des 3. ilb, wie es intern bei uns heißt, vorlegen. Dies ist ein kleines Wunder in diesen ökonomisch schwierigen Zeiten, aber vielleicht auch ein Zeichen der Ermutigung für andere, dass mit Enthusiasmus, Wille und guten Ideen heutzutage doch noch etwas zu bewegen ist, dass diese Haltungen und Energien doch überzeugender sind als Nörgelei, Neid, Eifersucht oder routinierte Bedenkenträgerei.

Ich spreche von Enthusiasmus. Auch wenn manche im Enthusiasmus nur Besessenheit erkennen können, glaube ich doch, dass es einer Verbindung von Vision und emotionaler Energie bedarf, um gegen die Macht der Gewohnheit im kulturellen Bereich etwas Neues Wirklichkeit werden zu lassen. Auf Kleinmütigkeit kann die Kultur verzichten, auf Enthusiasmus bestimmt nicht.

Aber auch notwendig will uns das Festival erscheinen. Notwendig, weil wir zutiefst davon überzeugt sind, dass Literatur, nach Inhalt und Form, menschliche Erfahrungen vermittelt, wie vielleicht keine Kunstform sonst. Trotz der universalen Vorherrschaft medialer und technischer Bilder bleibt die Sprache unsere wertvollste Verständigungs- und Widerstandsdimension dort, wo uns Verflachung und Kommerzialisierung an der Wahrnehmung der Welt hindern. Angesichts der Globalisierung müssen wir uns den Raum und die Zeit bewahren und neu erobern, die Erfahrungen vieler Sprachen, Traditionen und Kulturen zugänglich zu machen – nicht medial gefiltert, sondern gerade in Form authentischer Stimmen und Äußerungen. Eine Globalisierung, die kulturellen Realitäten gerecht werden will, muss auch mit der Erweiterung und Bereicherung von Welterfahrung einhergehen. Der Prozess der Globalisierung darf ja nicht nur heißen, dass die Welt überall gleichen Normen und Standards unterworfen wird, sondern muss bedeuten, dass sie eine Intensivierung der geistigen Verständigung, des Austauschs von kreativ gewendeten Erfahrungen möglich macht. Nur so kann sie uns helfen, den Reichtum der Verschiedenheit wahrzunehmen, anzuerkennen, kritisch zu reflektieren und auch zu genießen. Es geht bei diesem Festival um die Notwendigkeit freier, weltoffener Foren in literarischer Vielstimmigkeit. Das vielfältige Atmen der Welt vernehmbar zu machen, kann entscheidend dazu beitragen, eine Hauptstadt tatsächlich zu einer Weltmetropole zu machen. In diesem Geist haben wir uns bemüht, das Festival vorzubereiten.

Die überzeugenden Elemente der vergangenen Festivals haben wir beibehalten, so die unabhängige Jury des Programms »Literaturen der Welt«, die verschiedene Kompetenzen und Sensibilitäten vereint, sodann die beiden weiteren Hauptprogramme »Kaleidoskop« und »Internationale Kinder- und Jugendliteratur«, das intensiviert und erweitert wurde, sowie die bewährte Art, Lyrik- und Prosa-Autoren auf dem höchstmöglichen Niveau in konzentrierter Atmosphäre mithilfe von herausragenden Schauspielern und Moderatoren zu präsentieren. Es gelang zudem, neben dem Festival-Katalog den dritten Band der »Berliner Anthologie« herauszubringen. Die allseits hochgelobte Gedichtsammlung wurde dieses Mal nicht von einem belesenen Individuum, sondern von einigen der eingeladenen Autoren zusammengestellt wurde.

Wir haben wiederum versucht, aus den Kritiken zu lernen, indem wir auf manches verzichtet und anderes neu oder stärker akzentuiert haben. Zudem haben wir erstmals im Programm die Veranstaltungsreihe »Erinnerung, sprich«, die einlädt, bekannte und nahezu unbekannte Texte großer Autoren wieder oder erstmals zu hören.

Insgesamt, so glauben wir, bietet dieses Festival ein hochattraktives Programm. Neben den genannten drei Hauptprogrammen findet sich wiederum ein Länderschwerpunkt, der mit Griechenland dank der Unterstützung der Griechischen Kulturstiftung, dem Kulturministerium Griechenlands und Olympic Airways eine markante Farbe ins Festival bringen wird. Mit drei weiteren großen Festivals in Europa, die jährlich in Mantova, Hay in Wales und Molde in Norwegen stattfinden, bieten wir jungen Autoren in der Sparte »Scritture Giovani« die Möglichkeit, auch einem ausländischen Publikum bekannt zu werden.

Wir danken unseren vielen Unterstützern, die uns erst die Möglichkeit gaben, die gute Idee erneut umzusetzen, allen voran der Kulturstiftung des Bundes, die uns schon im vergangenen Jahr eine großzügige Förderung für das diesjährige Festival zusagte. Wir danken dem Auswärtigen Amt und dem Bundesministerium für wirtschaftliche Zusammenarbeit und Entwicklung sowie der Stiftung Preußische Seehandlung für ihre Unterstützung. Zudem danken wir den vielen Personen und Institutionen, die bei der Vorbereitung im In- und Ausland geholfen haben. Wiederum sind an erster Stelle Martin Mooij und Frank Berberich zu nennen sowie Michi Strausfeld, Ray-Güde Mertin und Hans Hütt. Markus Hayn und Tobias Willemeit danken wir für die Art Direction, Veruschka Götz für die Gestaltung des Katalogs (ihr haben wir auch unser Logo zu verdanken), Rebecca Horn für ihren Plakatentwurf, Amelie Deuflhard für die freundschaftliche Kooperation mit den sophiensæle n, Hermann Beil und Claus Peymann, Bernd Willms und Bettina Schültke, Thomas Ostermeier und Tobias Veit sowie Volker Hesse für ihre Gastfreundschaft, die uns erlaubt, in ihren Theatern die Autoren aus aller Welt vorzustellen – und zu feiern. Jürgen Michalski sei dank für seine jahrelange Unterstützung des Festivals mit werbewirksamen Ideen und Gestaltungsentwürfen und last but not least Eleftherios Ikonomou für die produktive Zusammenarbeit mit der Griechischen Kulturstiftung.

Dem Festival gelang es wiederum, Botschaften und ausländische Kulturinstitute, Hotels und Sponsoren aus der Wirtschaft zu gewinnen. Diese können hier nicht vollständig aufgezählt werden, aber einige möchte ich doch neben den bereits genannten noch hervorheben: DER SPIEGEL sponserte in großzügigster Weise Anzeigen, die Firma MIM den Auftritt auf einer großen Medienwand, die argonauten teilsponserten unser wunderbares Büro am Hackeschen Markt, nexum den website-Auftritt, TOTAL Deutschland, die Dresdner Bank und RANDOM HOUSE Geldbeiträge, Skoda den Shuttle-Service, illycaffé das Projekt Scritture Giovani, Vöslauer Mineralwasser und die Berliner Kindl Brauerei Getränke, Myllykowski Sales GmbH, Geese Papier und die Salzer Papier GmbH Papier. Wir danken naturgemäß auch den Kooperationspartnern und Freunden des Festivals für die vielfältige moralische und sachliche Unterstützung.

Mein großer Dank gilt auch dieses Jahr den Übersetzern, die mit ihrer Arbeit erst die Basis dafür schaffen, dass wir andere Literaturen überhaupt verstehen können. Vor allem aber danke ich allen Mitarbeiterinnen und Mitarbeitern sowie den zahlreicher gewordenen Praktikantinnen und Praktikanten, die keine Mühe scheuten, das Festival mit auf das Niveau zu bringen, das es heute hat.

Wir hoffen, dass unsere Gäste und ihr Publikum intensive, erfahrungsreiche, vergnügliche, intellektuell und ästhetisch anregende und auch streitsame Zeiten miteinander verbringen werden.

Ulrich Schreiber

foreword

Ulrich Schreiber

Welcome

to the 3rd international literature festival berlin.

After years setting up our project and the first two actual festivals, we are proud to present the programme of the 3rd ilb, as we call it internally. This is a small miracle in these economically troubled times, but perhaps also a signal to encourage others that it is still possible to get something done nowadays: with enthusiasm, willpower and good ideas. We would like to prove that these attitudes and efforts are more effective than grumbling, envy, jealousy or routine expressions of doubt.

What I am talking about is enthusiasm. Even if there are some who mistake enthusiasm for obsession, I believe that what we need to create something new against the force of habit in the cultural world is a combination of vision and emotional energy. Culture can do without faint-heartedness, but not by any means without enthusiasm.

But we would also like to think that the festival is necessary. Necessary because we are absolutely convinced that literature imparts, according to content and form, human experiences as perhaps no other art form can. In spite of the universal domination of medial and technical images, language remains our most valuable dimension of communication and resistance, wherever superficiality and commercialisation hinder us from grasping the world. In the face of globalisation, we have to preserve and reclaim space and time to make the experience of many languages, traditions and cultures accessible, not filtered through media, but in the very form of authentic voices and statements. A globalisation which aims to do justice to cultural realities must also be accompanied by an expansion and enrichment of world experience. The process of globalisation cannot simply mean that the world is subjected to the same norms and standards everywhere, but must also make an intensification of intellectual communication possible, an exchange of creatively appraised experiences. This is the only way that it can help us to perceive, recognise, critically reflect and also enjoy the wealth of diversity. This festival is all about the necessity of free, open-minded forums in a literary chorus of many different voices. Making the diverse spirit of the world tangible can play a decisive role in turning a capital city into a global metropolis. It is in this spirit that we have tried to organise the festival.

We have kept the convincing elements of the past festivals, such as the independent jury of the programme »Literatures of the World«, which unites differing competencies and sensibilities. In addition to this we have kept the other two main programmes, »Kaleidoscope« and »International Children's and Young People's Literature«, the latter having been intensified and extended, and have maintained presenting authors of poetry and prose, at the highest possible level, in a concentrated atmosphere with the help of actors, actresses and presenters.

We have also been able to publish the third volume of the »Berlin Anthology« alongside the festival catalogue. The highly-praised poetry collection, which for once has been compiled not by one well-read individual but by several of the invited authors themselves.

We have done our best to learn from criticism by giving up some aspects, and accentuating others differently or more strongly. We also have a new series of events in the programme, »Speak, Memory«, which invites visitors to hear famous and almost unknown texts by great authors once again, or for the very first time.

All in all, we are convinced that this festival offers a highly attractive programme. Alongside the three main programmes listed we will be placing an emphasis on one particular country – Greece – which will bring an unmistakable touch of colour into the festival, thanks to the support of the Greek Cultural Foundation, the Greek Ministry of Culture and Olympic Airways. In cooperation with three further large festivals in Europe which take place – naturally on a yearly basis – in Mantova, Hay in Wales and Molde in Norway, we are able to offer young authors the possibility to become known to an international audience with the programme »Scritture Giovani«.

We would like to thank our many supporters who have made it possible for us to put our good idea into practice, first and foremost the Kulturstiftung des Bundes, which guaranteed us a generous grant for this year's festival as early as last year. We would like to thank the Auswärtiges Amt and the Bundesministerium für wirtschaftliche Zusammenarbeit und Entwicklung, along with the Stiftung Preußische Seehandlung, for their support. We would also like to thank the many individuals and institutions in Germany and abroad who helped arrange the festival. Once again Martin Mooij and Frank Berberich are at the top of the list, as well as Michi Strausfeld, Ray-Güde Mertin and Hans Hütt. Thanks to Markus Hayn and Tobias Willemeit for the Art Direction, Veruschka Götz for the design of the catalogue (our logo is also of her doing), Rebecca Horn for her poster design, Amelie Deuflhard for the friendly cooperation with the sophiensæle, Hermann Beil and Claus Peymann, Bernd Willms and Bettina Schültke, Thomas Ostermeier and Tobias Veit, as well as Volker Hesse, for their hospitality, which enables us to introduce authors from across the globe in their theatres – and to celebrate them. Praise be to Jürgen Michalski for his longstanding support of the festival with ideas for publicity and design and, last but not least, thanks to Eleftherios Ikonomou for the productive cooperation with the Greek Cultural Foundation.

The festival has also been able to gain support from embassies and foreign cultural institutes, hotels and business sponsors. These are too numerous to list here, but I would like to name some of them specifically alongside those already mentioned: DER SPIEGEL most generously sponsored advertisements; MIM financed our appearance on a large media screen; die argonauten part-sponsored our wonderful office at Hackescher Markt; nexum the web appearance; TOTAL Deutschland, Dresdner Bank and RANDOM HOUSE donated sums of money; Skoda the shuttle service; illycaffé sponsored the project Scritture Giovani; Vöslauer Mineralwasser and the Berliner Kindl Brauerei have donated drinks; Myllykowski Sales GmbH, Geese Papier and the Salzer Papier GmbH paper. Naturally, we would also like to thank the cooperation partners and friends of the festival for their diverse moral and material support.

I would like to express my special gratitude to the translators once again this year, who create the basis for us all to be able to understand other literatures in the first place with their work. But most of all I thank all my co-workers and the larger than ever number of student volunteers, who have spared no pains to bring the festival up to the level of quality it has today.

We hope that our guests and their audiences will spend an intensive, experience-rich, pleasurable, intellectually and aesthetically stimulating, but also disputative time together.

Ulrich Schreiber

literaturen der welt

juan gustavo cobo borda | kolumbien
adolfo castañón
eduardo chirinos
darío jaramillo agudelo

alberto manguel | kanada | frankreich
anita desai
jabbar yassin hussin
susan swan

abdelwahab meddeb | tunesien | frankreich
mohammed bennis
lorand gaspar
josé maría ridao

martin mooij | niederlande
remco campert
clara janés
yôko ogawa

ljudmila petruschewskaja | russland
olga schamborant
viktorija tokarjewa
tatjana tolstaja

ilma rakusa | schweiz
gennadij ajgi
lászló darvasi
ryszard krynicki

véronique tadjo | elfenbeinküste | südafrika
fatou keïta
leïla marouane
lewis nkosi

shashi tharoor | indien
romesh gunesekera
lee siegel
o. v. vijayan

yvonne vera | simbabwe
achmat dangor
witi ihimaera
josé manuel prieto

eliot weinberger | usa
nuala ní dhomhnaill
semezdin mehmedinović
alberto ruy sánchez

herbert wiesner | deutschland
lászló márton
michèle métail
dieter wellershoff

gennadij ajgi
mohammed bennis
remco campert
adolfo castañón
eduardo chirinos
achmat dangor
lászló darvasi
anita desai
lorand gaspar
romesh gunesekera
jabbar yassin hussin
witi ihimaera
clara janés
darío jaramillo agudelo
fatou keïta
ryszard krynicki
leïla marouane
lászló márton
semezdin mehmedinović
michèle métail
nuala ní dhomhnaill
lewis nkosi
yôko ogawa
josé manuel prieto
josé maría ridao
alberto ruy sánchez
olga schamborant
lee siegel
susan swan
viktorija tokarjewa
tatjana tolstaja
o. v. vijayan
dieter wellershoff

gennadij ajgi
biography

The lyric poet Gennadi Aygi was born in 1934 as Gennadi Nikolayevich Lisin in Shaimursino in what today is the Chuvash Republic. He belongs to the Chuvash ethnic minority, an ethnic group distantly related to the Huns. His assumed Chuvash name means »he over there«, »the same one«.
His first poems in the 50's were published in the Chuvash language. The volume of poetry with which Gennadi Aygi wanted to conclude his studies in 1957, at the famous Gorki Literature Institute in Moscow, was declined. Inspired by his friend, the Russian poet Boris Pasternak, Gennadi Aygi has written exclusively in Russian since 1960 – in an attempt to use language to overcome his outsider position. In 1964 he was nevertheless banned from publication; this lasted for about 25 years. Despite this isolation Gennadi Aygi, who Roman Jakobson referred to as the greatest living Russian poet, soon made himself a name for himself in Germany and France. In Germany, the 1971 volume »Beginn der Lichtung« (t: Beginning of the Clearing) secured his position as an acclaimed poet. He has translated Dante and Lorca, Mayakovsky and Walt Whitman into his native language and he is editor of an anthology of Chuvash poetry. His poems have been published in 23 countries, translated into 44 languages and have received numerous prizes including – the lyric poetry prize of the Académie Française (1972), the Petrarca-Prize (1993), and the Boris Pasternak Prize (2000).
His poetry draws upon the Chuvash folk tradition and is rooted in deep orthodox faith. A multitude of literary influences can also be discerned in his work. These include French symbolists like Baudelaire and Rimbaud, and the Russian futurists around Mayakovsky. Characteristic of Aygi's composition principle is the extreme reduction and intensification of language, which has been made possible by breaking open classical poetical forms: Aygi is not interested in describing the world, but in »abstractly making phenomena in the world absolute by means of the poet«. He adds: »My works are not symbols, metaphors or allegories. My work is about being woken up by a piercing light, where a human pike – the word – intentionally becomes unclear, where the human being is reconciled with nature and the universe.«

Beginn der Lichtung
Suhrkamp
Frankfurt a. M., 1971
[Ü: Karl Dedecius]
Aus Feldern Rußland
Suhrkamp
Frankfurt a. M., 1991
[Ü: Felix Philipp Ingold]
Gruß dem Gesang
Rainer, Berlin, 1992
[Ü: Felix Philipp Ingold]
Veronikas Heft
Insel, Frankfurt a. M., 1993
[Ü: Felix Philipp Ingold]
Mit Gesang: Zur Vollendung
Ausgewählte Werke Bd. 1
edition per procura
Wien, 1995
[Ü: Felix Philipp Ingold]
Blätter in den Wind
Ausgewählte Werke Bd. 2
edition per procura
Wien, 1998
[Ü: Felix Philipp Ingold u. a.]
Wind vorm Fenster
Erker, St. Gallen, 1998
[Ü: Felix Philipp Ingold]

Der Lyriker Gennadij Ajgi wurde 1934 als Gennadij Nikolajewitsch Lisin in Schaimursino in der heutigen Republik Tschuwaschien geboren. Er gehört der ethnischen Minderheit der Tschuwaschen an, einer Volksgruppe, die entfernt mit den Hunnen verwandt ist. Sein angenommener tschuwaschischer Name bedeutet soviel wie »der dort«, »der selbige«. Seine ersten Gedichte in den fünfziger Jahren erschienen in tschuwaschischer Sprache. Der Gedichtband, mit dem Gennadij Ajgi 1957 sein Studium am berühmten Gorkij-Literaturinstitut in Moskau abschließen wollte, wurde abgelehnt. Durch den Dichterfreund Boris Pasternak angeregt, schrieb er seit 1960 ausschließlich auf Russisch – ein Versuch, die Ausgrenzung sprachlich zu überwinden. Doch schon 1964 erhielt er Publikationsverbot, das rund 25 Jahre gelten sollte. Trotz der Isolation war Gennadij Ajgi, den Roman Jakobson als den größten lebenden russischen Dichter bezeichnet hat, in Deutschland und Frankreich schon bald ein Begriff. 1971 wurde mit er dem Band »Beginn der Lichtung« in Deutschland zum vielbeachteten Lyriker. Er übersetzte Dante und Lorca, Majakowski und Walt Whitman in seine Muttersprache und ist Herausgeber einer Anthologie tschuwaschischer Lyrik.
Seine Gedichte erschienen in 23 Ländern, wurden in 44 Sprachen übersetzt und mit zahlreichen Preisen ausgezeichnet, unter anderem mit dem Lyrikpreis der Académie Française (1972), dem Petrarca-Preis (1993) und dem Boris Pasternak-Preis (2000).
Seine Dichtung speist sich aus tschuwaschischer Volksüberlieferung und wurzelt in einem tiefempfundenen orthodoxen Glauben. Zugleich lassen sich eine Vielzahl von literarischen Vorbildern in seinem Werk ausmachen. Hierzu gehören neben den französischen Symbolisten wie Baudelaire und Rimbaud die russischen Futuristen um Majakowski. Charakteristisches Kompositionsprinzip Ajgis ist die durch Aufbrechen klassischer dichterischer Formen möglich gewordene extreme Verkürzung und Verdichtung der Sprache: Es gehe ihm nicht um die Beschreibung der Welt, so Ajgi, sondern um die »abstrahierte Verabsolutierung von Welterscheinungen durch den Dichter«. Er sagt weiter: »Meine Arbeiten sind keine Symbole, keine Metaphern, keine Allegorien. Meine Arbeit ist Erwachen durch ein schrilles Licht, wo eine menschliche Spitze – das Wort – zum Dunstkreis wird, wo sich der Mensch mit der Natur und dem Universum vereinigt.«

То, что вызывает стихи... Это, очевидно, находится между „жалобами" и „молитвой", и желательно, чтобы первых было меньше, а вторая была бы скорее благодарственной, чем просительной.

Геннадий Айги

mohammed bennis

biography

Mohammed Bennis was born in Fès, Morocco in 1948. Even at an early age he was interested in literature, particularly lyrical poetry. During his studies at the Department of Philosophy in Fès he began corresponding with the Syrian poet Adonis (Ali Ahmad Said), who published Bennis's first poems in 1969. Since then numerous other collections of verse and essays have followed, not – as is so often the case in the Maghreb – in French, but in Arabic. Bennis's relationship to French culture is ambivalent. While he rejects the ideology of francophone policy – which for him represents a form of colonizing globalization – he does hold the French language in very high regard: »As a modern Arab poet I am committed to French culture and its modernity. The French language was the home of a poetic revolution and it gave my Arabic language a poetic strength, more valuable than any of the other modern languages.«
This close relationship, on which Arab poets are especially dependent if they want to be read outside of their own culture, is reflected in the translations of Bennis's own works. Several of his collections of poems have already been translated into French; among them »Le don du vide« (1992), for which he received the Moroccan literary award »Grand prix du livre« in 1993. In addition, Bennis has made a name for himself as the Arabic translator of Abdelwahab Meddeb, who writes in French, as well as the French poet Bernard Noël. Meddeb, for his part, translated Bennis's poems into French. In Germany, Bennis's poems can be found in two anthologies: »Zwischen Zauber und Zeichen – Moderne arabische Lyrik von 1945 bis heute« (2000, t: Between Signs and Magic – Modern Arab Lyric from 1945 to the Present) and »Die Farbe der Ferne« (2000, t: The Color of Distance). Bennis's efforts are aimed at the modernization of Arab poetry. He ranks among the most important voices in Arab literature. His writing is characterised by elements borrowed from traditional mysticism and surrealism. The result, that so distinguishes his verse, is at once radically succinct yet with several layers of meaning. In addition to his literary work, Bennis has always been active on a politico-cultural level. In 1974 he founded the magazine »Ath-Thaqâfa al-Djadîdah« (t: The New Cultures), which played an active role in the cultural life of Morocco until it was banned in 1984 after unrest in Casablanca. In 1985, together with university professors and writers, he established the poetry-based publishing house »Dâr Tubqâl«. In 1996 he became a founding member and president of »Maison de la Poésie« in Casablanca. Bennis lives in Rabat where he has taught Literature at the university since 1980.

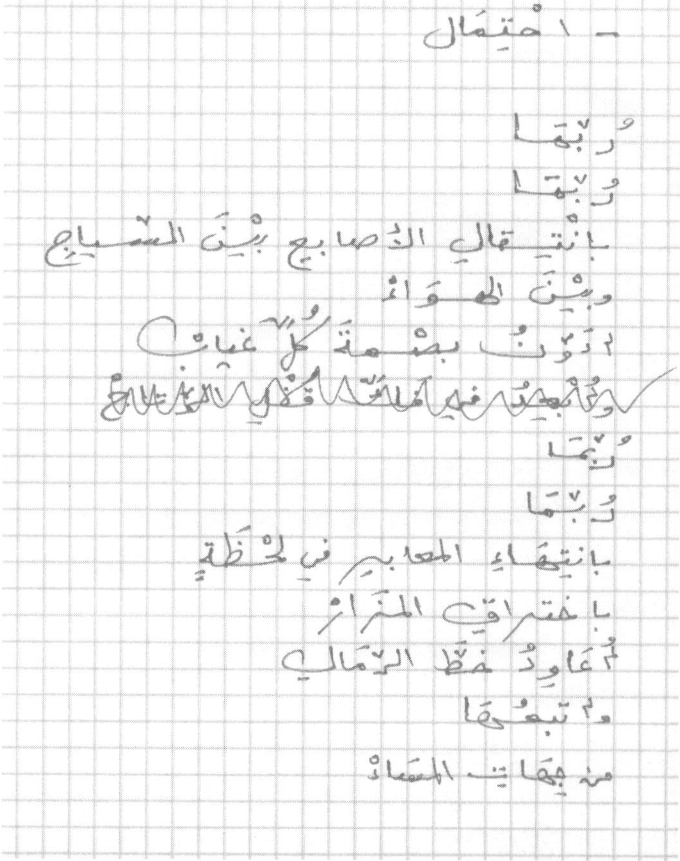

Chant pour un jardin de l'eau
Les patits classiques du grand pirate
Paris, 1999
[Ü: Abdellatif Laâbi]

Le don du vide
l'Escampette
Bordeaux, 1999
[Ü: Bernard Noël]

Désert au bord de la lumière
Al Manar, Neuilly, 1999
[Ü: Abdelwahab Meddeb]

Fleuve entre des funérailles
l'Escampette
Bordeaux, 2003
[Ü: Mostafa Nissabouri]

Mohammed Bennis wurde 1948 in Fès, Marokko, geboren. Schon früh entwickelte sich sein Interesse für Literatur, insbesondere für Lyrik. Während seines Studiums an der Philosophischen Fakultät in Fès begann er eine Korrespondenz mit dem syrischen Lyriker Adonis (eigentlich Ali Ahmad Said), der Bennis' erste Gedichte 1969 veröffentlichte. Bis heute folgten zahlreiche weitere Lyrik- sowie Essaybände – nicht, wie so oft im Maghreb, in französischer, sondern in arabischer Sprache. Bennis' Beziehungen zur französischen Kultur sind ambivalent. Während er die Ideologie der politischen Frankophonie, für ihn eine Form kolonialisierender Globalisierung, ablehnt, schätzt er doch die französische Sprache selbst sehr: »Als moderner arabischer Dichter bin ich der französischen Kultur und ihrer Modernität verpflichtet. Die französische Sprache war der Ort einer dichterischen Revolution, und sie hat meiner arabischen Sprache eine poetische Kraft gegeben, so wertvoll wie keine der ganzen Moderne.« Diese enge Beziehung spiegelt sich in den Übersetzungen der eigenen Werke wieder, auf die arabische Dichter in besonderer Weise angewiesen sind, wollen sie außerhalb ihres eigenen Kulturkreises gelesen werden. Bereits mehrere von Bennis' Gedichtsammlungen liegen in französischer Übersetzung vor, darunter »Le don du vide« (1992), für die er 1993 den marokkanischen Literaturpreis Grand prix du livre erhalten hatte. Zudem hat sich Bennis selbst als arabischer Übersetzer des französisch schreibenden Abdelwahab Meddeb sowie des französischen Dichters Bernard Noël einen Namen gemacht. Meddeb seinerseits hat Bennis' Gedichte ins Französische übertragen. In Deutschland sind Gedichte von Bennis derzeit in zwei Anthologien zu finden: »Zwischen Zauber und Zeichen. Moderne arabische Lyrik von 1945 bis heute« (2000) und »Die Farbe der Ferne« (2000). Bennis' Bemühungen gelten der Modernisierung der arabischen Dichtung. Er zählt zu den wichtigsten Stimmen der arabischen Literatur. Sein Schreiben ist geprägt durch Anleihen bei der traditionellen Mystik sowie beim Surrealismus. Im Ergebnis zeichnet sich seine Lyrik durch radikale Verknappung bei gleichzeitiger Vervielfältigung der Sinnebenen aus.
Neben seiner schriftstellerischen Tätigkeit hat Bennis stets auch kulturpolitisch gewirkt. 1974 gründete er die Zeitschrift »Ath-Thaqâfa al-Djadîdah« (Ü: Die neuen Kulturen), die eine aktive Rolle im kulturellen Leben Marokkos spielte, bis sie 1984 nach Unruhen in Casablanca verboten wurde. 1985 gründete er mit Hochschulprofessoren und Schriftstellern den auf Lyrik spezialisierten Verlag Dâr Tubqâl. 1996 wurde er Gründungsmitglied und Präsident des »Maison de la Poésie« in Casablanca. Bennis lebt in Rabat, wo er seit 1980 an der Universität Literatur lehrt.

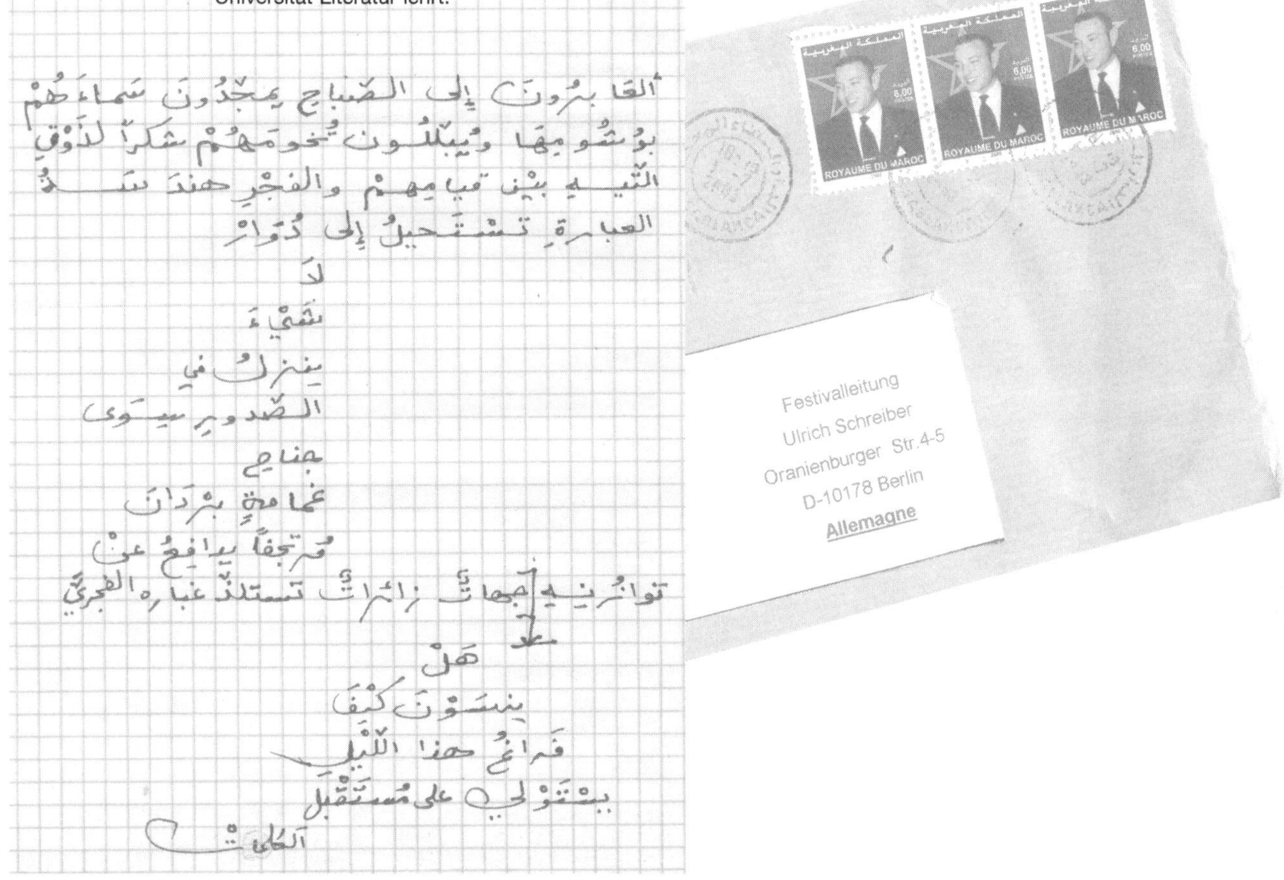

remco campert

biography

Remco Campert was born in The Hague, Netherlands, in 1929. He is the son of the journalist and poet Jan Campert, who was murdered in 1943 in the Neuengamme concentration camp. His mother was the actress Joekie Broedelet. Remco Campert started to write poetry at an early age and published his first book of verse »Vogels vliegen toch« (1951) at the age of 22; the title itself alludes to the fact that the author experiments with new forms.
Together with Rudy Kousbroek, he founded the magazine »Braak«, which helped lay the groundwork for the emergence of the 50's movement. Along with Bert Schierbeek, Gerrit Kouwenaar, Jan G. Elburg and Simon Vinkenoog, they brought about the most radical change in post-war Dutch literature to date. As the publisher of various newspapers and magazines including »Podium« and »Triade«, Remco Campert has significantly influenced the intellectual discourse in his country.
Characteristic of his openness and social involvement is that, unlike other writers of his generation, he made literature accessible to the »uninitiated«. He thus reached people who had never read literature before and became a youth idol.
His writing varies in scale and format. At first glance his poems, novels and stories appear to be easily accessible, but upon second glance they grow more refined and enigmatic. He addresses the shortcomings of life in a relaxed and humorous way. With ironic distance, Campert takes elitist rhetoric and juxtaposes it with immediacy and directness. His work alternates between disillusionment, philanthropy and melancholy, and in the Netherlands has earned him the honorary title of »Dichter« (t: poet), which is also the title of the anthology »Remco Campert – Dichter« published in 1995. Although Campert is primarily very popular as a poet in his native country, his novels, stories and thrice-weekly columns in the »Volkskrant« also reach a wide audience. In his involvement with the Poetry International Festival in Rotterdam, he played a decisive role even early on as a participant, translator, moderator and advisor, and was later made president of the International Advisory Board. In 1997 he co-founded the foundation Poets of all Nations (PAN). To date, although he is considered one of the most important representatives of Dutch poetry, only few of his poems have been translated into German.

Vogels vliegen toch
U. M. Holland
Amsterdam, 1951
Het leven is vurrukkulluk
De Bezige Bij
Amsterdam, 1961
Dichter
De Bezige Bij
Amsterdam, 1995
Ohi, hoho, bang, bang, of het lied van de vrijheid
De Bezige Bij
Amsterdam, 1995
Alle verhalen
De Bezige Bij
Amsterdam, 2001
Beschreven blad
De Bezige Bij
Amsterdam, 2002

Remco Campert wurde 1929 in Den Haag, Niederlande, geboren. Er ist der Sohn des Journalisten und Dichters Jan Campert, der 1943 im KZ Neuengamme ermordet wurde. Seine Mutter war die Schauspielerin Joekie Broedelet. Remco Campert befasste sich schon früh mit Poesie, veröffentlichte als 22-jähriger seinen ersten Lyrikband »Vogels vliegen toch« (1951), der schon ahnen ließ, dass hier ein Autor mit neuen Formen experimentierte. Zusammen mit Rudy Kousbroek gründete er das Magazin »Braak«, das Anschluß an die Bewegung der »Fünfziger« fand. Gemeinsam mit Bert Schierbeek, Gerrit Kouwenaar, Jan G. Elburg und Simon Vinkenoog brachten sie der niederländischen Literatur die bislang radikalste Veränderung der Nachkriegszeit bei. Als Herausgeber verschiedener Zeitschriften und Magazine wie »Podium« und »Triade« beeinflusste Remco Campert maßgeblich den intellektuellen Diskurs in seinem Land.
Seine Offenheit und sein sozialer Anspruch zeigen sich unter anderem darin, dass er, anders als viele Schriftsteller seiner Generation, auch den »Ungeweihten« Zugang zur Literatur ermöglichte. So erreichte er auch Menschen, die sich bislang nicht mit Literatur beschäftigten, und wurde zu einem Idol der Jugend.
Er bedient sich der großen und kleinen Formen gleichermaßen. Seine Gedichte, Romane und Erzählungen präsentieren sich auf den ersten Blick als leicht zugänglich, auf den zweiten aber als raffiniert und hintergründig. Er stellt sich der Auseinandersetzung mit den Unzulänglichkeiten des Lebens auf unverkrampfte, humorvolle Weise. Mit ironischer Distanz setzt Campert das Unmittelbare und Direkte gegen elitäre Rhetorik. Sein Werk changiert dabei zwischen Desillusionierung, Menschenfreundlichkeit und Melancholie. Das hat ihm in den Niederlanden den Ehrentitel »Dichter« eingebracht, wovon auch der Titel des 1995 erschienenen Sammelbandes »Remco Campert – Dichter« zeugt. Obwohl Campert in seiner Heimat vor allem als Lyriker große Popularität genießt, werden auch seine Romane, Erzählungen und die dreimal wöchentlich im »Volkskrant« publizierte Kolumne von einem großen Leserkreis wahrgenommen. Schon früh spielte er eine entscheidende Rolle beim Rotterdamer Poetry International Festival: als Teilnehmer, Übersetzer, Moderator, Berater, später auch als Präsident des International Advisory Board. 1997 war er Mitbegründer der Stiftung Poets of all Nations (PAN). Obwohl er als einer der wichtigsten Vertreter der neuen niederländischen Poesie gilt, sind in Deutschland bisher nur wenige seiner Gedichte übersetzt worden.

The poem makes the poet tick

Remco Campert

adolfo castañón
biography

Adolfo Castañón was born in Mexico City in 1952. He studied literature and philosophy at the autonomous university UNAM and was then engaged in literary research at the Institute for Philology. Since 1975 he has worked for the Mexican publisher Fondo de Cultura Económica (FCE), which he headed from 1985 to 2000. From 1992 to 1997, in cooperation with UNESCO, he directed the project »Periolibros« to publish the poetic and literary masterpieces of modern Iberoamerican writing. Over this period he coordinated the Mexican edition of the complete works of Octavio Paz in 15 volumes, which together with the Spanish »Círculo de Lectores« is published in Barcelona. He has worked as the editorial advisor on 12 Latin American cultural and literary magazines, including »Plural« (Mexico, from 1975), »Gradiva« (Columbia, 1986–89), »Vuelta« (Mexico, 1988–98) and »Letras Libres« (Mexico, since 1999). As guest editor, he has published dossiers on Mexican literature in the French magazine »Nouvelle Revue Française« (2000, 2001).
Adolfo Castañón is also a prolific and gifted writer whose work includes stories, essays, poetry and translations from both English (George Steiner) and French (Jean-Jacques Rousseau) as well as literary criticism. His love of transgression has led him to work with various literary genres like the fable, portrait, parable, legend, fragment and prose poem. His outstanding books of poetry include »La batalla perdurable« (1996, t: The Permanent Fight), a benchmark in Mexican modern prose poetry as well as »Tránsito de Octavio Paz/The Passing of Octavio Paz (1914-1998)«, a poetic-essayistic homage to the winner of the Nobel prize for literature, where the following is elegiacally and concisely stated: »No one knows how to explain his poems: the poet is dead.« He has recently published his collected poetry »La campana y el tiempo«.
»Por el país de Montaigne« (t: Through Montaigne's Country) is the name of his new book of essays, which was reprinted five times between 1995 and 2000. The geographic location of Perigord and the Loire area in France as well as the work of Michel de Montaigne as space and metaphor are his accomplices in his essayistic wanderings.

Por el país de Montaigne
Paidós, Mexiko, 1995
La otra mano del tañedor
Ediciones el Tucán de Virginia
Mexiko, 1996
La batalla perdurable
CNCA-Ediciones El Equilibrista
Mexiko, 1996
Grano de sal
Planeta, Mexiko, 2000
América Sintaxis
Aldus, Mexiko, 2000
Tránsito de Octavio Paz/ The Passing of Octavio Paz (1914-1998)
Mosaic Press
Oakville, Ontario, 2000
[Ü: Beatriz Zeller]

Adolfo Castañón wurde 1952 in Mexiko-Stadt geboren. Es studierte Literatur und Philosophie an der Autonomen Universität UNAM und war danach am Institut für Philologie in der Literaturforschung tätig. Seit 1975 arbeitet er im mexikanischen Verlagshaus Fondo de Cultura Económica (FCE), dessen Geschäftsführung er von 1985 bis 2000 übernahm. Zwischen 1992 und 1997 leitete er u. a. das Projekt »Periolibros« in Zusammenarbeit mit der UNESCO, um eine Ausgabe der literarischen Meisterwerke der iberoamerikanischen Moderne zu erarbeiten. Derzeit koordiniert er die mexikanische Werkausgabe sämtlicher Schriften von Octavio Paz in 15 Bänden, die gemeinsam mit dem spanischen »Círculo de Lectores« in Barcelona herausgegeben wird. Bei zwölf lateinamerikanischen Kultur- und Literaturzeitschriften war er bisher als Redaktionsbeirat tätig, darunter »Plural« (Mexiko, 1975f.), »Gradiva« (Kolumbien, 1986-89), »Vuelta« (Mexiko, 1988-98) und »Letras Libres« (Mexiko, seit 1999). Als Gastherausgeber veröffentlichte er Dossiers über mexikanische Literatur in der französischen Zeitschrift »Nouvelle Revue Française« (2000, 2001).

Adolfo Castañón hat sich auch selbst als Schriftsteller einen Namen gemacht, und zwar u. a. in den Bereichen der Erzählung, Essayistik, Lyrik, der Übersetzung aus dem Englischen (George Steiner) und aus dem Französischen (Jean Jacques Rousseau) sowie der Literaturkritik. Seine Vorliebe für Grenzgänge macht ihn zu einem Virtuosen der literarischen Gattungen, zu denen die Fabel, das Porträt, die Parabel, die Legende, das Fragment und das Prosagedicht gehören. Zu seinen herausragenden Lyrikbänden zählen »La batalla perdurable« (Ü: Der dauerhafte Kampf), der 1996 erschien – ein neuer Höhepunkt in der mexikanischen Tradition moderner Prosagedichte –, sowie »Tránsito de Octavio Paz (1914-1998)«, eine poetisch-essayistische Hommage auf den Literaturnobelpreisträger, in der es elegisch pointiert heißt: »Niemand weiß, wie man seinen Gedichten beibringt, dass der Dichter gestorben ist.« Zuletzt publizierte er gesammelte Gedichte unter dem Titel »La campana y el tiempo«.

»Por el país de Montaigne« (Ü: Durch das Land von Montaigne) nennt sich sein neuer Essayband, der zwischen 1995 und 2000 fünf erweiterte Auflagen erlebte. Sowohl die Landschaften des Perigord und Loiretales in Frankreich als auch das Werk von Michel de Montaigne als Raum und Metapher sind darin die Komplizen seiner essayistischen Rundgänge.

Certain lingüistic atmospheres make a tick to the puet I bring with me.

eduardo chirinos

biography

The poet Eduardo Chirinos was born in the Peruvian capital of Lima in 1960. He was the oldest of five siblings and he grew up in a house without any books. Reflecting on the paradoxical origins of his writing, Eduardo Chirinos laconically muses, »Poetry is a fate which one either accepts or does not.« He studied linguistics and cultural studies at the Catholic University in Lima and completed his doctoral studies in Spanish literature at Rutgers University in New Jersey, the U.S.A. Following several guest professorships in Venezuela and the U.S., he now lives in Missoula, where since 2000 he has taught literature at the University of Montana.

At the age of 17 Chirinos wrote his first poems, which four years later he published in his debut »Cuadernos de Horacio Morell« (1981; t: Notebooks of Horacio Morell) in Lima. Following a South American tradition, Chirinos played with the idea of a notional author, which he eventually concluded with the supposed suicide of Horacio Morell. Over the next 10 years he published seven books of poetry – four in Lima and three in Madrid. But he does not see himself as a prolific writer. According to his view, »every book is the verse of a single poem« that can never be completed. Although Chirinos is considered one of the most important poets of the Peruvian Generación del ochenta (80's generation), he paradoxically stands outside this heterogeneous group of intellectuals, which in realistic moments approximates to the charged jargon of the streets. Chirinos's early poems, by contrast, tended to focus on everyday matters in a calmer, more ironic fashion, while still incorporating dark and melancholic moods and frequently making use of classical elements of form. After a publication pause, five new volumes of poetry appeared between 1998 and 2003, including »El Equilibrista de Bayard Street« (1998, t: The Tightrope Walker of Bayard Street), which he wrote over a period of seven years, as well as »Abecedario del agua« (2000, t: Alphabet of Water) and »Escrito en Missoula« (2003, t: Written in Missoula). His later poems are increasingly influenced by US verse and language. His style becomes more concise and self-ironic, yet does so without dispensing with its central melancholic mood. For his book of poems »Breve historia de la música« (2001, t: A Brief History of Music), Chirinos received Madrid's Premio Casa de América (2001) in the category »innovative Latin American poetry«.

UNA LENTA Y VAGA MÚSICA

¿QUÉ ME LLAMA a escribir poesía? Durante años me he hecho esta pregunta qu —desde el punto de vista lógico— debería ser fácil ser contestada, pues el involucra el oficio al que, para bien o para mal, le he dedicado más de la mitad de mi vida. Ser incapaz de contestarla es, quiero creerlo, un saludable indicio de que voy a dedicarle la otra mitad que me queda. Ahora bien, esta incapacidad (a la que le debo varios libros poemas, ensayos, antologías, traducciones y mi vieja pasión por la enseñanza de la literatura) no me exime de la aproximación a algunas certezas que apuntala aunque sea de manera endeble, mi condición de escritor de poemas. Una de ellas tiene que ver con la música que a veces nos es dado escuchar. Una lenta y vaga música que se desprende de las cosas, de ciertas personas, de algunos recuerdos que provienen de la vida o de los libros (¿hay entre ell alguna diferencia?) que se apoderan de mi oído y, perdónenme el oxímoron, transforman en una visión que reclama convertirse en palabras. Se trata de una sensación física, de un azoro que sólo puede ser resuelto en el acto creativo, es decir (y perdónenme de nuevo el oxímoron) en esa comunión social que es la escritura solitaria de poesía. No estoy hablando aquí de experiencias "poéticas" y "no poéticas"; lo poético (si tal cosas existe) está en la mirada atenta a esa música con la que el mundo desea comunicars con nosotros y a través de nosotros. Tal vez este poema lo explique mejor que yo:

Selected Poems/ Selección poética
Luz Bilingual Publishing
Tarzana, Kalifornien, 1998
[Ü: Gary J. Racz]
Abecedario del agua
Pre-Textos, Valencia, 2000
Epístola a los transeúntes
Fondo Editorial de la Pontificia Universidad Católica del Perú
Lima, 2001
Breve historia de la música
Visor, Madrid, 2001
Escrito en Missoula
Pre-Textos, Valencia, 2003
El Fingidor
Fondo Editorial de la Pontificia Universidad Católica del Perú
Lima, 2003
Derrata del otoño (1978-2002)
Filodecaballos
Guadalajara, 2003

Der Lyriker Eduardo Chirinos wurde 1960 in der peruanischen Hauptstadt Lima geboren. Als ältestes von fünf Geschwistern verbrachte er seine Kindheit in einem Elternhaus, das keine Bücher kannte. »Die Poesie ist ein Schicksal, das man akzeptiert oder nicht«, resümiert Eduardo Chirinos lakonisch, wenn er die paradoxen Ursprünge seines Schreibens reflektiert. Er studierte an der Katholischen Universität von Lima Linguistik und Kulturwissenschaften und promovierte in Hispanischer Literatur an der Rutgers University in New Jersey in den USA. Nach mehreren Gastprofessuren in Venezuela und in den USA lebt er seit 2000 in Missoula, wo er an der University of Montana Literatur unterrichtet.
Chirinos verfaßte mit 17 Jahren die ersten Gedichte, die er vier Jahre später in dem Debütband »Cuadernos de Horacio Morell« (1981, Ü: Hefte von Horacio Morell) in Lima veröffentlichte. Chirinos spielte dabei, einer südamerikanischen Tradition folgend, mit einer fingierten Autorenpersönlichkeit, die er später mit dem vermeintlichen Selbstmord Horacio Morells wieder auflöste. In den folgenden zehn Jahren erschienen weitere sieben Gedichtbände, vier in Lima und drei in Madrid. Dennoch versteht er sich nicht als Vielschreiber. Seinem literarischen Selbstverständnis nach ist »jedes Buch der Vers eines einzigen Gedichts«, das nie vollendet werden kann. Obwohl Chirinos als einer der wichtigsten Dichter der peruanischen Generación del ochenta (Generation der achtziger Jahre) gilt, steht er paradoxerweise doch außerhalb dieser heterogenen Literatengruppe, die sich in realistischen Momenten dem aufgeregten Jargon der Straße annähert. Chirinos' frühe Gedichte dagegen widmen sich dem Alltag eher auf ruhige, ironische Weise, kennen auch dunkle und melancholische Stimmungen und weisen formal oftmals klassische Elemente auf. Nach einer Publikationspause legte er zwischen 1998 und 2003 fünf neue Lyrikbände vor, darunter »El Equilibrista de Bayard Street« (1998, Ü: Der Seiltänzer der Bayard Street), an dem er sieben Jahre geschrieben hat, sowie »Abecedario del agua« (2000, Ü: Alphabet des Wassers) und »Escrito en Missoula« (2003, Ü: In Missoula geschrieben). In diesen späten Gedichten macht sich zunehmend der Einfluss der US-amerikanischen Sprache und Lyrik bemerkbar. Sein Stil wird knapper, auch selbstironischer, ohne jedoch die melancholische Grundstimmung aufzugeben. Für seinen Gedichtband »Breve historia de la música« (2001, Ü: Kleine Musikgeschichte) erhielt Chirinos in der Kategorie »Innovative Lyrik Lateinamerikas« den Madrider Premio Casa de América (2001).

El silencio
invita al silencio.
a la contemplación de las montañas
que no son sino montañas,
a los ríos
que serpean azules como cualquier río.

Nunca pude con el silencio. Nunca
aprendí a escucharlo:
tras su blanca
pared escucho siempre una música.

Una lenta y vaga música
que luego se va sin decir nada.

Eduardo Chirinos

achmat dangor

biography

»I am an African with Asian and Dutch blood in me, I don't know what race I am, and I don't care« – with this description of himself, Achmat Dangor also describes the central themes of his literary work: heritage and a sense of belonging. He was born in an enviroment of Muslim and Indian traditions in Johannesburg, South Africa in 1948, the year that marked the beginning of apartheid in South Africa. As a result of the racial classification, he was considered a »coloured person«. He spoke Afrikaans and Sotho until he started school. Today he writes in English.

Dangor says about himself, »I write because I have to and because I love to; it is the closest I am to having an obsession«, and has committed himself to politics with the same fervor. At the time of his studies, he was a member of the group »Black Thoughts«, whose goal it was to strengthen the black movement through literature, theatre, and music. As a result of this involvement he was »banned« from 1973 to 1979; he was confined to Johannesburg and could not attend any social or political gatherings. In retrospect he sees this as an extremely productive period since it gave him the opportunity to write, even if he had to do secretly.

In the 80's, Dangor, one of the co-founders of the Congress of South African Writers, started to publish books in South Africa which were translated into five languages. His work comprises short stories, books of poetry and to date three novels, one of which, »Kafka's Curse« (1997), was published in German under the title »Kafkas Fluch« (2001). The central figure is a Muslim by birth named Omar Khan, who, as the supposed Jew Oscar Kahn, is married to a white woman. Using more than one voice, Dangor tells of the psychological consequences which emerge when the members of the affected family discover that his identity was a lie.

The novel thereby calls attention to the complex problems which the many ethnic and religious groups in South African society have to struggle with even today. The metamorphosis the hero goes through recalls Kafka as much as an Arabic legend, in which a gardener transforms himself into a tree because he dared to love a princess. Dangor's prose is lyrical and rich in metaphor. It is reminiscent of Salman Rushdie, who has been an influence on Dangor.

At the request of Bishop Tutu, he took over the direction of the newly founded Kagiso Trust, the largest foundation directed by blacks in South Africa, and politics again assumed a larger role in Dangor's life. Dangor was the director of the Nelson Mandela Children's Fund until the end of 2001 and has since then has lived in Johannesburg and New York, where his wife works for the United Nations.

Waiting for Leila
Ravan Press
Johannesburg, 1981
Bulldozer
Ravan Press
Johannesburg, 1983
Exiles Within
COSAW Publishing
Johannesburg, 1989
Z Town Trilogy
Ravan Press
Johannesburg, 1990
Private Voices
COSAW Publishing
Johannesburg, 1992
Kafkas Fluch
Knaus, München, 2001
[Ü: Gerhard Beckmann]
Bitter Fruit
Kwela Press
Kapstadt, 2001

Tick, Tick, Tick.

In the end he goes into the streets
As desperate as the hungry man on the corner,
Only ~~hungrier and~~ greedier-
He will search every sound shape, and
Rummage in the merest shadow
Until he finds that ~~glittering~~ dazzling prize:
A simple, illuminating word.

On good days he discovers one
That is whole, round, pure,
But he dare not ~~ignore~~ pass up
Those other flawed little things,
For they hold the promise
Of truly imagined riches.

There: that woman's laugh,
And the man who watches her mouth
Form its bold music,
The way they greet each other,
The tenderness of a hand half extended
Then quickly hidden behind the back,
One glistening, secretive word describes them:
Desire.

»Ich bin Afrikaner mit asiatischem und holländischem Blut, ich weiß nicht, zu welcher Rasse ich gehöre, und es interessiert mich auch nicht« – mit dieser Selbstcharakterisierung umreißt Achmat Dangor zugleich die zentralen Themen seines literarischen Schaffens: Herkunft und Zugehörigkeit. 1948, in dem Jahr, das den Beginn der Apartheid in Südafrika markiert, kam er in Johannesburg, Südafrika, in einer muslimisch und indisch geprägten Umgebung zur Welt. Der rassistischen Klassifizierung zufolge galt er als »Farbiger«. Bis zu seiner Einschulung sprach er Afrikaans und Sotho, heute schreibt er in Englisch.
Dangor, der von sich sagt: »Ich schreibe, weil ich es muß und weil ich es liebe; es ist das, was einer Obsession für mich am nächsten kommt«, hat sich mit der gleichen Intensität auch der Politik verschrieben. Schon während seines Studiums war er Mitglied der Gruppe »Black Thoughts«, die bestrebt war, durch Literatur, Theater und Musik die Bewegung der Schwarzen zu stärken. Für dieses Engagement wurde er von 1973 bis 1979 »festgesetzt«: Er durfte Johannesburg nicht verlassen und an keinen öffentlichen oder politischen Versammlungen teilnehmen. Eine Zeit, die er rückblickend jedoch als ungeheuer produktiv empfindet, da sie ihm Gelegenheit zum – wenn auch nur heimlichen – Schreiben gegeben hat. In den achtziger Jahren begann Dangor, einer der Mitbegründer des südafrikanischen Schriftstellerkongresses, in Südafrika Bücher zu veröffentlichen, die in fünf Sprachen übersetzt wurden: Kurzgeschichten, Gedichtbände und bislang drei Romane, von denen »Kafka's Curse« (1997) unter dem Titel »Kafkas Fluch« (2001) auf Deutsch erschienen ist. Die zentrale Figur ist der gebürtige Muslime Omar Khan, der als vorgeblicher Jude Oscar Kahn mit einer weißen Frau verheiratet ist. Dangor erzählt mehrstimmig von den psychologischen Konsequenzen, die das Aufdecken dieser Lebenslüge bei den Mitgliedern der betroffenen Familien zeitigt, und verweist damit auf die komplexen Probleme, mit denen die vielfältigen ethnischen und religiösen Gruppen im Miteinander der südafrikanischen Gesellschaft bis heute zu kämpfen haben. Die Metamorphose des Helden greift dabei auf Kafka wie auch auf eine arabische Legende zurück, in der ein Gärtner sich in einen Baum verwandelt, weil er es wagte, eine Prinzessin zu lieben. Dangors Prosa ist lyrisch und reich an Metaphern. Sie zeigt Anklänge an Salman Rushdie, von dem Dangor beeinflusst wurde.
Mit der auf Bitten Bischof Tutus übernommenen Leitung des neugegründeten Kagiso Trust, der größten von Schwarzen geführten Stiftung Südafrikas, nahm die Politik wieder mehr Raum in Dangors Leben ein. Dangor, der bis 2001 Direktor des Nelson Mandela Children's Fund war, lebt seit 2001 in Johannesburg und in New York, wo seine Frau für die Vereinten Nationen arbeitet.

He follows them to Grand Central,
Into the Campbell Apartment,
They drink champagne, and still,
~~Between them,~~ The sacred restraint.

He wonders where and when
Their moment of love will come,
Then struggles: this is wrong,
It is too soft and pliable,
Perhaps he should ask directly:
When is their hour for ~~fornicating~~? fucking?

Achmat Dangor
New York, ~~January~~, 2003.
~~Feb~~
March

lászló darvasi

biography

László Darvasi was born in the small town of Törökszentmiklós near Budapest in 1962. He spent most of his life in Szeged, a university city in the south of the country close to the Serbian border. In 1986 he gained a teaching diploma at the University of Szeged and taught at various elementary schools until 1989. Then he started to write, first as a journalist for a local daily newspaper; today he still writes soccer articles, television reviews and features. In 1990 he co-founded the literary magazine »Pompeji.« Since 1993 he has been the editor of the Budapest weekly newspaper »Élet és Irodalom« (t: Life and Literature). In 1991 Darvasi published his first book of poetry, which was followed by a rapid succession of prose pieces including stories, novellas and the novel »A könnymutatványosok legendája« (1999; t: The Legend of the Tear Showmen). His texts have been translated into German and seven other languages. He has received various awards for his literary work, including the scholarship from the DAAD's Berlin artist's programme (2000). Today Darvasi lives as a freelance writer in Szeged and Budapest.
»The Legend of the Tear Showmen,« which was influenced by the Balkan wars, collects episodes from the years when Turkey occupied Hungary in the 16th and 17th centuries. Within the context of Islamic, Christian and Talmudic written records, historical facts emerge, centering not on history's great figures but on five mysterious figures, who with a rickety vehicle travel through a world which, despite the historical framework, is oddly timeless. They are the tear showmen who travel as show people through the country and cry for those who are suffering. A burlesque joy in narration propels forward a fascinating richness in imagery and an impressive variety of characters and actions, which the author brings together, thereby creating a network of sorrow that is as fairytale-like as it is dreadful. This year Germany has seen the publication of two prose collections in which Darvasi continues to move between realism and fantasy as well as through various time periods while unceasingly speaking out against violence in the world.
In »The Dog-Hunters of Lo-Yang« the author places the idea of totalitarian rule within the context of an imaginary, older China, which in its parable-like quality is suddenly very contemporary. On the other hand, »Getting a Woman« is set against a backdrop which although borrowed from the Bosnian war is nonetheless surreal; the book is about the cruelty of war.

Horger Antal párisban
Holnap K.
Budapest, 1991
Das traurigste Orchester der Welt
Rowohlt, Berlin, 1995
[Ü: Agnes Relle]
Die Legende von den Tränengauklern
Suhrkamp
Frankfurt a. M., 2001
[Ü: Heinrich Eisterer]
Eine Frau besorgen. Kriegsgeschichten
Suhrkamp
Frankfurt a. M., 2003
[Ü: Terézia Mora
Agnes Relle]
Die Hundejäger von Lojang
Suhrkamp
Frankfurt a. M., 2003
[Ü: Heinrich Eisterer]

László Darvasi wurde 1962 in der Kleinstadt Törökszentmiklós in der Nähe von Budapest geboren. Den größten Teil seines Lebens verbrachte er in Szeged, einer Universitätsstadt an der Grenze zu Serbien im Süden des Landes. Dort schloss er 1986 sein Studium an der Pädagogischen Akademie ab und unterrichtete bis 1989 an verschiedenen Grundschulen. Danach begann er zu schreiben, zunächst als Journalist bei einer örtlichen Tageszeitung, für die er noch heute Fußballreportagen, Fernsehkritiken und Feuilletons verfasst. 1990 war er Mitbegründer der Literaturzeitschrift »Pompeji«, seit 1993 ist er Redakteur der Budapester Wochenzeitung »Élet és Irodalom« (Ü: Leben und Literatur). 1991 veröffentlichte Darvasi seinen ersten Gedichtband, seither erschienen in dichter Folge vor allem Prosastücke, darunter Erzählungen, Novellen und der Roman »A könnymutatványosok legendája« (1999; dt. »Die Legende von den Tränengauklern«, 2001). Seine Texte wurden ins Deutsche und in sieben weitere Sprachen übersetzt. Für sein literarisches Werk erhielt er verschiedene Auszeichnungen, unter anderem das Stipendium des Berliner Künstlerprogramms des DAAD (2000). Heute lebt Darvasi als freier Autor in Szeged und Budapest.
Die unter dem Eindruck der Balkankriege entstandene »Legende von den Tränengauklern« versammelt Episoden aus den Jahren der türkischen Besatzung Ungarns im 16. und 17. Jahrhundert. Vor dem Hintergrund islamischer, christlicher und talmudischer Überlieferungen werden historische Tatsachen sichtbar, in deren Mittelpunkt nicht die Großen der Geschichte, sondern fünf geheimnisvolle Gestalten stehen, die mit einem klapprigen Wagen durch eine trotz der historischen Rahmenhandlung merkwürdig zeitlose Welt reisen. Es sind die Tränengaukler, die als Schausteller durch die Lande ziehen und für die leidenden Menschen weinen. Eine burleske Erzählfreude treibt dabei einen faszinierenden Bilderreichtum und eine beeindruckende Personen- und Handlungsvielfalt voran, die der Autor zu einem ebenso märchenhaften wie schrecklichen Netz aus Trauer verflicht. In Deutschland sind in diesem Jahr zwei Prosasammlungen erschienen, mit denen sich Darvasi weiterhin im Fluss zwischen Realismus und Phantastik sowie quer durch den Strom der Zeiten bewegt und unermüdlich gegen die Gewalt in der Welt anschreibt: In »Die Hundejäger von Loyang« zeichnet der Autor das Bild der totalitären Herrschaft im imaginären China alter Zeiten, das in seiner Parabelhaftigkeit plötzlich ganz und gar gegenwärtig wird. »Eine Frau besorgen« hingegen setzt sich vor einer dem Bosnienkrieg entlehnten, immer wieder aber auch surrealen Kulisse mit der Grausamkeit des Krieges auseinander.

anita desai

biography

Anita Desai (originally Anita Mazumdar) was born to a German mother and an Indian father in Mussoorie, India, in 1937. When she was a child, German was spoken at home and Hindi outside of the family. But the language she learned to read and write was English, it is also the language in which she publishes her work. Very early on she set her heart on being a writer and published her first short story at the age of 9. After studying English at the University of New Delhi, she completely dedicated herself to writing. She has published novels, short stories, and children's books.

Anita Desai belongs to a generation of Indian authors for whom publishing in English was an experiment. That only changed in 1980 with the success of Salman Rushdie's »Midnight's Children«. Anita Desai's novels are mostly set against the background of a big city middle-class environment and focus on people, who, after the end of colonial rule, are trying to establish their lives anew, or live in a world that is no longer stable. The novels are snapshots of Indian life, which revolve around everyday relationships, the clash between traditional ways of life and power structures, as well as isolation and the longing for love; at the same time they present nuance-filled explorations of the soul. For instance »Fire on the Mountain« is about the isolation felt by an older woman and her solitary great granddaughter. Desai also frequently plays with the perspective of the social outsider or the foreigner to expose Western stereotypes about India; this is the case in »Baumgartner's Bombay«, the story of a Jewish immigrant family, and in »Journey to Ithaca« (1995).

Desai says that she writes to show what is fundamentally important, to discover the truth which has been covered up by so-called reality. If, early in her career, Desai still based her work on classic British and Russian writers like E. M. Forster, Virginia Woolf, Chekhov and Dostoyevski, later she increasingly took the concentration and intensity of poetry as her model. Her prose is concise and clear; it is characterised by a certain soberness and distance from the fictional events. Anita Desai has received several prizes and has been nominated three times for the Booker Prize. She lives in India and the U.S., where she teaches Creative Writing at the Massachusetts Institute of Technology.

Berg im Feuer
List, München, 1986
[Ü: Helga Pfetsch]
Baumgartners Bombay
Goldmann, München, 1993
[Ü: Peter Torberg]
Im hellen Licht des Tages
Lübbe
Bergisch Gladbach, 1996
[Ü: Ellen Krahe]
Reise ins Licht
Limes, München, 1996
[Ü: Regina Schneider]
Fasting, Feasting
Vintage, London, 2000
Spiele in der Dämmerung
Edition Kappa
München, 2001
[Ü: Helga Pfetsch;
Utta Roy-Seifert]

Once I was taught the letters at school, I found that by putting them down on paper and making words and sentences, I could give the chaotic, fragmented experience of life a shape and form that could be contemplated and understood. After that no experience, no sensation seemed complete till I had "shaped" it on paper. It is like an added sense, or dimension, to life and to lose it would mean becoming helpless, incomplete and unfulfilled.

Reading too makes sense of life and the world in the same way. I have always surrounded myself with books and since childhood wanted to live in the world of books.

Anita Desai wurde 1937 unter dem Namen Anita Mazumdar als Tochter einer Deutschen und eines Inders in Mussoorie, Indien, geboren. In ihrer Kindheit wurde zu Hause Deutsch und außerhalb der Familie Hindi gesprochen. Die Sprache, in der sie lesen und schreiben lernte, war jedoch Englisch – die Sprache, in der sie bis heute ihre Werke veröffentlicht. Ihr Ziel, Schriftstellerin zu werden, fasste Anita Desai früh ins Auge: Mit neun Jahren veröffentlichte sie ihre erste Kurzgeschichte. Nach dem Studium der Englischen Literatur an der Universität von Neu Delhi widmete sie sich dann ganz dem Schreiben. Sie hat Romane, Kurzgeschichten und Kinderbücher veröffentlicht.

Anita Desai gehört einer Generation indischer Autoren an, für die es noch keine Selbstverständlichkeit darstellte, auf Englisch zu publizieren. Dies änderte sich erst 1980 mit dem Erfolg von Salman Rushdies »Midnight's Children«. Im Zentrum der Romane von Anita Desai, die meist im großstädtischen Mittelschichtsmilieu angesiedelt sind, stehen Menschen, die nach dem Ende der Kolonialherrschaft versuchen, zu einer neuen, eigenen Ordnung zu finden oder sich in ihrer brüchig gewordenen Welt zu behaupten. Es sind Momentaufnahmen des indischen Lebens, die um familiäre Beziehungen, die Auseinandersetzung mit Traditionen und Machtstrukturen, um Vereinsamung und die Sehnsucht nach Liebe kreisen, zugleich aber auch nuancenreiche Erkundungen von Seelenlandschaften darstellen. »Fire on the Mountain« (1977; dt. »Berg im Feuer«, 1986) beispielsweise beschreibt die Isolation einer alten Frau und ihrer einzelgängerischen Urenkelin. Oft spielt Desai auch mit der Perspektive des sozialen Außenseiters oder des Fremden, um den stereotypen westlichen Blick auf Indien bloßzulegen, etwa in »Baumgartner's Bombay« (1988; dt. »Baumgartners Bombay«, 1989), der Geschichte einer jüdischen Emigrantenfamilie, oder in »Journey to Ithaca« (1995; dt. »Reise ins Licht«, 1996).

Desai sagt, sie schreibe, um das Wesentliche kenntlich zu machen, um die unter dem Eisberg der sogenannten Realität verborgene Wahrheit zu erkunden. Orientierte sich die Autorin anfangs noch an britischen und russischen Klassikern wie E. M. Forster, Virginia Woolf, Tschechow und Dostojewski, so nahm sie sich später zunehmend die Verdichtung und Intensität der Lyrik zum Vorbild für ihre eigenen Arbeiten. Ihre Prosa ist knapp und klar, von Nüchternheit und Distanz zum fiktionalen Geschehen geprägt. Anita Desai wurde mit vielen Preisen ausgezeichnet und dreimal für den Booker Prize nominiert. Sie lebt in Indien und in den USA, wo sie am Massachusetts Institute of Technology Kreatives Schreiben unterrichtet.

Once I was taught the letters at school, I found that by putting them down on paper and making words and sentences, I could give the chaotic, fragmented experience of life a shape and form that would be contemplated and understood. After that no experience, no sensation seemed complete till I had "shaped" it on paper. It is like an added sense, or dimension, to life and to lose it would mean becoming helpless, incomplete and unfulfilled.

Reading too makes sense of life and the world in the same way. I have always surrounded myself with books and since childhood worked to live in the world of books.

lorand gaspar

biography

Lorand Gaspar was born in Marosvàsàrhely (Transsylvania), Romania, in 1925. He grew up in a Jewish home speaking three languages (Hungarian, Romanian and German) and also had French lessons from an early age. He was fascinated by Rimbaud's poetry, as well as by Einstein's theory of relativity. As a child he wanted to become a physicist and a writer; in fact he became a surgeon and a poet. He began to study sciences in Budapest in 1943 but was soon called up to serve in the war. After Hungary was occupied by the Germans, Lorand Gaspar was deported to a labour camp in the south of Germany. He was able to escape to a French camp in March 1945. He later assumed French nationality and studied medicine in Paris. In 1954 he went to Israel as a young doctor. While a surgeon in Jericho, Jerusalem and Bethlehem, he came into close contact with the Palestinian population. It was through the Palestinians that he first got to know the desert, which was to have such a lasting influence on him, forming the most important source of inspiration for his poetry over a long period of time. From 1970 until his retirement, he worked in a hospital in Tunis. His first poetry collection was published in 1966 under the title »Le Quatrième état de la matière« (t: The Fourth State of Material). Further collections of poems followed, most recently »Patmos et autres poèmes« (2001, t: Patmos and Other Poems). Gaspar approaches the sublimity of nature with precise diction and a keen eye for detail, taking in the substance, surface and structure of a material in order to communicate its metaphysical nature. In »Patmos« he frees himself of the material aspect in favour of floating, light and colours. His poems are often fragmentary and elliptic in construction, as if to allow the meaning to shine through between the lines.

In addition to his poems he has also written travel diaries on the Middle East and the eastern Mediterranean illustrated with his own photography, among which is included a history of Palestine (1968, »Histoire de la Palestine«). He has translated poetry from various languages, including Rilke, János Pilinszky, D. H. Lawrence and George Seferis. Lorand Gaspar is recognised as one of France's most important contemporary poets. His work has won the Grand Prix de Poésie de la Ville de Paris (1987) and the Grand Prix national de Poésie (1994). Lorand Gaspar lives in Paris and Tunis.

Sol absolu
Gallimard, Paris, 1982
Carnes de Patmos
Le Temps Qu'il Fait
Cognac, 1991
Égée, Judée
Gallimard, Paris, 1993
Apprentissage
Deyrolle, Paris, 1994
Arabie Heureuse
Deyrolle, Paris, 1997
Carnets de Jérusalem
Le Temps Qu'il Fait
Cognac, 1997
Patmos
Gallimard, Paris 2001

La vie. Ma vie.
Avoir conscience de ma vie finie.
De l'infinité infinie immanente
des mondes.
De la relativité de toute connaissance
humaine.

Le plaisir et le déplaisir, parfois
de regarder, d'entendre
de sentir et de penser les choses,
humaines et non humaines,
l'obscurité et la lumière.
Trouver les mots pour essayer de le
dire
Ecrire ce quelque chose qu'on appelle
un poème,
sachant qu'on ne sait pas ce que c'est—

Lorand Gaspar wurde 1925 in Marosvàsàrhely (Transsylvanien), Rumänien, geboren. In seinem jüdischen Elternhaus wuchs er mit drei Sprachen auf (ungarisch, rumänisch und deutsch), zusätzlich erhielt er schon früh Unterricht in Französisch. Rimbauds Lyrik faszinierte ihn ebenso wie Einsteins Relativitätstheorie. Sein damaliger Berufswunsch: Physiker und Schriftsteller. Er wurde Chirurg und Dichter. Zunächst begann er 1943 ein naturwissenschaftliches Studium in Budapest, doch schon bald wurde er zum Kriegsdienst einberufen. Während der deutschen Besatzung Ungarns wurde Lorand Gaspar in ein Arbeitslager nach Süddeutschland deportiert. Im März 1945 gelang ihm die Flucht in ein französisches Lager. Später nahm er die französische Staatsangehörigkeit an und studierte in Paris Medizin.

1954 ging der junge Arzt nach Israel. Als Chirurg in Jericho, Jerusalem und Bethlehem hatte er nahen Kontakt zur palästinensischen Bevölkerung. Dadurch lernte er die Wüste kennen, die ihn so nachhaltig beeindruckte, dass sie über lange Zeit die wichtigste Inspirationsquelle für seine Lyrik war. Von 1970 bis zu seiner Pensionierung arbeitete er in einem Krankenhaus in Tunis.

1966 wurde seine erste Gedichtsammlung unter dem Titel »Le Quatrième état de la matière« (Ü: Der vierte Zustand der Materie) veröffentlicht. Weitere Gedichtbände folgten, zuletzt »Patmos et autres poèmes« (2001; Ü: Patmos und andere Gedichte). Gaspar nähert sich dem Erhabenen der Natur mit präziser Wortwahl und einem detailgenauen Blick auf die Physis, die Oberflächen und Strukturen der Materie, um eine Idee des Metaphysischen zu vermitteln. In »Patmos« löst er sich vom Materiellen und bewegt sich hin zum Schwebenden, zum Licht und zu den Farben. Seine Gedichte sind oft fragmentarisch und elliptisch angelegt, so dass gleichsam der Sinn zwischen den Worten hindurchscheinen kann. Neben poetischen Texten schrieb er Reisetagebücher, illustriert mit eigenen Fotografien, über den Nahen Orient und den östlichen Mittelmeerraum, darunter u. a. eine Geschichte Palästinas (1968; »Histoire de la Palestine«). Auch übersetzte er Lyrik aus verschiedenen Sprachen, z. B. Rilke, János Pilinszky, D. H. Lawrence und George Seferis. In Frankreich zählt Lorand Gaspar zu den wichtigsten zeitgenössischen Dichtern. Seine Werke wurden mit dem Grand Prix de Poésie de la Ville de Paris (1987) und dem Grand Prix national de Poésie (1994) ausgezeichnet. Lorand Gaspar lebt heute in Paris und Tunis.

La vie. Ma vie.
Etre conscient de ma vie finie –
De l'infinité infinie, immanente
des mondes –
De la relativité de toute
connaissance humaine,
l'obscurité et la lumière –
Trouver des mots pour essayer
de le dire.

Ecrire ce quelque chose
qu'on appelle un poème,
sachant que je ne sais pas
ce que c'est –

Lorand Gaspar

romesh gunesekera

biography

Romesh Gunesekera was born in Colombo, Sri Lanka, in 1954, where he also spent his early childhood. He grew up bilingual speaking English and Singhalese, the official language of Sri Lanka. His family moved from Sri Lanka to the Philippines before settling in London in 1972. Gunesekera studied English Literature and Philosophy at the University of Liverpool.

Gunesekera started writing at the age of 14. He published the short story collection »Monkfish Moon« in 1992. His first novel »Reef« was published in 1994 and was nominated for the Booker Prize. »Reef« is a love story set against the background of a threatened paradise. The story is told by Triton, who, at the age of eleven, becomes the servant of Sagaldos, a marine biologist obsessed by his scientific work. Triton is a descriptive name – originally borrowed from Greek mythology, where it is the name of Neptune's son, but at the same time the name of the largest moon of the second-to-last planet in our solar system – it alludes to the relationship between the two main characters and their dream-like detachment from the world. Sagaldos's house is a self-contained microcosm whose nature is determined by Triton's culinary skills, and whose magic garden allows nothing of the ethnic and social conflicts of Sri Lanka to penetrate. But this apparently Elysian state of being cannot last; when political reality catches up with the two men, the reef, which is the object of Sagaldos's research and the centre of his life, also falls victim to destruction as a marketable resource. Far from home, the now-adult narrator realises that he had relied on a weak, naïve, unworldly man. The distinctive voice of the narrator, innocent and at the same time alert, dissolves into the adult perspective with ease and seemingly causes the concepts of familiarity and estrangement to switch places. This impression is intensified by the use of Singhalese words, which are left unexplained (in the German translation the words are explained in a glossary). The tone is lyrical, towards the end increasingly elegiac, and it becomes apparent that the outside influences that swept into the country too quickly and diversely did not play a wholly innocent role in the end of this world.

Gunesekera has published two further novels: »The Sandglass« (1998), a reflection on melancholy and decay set against the background of two enemy families, and »Heaven's Edge« (2002). Gunesekera also writes poetry, which has been published in various anthologies. His work has been translated into many languages and won numerous prizes. He lives in London.

Monkfish Moon
Granta, London, 1992
Riff
Unionsverlag, Zürich, 1998
Sandglas
Unionsverlag, Zürich, 1999
Heaven's Edge
Bloomsbury, London, 2002

Romesh Gunesekera wurde 1954 in Colombo, Sri Lanka, geboren, wo er auch seine frühe Kindheit verbrachte. Er wuchs zweisprachig auf, mit Englisch und Singhalesisch, der Amtssprache Sri Lankas. Von Sri Lanka zog die Familie auf die Philippinen, bevor sie sich 1972 in London niederließ. Gunesekera hat Englische Literatur und Philosophie an der University of Liverpool studiert.

Gunesekera begann bereits im Alter von 14 Jahren mit dem Schreiben. 1992 veröffentlichte er die Erzählsammlung »Monkfish Moon« (Ü: Seeteufel Mond). Sein erster Roman, »Reef«, (dt. »Riff«, 1998) erschien 1994 und wurde für den Booker Prize nominiert. »Riff« ist eine Liebesgeschichte, die in einem bedrohten Paradies angesiedelt ist. Erzählt wird sie von Triton, der mit elf Jahren in die Dienste Sagaldos tritt, eines in seine Wissenschaft vertieften Meeresbiologen. Triton ist ein sprechender Name: Ursprünglich der antiken Mythologie entlehnt, wo er den Sohn Neptuns bezeichnet, zugleich aber auch der Name des größten Mondes des vorletzten Planeten unseres Sonnensystems, verweist der Name auf das Verhältnis zwischen den beiden Hauptfiguren und ihre Entrücktheit von der Welt. Das Haus Sagaldos ist ein sich selbst genügender Mikrokosmos, der von Tritons Kochkünsten bestimmt wird und durch dessen Zaubergarten nichts von den ethnischen und sozialen Konflikten Sri Lankas dringt. Aber dieser scheinbar elysische Zustand ist nicht von Dauer, die politische Realität holt beide ein, und auch das Riff, Forschungsobjekt und Lebensinhalt Sagaldos, fällt als vermarktbare Ressource der Zerstörung zum Opfer. Fern der Heimat muss der erwachsen gewordene Erzähler erkennen, dass er auf einen schwachen und naiven, weltfremden Mann gebaut hatte. Die markante Stimme des Erzählers, naiv und wach zugleich, die bruchlos in die erwachsene Perspektive überblendet, verkehrt die Bedeutung von Vertrautheit und Fremde. Verstärkt wird dieser Eindruck durch das Einflechten unkommentierter singhalesischer Begriffe, (in der deutschen Übersetzung werden die Begriffe in einem Glossar erläutert). Der Ton ist lyrisch, gegen Ende zunehmend elegisch, und es scheint die Erkenntnis auf, dass die fremden Einflüsse, die zu schnell und vielgestaltig in das Land eingedrungen sind, nicht ganz unschuldig sind am Untergang dieser Welt.

Gunesekera hat zwei weitere Romane veröffentlicht: »The Sandglass« (1998; »Sandglas«, 1999), eine Reflexion über Schwermut und Verfall vor dem Hintergrund der Geschichte zweier verfeindeter Familien, und »Heaven's Edge« (2002; Ü: Himmelsrand). Gunesekera verfasst auch Lyrik, mit der er in verschiedenen Anthologien vertreten ist. Sein Werk wurde in viele Sprachen übersetzt und mit zahlreichen Preisen ausgezeichnet. Er lebt in London.

jabbar yassin hussin

biography

Jabbar Yassin Hussin was born in Baghdad, Iraq in 1954. He grew up in a laicised and politically left-wing environment. After the Ba'ath Party took over power in 1968 (with Saddam Hussein as head of the ministry for state security), he joined the Communist Party at the age of 14. He was arrested and tortured several times while still at school because of his political activities, which included holding the chair of the young communists of Baghdad. He withdrew his membership in 1973, when the Communist Party was taken over by the Ba'ath Party. From then on he was under constant observation by Saddam Hussein's regime. He was a student at the University of Baghdad and worked as a journalist for a short period but was not allowed to continue either his studies or his journalistic work. Instead, he wrote novellas, short stories and fairy stories for children. In 1976 he was threatened with further arrest, and had to flee the country for France. There, together with others in exile he founded the magazine »Aswat« (t: The Voice), a publication which took a critical stance on Saddam Hussein.
As well as short stories, Jabbar Yassin Hussin also writes articles for various newspapers and magazines. His texts are primarily concerned with the traumatic experience of exile, the loss of home and identity. »I wrote so as to remember what I had left behind.« He works in Arabic – both a conscious and an emotional decision, as his power of expression in his native language was relativised by the dominance of the exile language French. His books have been published in France since the early 90's and include »Adieu, l'enfant« (1996), a very personal approach to the stories and memories of his childhood. His stories »Le lecteur de Bagdad. Contes et nouvelles« (2000) and »Histoires de jour, contes de nuit« (2003) recall his life in his home country. Published the same year, »Paroles d'argiles – Un Irakien en exile« is a collection of articles, commentaries and speeches on the current situation in Iraq that were originally printed in the Arabic press. His texts have been translated into eight European languages. Jabbar Yassin Hussin had lived near La Rochelle in France since 1992. After 27 years in French exile, Jabbar Yassin Hussin returned to Baghdad in May 2003.

Aux Rives de la folie
L'Harmattan, Paris, 1991
Un Ciel assombri d'étoiles
Atelier du Gué
Villelongue d'Aude, 1993
Adieu l'enfant
Atelier du Gué
Villelongue d'Aude, 1996
Yémen-Détours
L'Esprit des Péninsules
Paris, 2000
Le Lecteur de Bagdad
Atelier du Gué
Villelongue d'Aude, 2000
Histoires de jour, contes de nuit
Atelier du Gué
Villelongue d'Aude, 2002
Paroles d' argile
Atelier du Gué
Villelongue d'Aude, 2003

Jabbar Yassin Hussin wurde 1954 in Bagdad, Irak, geboren. Er wuchs in einem laizistischen und politisch links orientierten Umfeld auf. Nachdem die Ba'ath-Partei 1968 die Macht übernommen hatte (mit Saddam Hussein als Chef des Ministeriums für Staatssicherheit), schloss er sich im Alter von 14 Jahren der Kommunistischen Partei an. Wegen seiner politischen Aktivitäten, u. a. als Vorstand der kommunistischen Jugend Bagdads, wurde er bereits in seiner Schulzeit mehrmals inhaftiert und gefoltert. Als 1973 die Kommunistische Partei von der Ba'ath-Partei vereinnahmt wurde, gab er seine Mitgliedschaft auf. Seither stand er unter ständiger Beobachtung des Regimes von Saddam Hussein. Er war an der Universität in Bagdad eingeschrieben und kurze Zeit als Journalist tätig, durfte jedoch weder sein Studium noch seine Arbeit fortsetzen. Stattdessen schrieb er Novellen, Erzählungen und Märchen für Kinder. 1976 drohte ihm eine erneute Inhaftierung, weshalb er das Land überstürzt verlassen musste. Er floh nach Frankreich. Dort gründete er mit befreundeten Exilanten die Zeitschrift »Aswat« (Ü: Die Stimme), die sich kritisch gegenüber Saddam Hussein äußerte.
Jabbar Yassin Hussin schreibt neben Kurzgeschichten und Erzählungen auch Artikel für diverse Zeitungen und Magazine. Er behandelt in seinen Texten vor allem die traumatische Erfahrung des Exils, den Verlust von Heimat und Identität. »Ich schrieb, um mich an das zu erinnern, was ich verlassen hatte.« Er verfasst seine Texte auf arabisch – eine ebenso bewusste wie emotionale Entscheidung, da seine Muttersprache durch die Dominanz der Exilsprache Französisch in ihrer Ausdruckskraft relativiert wurde. Seit Anfang der neunziger Jahre wurden seine Bücher in Frankreich veröffentlicht, darunter »Adieu, l'enfant« (1996), eine sehr persönliche Annäherung an die Geschichten und Ereignisse seiner Kindheit.
Seine Erzählungen »Le lecteur de Bagdad. Contes et nouvelles« (2000) und »Histoires de jour, contes de nuit« (2003) thematisieren sein Leben in der Heimat. Im selben Jahr erschien »Paroles d'argiles. Un Irakien en exile«, eine Sammlung von Artikeln, Kommentaren und Reden zur aktuellen Situation im Irak, die in der arabischen Presse veröffentlicht wurden. Seine Texte wurden in acht europäische Sprachen übersetzt.
Jabbar Yassin Hussin lebte seit 1992 in der Nähe von La Rochelle in Frankreich. Nach 27 Jahren im französischen Exil kehrte Jabbar Yassin Hussin im Mai 2003 nach Bagdad zurück.

L'embryon renfermé dans une coquille d'oeuf déforme la vision du poussin à venir. La poésie peut corriger la vision puisque le monde insolite, le monde des essences, ne peut être vu à travers la loupe, mais à travers les mots qui sont miraculeusement accordés. Nous ne savons pas pourquoi nous sommes atteints de cette maladie. Mais nous savons que le monde visible n'est pas le monde réel que nous avons voulu voir lorsque nous étions encore embryons. Le mot ver en arabe a le même sens et la même orthographe que le mot maison. Et puisque le monde réel nous chasse, alors nous retournons à la maison qui nous rappelle la coquille qui enveloppait l'embryon que nous étions. C'est encore le mythe de l'origine.

Jabbar YASSIN HUSSIN

witi ihimaera
biography

Witi Ihimaera is the first Maori writer to have his works published and made accessible to a larger public. He was born in Gisborne, New Zealand, in 1944. In 1972, a year after graduating in English, he enjoyed the success of his first publication before embarking upon a diplomatic career.
In his first works, he was primarily interested in describing »the emotional landscape of the Maori people«. In the late 70's he became aware of the fact that his books were read as the definitive portrayal of the world of the Maori. He then became convinced that his portrayals no longer did justice to the real social and political changes which were taking place. In 1977 he therefore decided to take a break from writing. In the 80's his creative period is characterised by the conflict-filled political and social reality of New Zealand society. »The Whale Rider« (1987), his novel which is probably most appreciated by the Maori, stems from this time and tells the fairytale-like story of Kahutia Te Rangi, who, through her friendship with a whale, makes contact with her ancestors, thus preventing the break-up of her tribe. The film »Whale Rider« was shown in 2003. In New Zealand, his adaptations of short stories by Katherine Mansfield from a Maori perspective received scathing reviews but were well received internationally (»Dear Miss Mansfield«, 1989). With »Nights in the Gardens of Spain« (1995) his writing takes a new turn: the novel is the expression and admission of his homosexuality. Ihimaera is considered one of the most important native New Zealand voices. He sees himself as a mediator between the Maori and the Pakeha, the New Zealanders who are descended from the Europeans.
His English language texts are characterised by a simple language, a linear narrative technique, and draw on material which has been handed down orally; he also uses many Maori terms for which there are no English equivalents. He has received the Wattie (now Montana) Book of the Year Award, New Zealand's most important literature prize, more than once. He is the editor of numerous anthologies and non-fiction books, and the author of several opera libretti and the theatre piece »Woman Far Walking« (2000). The book of stories »Aroha. Maori-Geschichten aus dem Jadeland« offers the German reader a selection of his work. Ihimaera lives in Auckland, where he has taught since 1990.

The Dream Swimmer
Penguin, Auckland, 1997
Aroha
Edition Isele
Eggingen, 1999
[Ü: Maria von der Ahé]
The Uncle's Story
Penguin, Auckland, 2000
Woman Far Walking
Reed, Auckland, 2000
Nights In the Gardens of Spain
Reed, Auckland, 2001
Pounamu, Pounamu
Heinemann, Auckland, 2002
Sky Dancer
Penguin, Auckland, 2003
Whalerider
Rowohlt, Reinbek, 2003
[Ü: Sabine Schulte]

Witi Ihimaera ist der erste Maori-Schriftsteller, dessen Arbeiten veröffentlicht und so einem breiten Publikum zugänglich gemacht wurden. Er wurde 1944 in Gisborne, Neuseeland, geboren. Nach dem Erfolg seiner ersten Publikation, die 1972, ein Jahr nach Abschluss seines Anglistikstudiums, erschien, begann er eine diplomatische Karriere.
In seinen ersten Werken ging es ihm vor allem darum, die »emotionale Landschaft der Maori« zu schildern. Gegen Ende der siebziger Jahre wurde ihm bewusst, dass seine Bücher als endgültiges Porträt der Welt der Maori gelesen wurden. Er selbst war inzwischen jedoch zu der Überzeugung gelangt, dass seine Darstellungen nicht mehr den realen Veränderungen der gesellschaftlichen und politischen Situation gerecht wurden und beschloss 1977 deshalb, mit dem Schreiben auszusetzen. Die Schaffensperiode der achtziger Jahre ist durch die konfliktreiche politische und soziale Realität der neuseeländischen Gesellschaft geprägt. Sein bei den Maori am meisten geschätzter Roman »The Whale Rider« (1987; dt. 2003) stammt aus dieser Zeit und erzählt die märchenhafte Geschichte Kahutia Te Rangis, die durch ihre Freundschaft mit einem Wal Verbindung zu ihren Ahnen aufnimmt und so ihren Stamm vor dem Auseinanderbrechen bewahrt. Eine Verfilmung des Romans kam 2003 in die Kinos. Seine Adaption von Kurzgeschichten Katherine Mansfields aus Maori-Perspektive erhielt in Neuseeland vernichtende, international jedoch enthusiastische Rezensionen (»Dear Miss Mansfield«, 1989). Eine erneute Zäsur in seinem Schaffen bezeichnet »Nights in the Gardens of Spain« (1995): Der Roman ist Ausdruck und Bekenntnis seiner Homosexualität. Ihimaera gilt als eine der wichtigsten Stimmen der neuseeländischen Ureinwohner. Er selbst versteht sich als Mittler zwischen den Maori und den Pakeha, den europäischstämmigen Neuseeländern. In seinen englischsprachigen Texten, die durch eine schnörkellose Sprache und eine lineare Erzählweise geprägt sind, greift er auf mündlich tradierte Stoffe der Ureinwohner zurück und lässt vielfach Maori-Begriffe einfließen, für die es im Englischen keine Entsprechung gibt. Er wurde mehrfach mit dem Wattie (jetzt Montana) Book of the Year Award, dem wichtigsten Literaturpreis Neuseelands, ausgezeichnet. Er ist Herausgeber zahlreicher Anthologien und Sachbücher, Autor mehrerer Opernlibretti und des Theaterstücks »Woman Far Walking« (2000). Dem deutschen Leser bietet der Erzählband »Aroha. Maori-Geschichten aus dem Jadeland« (1999) einen Querschnitt durch sein erzählerisches Schaffen. Ihimaera lebt in Auckland, wo er seit 1990 lehrt.

Tick tock, hickory dock,
The poet ran up the clock,
While he was there he found despair
Wrote his poem, readers beware!
Hickory dickory dock

Tick tock hickory dock,
The poet (again) ran up the clock,
This time he found ... inspiration!
The clock struck twelve,
The poet ran down,
Hickory dickory
dock

clara janés

biography

Clara Janés was born in Barcelona in 1940, the daughter of the poet and lecturer Josep Janés. She studied philosophy and literature at the Universities of Barcelona and Pamplona, and later comparative literature and Czech at the Sorbonne in Paris. She has been living in Madrid ever since.
Clara Janés's literary work displays an unusual diversity. While she is particularly well known as a poet, her numerous publications also include novels, essays, biographies (»La vida callada de Federico Mompou«, 1975; t: The Silent Life of Federico Mompou), autobiographical narrations (»Jardín y Laberinto«, 1990; t: Garden and Labyrinth), travel reports and translations. In her translation work, she has concentrated in particular on Czech poetry (above all on Vladimír Holan) but has also translated from French (Marguerite Duras, Nathalie Sarraute) and English (Katherine Mansfield, William Golding). She has recently devoted herself to Persian and Turkish verse. Moreover, she has published the works of various Spanish authors and, in the year 2001, also a Spanish edition of a volume of poetry by Johannes Bobrowski, translated by her daughter Adriana. Janés has received several awards for her poetry and for prose and translations alike; she was recently awarded the renowned Premio Jaime Gil de Biedma in 2002. Her works have been translated into just under twenty languages, including Arabic, Persian and Icelandic.
Clara Janés belongs to Spanish literature's feminist avantgarde, which has gained in importance since the 80's and established itself in a hitherto male-dominated Spanish society that is characterized by an indelible Catholicism. Her poems in particular reflect her constant preoccupation with her own dual role as woman and poet. If she approached this topic in her initial poems (»Las estrellas vencidas«, 1964; t: The Defeated Stars) under a rather general perspective, she plumbed the depths of femininity in the following decades in ever more intimate ways. The collection »Kampa« (1986, written in the 70's) is considered to be the turning point toward an assertive erotic literature in which the author links female self-confidence with erotic fulfillment for the first time. This vein is continued in »Eros« (1981) and »Vivir« (1983, t: Life) with such explicitness and desire that Rosa Chacel called Janés »one of the great love poets«. In her more recent texts she examines and re-examines new variants of the relationship between the feminine self, the body, sensuality and eroticism – for example in the connection between Eros and death in »Arcángel de sombra« (1998, t: Archangel of the Shadow).

Desintegración
Editorial Eucar
Madrid, 1969
Eros
Hiperión, Madrid, 1981
Vivir
Hiperión, Madrid, 1983
Los caballos del sueño
Ed. Anagrama
Barcelona, 1989
El hombre de Adén
Editorial Anagrama
Barcelona, 1991
Arcángel de sombra
Visor, Madrid, 1999
Los secretos del bosque
Visor, Madrid, 2002

Clara Janés wurde 1940 in Barcelona als Tochter des Lyrikers und Lektors Josep Janés geboren. An den Universitäten von Barcelona und Pamplona studierte sie Philosophie und Literatur, später Vergleichende Literaturwissenschaft und Tschechisch an der Sorbonne in Paris. Seither lebt sie in Madrid.
Das literarische Werk von Clara Janés ist ausgesprochen facettenreich. Zwar ist sie vor allem als Lyrikerin bekannt, doch umfassen ihre zahlreichen Publikationen auch Romane, Essays, Biographien (1975; »La vida callada de Federico Mompou«, Ü: Das schweigsame Leben des Federico Mompou), autobiographische Erzählungen (1990; »Jardín y Laberinto«, Ü: Garten und Labyrinth), Reiseberichte und Übersetzungen. Einen Schwerpunkt bildet dabei die tschechische Lyrik (vor allem Vladimír Holan), aber auch aus dem Französischen (Marguerite Duras, Nathalie Sarraute) und Englischen (Katherine Mansfield, William Golding) hat sie übersetzt. Neuerdings widmet sie sich persischer und türkischer Lyrik. Darüber hinaus hat sie Werke verschiedener spanischer Autoren herausgegeben, 2001 auch eine von ihrer Tochter Adriana übersetzte spanische Ausgabe eines Lyrikbandes von Johannes Bobrowski. Janés wurde sowohl für ihre Lyrik als auch für Prosa und Übersetzungen mehrfach ausgezeichnet, zuletzt 2002 mit dem renommierten Premio Jaime Gil de Biedma. Ihre Werke wurden in knapp zwanzig Sprachen übersetzt, darunter ins Arabische, Persische und Isländische. Clara Janés gehört zur feministischen Avantgarde der spanischen Literatur, die seit den achtziger Jahren an Bedeutung gewann und die sich in der bis dahin von Männern dominierten und nachhaltig katholisch geprägten spanischen Gesellschaft behaupten konnte. Insbesondere ihre Lyrik spiegelt die ständige Beschäftigung mit der eigenen Doppelrolle als Frau und Dichterin wieder. Näherte sie sich diesem Thema in den ersten Gedichten (1964; »Las estrellas vencidas«, Ü: Die besiegten Sterne) unter einer eher allgemeinen Perspektive, lotete sie die Weiblichkeit in den folgenden Jahrzehnten auf immer intimere Weise aus. Als Wendepunkt hin zu einer offensiv erotischen Literatur gilt die Sammlung »Kampa« (1986, geschrieben bereits in den siebziger Jahren), in der die Autorin zum ersten Mal weibliches Selbstbewusstsein mit erotischer Erfüllung verknüpft. Diese Linie setzt sich in »Eros« (1981) und »Vivir« (1983; Ü: Leben) so explizit und lustvoll fort, dass Rosa Chacel Janés »eine der großen Liebesdichterinnen« nannte. Auch in jüngsten Texten werden immer wieder neue Varianten der Beziehung von weiblichem Selbst, Körper, Sinnlichkeit und Erotik erforscht, in »Arcángel de sombra« (1998; Ü: Erzengel des Schattens) etwa in der Verbindung von Eros und Tod.

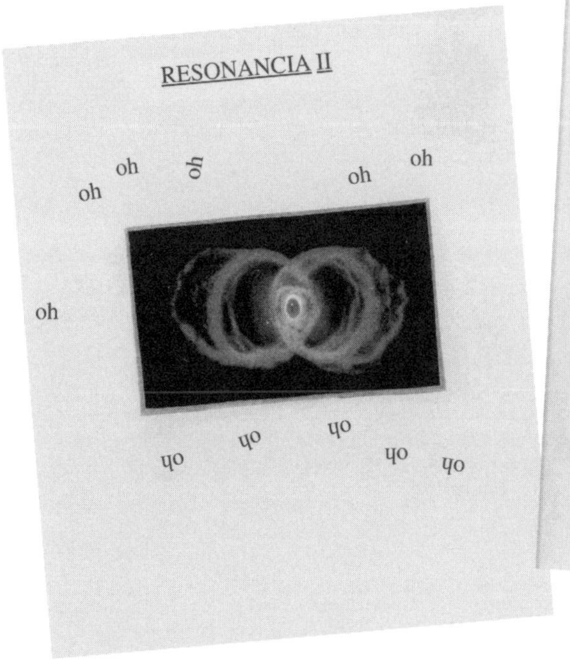

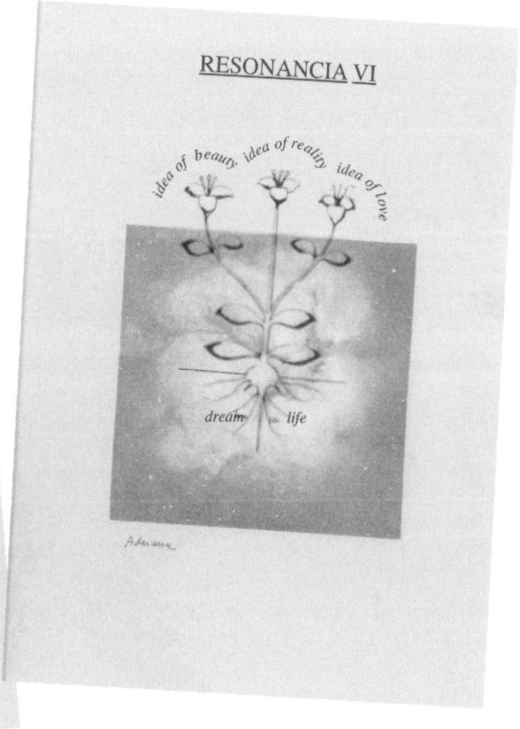

darío jaramillo agudelo

biography

Darío Jaramillo Agudelo was born in Santa Rosa de Osos in the province of Antioquia in northwest Colombia in 1947. He studied Law and Economics at the Universidad Javeriana in Bogotá. Dario Jaramillo Agudelo published his first book of poetry »Historias« in 1974. Four years later his second book of verse »Tratado de retórica« received the Premio Nacional de Poesía. His debut novel, 1983's »La muerte de Alec« was followed by five more novels, including »Cartas cruzadas«, »Guía para viajeros« and »Memorias de un hombre feliz«, which proved him also to be a remarkable prose writer. In spite of this, as a writer, Darío Jaramillo Agudelo did not want to have to depend on royalties, scholarships and prize money, which is why since 1985 he has earned his living as a cultural representative for the National Bank of Columbia. In 1995 Jaramillo Agudelo was made a corresponding member of the Colombian Academy of Languages. He lives in Bogotá.

Darío Jaramillo Agudelo's writing overcomes the gap which today separates poetry and prose; he lets the poetic stimulate his literature. In an interview with the Mexican newspaper »La Jornada« he admitted, »I'm convinced that the only literary genre is that of poetry. A novel, an essay, a reportage is only valuable if it conveys poetic emotion.« But his novels are not sentimental. They are dominated by topics having to do with the violent nature of everyday Columbian life, a subject that is also pursued by Columbia's own literary movement, the »literatura de la violencia«. Dario Jaramillo Agudelo became popular above all through his series »Poemas de amor«. Together with Juan Gustavo Cobo Borda, Juan Manuel Roca, Giovanni Quessep, Henry Luque Muñoz, Raúl Henao, María Mercedes Carranza and Elkin Restrepo, Darío Jaramillo Agudelo belongs to the so-called »Generación sin Nombre« (»Generation without a Name«). He nonetheless does not see Latin and South American literature as experiencing a creative crisis. Instead, in Colombia's very dynamic literature scene and publishing landscape a »wide array of possibilities« (Patricia Salazar) are unfolding.

Historias
La Soga al cuello
Bogotá, 1974
Tratado de Retórica
Centro Editorial Universidad
Nacional de Colombia
Bogotá, 1987
Cartas cruzadas
Alfaguara
Santafé de Bogotá, 1995
La muerte de Alec
Alfaguara, Bogotá, 1999
**Memorias de
un hombre feliz**
Alfaguara, Bogotá, 2000
Cantar por cantar
Pre-Textos, Madrid, 2001
El juego del alfiler
Pre-Textos, Madrid, 2002

Darío Jaramillo Agudelo wurde 1947 in Santa Rosa de Osos, in der Provinz Antioquia im Nordwesten Kolumbiens, geboren. Er studierte Jura und Wirtschaftswissenschaften an der Universidad Javeriana in Bogotá. Bereits 1974 veröffentlichte Darío Jaramillo Agudelo seinen poetischen Erstling »Historias« und erhielt vier Jahre später für seinen zweiten Gedichtband »Tratado de retórica« den Premio Nacional de Poesía (1978). Sein Romandebüt des Jahres 1983, »La muerte de Alec«, dem bislang fünf weitere Romane folgten, darunter »Cartas cruzadas«, »Guía para viajeros« und »Memorias de un hombre feliz«, brachte schließlich ein beachtenswertes Doppeltalent zum Vorschein. Dennoch wollte Darío Jaramillo Agudelo als Autor stets von Tantiemen, Stipendien und Preisgeldern unabhängig bleiben, weshalb er seinen Lebensunterhalt seit 1985 als Kulturbeauftragter der Nationalbank Kolumbiens verdient. 1995 wurde Jaramillo Agudelo zum korrespondierenden Mitglied der Kolumbianischen Akademie für Sprache gewählt. Er lebt in Bogotá.

Die Kluft, die Poesie und Prosa, Dichter und Schriftsteller heute voneinander trennt, ist bei Darío Jaramillo Agudelo einer dichterischen Befruchtung der Literatur gewichen. In einem Interview mit der mexikanischen Zeitung »La Jornada« bekannte er: »Ich bin davon überzeugt, dass die einzige literarische Gattung die Poesie ist. Ein Roman, ein Essay, eine Reportage sind erst dann wertvoll, wenn sie eine beliebige poetische Emotion vermitteln.« Gefühlsselig sind seine Romane darum nicht. In ihnen dominieren die Themen des von Gewalt geprägten kolumbianischen Alltags, mit dem sich in Kolumbien eine eigene Literaturrichtung, die »literatura de la violencia«, befasst. Seine Popularität erlangte Darío Jaramillo Agudelo vor allem durch seinen Zyklus »Poemas de amor«. Darío Jaramillo Agudelo gehört mit Juan Gustavo Cobo Borda, Juan Manuel Roca, Giovanni Quessep, Henry Luque Muñoz, Raúl Henao, María Mercedes Carranza und Elkin Restrepo zur so genannten »Generación sin Nombre« (»Generation ohne Namen«). Dennoch erkennt er keine kreative Krise der lateinund südamerikanischen Literatur, vielmehr entfaltet sich in der überaus dynamischen Literaturszene und Verlagslandschaft Kolumbiens für ihn ein »breiter Fächer der Möglichkeiten« (Patricia Salazar).

fatou keïta
biography

Fatou Keïta was born in Soubré on the Ivory Coast. Due to family reasons, she lived in France well into elementary school and then returned to her homeland with her parents. From 1976 to 1981 she studied English language and literature at the Polytechnic of Central London and at the Université d'Abidjan-Cocody in the capital of the Ivory Coast. She completed her doctoral studies three years later at the Université de Caen in France. Keïta has since lived in Abidjan, where she teaches in the English Department.
In the 90's, in addition to teaching, Fatou Keïta started to write children's books. Her debut, »Le petit garçon bleu« is about a little boy who is not accepted by the other children because of his unusual skin colour; only slowly do the children learn to see his specialness as enriching for them as well. The book is a hymn to racial tolerance and has won awards, including the first prize from the Agence de Coopération Culturelle et Technique (1994). »La voleuse de sourires«, Keïta's second book from the same year, is also about the joys of being different and was received very positively.
A Fulbright scholarship, which in 1995 brought Keïta to the University of Virginia in Charlottesville in the US, marked the start of a new phase in her scholarly and literary work. She discovered the works of Alice Walker and Toni Morrison and became aware of the American discussion on mutilation practices in Africa. Shortly thereafter Keïta began work on her first novel, which she would like to see understood as a protest against this awful ritual, yet also against stereotypical Western criticism of the »barbaric« black continent. In courageous and direct terms, »Rebelle« addresses the living conditions of African women. Malimouna, the young hero of the novel, flees a forced marriage and mutilation, leaving her village for Paris. There she learns what life is like in the housing settlements for immigrants; she also learns about racism, holding on to traditions that have been handed down and the daily violence against women. When her own marriage ends in a fiasco, she finds the courage to rebel against her maltreatment and encourages other women to finally overcome the shame and to break the silence about their suffering.
After her successful debut as a novelist, Fatou Keïta continues to remain committed to children's literature. Six more stories were published, most recently »Les billes de Karim« in 2001.

Sinabani, la petite dernière
Ed. Nouv. Ivoiriennes
Abidjan, 1997
Le coq qui ne voulait pluschanter
Ed. Nouv. Ivoiriennes
Abidjan, 1999
Die Diebin des Lächelns
KiK-Verlag
Berg am Irchel, 1999
[Ü: Yvonne Lüssi]
Der kleine blaue Junge
KiK-Verlag
Berg am Irchel, 1999
[Ü: Yvonne Lüssi]
Les billes de Karim
Ed. Nouv. Ivoiriennes
Abidjan, 2001
Die stolze Rebellin
Ullstein, München, 2003
[Ü: Sigrid Groß]

Fatou Keïta wurde in Soubré, Elfenbeinküste, geboren. Bis in die Grundschulzeit hinein lebte sie aus familiären Gründen in Frankreich, dann kehrte sie mit ihren Eltern in die Heimat zurück. Von 1976 bis 1981 studierte sie englische Sprache und Literatur an der Polytechnic of Central London und der Université d'Abidjan-Cocody in der Hauptstadt der Elfenbeinküste. Drei Jahre später folgte ihre Promotion an der Université de Caen in Frankreich. Seitdem lebt Keïta wieder in Abidjan und unterrichtet am dortigen Lehrstuhl für Anglistik.
In den neunziger Jahren begann Fatou Keïta neben ihrer akademischen Lehrtätigkeit Kinderbücher zu schreiben. Ihr Erstling aus dem Jahr 1994, »Le petit garçon bleu« (dt. »Der kleine blaue Junge«, 1999), erzählt die Geschichte eines kleinen Jungen, der wegen seiner ungewöhnlichen Hautfarbe von den anderen Kindern abgelehnt wird; erst ganz allmählich begreifen sie, dass seine Besonderheit auch für sie eine Bereicherung ist. Das Buch ist eine Hymne an die Toleranz und wurde unter anderem mit dem ersten Preis der Agence de Coopération Culturelle et Technique (1994) ausgezeichnet. Auch »La voleuse de sourires« (dt. »Die Diebin des Lächelns«, 1999), Keïtas zweites Buch aus demselben Jahr, handelt vom Segen der Andersartigkeit und wurde überaus positiv aufgenommen.
Ein Fulbright-Stipendium, das sie 1995 an die University of Virginia in Charlottesville, USA, führte, markierte für Fatou Keïta den Beginn einer neuen Phase in ihrem wissenschaftlichen und literarischen Denken. Sie entdeckte die Werke von Alice Walker und Toni Morrison und wurde auf die amerikanische Diskussion über die Beschneidungspraktiken in Afrika aufmerksam. Kurz darauf begann Keïta mit der Arbeit an ihrem ersten Roman, den sie als einen Aufschrei gegen dieses grausame Ritual, aber auch gegen die westlich-stereotype Kritik am »barbarischen« schwarzen Kontinent verstanden wissen will. »Rebelle« (dt. »Die stolze Rebellin«, 2000) setzt sich auf couragierte und geradlinige Art mit den Lebensbedingungen afrikanischer Frauen auseinander. Malimouna, die junge Heldin des Romans, flieht vor Beschneidung und Zwangsheirat aus ihrem Dorf nach Paris. Dort lernt sie das Leben in den Immigrantensiedlungen kennen, den Rassismus, das Festhalten an überkommenen Traditionen und die alltägliche Gewalt gegen Frauen. Als auch ihre eigene Ehe im Fiasko endet, findet sie den Mut, sich gegen die Misshandlungen aufzulehnen, und ermuntert auch andere Frauen, die Scham zu überwinden und das Schweigen über ihr Leiden zu brechen.
Fatou Keïta ist auch nach ihrem erfolgreichen Debüt als Romanschriftstellerin der Kinderliteratur treu geblieben. Es erschienen sechs weitere Erzählungen, zuletzt »Les billes de Karim« im Jahr 2001.

Quand j'ai mal...
Quand l'envie de partager la vie
Si fort se fait sentir
Quand tout va si mal
Quand le bonheur est pâle
Ou qu'on le sent revivre...
Quand la vie soupire
Il me faut bien le dire!
Alors ma plume
De cette envie de dire
Se fait l'avol

Fatou Keïta

ryszard krynicki

biography

Ryszard Krynicki was born in Sankt Valentin (Wimberg camp), Austria, in 1943. His Polish parents were forced labourers. After graduating in Polish Studies at the Adam Mickiewiecz University in Poznan, he worked as a librarian and as editor of the magazine »Student«, a job that he had to give up due to his involvement in the civil rights movement. Krynicki is one of the most important of the now-renowned »new wave« group of poets, a collective formed in the late 60's to oppose the ideology and language of the prevailing political system. In the late 70's, his activities in this group as well as in the democratic movement led to his being banned from publication for several years. The poet has translated many German authors including Nelly Sachs, Celan, Brecht and Reiner Kunze, and has received many prizes, most recently the Friedrich Gundolf Prize in 2000 for his contribution to gaining recognition for German art abroad.

Ryszard Krynicki's early poems are strikingly different from his later work. In the first poems, written just after his debut in 1966, the language displays a density of metaphor and opulent imagery, through which the world is comprehended as a terror-invoking maelstrom. Uncertainty and fear characterise the figures in this world, who attempt to flee as a way out. Both in terms of content and language, Krynicki is able to write in a way that renounces the ideological model of society and its prescribed use of language. This critique does not lead to nihilistic despair, but instead keeps »the conscience, which is constantly endangered by outer constraints and the possibility of inner stultification, alert and thereby hopes to heal the disturbed, sickened sense of self-esteem« (Karl Dedecius). The more recent texts (such as »Wunde der Wahrheit«, 1991) are more minimal and laconic. Just a few lines long, the clarity of language has an almost ascetic effect in comparison to the first poems. Krynicki proves himself to be a relentless critic of reality, a sceptical observer of language and its poetical as well as political potential. »Escape«, writes one critic, commenting on the change in Krynicki's tone, »is replaced by a resolute spiritual pilgrimage.« Krynicki even thoroughly reworks his older poems, minimising the previously lavish language and showing that there is considerable truth in the sentiment that a poem is never finished.

Krynicki lives in Krakow where, together with his wife, he runs the publishing house a5.

Akt urodzenia
Wydawnictwo Poznażskie
Poznan, 1969
Nasze życie rożnie
Instytut Literacki, Paris 1978
Niepodlegli nicożci
Niezależna Oficyna
Wydawnicza
Warschau, 1988
Um niemanden zu verletzen
Edition Tiessen
Neu-Isenburg, 1991
[Ü: Karl Dedecius]
Wunde der Wahrheit
Suhrkamp
Frankfurt a. M., 1991
[Ü: Karl Dedecius]
Magnetyczny punkt
CiS, Warschau, 1996
Stein aus der Neuen Welt
Rospo, Hamburg, 2000
[Ü: Esther Kinsky]

Ryszard Krynicki wurde 1943 in Sankt Valentin (Lager Wimberg) in Österreich als Kind polnischer Zwangarbeiter geboren. Nach seinem Studium der Polonistik an der Adam-Mickiewiecz-Universität in Posen arbeitete er als Bibliothekar und als Redakteur der Zeitschrift »Student«, die er jedoch aufgrund seines Engagements in der Bürgerrechtsbewegung verlassen musste. Krynicki ist einer der bedeutendsten Dichter der als »Neue Welle« bekanntgewordenen Gruppe von Lyrikern, die sich in in den späten sechziger Jahren in Opposition zur Ideologie und Sprache des herrschenden politischen Systems formiert hatte. Seine Aktivitäten in dieser Gruppe wie auch in der demokratischen Bewegung führten Ende der siebziger Jahre dazu, dass er mehrere Jahre mit einem Publikationsverbot belegt wurde. Der Lyriker hat viele Autoren aus dem Deutschen übersetzt, darunter Nelly Sachs, Celan, Brecht und Reiner Kunze, und wurde mit zahlreichen Preisen ausgezeichnet, zuletzt 2000 mit dem Friedrich-Gundolf-Preis für die Vermittlung deutscher Kunst im Ausland.

Das Werk Ryszard Krynickis ist von einem auffälligen Bruch durchzogen. Die ersten Gedichte, die nach dem Debüt 1966 erschienen, zeichnen sich aus durch eine dichte Bildsprache und opulente Metaphorik, in der die Welt als schreckenerregendes Chaos erscheint. Unsicherheit und Angst prägen die Figuren, die sich in dieser Welt bewegen, Flucht wird als Ausweg erprobt. Sowohl inhaltlich als auch auf sprachlicher Ebene vollzieht Krynicki damit die Abwendung von der ideologisierten Gesellschaft und der ihr oktroyierten, vereinheitlichten Sprache. Dabei mündet diese Kritik jedoch nicht in Nihilismus und Verzweiflung, sondern hält »die durch äußeren Zwang und innere Verödung beständig gefährdeten Gewissen wach und hofft, damit das gestörte, krank gemachte Selbstwertgefühl zu heilen.« (Karl Dedecius)

Die neueren Texte (etwa in »Wunde der Wahrheit«, 1991) präsentieren sich dagegen sparsamer und lakonischer. Nur noch wenige Zeilen lang und in klarer Sprache formuliert, wirken sie im Vergleich zu den ersten Gedichten beinahe asketisch. Krynicki weist sich als unnachgiebiger Kritiker der Realität aus, als skeptischer Beobachter der Sprache und ihres poetischen wie politischen Potentials. »Flucht«, so ein Kritiker zum Wandel in Krynickis Ton, »wurde ersetzt durch eine entschlossene spirituelle Pilgerreise.« Selbst seine älteren Gedichte unterzieht Krynicki einer grundlegenden Überarbeitung, minimiert die einst üppige Sprache – und gibt damit der Vermutung Recht, dass ein Gedicht niemals fertig ist.

Krynicki lebt in Krakau, wo er zusammen mit seiner Frau den Verlag a5 leitet.

leïla marouane

biography

Leïla Marouane was born in Algeria in 1960. She studied medicine and literature in Algiers and then worked as a journalist. Due to the tense situation in Algeria, she has lived and worked as a freelance writer in Paris since 1990. To date she has published three novels. All her works are about the oppression of women in her native country and the slow decay of Algeria's once blossoming cities, where Western modernity and Islamic fundamentalism collide.

Set against the background of political events in Algeria in the late 80's, »La fille de la casbah« (1996; t: The Girl from the Casbah) tells the story of a young teacher who successfully defends herself against her parents' plans but then fails at realising her own goals in life. Neither Islam nor the Western way of life offer her the stability she needs, until finally her life ends in a bloody nightmare.

Marouane identifies with neither Islam, Judaism, nor Christianity. In her opinion they all place the woman in a subordinate role. In her second novel »Le Ravisseur« (1999; t: The Kidnapper), which describes the fate of an Algerian woman, she sharply criticises the right of the man in Islam to disown his wife. With linguistic sensitivity she discusses the consequences of a traditional and increasingly anachronistic legal maxim.

In Algeria, Marouane was herself singled out for attacks against her person since, as a columnist and social critic, she sympathised with the Algerian women's rights movement. She wrote her third novel »Le châtiment des hyprocrites« (2001; t: The Punishment of the Hypocrites) to keep an act of violence which was largely hushed up, the murder of a friend, from being forgotten. It tells the story of Fatima Kosra, who was abducted, abused and impregnated by Islamists. She cannot get over the traumatic experience, but it temporarily recedes into the background when she meets the great love of her youth. The man, who lives in Paris, takes her to France with him, where her past eventually catches up with her and she becomes a murderer.

Das Mädchen aus der Kasbah
Zsolnay, Wien, 1998
[Ü: Rolf und Hedda Soellner]
Le châtiment des hypocrites
Éditions du Seuil
Paris, 2001
Entführer
Haymon, Innsbruck, 2003
[Ü: Regina Keil-Sagawe]

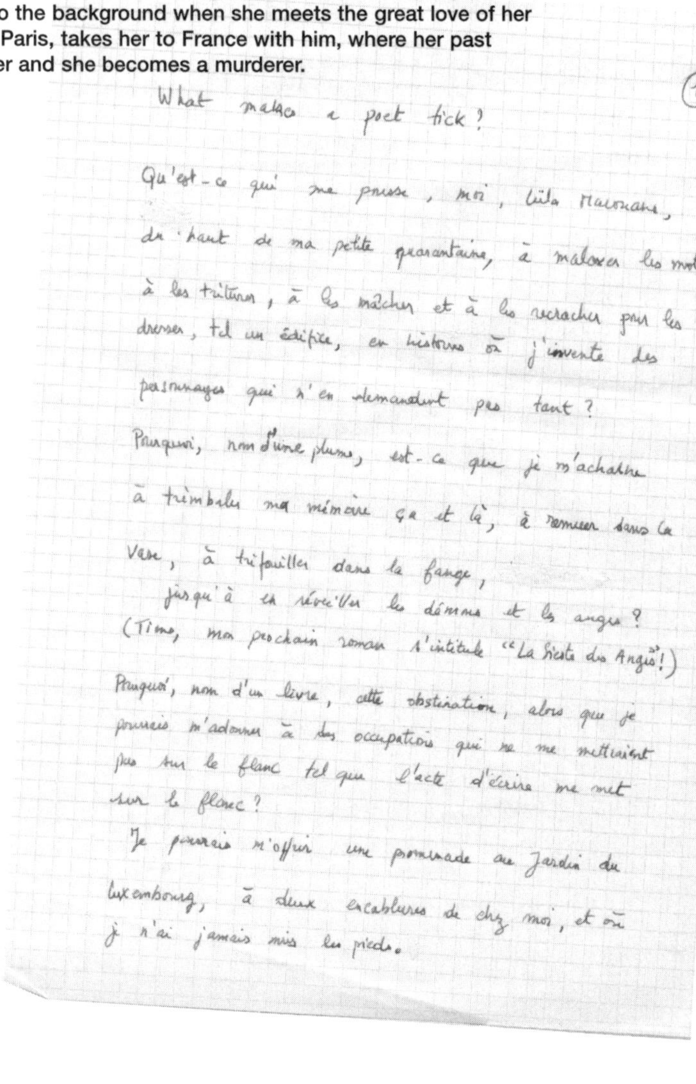

(1)

What makes a poet tick?

Qu'est-ce qui me pousse, moi, Leïla Marouane, du haut de ma petite quarantaine, à malaxer les mots, à les triturer, à les mâcher et à les recracher pour les dresser, tel un édifice, en histoires où j'invente des personnages qui n'en demandent pas tant?

Pourquoi, nom d'une plume, est-ce que je m'acharne à trimbaler ma mémoire ça et là, à remuer dans la vase, à trifouiller dans la fange, jusqu'à en réveiller les démons et les anges? (Timo, mon prochain roman s'intitule "La Sieste des Anges"!)

Pourquoi, nom d'un livre, cette obstination, alors que je pourrais m'adonner à des occupations qui ne me mettraient pas sur le flanc tel que l'acte d'écrire me met sur le flanc?

Je pourrais m'offrir une promenade au Jardin du Luxembourg, à deux encablures de chez moi, et où je n'ai jamais mis les pieds.

Leïla Marouane wurde 1960 in Algerien geboren. Sie studierte in Algier Medizin und Literaturwissenschaft und arbeitete anschließend als Journalistin. Aufgrund der angespannten Situation in Algerien lebt und arbeitet sie seit 1990 als freie Schriftstellerin in Paris. Drei Romane sind seither erschienen. Darin schildert die Autorin die Unterdrückung der Frau in ihrer Heimat und den schleichenden Verfall der einst blühenden Städte Algeriens, in denen westliche Moderne und islamischer Fundamentalismus aufeinanderprallen.

»La fille de la casbah« (1996; dt. »Das Mädchen aus der Kasbah«, 1998) erzählt vor dem Hintergrund der politischen Ereignisse im Algerien der späten achtziger Jahre die Geschichte einer jungen Lehrerin, die sich zwar gegen die Pläne ihrer Eltern zur Wehr setzt, aber dennoch daran scheitert, ihren eigenen Lebensentwurf zu verwirklichen. Weder der Islam noch die westliche Lebensweise bieten ihrem Inneren ausreichenden Halt, bis ihr Leben in einem blutigen Alptraum endet.

Auch in ihrem zweiten Roman, »Le Ravisseur« (1999; dt. »Entführer«, 2003), schildert Marouane, die sich weder mit der islamischen, jüdischen noch mit der christlichen Religion identifizieren kann, da sie alle ihrer Ansicht nach der Frau nur eine untergeordnete Rolle zuweisen, ein algerisches Frauenschicksal. Sie nimmt dabei das Recht des Mannes im Islam aufs Korn, das es ihm erlaubt, seine Frau zu verstoßen. Mit großer sprachlicher Sensibilität entwickelt sie die Konsequenzen eines überkommenen und mittlerweile anachronistischen Rechtsgrundsatzes.

Marouane war in Algerien Angriffen gegen ihre Person ausgesetzt, da sie als gesellschaftskritische Kolumnistin mit der algerischen Frauenrechtsbewegung sympathisierte. Um die weitgehend kaschierte Gewalt, so den Mord an einer Freundin, der Vergessenheit zu entreißen, verfasste sie ihren dritten Roman, »Le châtiment des hypocrites« (2001; Ü: Bestrafung der Scheinheiligen). Er erzählt die Geschichte von Fatima Kosra, die von Islamisten verschleppt, missbraucht und geschwängert wird. Zwar kann sie das traumatische Erlebnis nicht verwinden. Doch zumindest vorübergehend tritt es in den Hintergrund, als sie die große Liebe ihrer Jugendtage wiedertrifft. Der in Paris lebende Mann nimmt sie zu sich nach Frankreich, wo ihre Geschichte sie zuletzt wieder einholt und sie zur Mörderin wird.

(2)

Je pourrais me laisser porter par les vagues de l'Atlantique, à une heure de Paris. J'aurais pu tout récemment aller crapahuter dans le Massif Central, où des amis m'ont gentiment invitée. Et, plus prosaïquement, j'aurais pu procréer et ainsi contribuer à la pérennité de l'Homme, et par la même assouvir ce besoin de maternité qui taraude toute femme « normalement constituée. »

Quoi qu'il en soit, jour après jour, page après page, chapitre après chapitre, livre après livre, dans la dispersion des mots, dans le tumulte des personnages, je m'aperçois que l'acte d'écrire, ce besoin entêtant, me permet de « dire » De dire ce que je ne peux pas « hurler ». Toute cette encre, ce papier, cette énergie et ce temps, pour essayer de comprendre ce qui m'habite et me possède? Pour trouver ma voix/voie dans les dédales de mes souvenirs refoulés ou à fleur de peau? Pour expulser ces acouphènes, doux ou violents, et les rendre audibles par tous?

Qu'importe! Puisqu'au final, j'éprouve le sentiment d'avoir donné libre cours aux

(3)

émotions dont j'ai besoin soit pour échapper à la folie, soit pour perdre (à jamais) la raison soit tout simplement pour régler mes comptes, disons avec poésie. Et peut-être aussi, qu'à travers mes propres comptes, suis-je en train de régler ceux de l'humanité. En toute humilité.

Leïla Marouane

Paris, juillet 2003

lászló márton

biography

László Márton was born in Budapest, Hungary, in 1959. He studied Hungarian, German and Sociology at the Loránd-Eötvös University in Budapest. From 1983 to 1990 he worked as an editor at Helikon Publishing in Budapest and then started to work as a freelance writer. In the 90's he lived in Berlin: from 1995 to 1996 by invitation of the Literary Colloquium Berlin, and from 1998 to 1999 as a guest of the Berlin artists' programme of the DAAD.

Since his literary debut in 1983 Márton has published novels, stories, dramas and essays and received numerous prizes. He has also made a name for himself as a translator. He translated Novalis' »Heinrich von Ofterdingen«, Kleist's »Michael Kohlhaas«, and Goethe's »Faust« into Hungarian. Working closely on these texts clearly influenced his writing. The novel »Jacob Wunschwitz igaz története« (1997) is a historical parable about power and powerlessness in times of despotic rule, which shows clear parallels with Kohlhaas. In the year 1603 the fabric dyer Jacob Wunschwitz is travelling on business in Lower Lusatia and unbeknowingly gets caught up in the machinations of spiritual and worldly powers. Márton's lavish language uses elaborate multi-clause sentences and almost completely renounces the use of direct speech; his narrator comments extensively on the events and makes philosophical observations. Transmitting historical and encyclopedic knowledge is just as characteristic of Márton's writing as is his predilection for intricate narrations and various time levels – as someone who travels between different times and worlds, Wunschwitz is a victim of the Spartacus revolt of 1919 in Berlin and at the same time one of the founders of the Sozialistische Einheitspartei Deutschlands (Socialist Unity Party of Germany).

His second novel to be published in German, »Árnyas főutca« (1999), takes as its point of departure the missing portraits of people and landscapes taken by photographer Ignác Halász in a small town in Hungary in the first half of the 20th century. From these fleeting memories Márton reconstructs the everyday life and fate of the Jewish residents, whose lives were destroyed by National Socialism and Soviet rule. After escape and expulsion, only the memory remains of Jews and Christians living peacefully side by side together. Péter Esterházy praised this novel as »unusually original and radical«, which secured Márton a place with established Hungarian writers like Imre Kertész and Péter Nádas. Márton lives in Budapest.

Nagy-budapesti Rém-üldözés
Magvető, Budapest, 1984
Tudatalatti megálló
Holnap, Budapest, 1990
Nagy-budapesti Rém-üldözés és más történetek
Jelenkor, Pécs, 1995
Die fliehende Minerva oder Die letzten Tage des Verbannten
Ed. Thanhäuser Ottensheim a. d. Donau 1997
Die wahre Geschichte des Jacob Wunschwitz
dtv, München, 2002
[Ü: Hans-Henning Paetzke]
Die schattige Hauptstraße
Zsolnay, Wien, 2003
[Ü: Agnes Relle]

hiermit schicke ich Ihnen eine kleine Collage als Antwort auf die Frage "What makes the poet tick?". Ich bin in im Sinne von Giambattista Vico verfahren, der meint, die Poesie sei eine bildhafte, also weisende und nicht be-weisende Sprache.

Herzliche Grüße von

László Márton wurde 1959 in Budapest, Ungarn, geboren. Er studierte dort an der Loránd-Eötvös Universität Hungarologie, Germanistik und Soziologie. Von 1983 bis 1990 arbeitete er als Lektor beim Budapester Helikon-Verlag. Seither ist er freier Schriftsteller. In den neunziger Jahren lebte er in Berlin, von 1995 bis 1996 auf Einladung des Literarischen Colloquiums Berlin und von 1998 bis 1999 als Gast des Berliner Künstlerprogramms des DAAD.
Seit seinem literarischen Debüt 1983 hat Márton Romane, Erzählungen, Dramen und Essays publiziert und dafür zahlreiche Auszeichnungen erhalten. Daneben hat er sich als Übersetzer einen Namen gemacht. Er übertrug Novalis' »Heinrich von Ofterdingen«, Kleists »Michael Kohlhaas« und Goethes »Faust« ins Ungarische. Die Auseinandersetzung mit diesen Werken war für sein eigenes Schaffen prägend. Der Roman »Jacob Wunschwitz igaz története« (1997; dt. »Die wahre Geschichte des Jacob Wunschwitz«, 2002) ist eine historische Parabel über Macht und Ohnmacht in Zeiten der Willkürherrschaft, die Parallelen zum Kolhaas-Stoff erkennen lässt. Der Tuchfärber Jacob Wunschwitz ist im Jahr 1603 geschäftlich in der Niederlausitz unterwegs und gerät dabei unversehens in das Räderwerk geistlicher und weltlicher Mächte. Mártons opulente Sprache bedient sich kunstvoller Schachtelsätze und verzichtet fast vollständig auf direkte Rede, sein Erzähler kommentiert ausschweifend das Geschehen und stellt philosophische Betrachtungen an. Die Ausbreitung historischen und enzyklopädischen Wissens ist ebenso kennzeichnend für Mártons Schreiben wie die Vorliebe für verzweigte Handlungsstränge und unterschiedliche Zeitebenen: Als Reisender zwischen den Zeiten und Welten ist Wunschwitz Opfer des Spartakusaufstandes 1919 in Berlin und zugleich einer der Gründer der Sozialistischen Einheitspartei Deutschlands.
Sein zweiter auf Deutsch erschienener Roman »Árnyas főutca« (1999; dt. »Die schattige Hauptstraße«, 2003) nimmt seinen Ausgang in den verschwundenen Porträts von Menschen und Landschaften, die der Fotograf Ignác Halász in der ersten Hälfte des 20. Jahrhunderts in einer ungarischen Kleinstadt anfertigte. Márton rekonstruiert aus diesen Schemen der Erinnerung Alltag und Schicksal der jüdischen Bewohner, deren Leben durch Nationalsozialismus und Sowjetherrschaft zerstört wurde. Nach Flucht und Vertreibung ist allein die Erinnerung an ein friedliches Zusammenleben von Juden und Christen geblieben.
Als »außergewöhnlich originell und radikal« pries Péter Esterházy diesen Roman, mit dem sich Márton endgültig einen Platz neben etablierten ungarischen Schriftstellern wie Imre Kertész oder Péter Nádas gesichert habe. Márton lebt in Budapest.

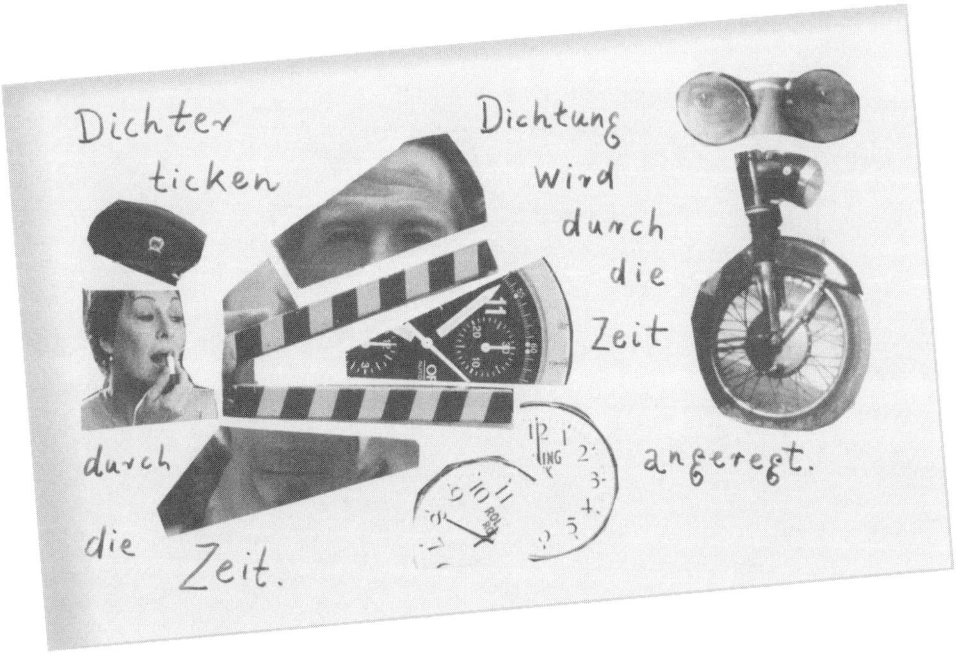

semezdin mehmedinović

biography

Semezdin Mehmedinović was born in Kiseljak, Bosnia-Herzegovina, in 1960. After studying Comparative Literature and Librarianship in Sarajevo, he worked as an editor for the opposition magazines for young people »Lica« and »Walter«. He also did performance art. He published his first book of poetry »Modrac« in 1984, and his second book »Emigrant« in 1990. In 1991 he founded the cultural magazine »Fantom slobode« (t: Phantom of Freedom), of which only six issues appeared – three pre-war and three war editions. When war broke out in 1992, Mehmedinović remained with his family in Sarajevo during the attacks. In this year he published an early version of »Sarajevo Blues«; the more extensive version was published in Zagreb in 1995. With friends he founded the weekly political magazine »Dani« (t: Days) in 1992, to create a voice for democracy and pluralism in times of genocide. Today, its objectivity and lucidity still make it Bosnia's best magazine.

In 1996 Mehmedinović emigrated to the US and now lives in Alexandria, Virginia. »Sarajevo Blues« was published in English in 1998 and was praised by the »Washington Post« as one of the best literary documents on the Bosnian war. »Sarajevo Blues« was translated into German in 1999. In 2002 Mehmedinović published another book of poems entitled »Devet Alexandrija«, in Zagreb, Croatia. This autumn the book will be available in English translation under the title »Nine Alexandrias.«

Modrac
Svjetlost
Sarajevo, 1984
Emigrant
Zadrugar
Sarajevo, 1990
Sarajevo Blues
Hainholz
Göttingen, 1999
[Ü: Harris Džajić]
Devet Alexandrija
Durieux, Zagreb, 2002

Semezdin Mehmedinović wurde 1960 in Kiseljak in Bosnien-Herzegowina geboren.
Im Anschluss an sein Studium der Vergleichenden Literaturwissenschaft und Bibliothekswissenschaften in Sarajevo arbeitete er als Redakteur der oppositionellen Jugendzeitschriften »Lica« und »Valter« und trat als Performancekünstler auf. Seinen ersten Gedichtband »Modrac« veröffentlichte er 1984. Im Jahr 1991 gründete er die Kulturzeitschrift »Fantom slobode« (Ü: Phantom der Freiheit), von der insgesamt nur sechs Ausgaben erschienen – drei Vorkriegs- und drei Kriegsausgaben. Bei Ausbruch des Krieges 1992 blieb Mehmedinović mit seiner Familie im belagerten Sarajevo. In diesem Jahr veröffentlichte er eine frühe Fassung von »Sarajevo Blues«, einer Sammlung von Texten über den Krieg, die 1995 in einer erweiterten Ausgabe in Zagreb erschien. Mit Freunden gründete er die politische Wochenzeitschrift »Dani« (Ü: Tage), um eine Stimme der Demokratie und des Pluralismus in Zeiten des Genozids zu schaffen. Sie gilt noch heute aufgrund ihrer Objektivität und Klarsicht als die beste Zeitschrift Bosniens.
1996 emigrierte Mehmedinović in die Vereinigten Staaten, wo er mittlerweile in Alexandria, Virginia, lebt. »Sarajevo Blues«, sein international am stärksten beachtetes Werk (in deutscher Übersetzung 1999 unter dem gleichen Titel erschienen), war 1998 in englischer Übersetzung herausgekommen und wurde von der »Washington Post« als eines der besten literarischen Dokumente über den Bosnien-Krieg hervorgehoben. 2002 veröffentlichte Mehmedinović einen weiteren Gedichtband mit dem Titel »Devet Alexandrija« (Ü: Neun Alexandrien). Noch in diesem Jahr wird der Band unter dem Titel »Nine Alexandrias« in englischer Übersetzung vorliegen.

michèle métail

biography

The poet Michèle Métail was born in Paris in 1950. She studied German language and literature and sinology and wrote a dissertation on variations in form in classical Chinese verse.

Métail occasionally makes use of formats taken from other media when composing her poems. In her book »Les horizons du sol« (1999) she describes geological formations using a single sentence without any punctuation. In 2001 as a guest of the DAAD's Berlin artists' programme, she wrote fragmentary snapshots of the city using a 10 x 15 photo format (which means 10 lines, each with 15 letters). The translator Elfriede Czurda translated them into German in the fictitious 10 x 17 photo format in order to accomodate the particularities of the German language (»Gehen und Schreiben. Gedächtnis-Inventar,« 2002). The diary-like notes are supplemented with photos, which also adhere to a certain structure. They are illustrations of buildings, for the most part of glass buildings, in which other buildings are reflected and whose architectonic forms are linear and cage-like. The 24 illustrations and 36 texts, which in turn refer to the given film formats, are juxtaposed with one another, but in terms of content do not refer to one another. As in previous works, a polyphonic statement emerges. The group »Les arts contigus«, which she founded with Louis Roquin, is also interested in the confrontation between various forms of expression such as sculpture, literature, music, dance, performance, and installations.

In addition to always being interested in form, Métail's verse is characterised by an interest in spoken and visual forms that attempt to explore time, space and sound. Since 1973 many of Métail's poems have only been published orally in so-called »publications orales«. In her readings, which are frequently accompanied by slide shows and performance elements, she musically modulates her voice by varying the tempo, nuance, and tone. The text functions like a score and the reading as the final creative stage in the process. The conviction that »articulating the word in the room represents writing's highest level« has brought the author to countless readings and exhibitions in Europe and Canada.

Her scholarly research is dedicated to older Chinese verse, which she also translates into French. Métail, who has received numerous awards for her work, lives in Lasalle, France.

Portraits-Robots
Ramsay, Paris, 1987
Cinquante Poèmes oscillatoires
Ramsay, Paris, 1987
Cent pour cent
Despalles, Paris, 1998
Les Horizons du sol – Panorama
Centre international de poésie Marseille, 1999
Toponyme: Berlin. Dédale – cadastre – jumelage – panorama
Ed. Tarabuste Saint-Benoît-du-Sault, 2002
Gehen und Schreiben
DAAD, Berlin, 2002 [Ü: Elfriede Czurda]
Poème infini. Extrait
Ed. C. Moreau, Paris, 2003

la ligne-*vers*----

Die Lyrikerin Michèle Métail wurde 1950 in Paris geboren. Sie studierte Germanistik und Sinologie und promovierte mit einer Arbeit zu Formvariationen in der klassischen chinesischen Lyrik.
Métail erlegt ihren Gedichten bisweilen Formate auf, die sie aus anderen Medien übernahm. So beschreibt sie in ihrem Band »Les horizons du sol« (1999) geologische Formationen in einem einzigen Satz ohne jede Interpunktion. Als Gast des Berliner Künstlerprogramms des DAAD 2001 verfasste sie fragmentarische Momentaufnahmen der Stadt im Fotoformat 10 x 15 (d. h. 10 Zeilen à 15 Buchstaben). Die Übersetzerin Elfriede Czurda übertrug sie im Deutschen in das fiktive Fotoformat 10 x 17, um so deutschen Spracheigenheiten gerecht zu werden (»Gehen und Schreiben. Gedächtnis-Inventar«, 2002). Die tagebuchartigen Skizzen werden durch Fotos ergänzt, die ebenfalls einer bestimmten Struktur folgen. Es sind Abbildungen von Gebäuden, zumeist Glasbauten, in denen sich andere Gebäude spiegeln und die von linien- und gitterartigen architektonischen Formen geprägt sind. Die 24 Abbildungen und 36 Texte, die wiederum Bezug auf gegebene Filmformate nehmen, werden einander gegenübergestellt, sind aber inhaltlich nicht aufeinander bezogen. So entsteht, wie schon in anderen Werken zuvor, eine polyphone Aussagedimension. Auch der Gruppe »Les arts contigus«, die sie mit Louis Roquin begründete, geht es um die Konfrontation verschiedener Ausdrucksformen wie Bildhauerei, Literatur, Musik, Tanz, Performance und Installationen. Neben dieser anhaltenden Beschäftigung mit der Form ist Métails Lyrik geprägt von ihrer Auseinandersetzung mit Mündlichkeit und visuellen Formen, die sich als Versuch versteht, Zeit, Raum und Klang auszuloten. Seit 1973 werden viele Gedichte Métails nur mündlich, in sogenannten »publications orales«, veröffentlicht. Ihr Lesevortrag, der oft durch Diaprojektionen und Performance-Elemente begleitet wird, basiert auf der musikalischen Modulation der Sprechstimme durch Variationen von Tempo, Nuance und Ton. Der Text gilt ihr dabei als Partitur, der mündliche Vortrag als kreative Endstufe des Prozesses. Die Überzeugung, dass »der Wurf des Wortes in den Raum die höchste Stufe des Schreibens darstellt«, hat die Autorin auf unzählige Lesungen und Ausstellungen in Europa und Kanada geführt. Ihre wissenschaftlichen Forschungen widmen sich älterer chinesischer Lyrik, die sie auch ins Französische überträgt. Métail, die für ihr Werk zahlreiche Auszeichnungen erhielt, lebt in Lasalle, Frankreich.

------------l'horizon

nuala ní dhomhnaill
biography

Nuala Ní Dhomhnaill was born in St. Helens in the English county of Lancashire in 1952. Her parents were Irish. As a writer she draws tremendous inspiration from the culture of her ancestors, which she got to know at age 5 when the family moved to Dingle Gaeltacht in the Irish county of Kerry – one of the few places in Ireland where Gaelic is still spoken today. From 1969 to 1973 she studied English and Irish at the University College in Cork. She lived in the Netherlands and in Turkey for a few years with her husband, the Turkish geologist Dogan Leflef, before moving to Dublin in the early 80's. Since 2001 the poet, who also teaches on the side, has held Ireland's renowned Chair of Poetry.
Ní Dhomhnaill wrote her first poems in English; two early poems were published in a school newspaper. She soon realised that the English language did not suit her Irish poetry. She started to translate her poems into Irish and quickly won an award in a literature competition held by the »Irish Times«. »I had chosen my language, or more rightly, perhaps, at some very deep level, the language had chosen me«, is what Ní Dhomhnaill writes about how she found herself as a writer. Her own country is critical of her decision to write poetry in a language which, even in Ireland, is only spoken by a third of the population. In her essays, the poet always writes about the mythical power of this traditional language. She feels that the linguistic inheritance of her people carries a connection to the natural, rural Ireland of the past. In her verse, the fairytale-like and mythological figures of this past are confronted with the problems of modern everyday life, problems which are frequently tinged with feminism. The proximity to the earth, which forges the poetic link to today's world, also finds expression in Ní Dhomhnaill's poetic language, which, far from using flowery metaphor, works with simple images borrowed from nature.
In addition to books of poetry and essays, Nuala Ní Dhomhnaill has also written screenplays and theatre pieces for children and has distinguished herself as a translator and editor of Irish verse. That her decision to focus on what is traditionally Irish did not harm her career is made clear by the international acclaim for her work – her books of poetry have received many awards and have been translated into several languages.

An Dealg Droighin
Cló Mercier, Dublin, 1981
Féar Suaithinseach
An Sagart
Daingean, 1984
Pharaoh's Daughter
Gallery Press
Oldcastle, 1990
[Ü: Medbh McGuckian
Seamus Heaney u. a.]
The Astrakhan Cloak
Gallery Press
Oldcastle, 1992
[Ü: Paul Muldoon]
Cead Aighnis
An Sagart, Daingean, 1998
The Water Horse
Gallery Press
Oldcastle, 1999
[Ü: Medbh McGuckian
Eiléan Ní Chuilleanáin]
**Selected Poems:
Rogha Dánta**
New Island Books
Dublin, 2000
[Ü: Michael Hartnett]

Nuala Ní Dhomhnaill wurde 1952 als Tochter irischer Eltern in St. Helens, im englischen Lancashire, geboren. Die Kultur ihrer Vorfahren, die für ihr Schreiben so außerordentlich inspirierend sein sollte, lernte sie im Alter von fünf Jahren kennen, als die Familie nach Dingle Gaeltacht in der irischen Grafschaft Kerry übersiedelte – eine der wenigen Gegenden Irlands, wo auch heute noch Gälisch gesprochen wird. Von 1969 bis 1973 studierte sie Englisch und Irisch am University College Cork. Mit ihrem Ehemann, dem türkischen Geologen Dogan Leflef, lebte sie einige Jahre in den Niederlanden und in der Türkei, bevor sie sich in den frühen achtziger Jahren in Dublin niederließ. Seit 2001 hat die Dichterin, die nebenberuflich stets auch Lehraufträge übernommen hat, den renommierten Ireland Chair of Poetry inne.
Ihre ersten lyrischen Gehversuche machte Ní Dhomhnaill im Englischen, zwei frühe Gedichte wurden in einer Schülerzeitung veröffentlicht. Bald aber wurde ihr bewusst, dass die englische Sprache nicht mit ihrer irischen Poesie korrespondiert. Sie begann, ihre Gedichte ins Irische zu übertragen, und wurde prompt bei einem Literaturwettbewerb der »Irish Times« ausgezeichnet. »Ich habe meine Sprache gewählt, oder vielleicht sollte ich besser sagen, auf eine unergründliche Weise hat die Sprache mich gewählt«, schreibt Ní Dhomhnaill über ihre literarische Selbstfindung. Ihre Entscheidung, Gedichte in einer Sprache zu schreiben, die selbst in Irland nur noch knapp ein Drittel der Bevölkerung spricht, wird im eigenen Land durchaus kritisch gesehen. Die Dichterin beruft sich in ihren Essays immer wieder auf die mythische Kraft dieser traditionsreichen Sprache. Das sprachliche Erbe ihres Volkes stellt für sie die Verbindung her zu dem ungezwungenen und ländlich-sinnlichen Irland der Vergangenheit, dessen märchenhafte Gestalten und mythologische Figuren in ihrer Lyrik mit den häufig feministisch eingefärbten Problemstellungen des modernen Alltags konfrontiert werden. Die Erdverbundenheit, die diesen poetischen Brückenschlag in die heutige Erlebniswelt trägt, schlägt sich auch in Ní Dhomhnaills lyrischer Sprache nieder, die fernab aller blumigen Metaphorik mit schlichten, der Natur entlehnten Bildern operiert.
Nuala Ní Dhomhnaill hat neben Gedichtbänden und Essays auch Drehbücher und Theaterstücke für Kinder geschrieben und sich als Übersetzerin und Herausgeberin irischer Lyrik hervorgetan. Dass die Konzentration auf das traditionell Irische ihrer literarischen Karriere nicht geschadet hat, beweist das internationale Interesse an ihren Werken: Ihre Gedichtbände sind vielfach prämiert und mittlerweile in zahlreiche Sprachen übersetzt.

what makes the poet tick----
well a profound sense that I eavesdropped as a
small child in the Kerry Gaeltacht on a level
of language of an idiomatic richness and sensitivity
of expression that I have yet to meet again and so
I feel in honour bound to try and re-create it.

lewis nkosi

biography

Lewis Nkosi, who was born in Durban, South Africa, in 1936 is considered one of Africa's most important authors as well as literature and culture critics. He has provided hard-edged commentary on the cultural and political developments in his country and on the African continent since the 50's when, still in Johannesburg, he wrote for the legendary magazine »Drum«. Nkosi was soon prevented from writing his criticisms of the regime from inside his country. When in 1961 he received a scholarship to study at Harvard, he was forbidden by the South African government to return to his country. From this point on, Nkosi resided as a literature scholar in the US, in Zambia, and in England, where he wrote and commented on the events in his homeland.

In addition to essays and scholarly writings, Nkosi has written short stories, theatre pieces as well as to date two novels. In the novel »Mating Birds«, which was translated into ten languages, the author thematises the explosive political force that sexual relationships between blacks and whites have in a regime under apartheid. In his death cell, the first-person narrator Sibiya looks back and tells about his relationship with the white Veronica, who has accused him of raping her. Nkosi contrasts the main theme, the segregation of sexual partners on the basis of their skin colour, with the background motif of the birds visible to Sibiya from his cell window as they pair up freely with oneanother in flight.

In this novel the sharp racial division is portrayed at the time of its appearance which rendered white South Africans incapable of fully understanding the plight of black South Africans. This is explicitly underlined in Sibiya's relationship to the psychologist Dufré, when the protagonist reflects amusedly on how the whites often attempt to to interpret foreign cultures by means of European models of understanding, in Dufré's case by using the psychoanalytical ideas of Freud. He remembers his father's warning: »Our ways are not the ways of white people, their speech is not ours. White people are as smooth as eels, but they devour us like sharks.« In its structure as a prison report, as well as in the distanced and detached way that the protagonist follows his uncertain destiny and tells his story, the novel is clearly reminiscent of »The Outsider« by Albert Camus. The text also employs postmodern narrative techniques – for instance, when Sibiya reflects on his own narration, taking an interest in the unfolding of events as if he himself were uncertain of what happened. The style is precise and laconic, emphasising the opacity of events.

Nkosi's second novel »Underground People« was published to unanimous acclaim in 2002, and was shortlisted for the Herman Boesman Prize. Nkosi divides his time between Basel, Switzerland, and South Africa.

The Rhythm of Violence
Oxford University Press
London, 1964

The Transplanted Heart
Ethiope Publishing
Corporation
Nigeria, 1975

Underground People
Kwela Books
Kapstadt, 2002

Weiße Schatten
dtv, München, 2003
[Ü: Eva Bornemann]

Der 1936 im südafrikanischen Durban geborene Lewis Nkosi gilt als einer der bedeutendsten Autoren sowie Literatur- und Kulturkritiker Afrikas. Seit den fünfziger Jahren, als er noch in Johannesburg für die legendäre Zeitschrift »Drum« schrieb, kommentiert er mit scharfer Feder die kulturelle und politische Entwicklung seines Landes und des Kontinents. Schon bald durfte Nkosi seine Kritik nicht mehr in seinem Heimatland äußern. Als er 1961 mit einem Stipendium zum Studium nach Harvard ging, verweigerte ihm die südafrikanische Regierung die Wiedereinreise. Fortan lebte Nkosi als Literaturwissenschaftler unter anderem in den USA, in Sambia und England, von wo aus er zu den Ereignissen in seiner Heimat Stellung bezog. Neben Essays und wissenschaftlichen Schriften hat Nkosi Kurzgeschichten, Theaterstücke sowie bislang zwei Romane verfasst. In dem in zehn Sprachen übersetzten Roman »Mating Birds« (1983; dt. »Weiße Schatten«, 1987) thematisiert der Autor die politische Sprengkraft sexueller Beziehungen zwischen Schwarzen und Weißen unter dem Apartheid-Regime. Der Ich-Erzähler Sibiya berichtet in der Todeszelle rückblickend von seiner Beziehung zu der Weißen Veronica, die ihn der Vergewaltigung angeklagt hat. Dem Thema der Segregation der Geschlechtspartner auf Grundlage ihrer Hautfarbe in der Binnenhandlung stellt Nkosi in der Rahmenhandlung das Motiv der sich frei im Flug paarenden Vögel gegenüber, die Sibiya von seinem Zellenfenster aus beobachtet. Der Roman zeichnet die scharfe Rassentrennung zur Zeit seiner Entstehung nach, die es weißen Südafrikanern unmöglich machte, die Not der schwarzen Bevölkerung wirklich zu begreifen. Dies zeigt sich besonders deutlich in Sibiyas Verhältnis zum Psychologen Dufré, als der Protagonist amüsiert darüber nachdenkt, wie die Weißen oft fremde Kulturen mit Hilfe europäischer Deutungsmuster – in Dufrés Fall mit Freuds psychoanalytischen Ideen – zu verstehen versuchen. Dabei klingt in ihm die Warnung seines Vaters nach: »Wir leben anders als die Weißen; wir sprechen eine andere Sprache. Die Weißen sind glatt wie Aale, aber sie zerreißen uns wie die Haie.« In seiner Anlage als Gefängnisbericht wie auch in der distanziert-unbeteiligten Haltung, mit der der Protagonist sein ungewisses Schicksal verfolgt und erzählt, zeigt der Roman deutliche Anklänge an Albert Camus' »Der Fremde«. Zugleich treibt der Text sein Spiel mit postmodernen Erzählweisen, so etwa, wenn Sibiya immer wieder sein eigenes Erzählen reflektiert und sich am eigentlichen Hergang des Vorfalls in einer Weise interessiert zeigt, als wäre er selbst sich des Geschehenen nicht sicher. Die Diktion ist knapp und lakonisch und unterstreicht die Undurchsichtigkeit des Geschehens. Nkosis zweiter Roman »Underground People« (2002) wurde einhellig gelobt und für den Herman Boesman Prize nominiert. Nkosi lebt in Basel und Südafrika.

yôko ogawa

biography

Yôko Ogawa was born in the prefect of Okayama, Japan in 1962. Shintoism, which understands all parts and aspects of reality as divine, had a strong spiritual influence on her youth. In the early 80s she studied literature and art at Waseda University in Tokyo. After completing her studies, she returned to Okayama where she worked at a medical university for a while. Shortly thereafter she married. At the same time she began to write. In 1988 she received the Kaien Prize for young authors for her story »Agehachô ga kowareru toki«. Her ensuing works were also well received: With »Kampekina Byôshitsu«, »Daibingu Puru«, and »Samenai Kôcha«, she was nominated for three consecutive years for Japan's most prestigious literature prize, the Akutagawa Prize. She received this important award again in 1991 for »Ninshin Karenda«. Today with her numerous novellas, short stories, essays and novels, she is considered one of Japan's most important contemporary authors. In Europe, Yôko Ogawa was first only read in France, where since 1995 ten of her books have appeared in translation. To date the novels »Hoteru Airisu«, »Kusuriyubi«, as well as a book of stories are available in German.
Yôko Ogawa surprises her readers with a cool, minimal narrative style, which offers them all the more room to use their imaginations and make associations. Her simple sentences, the detailed descriptions and the linear narrative style intensify into an unusual, diffuse atmosphere. The characters in Ogawa's unsettling, mysterious worlds are reduced to just a few characteristics. The author primarily narrates from the viewpoint of a young, rather passive woman, who freely subordinates her actions and existence to the dominance of a man. This is also the case in »Hotel Iris«, where it is simply the dominating voice of a significantly older man that fascinates the 17 year-old Mari to such a degree that she enters into a sadomasochistic relationship with him. Ogawa's approach is neither voyeuristic nor does she pass moral judgment; she instead focuses on a subtle account of mutual dependency. Yôko Ogawa lives with her family in the Japanese prefect of Hyôgo.

Hotel Iris
Liebeskind, München, 2001
[Ü: Ursula Gräfe und
Kimiko Nakayama-Ziegler]
Der Ringfinger
Liebeskind, München, 2002
[Ü: Ursula Gräfe und
Kimiko Nakayama-Ziegler]
Schwimmbad im Regen
Liebeskind, München, 2003
[Ü: Ursula Gräfe und
Kimiko Nakayama-Ziegler]

Yôko Ogawa wurde 1962 in der Präfektur Okayama, Japan, geboren. Einen starken spirituellen Einfluss übte in ihrer Jugend der Shintoismus aus, der alle Teile und Bereiche der Wirklichkeit als göttlich begreift. Anfang der achtziger Jahre studierte sie Literatur und Kunst an der Waseda Universität Tokio. Nach dem Studium kehrte sie nach Okayama zurück, wo sie eine Zeitlang an einer medizinischen Universität arbeitete und bald darauf heiratete. Gleichzeitig begann sie mit dem Schreiben. 1988 wurde sie für die Erzählung »Agehachô ga kowareru toki« (Ü: Als der Schwalbenschwanz zerbrach) mit dem Kaien-Preis für junge Autoren ausgezeichnet. Auch ihre nachfolgenden Werke fanden große Beachtung: mit »Kampekina Byôshitsu« (Ü: Das perfekte Krankenzimmer), »Daibingu Puru« (Ü: Diving Pool) und »Samenai Kôcha« (Ü: Schwarzer Tee, der nie abkühlt) war sie drei Jahre in Folge für den renommiertesten Literaturpreis Japans, den Akutagawa-Preis, nominiert. Diese bedeutende Auszeichnung erhielt sie schließlich 1991 für »Ninshin Karenda« (dt. »Tagebuch einer Schwangerschaft«, in: »Schwimmbad im Regen«, 2003). Heute zählt sie mit ihren zahlreichen Novellen, Kurzgeschichten, Essays und Romanen zu den wichtigsten zeitgenössischen Autorinnen Japans.

In Europa wurde Yôko Ogawa zunächst nur in Frankreich wahrgenommen, wo seit 1995 zehn Titel von ihr in Übersetzung erschienen sind. In deutscher Sprache liegen bisher die Romane »Hoteru Airisu« (dt. »Hotel Iris«, 2001), »Kusuriyubi« (dt. »Der Ringfinger«, 2002) sowie ein Band mit Erzählungen vor.

Yôko Ogawa überrascht mit einem kühlen, minimalistischen Erzählstil, der umso mehr Raum für die Phantasien und Assoziationen ihrer Leser bietet. Ihre einfachen Sätze, die detaillierten Beschreibungen und die Linearität der Handlung verdichten sich zu einer seltsam diffusen Atmosphäre. Die Charaktere in Ogawas beunruhigenden, rätselhaften Welten bleiben auf wenige Merkmale reduziert. Meist erzählt die Autorin aus der Sicht einer jungen, eher passiven Frau, die ihr Handeln und Sein freiwillig der Dominanz eines Mannes unterordnet. So auch in »Hotel Iris«, wo die 17-jährige Mari allein vom gebieterischen Klang der Stimme eines wesentlich älteren Mannes so fasziniert ist, dass sie sich auf eine sado-masochistische Beziehung mit ihm einlässt. Ogawa vermeidet hier einen voyeuristischen Blick ebenso wie eine moralische Wertung und konzentriert sich stattdessen auf die subtile Schilderung einer gegenseitigen Abhängigkeit. Yôko Ogawa lebt mit ihrer Familie in der japanischen Präfektur Hyôgo.

Überraschungen in kleinen Szenen meines Alltags "make me tick".

josé manuel prieto

biography

José Manuel Prieto was born in 1962 in Havana. At age 19, after taking his school-leaving exam, he left Cuba and went to Novosibirsk to study electronic engineering, which is where he met his future wife Elena. During Perestroika he lived with his wife in St. Petersburg, where their daughter Alicia was born. He has lived in Mexico City since 1995.

In 1996 his first book of stories »Nunca antes habías visto el rojo« (t: You have never seen red before) was published in Cuba. He published his first novel »Enciclopedia de una vida en Rusia« (t: Encyclopedia of a life in Russia) in 1998 in Mexico; an excerpt from the novel can be found in the anthology »Cubanísimo. Junge Erzähler aus Kuba« (t: Cubanísimo. Young writers from Cuba). His second novel »Livadia« (»Nocturnal Butterflies of the Russian Empire«, 2001) which was published in Barcelona in 1999, has been translated into seven languages including German (to appear in February 2004).

The novel has been praised as a jewel by literary critics among others in the »New York Times« and the »New York Review of Books«. This is not only because an intelligent interlinear network of literary references and allusions runs through the narrative texture in an original way, recalling Nabokov's greatest moments, but also for his convincing portrayal of post-soviet Russia. José Manuel Prieto has also distinguished himself as a brilliant translator of Russian literature into Spanish. His translation work includes poems by Gennadi Aygi, Anna Akhmatova, Marina Cvetaeva, and Josef Brodsky as well as prose by Andre Platonov, Victor Pelevin, Vladimir Mayakovsky, Alexander Solzhenitsyn, and Vladimir Nabokov. In 2002 he published two new books: in Mexico his second book of stories »El tartamudo y la rusa« (t: The stutterer and the russian) and in Barcelona his first travel book »Treinta días en Moscú« (t: Thirty days in Moscow). In 2002 he received a fellowship from the John Simon Guggenheim Foundation.

Nunca antes habías visto el rojo
Letras Cubanas
La Habana, 1996
Enciclopedia de una vida en Rusia
CNCA, Mexiko, 1998
Livadia
Mondadori, Barcelona, 1999
Treinta días en Moscú
Mondadori, Barcelona, 2001
El tartamudo y la rusa
Tusquets, Mexiko, 2002
Liwadija
Suhrkamp, Frankfurt a. M., erscheint 2004

What makes the poet tick?

May be the right answer will be if you put one page from Swan's way by Proust. Is in the first book (the are 7) and the first part of this book, the first volume, is a chapter "Combray" then follow "Swan's love".

José Manuel Prieto wurde 1962 in Havanna geboren. Nach seinem Schulabschluss verließ er Kuba mit 19 Jahren und ging zum Studium der Elektrotechnik nach Nowosibirsk, wo er seine spätere Frau Elena kennenlernte. In den Zeiten der Perestroika wohnte er mit seiner Frau in Sankt Petersburg, wo die gemeinsame Tochter Alicia geboren wurde. Seit 1995 lebt er in Mexiko-Stadt.

1996 erschien in Kuba sein erster Erzählband »Nunca antes habías visto el rojo« (Ü: Nie zuvor sahst du das Rote). Seinen Romanerstling »Enciclopedia de una vida en Rusia« (Ü: Enzyklopädie eines Lebens in Russland) veröffentlichte er 1998 in Mexiko. Ein Ausschnitt davon erschien in der Anthologie »Cubanísimo. Junge Erzähler aus Kuba« (2000). Sein zweiter Roman »Livadia« (dt. »Liwadija«, erscheint 2004), der 1999 in Barcelona herauskam, wurde inzwischen in sieben Sprachen übersetzt. Der Roman wurde von der Literaturkritik als Entdeckung gefeiert, u. a. in der »New York Times« und der »New York Review of Books«. Dies nicht nur allein, weil seine Texte ein klug gespanntes Netz an literarischen Bezügen und Anspielungen auf originelle Weise durchzieht, sondern auch, weil ihm eine eindrucksvolle Schilderung des postsowjetischen Russland gelang.

José Manuel Prieto ist außerdem als Übersetzer russischer Literatur ins Spanische hervorgetreten, darunter Gedichte von Gennadij Ajgi, Anna Achmatowa, Marina Zwetajewa und Josef Brodsky sowie Prosa von Andrej Platonow, Victor Pelewin, Wladimir Majakowski, Alexander Solschenizyn und Vladimir Nabokov.

2002 veröffentlichte er zwei neue Bücher, in Mexiko seinen zweiten Erzählband »El tartamudo y la rusa« (Ü: Der Stotterer und die Russin) und in Barcelona sein erstes Reisebuch »Treinta días en Moscú« (Ü: Dreißig Tage in Moskau). Im selben Jahr erhielt er ein Stipendium der John Simon Guggenheim-Stiftung.

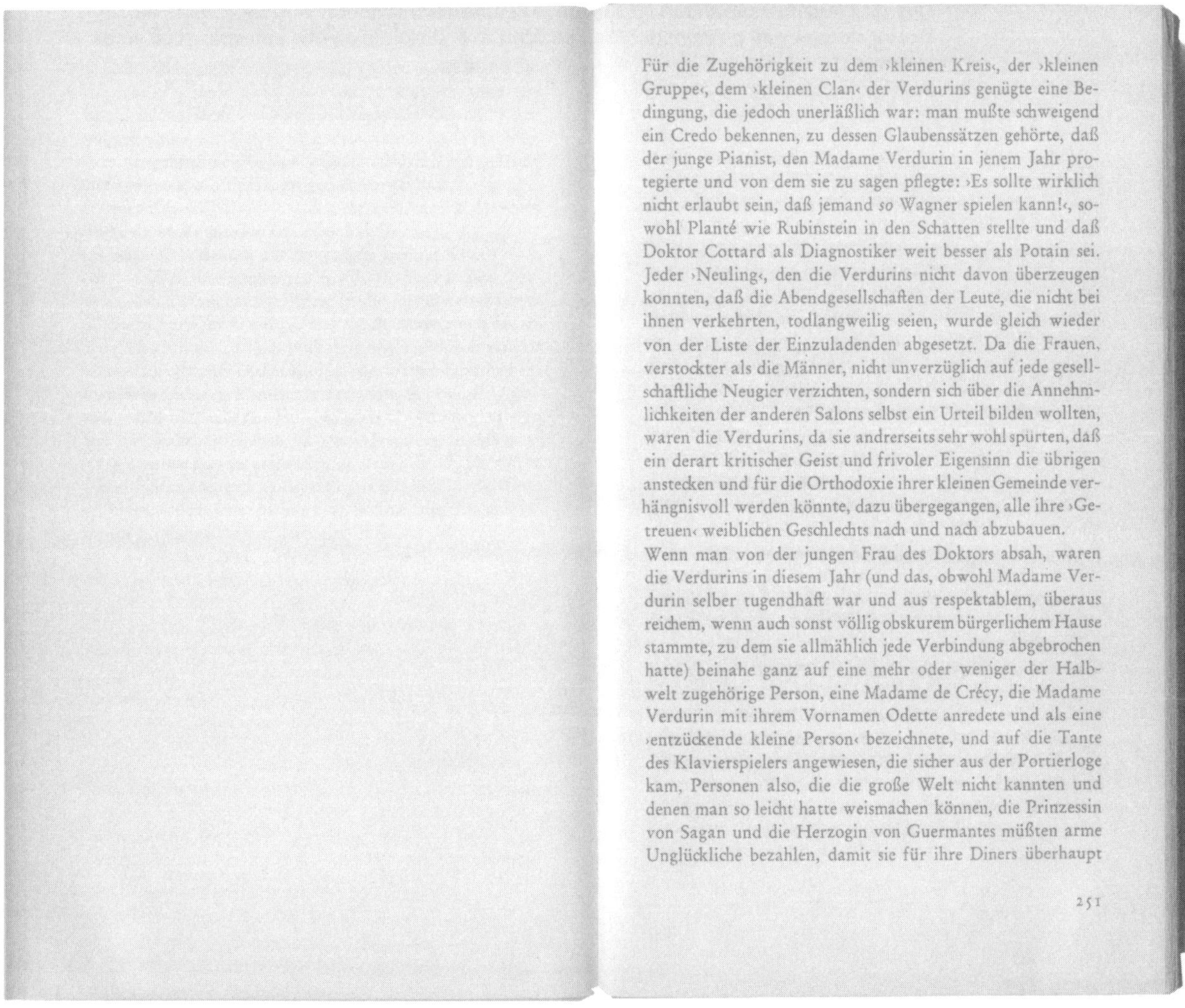
Für die Zugehörigkeit zu dem ›kleinen Kreis‹, der ›kleinen Gruppe‹, dem ›kleinen Clan‹ der Verdurins genügte eine Bedingung, die jedoch unerläßlich war: man mußte schweigend ein Credo bekennen, zu dessen Glaubenssätzen gehörte, daß der junge Pianist, den Madame Verdurin in jenem Jahr protegierte und von dem sie zu sagen pflegte: ›Es sollte wirklich nicht erlaubt sein, daß jemand *so* Wagner spielen kann!‹, sowohl Planté wie Rubinstein in den Schatten stellte und daß Doktor Cottard als Diagnostiker weit besser als Potain sei. Jeder ›Neuling‹, den die Verdurins nicht davon überzeugen konnten, daß die Abendgesellschaften der Leute, die nicht bei ihnen verkehrten, todlangweilig seien, wurde gleich wieder von der Liste der Einzuladenden abgesetzt. Da die Frauen, verstockter als die Männer, nicht unverzüglich auf jede gesellschaftliche Neugier verzichten, sondern sich über die Annehmlichkeiten der anderen Salons selbst ein Urteil bilden wollten, waren die Verdurins, da sie andrerseits sehr wohl spürten, daß ein derart kritischer Geist und frivoler Eigensinn die übrigen anstecken und für die Orthodoxie ihrer kleinen Gemeinde verhängnisvoll werden könnte, dazu übergegangen, alle ihre ›Getreuen‹ weiblichen Geschlechts nach und nach abzubauen.
Wenn man von der jungen Frau des Doktors absah, waren die Verdurins in diesem Jahr (und das, obwohl Madame Verdurin selber tugendhaft war und aus respektablem, überaus reichem, wenn auch sonst völlig obskurem bürgerlichem Hause stammte, zu dem sie allmählich jede Verbindung abgebrochen hatte) beinahe ganz auf eine mehr oder weniger der Halbwelt zugehörige Person, eine Madame de Crécy, die Madame Verdurin mit ihrem Vornamen Odette anredete und als eine ›entzückende kleine Person‹ bezeichnete, und auf die Tante des Klavierspielers angewiesen, die sicher aus der Portierloge kam, Personen also, die die große Welt nicht kannten und denen man so leicht hatte weismachen können, die Prinzessin von Sagan und die Herzogin von Guermantes müßten arme Unglückliche bezahlen, damit sie für ihre Diners überhaupt
251

josé maría ridao

biography

The diplomat, essayist and writer José María Ridao was born in Madrid in 1961. After completing a degree in Law and Arabic studies he entered the diplomatic service in 1987. In the following years his work took him to Angola and Equatorial Guinea as an embassy counsellor and to Moscow as a consul.
Ridao does not regard literature and politics as being fundamentally different things. He feels close to authors such as Günter Grass and quotes Manuel Azaña, president of the Spanish republic from 1936 to 1939, by way of explanation for how he sees his own role: »History is the highest level of our culture.« Ridao proves himself a keen analyst and eloquent critic, who, in his work, uses poetic means to examine the root causes of thought patterns that have formed our present culture.
His most recent book »El pasajero de Montauban« (2003; t: The Traveller of Montauban) is at once an essay and a fictional travel report, whose title is another reference to Azaña. Ridao traces the footsteps of prominent intellectuals who have travelled in Spain – alongside Azaña for example Walter Benjamin – in an attempt to revise current Spanish discourse, which Ridao himself describes as historical pasticcio. The novel »El mundo a media voz« (2001; t: The World in a Hushed Voice), to be published in German translation next year, is the story of a man who researches his family history to find out why his grandfather emigrated to Angola. His discoveries fall short of his expectations – he does not find the endangered Franco opponent that he had imagined his grandfather to be, but instead a picture of a convinced colonialist comes together. Ridao writes on the loss of innocence with great narrative talent. His prose is precise and subtle; it has occasionally been associated with the Spanish realism of the 50's and 60's.
His essays were first published in various newspapers, including in »El País«. A collection was published under the title »La desilusión permanente« (t: The Permanent Disappointment) in 2000. Further essay collections followed. Ridao started writing at an early age but did not publish his first novel until 1998 (»Agosto en el Paraíso«; t: August in Paradise). One year later the short story collection »Excusas para el doctor Huarte« (t: Excuses for Doctor Huarte) was published. Ridao decided to end his diplomatic career in 2000 so as to devote himself to writing. He now lives in Madrid.

Agosto en el paraíso
Montesinos
Barcelona, 1998
Excusas para el doctor Huarte
Montesinos
Barcelona, 1999
La desilusión permanente
Montesinos
Barcelona, 2000
La elección de la barbarie
Tusquets Editores
Barcelona, 2002
El passajero de Montauban
Galaxia Gutenberg
Barcelona, 2003

Der Diplomat, Essayist und Schriftsteller José María Ridao wurde 1961 in Madrid geboren. Nach Abschluss seines Jura- und Arabistik-Studiums trat er 1987 in den diplomatischen Dienst ein. Dieser führte ihn in den folgenden Jahren als Botschaftsrat nach Angola und Äquatorial-Guinea sowie als Konsul nach Moskau.
Ridao begreift Literatur und Politik nicht als grundverschiedene Dinge. Er fühlt sich Autoren wie etwa Günter Grass nahe und zitiert Manuel Azaña, den Präsidenten der spanischen Republik von 1936 bis 1939, um sein Selbstverständnis zu verdeutlichen: »Politik ist die höchste Stufe unserer Kultur.« Ridao erweist sich als scharfer Analytiker und eloquenter Kritiker, der in seinem Werk mit poetischen Mitteln die Ursprünge unserer Denkmuster hinterfragt, die noch die gegenwärtige Kultur prägen.
Sein neuestes Buch, »El pasajero de Montauban« (2003; Ü: Der Reisende von Montauban), ist Essay und fiktiver Reisebericht zugleich und spielt im Titel wiederum auf Azaña an. Ridao wandelt auf den Spuren prominenter Intellektueller, die Spanien bereist haben – neben Azaña beispielsweise Walter Benjamin –, um eine Revision des aktuellen Diskurses in Spanien zu versuchen, den Ridao selbst als Geschichtsklitterung bezeichnet. Der Roman »El mundo a media voz« (2001; Ü: Die Welt mit gedämpfter Stimme), der im nächsten Jahr in deutscher Übersetzung erscheinen wird, ist die Geschichte eines Mannes, der in der Vergangenheit seiner Familie forscht, um zu ergründen, weshalb sein Großvater einst nach Angola emigriert ist. Seine Entdeckungen entsprechen nicht seiner Erwartung: Er findet nicht den bedrohten Franco-Gegner, zu dem er den Großvater stilisiert hatte, sondern das Bild eines überzeugten Kolonialisten. Ridao schreibt mit großem erzählerischen Können vom Verlust der Unschuld. Seine Prosa ist präzise und subtil, bisweilen wurde sie mit dem spanischen Realismus der fünfziger und sechziger Jahre assoziiert.
Das essayistische Werk erschien zunächst in verschiedenen Zeitungen, u. a. in »El País«, und wurde 2000 in einer Auswahl unter dem Titel »La desilusión permanente« (Ü: Die permanente Enttäuschung) herausgebracht. Weitere Essaybände folgten. Ridao begann schon sehr früh mit dem Schreiben, veröffentlichte seinen ersten Roman jedoch erst 1998 (»Agosto en el Paraíso«; Ü: August im Paradies). Ein Jahr später erschien der Erzählband (»Excusas para el doctor Huarte«; Ü: Entschuldigungen für den Doktor Huarte). Ridao entschloss sich 2000, seine diplomatische Laufbahn zu beenden, um sich ganz dem Schreiben widmen zu können, und lebt heute in Madrid.

alberto ruy sánchez

biography

Alberto Ruy Sánchez was born in Mexico City in 1951. After studying information and communication studies at the Iberoamericana University in Mexico City, he lived in Paris, where from 1975 to 1982 he continued his studies under Roland Barthes, Gilles Deleuze and Jacques Rancière, focusing in particular on film and philosophy. He received his Ph.D. in 1980 and has since worked as a writer and publisher. From 1984 to 1986 he was editorial secretary on the legendary magazine »Vuelta« published by Octavia Paz. Since 1988 he has been the publisher of the renowned art magazine »Artes de México« and director of the publishing house of the same name in Mexico City.
Ruy Sánchez's literary influences include »On the Road« by Jack Kerouac and the works of Herman Melville, Ezra Pound, William Carlos Williams, Langston Hughes and Robert Frost. To date Ruy Sánchez has published 20 works. They have won numerous awards and have been translated into various languages including French and Arabic. Shortly after its publication in 1987, his first novel »Los nombres del aire« (German: »Mogador«, 1992) received Mexico's most important literary award, the Xavier Villaurrutia Prize. It has since attained cult status and is reprinted annually. The novella describes the awakening desire of a young Muslim woman and her restless expeditions through the city of Mogador in search of erotic fulfillment. Ruy Sánchez links elements of magic realism with Arabic mysticism, invoking a sensual and spirtual mood in everyday Islamic life. Mogador is the ancient name of the city of Essaouria on the Moroccan Atlantic coast, and forms the imaginary centre of the narrative labyrinth of Ruy Sánchez's work, a point to which he often returns in later works such as the short story »De cómo llegó a Mogador la Melancolía« (1999, t: How Melancholy Came to Mogador). In his prose work, which revolves around the city of Mogador, Ruy Sánchez aims to reconstruct the Arabic roots of Hispanic culture and identity by way of fiction.
In addition to novels and stories, Ruy Sánchez has also published poems, including a Haiku cycle, as well as extensive collections of essays. His writing on literature, art, philosophy, eroticism and film has earned him a reputation as »one of our [Mexico's] best essayists« (Octavio Paz). The outstanding monograph »Octavio Paz: Leben und Werk – Eine Einführung« (1991) has also been published in German. The author lives in Mexico City.

Los demonios de la lengua
La Orquesta, Mexiko, 1987
Los nombres del aire
Joaquín Mortiz
Mexiko, 1987
La inaccesible
Taller Martín Pescador
Mexiko, 1990
Octavio Paz – Leben und Werk
Suhrkamp
Frankfurt a. M., 1991
[Ü: Thomas Brovot]
En los labios del agua
Alfaguara, Mexiko, 1996
La huella del grito
Solar editores, Mexiko, 2002
Los jardines secretos de Mogador
Alfaguara, Madrid, 2002

Alberto Ruy Sánchez wurde 1951 in Mexiko-Stadt geboren. Nach dem Studium der Informations- und Kommunikationswissenschaften an der Universidad Iberoamericana in Mexiko-Stadt lebte er von 1975 bis 1982 in Paris, wo er bei Roland Barthes, Gilles Deleuze und Jacques Rancière seine Studien u. a. in den Bereichen Film und Philosophie erweiterte und 1980 promovierte. Seitdem arbeitet Ruy Sánchez als Schriftsteller und Herausgeber. Von 1984 bis 1986 war er Redaktionssekretär der legendären, von Octavio Paz herausgegebenen Zeitschrift »Vuelta«. Seit 1988 ist er Herausgeber der renommierten Kunstzeitschrift »Artes de México« und Leiter des gleichnamigen Verlags in Mexiko-Stadt.
Zu der Literatur, die Ruy Sánchez beeinflußt hat, gehörten der Roman »Unterwegs« von Jack Kerouac sowie die Werke von Herman Melville, Ezra Pound, William Carlos Williams, Langston Hughes und Robert Frost. Ruy Sánchez hat bislang knapp 20 Werke veröffentlicht, die in verschiedene Sprachen übersetzt worden sind, u. a. ins Französische und Arabische. Sein Romanerstling »Los nombres del aire« (Ü: Die Namen der Luft) wurde 1987, noch im Jahr des Erscheinens, mit dem Premio Xavier Villaurrutia, dem wichtigsten Literaturpreis Mexikos, ausgezeichnet und gilt seither als Kultbuch, das jährlich Neuauflagen erlebt. Der Kurzroman beschreibt das erwachende Begehren einer jungen Muslimin und ihre rastlosen Streifzüge durch die Stadt Mogador auf der Suche nach erotischer Erfüllung. Ruy Sánchez verbindet hier Elemente des magischen Realismus mit arabischer Mystik und beschwört eine Stimmung von Sinnlichkeit und Spiritualität im islamischen Alltag. Mogador ist der alte Name der Stadt Essaouria an der marokkanischen Atlantikküste und bildet den imaginären Mittelpunkt des narrativen Labyrinths in Ruy Sánchez' Werk, zu dem er in späteren Erzählungen immer wieder zurückkehrt, z. B. in »De cómo llegó a Mogador la Melancolía« (1999, Ü: Wie die Melancholie nach Mogador kam). Ruy Sánchez sucht in seinem stetigen Kreisen um die Stadt Mogador die arabischen Wurzeln hispanischer Kultur und Identität auf fiktive Weise zu rekonstruieren.
Neben Romanen und Erzählungen hat Ruy Sánchez auch Gedichte, darunter einen Haiku-Zyklus und umfangreiche Essaysammlungen veröffentlicht. Seine Arbeiten zur Literatur, Kunst, Philosophie, zur Erotik und zum Film haben ihm den Ruf »eines der besten Essayisten Mexikos« (Octavio Paz) eingebracht. Auf Deutsch ist von Ruy Sánchez 1991 die ebenfalls ausgezeichnete Monographie »Octavio Paz: Leben und Werk.« erschienen. Der Autor lebt in Mexiko-Stadt.

Alberto Ruy-Sánchez

**Nueve respuestas serpentinas
que se muerden la cola,
para saber que hace click en el poeta.**

1. Sentir que el cuerpo es una casa llena de fantasmas.
2. Comprobar que nunca acaba el beso que incendia al mundo.
3. Pero también, de pronto, sentir el beso de la muerte.
2. Despertar dentro del sueño.
3. Mirar con otros ojos otras vidas.
4. Ser mirado con los ojos cerrados de la persona amada.
5. Entre la rabia y el asombro, saber insoportable el aliento contenido.
6. Estar seguro, por un instante al menos, de que la magia de las palabras algo cambia en el mundo.
7. Conocer la fiebre en la sombra cuando se vuelve voz y se vuelve viento.
8. Sentir en la boca un torbellino o la aguda presencia de la nada.
9. Dejarse navegar por el deseo como se lleva en la sangre una nave pirata.

olga schamborant

biography

Olga Shamborant was born in Moscow in 1945. Since completing her studies in biology at the state university in Moscow in 1969, she has worked at the Institute for Bioorganic Chemistry (RAN).
She began writing her first poems in early adolescence, an endeavour that her family did not praise, but rather looked down upon slightly. Referring back to this time, the author notes that as a child she was already fascinated by the monotonous intonation of Stalinist rhetoric. Her output in the years that followed consisted only of occasional texts, which she nevertheless did not publish because she was afraid of censorship. It was only after Perestroika, in the early 90's, that she began to continuously write prose poems and essays. Some of these were published for the first time in 1992 in the »Niezavisimaja Gazeta«. Since then her texts have appeared regularly in Russian periodicals like »Nowoje Russkoje Slowo«, »Nowj Mir«, »Postskriptum«, »Itogi« and »Rossija«. In addition to her own literary works, she regularly writes literary criticism. Her literary influences include Marina Zwetajewa, Joseph Brodsky, Vladimir Nabokov and Kurt Vonnegut. Her scientific background is apparent in her works – in the microscopic attention with which she diagnoses daily life. Here, her concern is not so much with the events themselves but with taking an in-depth look at life, which unfolds in stages like an experiment. In 1998 she published a book of selected essays entitled »Priznaki Schisni« in St. Petersburg. Her second book »Srok godnosti« includes the essays »Svidetelstvo o smerti« and »Tainstvo ili podljanka« – the latter was written in the wake of the sinking of the Russian submarine »Kursk« in August 2000 – both of which reflect on the post-communist Russian individual's limited aptitude for learning as far as the subject of mortality is concerned.

Prisnaki Schisni
Puschkinski Fond
St. Petersburg, 1998
Srok godnosti
Puschkinski Fond
St. Petersburg, 2003

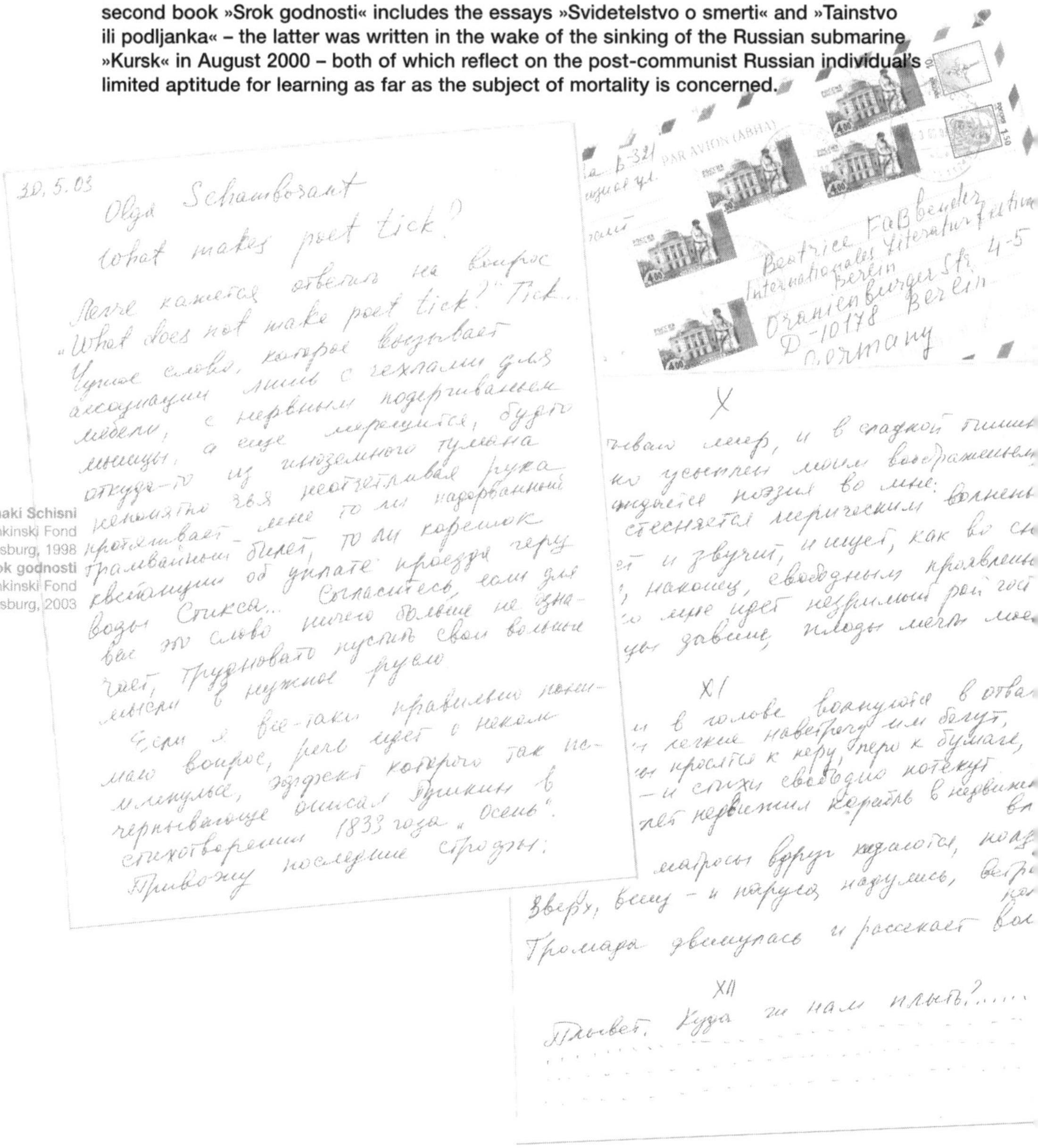
30.5.03
Olga Schamborant
What makes poet tick?
Мне кажется ответить на вопрос „What does not make poet tick?" Tick... Чужое слово, которое вызывает ассоциации лишь с тахтами для мебели, с нервным подергиванием мышцы, а еще мерещится, будто откуда-то из иноземного тумана непонятно чья неотчетливая рука протягивает мне то ли надорванный трамвайный билет, то ли корешок квитанции об уплате проезда через воды Стикса... Согласитесь, если для вас это слово ничего больше не значит, трудновато пустить свои вольные мысли в нужное русло.
Если я все-таки правильно понимаю вопрос, речь идет о неком эффекте, который так исчерпывающе описал Пушкин в стихотворении 1833 года „Осень". Привожу последние строфы:

X
...ваю мир, и в сладкой тишин...
...ко усыплен моим воображень...
...ждается поэзия во мне:
...стесняется лирическим волнень...
...ет и звучит, и ищет, как во сн...
..., наконец, свободным проявлень...
...о мне идет незримый рой гост...
...цы давние, плоды мечты мое...

XI
...и в голове волнуются в отва...
...легкие навстречу им бегут,
...ся просятся к перу, перо к бумаге,
... – и стихи свободно потекут.
...пит недвижим корабль в недвижн...
...матросы вдруг кидаются, полз...
вверх, вниз – и паруса надулись, ветр...
Громада двинулась и рассекает вол...

XII
Плывет. Куда ж нам плыть?......

Olga Schamborant wurde 1945 in Moskau geboren. Seit dem Abschluss ihres Biologiestudiums an der Staatlichen Universität Moskau 1969 ist sie am Institut für Bioorganische Chemie (RAN) tätig.
Schon in frühester Jugend schrieb sie erste Gedichte, die ihr allerdings statt der Anerkennung der Familie lediglich milden Spott einbrachten. Die Autorin bemerkt im Rückblick auf diese Zeit, dass sie schon als Kind fasziniert der immergleichen Intonation der stalinistischen Rhetorik lauschte. In den darauf folgenden Jahren verfasste sie nur gelegentlich Texte, die sie jedoch nicht veröffentlichte, weil sie die Zensur fürchtete. Erst nach der Perestroika, Anfang der neunziger Jahre, begann sie kontinuierlich Prosagedichte und Essays zu schreiben, von denen erstmals 1992 einige in der »Niezavisimaja Gazeta« publiziert wurden. Seitdem erscheinen ihre Texte regelmäßig in russischen Periodika wie »Nowoje Russkoje Slowo«, »Nowj Mir«, »Postskriptum«, »Itogi« und »Rossija«. Neben ihren eigenen literarischen Arbeiten schreibt sie regelmäßig Literaturkritiken. Zu ihren literarischen Gewährsleuten zählt sie Marina Zwetajewa, Joseph Brodsky, Vladimir Nabokov und Kurt Vonnegut. Ihre berufliche Erfahrung als Wissenschaftlerin findet sich in ihren Werken wieder – mit mikroskopischem Blick diagnostiziert sie den Alltag. Dabei gilt ihre Aufmerksamkeit nicht der Handlung, vielmehr vertieft sie sich in die Betrachtung des Lebens, das wie in einer experimentellen Anordnung abläuft. 1998 erschien ein Band mit ausgewählten Essays unter dem Titel »Priznaki Schisni« (Ü: Anzeichen des Lebens) in Sankt Petersburg. Ihr zweites Buch mit dem Titel »Srok godnosti« (Ü: Haltbarkeitsdauer) enthält Essays wie »Svidetelstvo o smerti« (Ü: Todesbescheinigung) und »Tainstvo ili podljanka« (Ü: Der Tod als Mysterium und als Beschiss) – letzterer geschrieben anlässlich des Untergangs des russischen U-Boots »Kursk« im August 2000 –, in denen die eingeschränkte Lernfähigkeit des postkommunistischen russischen Menschen in Bezug auf seine Sterblichkeit reflektiert wird.

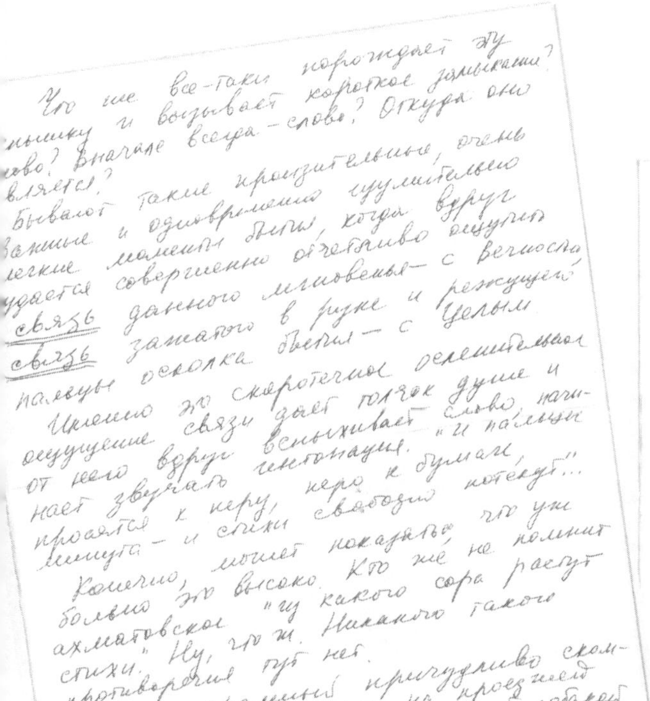
Что же все-таки порождает эту
…нышку и вызывает короткое замыкание?
…ово? Вначале всегда — слово? Откуда оно
…вляется?
Бывают такие поразительные, очень
важные и одновременно удивительно
легкие моменты бытия, когда вдруг
удается совершенно отчетливо ощутить
связь данного мгновенья — с вечностью,
связь зажатого в руке и режущего
пальцы осколка бытия — с целым.
Именно это скоротечное осязаемое
ощущение связи дает толчок душе и
от него вдруг вспыхивает слово, начи-
нает звучать интонация. „И пальцы
просятся к перу, перо к бумаге,
минута — и стихи свободно потекут"...
Конечно, может показаться, что уж
больно это высоко. Кто же не помнит
ахматовское „Из какого сора растут
стихи". Ну, что ж. Никакого такого
противоречия тут нет.
Если огромный причудливо скомканный лист бумаги на проезжей
части показался вам сбитой собакой
— огромное облегчение, которое вы
испытаете, подобно блику, может дать
вам ту самую энергию, тот импульс,

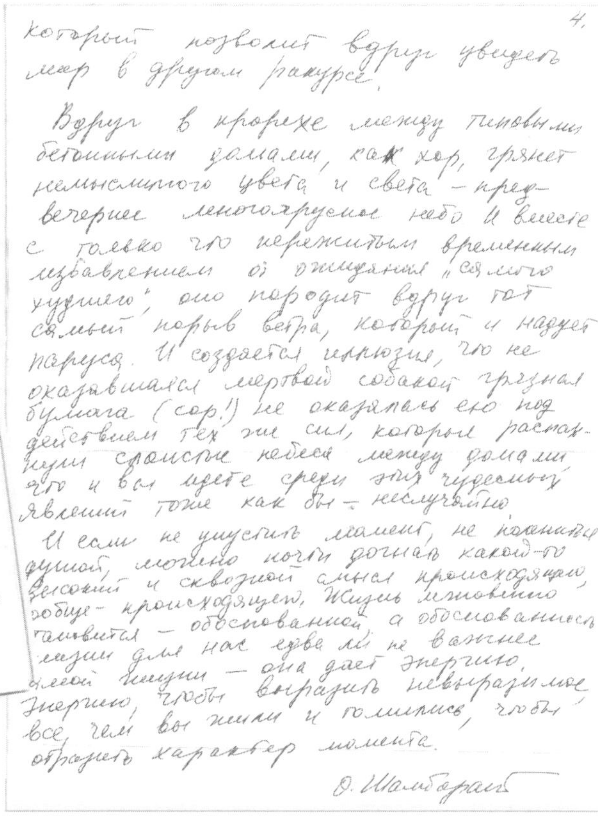
4.
который позволит вдруг увидеть
мир в другом ракурсе.
Вдруг в прорехе между типовыми
бетонными домами, как хор, грянет
немыслимого цвета и света — пред-
вечернее многоярусное небо и вместе
с только что пережитым временным
избавлением от ожидания „самого
худшего", оно породит вдруг тот
самый порыв ветра, который и надует
паруса. И создается иллюзия, что не
оказавшаяся мертвой собакой грязная
бумага (сор!) не оказалась ли под
действием тех же сил, которые растащили
сплошные небеса между домами,
что и вся идея среди этих чудесных
явлений тоже как бы — неслучайна.
И если не упустить момент, не поленится
душой, можно почти догнать какой-то
высокий и сквозной смысл происходящего,
вообще — происходящего. Жизнь мгновенно
становится — обоснованной, а обоснованность
жизни для нас едва ли не важнее
самой жизни — она дает энергию,
энергию, чтобы выразить невыразимое
все, чем вы жили и томились, чтобы
отразить характер момента.
О. Шамборант

lee siegel

biography

Lee Siegel was born in Los Angeles, California, in 1945. He studied comparative literature at the University of California in Berkeley, and fine arts at Columbia University in New York. After completing his doctoral dissertation in the field of Sanskrit at Oxford University, he was engaged by the University of Hawaii, where he has since worked as a Professor of Religious Studies.

Siegel's scholarly examinations of Indian love poetry, comedy, horror and magic have won many awards. His interest in, knowledge of, and fascination with the culture of India influence and inform his fiction. Siegel's first novel »Love in a Dead Language« (1999), a »New York Times« Notable Book of the Year, is the story of a professor of Indology who, imagining that he will only be able to fully understand Indian culture when he has had an affair with an Indian woman, falls obsessively and disastrously in love with a young American student of Indian descent. The book is a satire of the American academy, a parody of western fantasies about Oriental understandings of sexual passion, and a burlesque of the many ways of writing about erotic love.

Siegel's most recent novel, »Love and Other Games of Chance« (2003), beginning on the shores of the Dead Sea and ending on the summit of Mount Everest, maps an allegorical journey from the lowest place on earth to the highest. This comic tale is flamboyantly spun by a vagrant showman, Isaac Schlossberg, as he waits in Hawaii for World War II to end so that he can attempt to become the first person to conquer Everest. The entertainer organizes his memories into one hundred squares on the childhood game of Snakes and Ladders, one hundred narrative blocks that form a patchwork picaresque. The son of Jewish immigrants to America at the beginning of the 20th century, Isaac's first recollection is of himself as Samoo the Amazing Snake Boy in his father's travelling sideshow. Starting as Wild-West performers, the Schlossbergs work their way up the game through circus, vaudeville, and early films. From California, Isaac travels to Calcutta and there assembles a troupe, to go on tour in England. Via the Soviet Union and Paris he finally returns to the United States.

As Isaac travels geographically around the world and up and down the board, he moves sentimentally from the beginnings of love, through many of its most painful and joyous, noble and ridiculous manifestations, to finally almost achieve its realization. »It is a story,« Isaac insists, »about love and death and trying to have a good time anyway.«

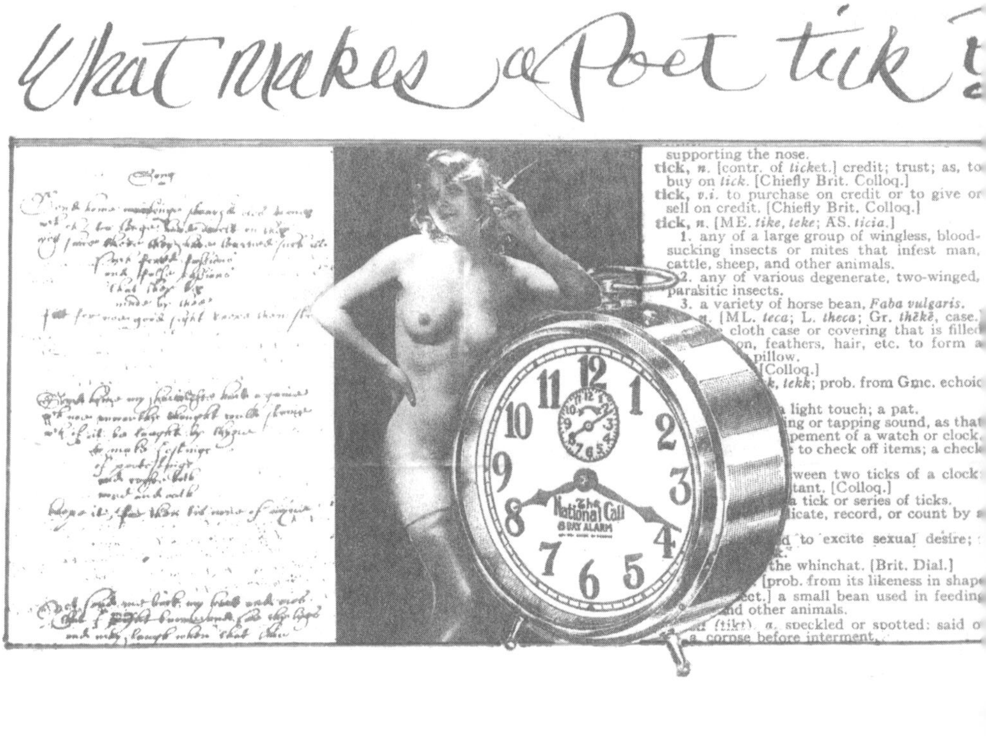

Sacred and Profane Dimensions of Love in Indian Traditions
Oxford University Press
Delhi; New York, 1978
Fires of Love, Waters of Peace. Passion and Renunciation in Indian Culture
University of Hawaii Press
Honolulu, 1983
Laughing Matters. Comic Tradition in India
University of Chicago Press
Chicago, 1987
Net of Magic. Wonders and Deceptions in India
University of Chicago Press
Chicago, 1991
City of Dreadful Night. A Story about Horror & the Macabre in India
University of Chicago Press
Chicago, 1995
Love in a Dead Language
University of Chicago Press
Chicago, 1999
Love and Other Games of Chance
Viking, New York, 2003

Lee Siegel wurde 1945 in Los Angeles, Kalifornien, geboren. Er studierte Vergleichende Literaturwissenschaft an der University of California in Berkeley und Kunst an der Columbia University in New York. Nachdem er in Oxford im Fachgebiet Sanskrit promovierte, erhielt er einen Ruf an die University of Hawaii, wo er seither als Professor für Religionswissenschaften tätig ist.
Siegels wissenschaftliche Arbeiten zur Liebeslyrik, Komödie, Horror und Magie Indiens wurden mehrfach ausgezeichnet. Sein Interesse und seine Faszination an Indien, sein Wissen über diese Kultur beeinflussen und prägen seine literarischen Texte. Siegels erster Roman »Love in a Dead Language« (1999) – Notable Book of the Year der »New York Times« – erzählt die Geschichte eines Professors für Indologie, der glaubt, erst nach einer Affäre mit einer Inderin die Kultur des Landes verstehen zu können, und der sich aus dieser Vorstellung heraus so obsessiv wie verhängnisvoll in eine junge Amerikanerin indischer Herkunft verliebt. Das Buch ist sowohl eine Satire auf den amerikanischen Lehrbetrieb als auch eine Parodie westlicher Phantasien über das orientalische Verständnis sexueller Leidenschaft und eine Karikatur der Möglichkeiten, von erotischer Liebe zu schreiben.
Siegels jüngster Roman, »Love and Other Games of Chance« (2003), führt von den Ufern des Roten Meeres bis auf den Gipfel des Mount Everest und kartographiert so eine Reise vom tiefsten bis zum höchsten Punkt der Erde. Diese komische Erzählung wird raffiniert verwoben von dem umherziehenden Schausteller Isaac Schlossberg, der in Hawaii auf das Ende des Zweiten Weltkriegs wartet, damit er als erster Mensch den Mount Everest besteigen kann. Er ordnet seine Erinnerungen in die hundert Felder des Kinderbrettspiels Schlangen und Leitern, in hundert Erzählblöcke eines patchworkartigen Schelmenromans. In einer ersten Erinnerung sieht Isaac, Sohn jüdischer Immigranten im frühen 20. Jahrhundert, sich selbst in der fahrenden Varietéshow seines Vaters als Samoo, den wundersamen Schlangenjungen. Als Wild-West-Darsteller beginnend, arbeiten sich die Schlossbergs im Spiel hinauf durch Zirkus, Vaudeville und frühe Filme. Isaac selbst reist von Kalifornien nach Kalkutta, als Darsteller einer Schauspielertruppe weiter nach England, in die Sowjetunion und nach Paris, bis er schließlich nach Amerika zurückkehrt.
So wie Isaac durch die Welt und über das Spielbrett reist, bewegt er sich auch wehmütig von den Anfängen der Liebe durch ihre schmerzvollsten und fröhlichsten, edelsten und lächerlichsten Formen, bis er endlich beinahe ihre Erfüllung findet. »Es ist«, beharrt Isaac, »eine Geschichte über Liebe und Tod und den Versuch, dennoch Spaß zu haben.«

Credit, trust, wingless, blood-sucking insects, mites, degenerate, two-winged parasites, horse beans, cloth cases, feathers, hair, pillows, light touches, tapping sounds, watches, clocks, checks, records, sexual desire, whinchats, small beans and corpses before interment.

susan swan

biography

Susan Swan was born in 1945 in Midland, Ontario, a small town for tourists close to the Great Lakes in Canada. Her later work was strongly influenced by the years she spent at a girls boarding school, where she grew up at a time of tension spanning the conformist 50's and the protest movements of the ensuing decade. After studying English Literature at McGill University in Montreal, she worked for a daily newspaper in Toronto. In 1973, after the birth of her daughter, she began to write literature. Susan Swan is also known internationally as a poet and dramatist. Since 1983 she has taught Creative Writing at Canadian colleges and is currently a professor at York University in Toronto.
Her novels have been published in 16 countries. Writing in an entertaining and provocative way, she is above all concerned with questions of gender roles. Creating »strong female characters with mythical power,« who »show new ways to be a woman« is how she herself describes her literary concerns. Her first novel »The Biggest Modern Woman of the World«, now a classic in Canada, is indeed about an unusual woman. It tells the life story of the giant Anna Swan (1846–1888), who is put on exhibition in New York as the »largest woman in the world« and becomes internationally famous. But when she later wants to lead a »normal« life in the Midwest, she realizes that she is not satisfied with the conventions of the time. Swan describes the giant woman as a mythical figure, who is more than just literally »too big« for the confines of a woman's role in a male-dominated world. The passions and the rebellion of two very different female friends, who find the idea of life as a boy more appealing, forms the background to »The Wives of Bath« (1993). Through the eyes of the main figure, Mary, who with black humour and self-irony examines the tragic events that took place while she was at boarding school, a clear picture of how young girls grew up in Canada in the 60's emerges. In this book Swan is also interested in strange figures who open the way to a different, deeper reality. The feature film based on Swan's novel »Lost and Delirious« (2001) – which was also shown in German cinemas under the same title – was well received at the Sundance Film Festival in Utah and at the Berlinale Film Festival in 2001.

The Biggest Modern Woman of the World
Lester & Orpen Dennys
Toronto, 1983
The Last of the Golden Girls
Lester & Orpen Dennys
Toronto, 1989
Stupid Boys Are Good to Relax With
Somerville House Publishing
Toronto, 1996
Böse Mädchen
Piper, München, 1997
[Ü: Heimo Mitterer]
What Casanova Told Me
Knopf Canada
Toronto, erscheint 2004

Susan Swan wurde 1945 in Midland, Ontario, einem kleinen Touristenort am Rand der Great Lakes in Kanada, geboren. Großen Einfluss auf ihr späteres Werk sollten die Jahre in einem Mädcheninternat haben, wo sie im Spannungsfeld der konformistisch geprägten fünfziger Jahre und der Protestbewegung des darauffolgenden Jahrzehnts aufwuchs. Nach dem Studium der Englischen Literatur an der McGill University in Montreal war sie zunächst für eine Tageszeitung in Toronto tätig, ehe sie 1973, nach der Geburt ihrer Tochter, mit dem literarischen Schreiben begann. Inzwischen ist Susan Swan auch als Lyrikerin und Dramatikerin international bekannt. Seit 1983 lehrt sie an kanadischen Hochschulen Kreatives Schreiben und ist derzeit Professorin an der York University in Toronto.
In ihren Romanen, die in 16 Ländern erschienen sind, beschäftigt sich Susan Swan auf unterhaltsame und provozierende Weise vor allem mit der Frage der Geschlechterrollen. »Starke weibliche Charaktere mit mythischer Kraft« zu erschaffen, die »neue Wege aufzeigen, eine Frau zu sein« – so charakterisiert sie selbst ihr schriftstellerisches Anliegen. Eine solche außergewöhnliche Frau steht auch im Zentrum ihres ersten Romans »The Biggest Modern Woman of the World« (1983), der in Kanada mittlerweile als Klassiker gilt. Erzählt wird die groteske Lebensgeschichte der Riesin Anna Swan (1846-1888), die als »größte Frau der Welt« in New York zur Schau gestellt wurde und internationale Berühmtheit erlangte. Als sie später im Mittleren Westen ein »normales« Leben führen will, muss sie jedoch erkennen, dass sie den Konventionen ihrer Zeit nicht genügen kann. Swan beschreibt die Riesin als mythische Figur, die sich nicht nur im wörtlichen Sinn als »zu groß« für das enge Frauenbild einer von Männern dominierten Welt erweist.
Die Leidenschaften und das Aufbegehren zweier ungleicher Freundinnen, denen ein Leben als Junge verlockender erscheint, bilden den Hintergrund von »The Wives of Bath« (1993; dt. »Böse Mädchen«, 1997). Aus der Perspektive der Hauptfigur Mary, die mit schwarzem Humor und Selbstironie den tragischen Ereignissen ihrer Internatszeit auf die Spur geht, wird ein plastisches Bild vom Erwachsenwerden junger Mädchen im Kanada der sechziger Jahre gezeichnet. Doch auch in diesem Buch zeigt sich Swans Interesse an skurrilen Gestalten, die dem Leser jenseits des Vertrauten den Blick auf eine andere, tiefere Realität eröffnen. Der auf Swans Roman basierende Spielfilm »Lost and Delirious« (2001) – der unter diesem Titel auch in den deutschen Kinos lief – fand beim Sundance Film Festival in Utah und bei der Berlinale 2001 große Beachtung.

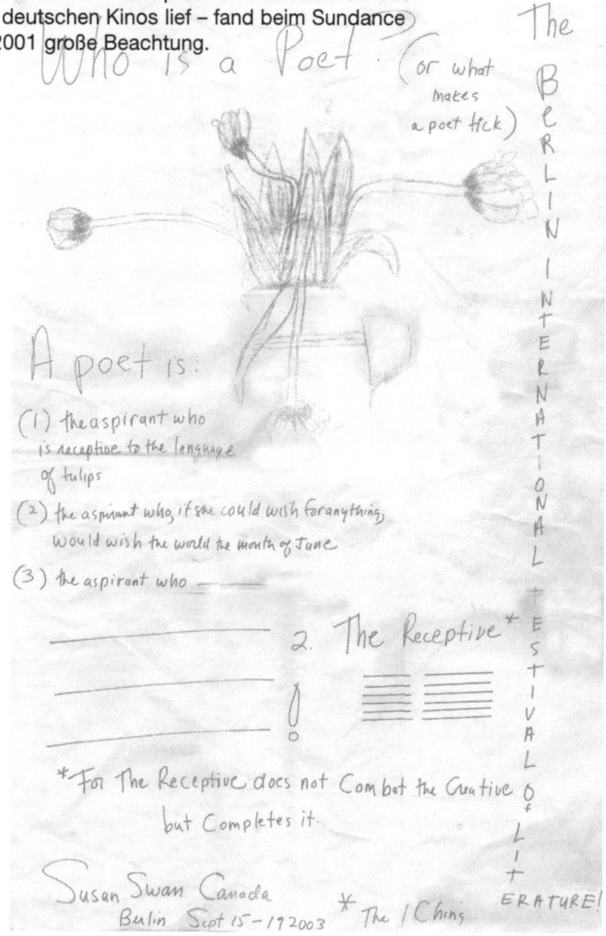

viktorija tokarjewa

biography

Victoria Tokarjeva was born in Leningrad in 1937. At the age of 18 she was awarded a diploma as a pianist at the Leningrad college of music. After marrying a physicist she moved to Moscow, where she worked as a piano teacher for three years. She had started writing young and so enrolled to study screenplay writing at the Moscow film school to escape the life of a piano teacher. She was awarded her diploma in 1968. Fifteen of her scripts have been filmed to date. Victoria Tokarjeva has twice won first prize at the Moscow international film festival for her screenplays, and in 1981 she was awarded first prize at the international documentary film festival.
She published her first short story »Den' bez vranja« (t: One Day without a Lie) in the magazine »Molodaja gvardija« in 1964 – shortly before Khrushchev's resignation and the end of the thaw in Soviet politics – and was immediately successful. She remained largely exempt from Soviet censorship despite the fact that her stories, which mostly revolve around the theme of love, insist on the right to privacy and intimacy. She had numerous short stories published before Perestroika and is extremely popular in Russia. Ten of her short story collections have been translated into German. Diogenes are shortly to publish »Eine Liebe fürs ganze Leben« (t: A Lifelong Love) in Germany.
Tokarjeva's stories are set in the Russian metropolis. The people there, whose lives are steeped in everyday banality, occasionally dream the dream of true love, intensive feelings and a life with a purpose, fear loneliness, or yearn for life. There is the girl who loves her piano teacher – but doesn't dare tell him (»Raraka«); the star pianist in a midlife crisis (»Ne sotvori«); and the man-eating new Russian woman who ends up falling in love again (»Pervaja popytka«). Her characters are usually robbed of their illusions in the end, but gain a tiny piece of wisdom and, at times, even something like happiness.
Tokarjeva's film-industry background is evident in her short stories: images are lined up one after another in simple, unpretentious language, and the scene is set with a few strokes of the pen. The figures are enriched with character through their gestures and through small, everyday actions. Like her idol Chekhov, Tokarjeva observes life with both great sensitivity and cool distance. She writes a »Russian sociology en miniature«, typically melancholy, but with ever-present laconic humour.

Zickzack der Liebe
Diogenes, Zürich, 1990
[Ü: Monika Tantzscher]
Happy-End
Diogenes, Zürich, 1994
[Ü: Angelika Schneider]
Die Diva
Diogenes, Zürich, 1995
[Ü: Angelika Schneider u. a.]
Sentimentale Reise
Diogenes, Zürich, 1997
[Ü: Angelika Schneider]
Der Pianist
Diogenes, Zürich, 2002
[Ü: Angelika Schneider]
Lampenfieber
Diogenes, Zürich, 2003
[Ü: Angelika Schneider]

Viktorija Tokarjewa wurde 1937 in Leningrad geboren. Mit 18 diplomierte sie an der Leningrader Musikhochschule als Pianistin. Nach ihrer Hochzeit mit einem Physiker zog sie nach Moskau um, wo sie drei Jahre als Klavierlehrerin arbeitete. Sie begann früh zu schreiben. Daher immatrikulierte sie sich, um einem Leben als Klavierlehrerin zu entkommen, schließlich an der Moskauer Filmhochschule im Drehbuchfach, das sie 1968 mit einem Diplom abschloss. Fünfzehn ihrer Drehbücher wurden bislang verfilmt. Viktorija Tokarjewa erhielt für ihre Drehbücher zweimal den ersten Preis beim Internationalen Moskauer Filmfestival sowie 1981 den ersten Preis beim Internationalen Dokumentarfilmfestival.
1964 – kurz vor dem Rücktritt Chruschtschows und damit dem Ende der Tauwetterperiode – veröffentlichte sie in der Zeitschrift »Molodaja gvardija« ihre erste Erzählung »Den' bez vranja« (Ü: Ein Tag ohne Lüge), mit der ihr sogleich der Durchbruch gelang. Von der sowjetischen Zensur blieb sie weitgehend verschont, obwohl ihre Erzählungen, die meist um das Thema Liebe kreisen, auf dem Anspruch nach Privatem, Intimem beharren. Schon vor der Perestrojka wurden zahlreiche ihrer Erzählungen publiziert; sie ist in Russland außerordentlich populär. Heute sind bereits zehn ihrer Erzählbände ins Deutsche übersetzt. Demnächst erscheint bei Diogenes »Eine Liebe fürs ganze Leben«.
Den Schauplatz von Tokarjewas Erzählungen bildet die russische Großstadt. Die Menschen dort, die ihr Leben im Alltäglichen fristen, träumen gelegentlich den Traum von wahrer Liebe, großen Gefühlen und einem sinnerfüllten Leben, haben Angst vor der Einsamkeit oder sie gieren nach Leben. Da gibt es das Mädchen, das den Klavierlehrer liebt, aber nie ein Wort zu sagen wagt (»Raraka«), den Starpianisten in der Midlife-Crisis (»Ne sotvori«, dt. »Die Diva«, 1995) und die männerverschlingende neue Russin, die sich dann doch einmal verliebt (»Pervaja popytka«, dt. »Mara«, 1993). Am Ende werden meist die Figuren ihrer Illusionen beraubt, gewinnen aber ein kleines Stück Weisheit und manchmal auch so etwas wie Zufriedenheit.
Tokarjewas Erzählungen ist die filmische Ausbildung der Autorin anzumerken: In schlichter, schnörkelloser Sprache werden Bilder aneinandergereiht und mit wenigen Strichen die Szenen skizziert. Die Figuren gewinnen ihren Charakter durch ihre Gesten, durch kleine, alltägliche Handlungen. Wie ihr Vorbild Tschechow beobachtet sie mit großer Sensibilität und zugleich kühler Distanz. Sie schreibt eine »russische Soziologie en miniature«, meist melancholisch, aber stets mit lakonischem Humor.

Jedes Schaffen ist ein Instinkt der Übergabe von Information.

Der Poet lebt, bewogen von diesem Instinkt.

Außerdem – Erfolg.

Der Poet lebt vom Erfolg.

tatjana tolstaja

biography

Tatjana Tolstaja was born in St. Petersburg (Leningrad), Russia, in 1951. She studied Classical philology in Leningrad. Thereafter she worked briefly as an editor before going to Moscow to work as an author. Her famous ancestors include Leo Tolstoy. She herself began to write relatively late. Her first collection of stories (1987; German »Stelldichein mit einem Vogel«, 1989) was a great literary success which turned her into the Soviet Union's best-known author overnight. In 1989 she left Moscow and went to the US In the 90's she taught at Princeton University and at Skidmore College, which are both in New Jersey, while writing numerous essays on Russian literature and politics for magazines including »The New York Review of Books«. Some of the essays were critical, others humorous. Twenty of these essayistic texts were recently published in the US under the title »Pushkin's Children – Writings on Russia and Russians«. In 2000 she returned to Russia. Within a month she completed her first novel »Kys«, which she had already started to work on 14 years earlier in 1986.

In »Kys« Tatjana Tolstaja sketches the dismal, bizarre world of a future Russia. This realm is ruled by a dictator and populated by misshapen people and mutations, who live in fear of the cruel creature Kys. Owning books is not allowed, but for the protagonist Benedikt reading is a drug. Tolstaja unfolds the fairytale-like magic of her narrative technique, draws on Russian narrative tradition, plays with old Cyrillic letters, invents new words, indulges in literary allusions and cites, alongside Gogol, Chekhov, Tolstoy and Pushkin, other great writers of world literature. »The texts I incorporated into my book came up unconsciously while writing.«

In addition to »Kys« (2003), several other books of stories have been published in German: »Stelldichein mit einem Vogel« (1989), »Sonja« (1991) and »Und es fiel ein Feuer vom Himmel« (1992). It is not only as a writer and essayist that Tatjana Tolstaja comments critically and ironically on the state of her country, she is also a television anchorwoman. She lives in Moscow, New York and St. Petersburg.

Stelldichein mit einem Vogel
Luchterhand
Frankfurt a. M., 1989
[Ü: Sylvia List]
Sonja
Luchterhand
Frankfurt a. M., 1991
[Ü: Sylvia List]
Und es fiel ein Feuer vom Himmel
Rowohlt, Berlin, 1992
[Ü: Sylvia List]
Kys
Rowohlt, Berlin, 2003
[Ü: Christiane Körner]

Tatjana Tolstaja wurde 1951 in St. Petersburg (Leningrad), Russland, geboren. Sie studierte Altphilologie in Leningrad. Anschließend war sie für kurze Zeit als Lektorin tätig, bevor sie nach Moskau ging, um dort als Autorin zu arbeiten. Zu ihren berühmten Vorfahren zählt Leo Tolstoi. Sie selbst begann erst relativ spät mit dem Schreiben. Ihre erste Sammlung von Erzählungen (1987; dt. »Stelldichein mit einem Vogel«, 1989), war ein großer literarischer Erfolg, der sie über Nacht zu einer der bekanntesten Schriftstellerinnen der Sowjetunion machte.
1989 verließ sie Moskau und ging in die USA. In den neunziger Jahren lehrte sie an der Princeton University in New York und am Skidmore College in New Jersey, während sie für Magazine wie »The New York Review of Books« zahlreiche, teils kritische, teils humorvolle Essays zur russischen Literatur und Politik verfasste. Zwanzig dieser essayistischen Texte wurden jüngst unter dem Titel »Pushkin's Children. Writings on Russia and Russians« in den USA veröffentlicht. Im Jahr 2000 kehrte sie nach Russland zurück. Dort vollendete sie innerhalb eines Monats ihren ersten Roman »Kys«, den sie bereits 1986 zu schreiben begonnen hatte.
Tatjana Tolstaja entwirft in »Kys« die düstere, bizarre Welt eines zukünftigen Russland. Dieses Reich wird beherrscht von einem Diktator und bevölkert von missgestalteten Menschen und Mutationen, die in Schrecken vor der grausamen Kreatur Kys leben. Der Besitz von Büchern ist verboten, doch für den Protagonisten Benedikt ist das Lesen eine Droge. Tolstaja entfaltet den märchenhaften Zauber ihrer Erzählkunst, bezieht sich auf russische Erzähltraditionen, spielt mit alten kyrillischen Buchstaben, erfindet neue Wörter, schwelgt in literarischen Anspielungen und zitiert überdies neben Gogol, Tschechow, Tolstoi und Puschkin andere Größen der Weltliteratur. »Ich habe die Texte in mein Buch aufgenommen, die beim Schreiben aus meinem Unbewussten aufgetaucht sind.«
In deutscher Sprache sind neben »Kys« (2003) mehrere Bände mit Erzählungen von ihr erschienen: »Stelldichein mit einem Vogel« (1989), »Sonja« (1991) sowie »Und es fiel ein Feuer vom Himmel« (1992). Tatjana Tolstaja kommentiert nicht nur als Schriftstellerin und Essayistin, sondern auch als Fernsehmoderatorin kritisch-ironisch die Lage ihrer Nation. Sie lebt in Moskau, New York und St. Petersburg.

o. v. vijayan

biography

O. V. Vijayan was born in Palakkad in the southern Indian state of Kerala in 1930. His father was a senior police officer in the Malabar special forces and he grew up in several barracks. Because of his weak health, he did not start school until the age of 12. In 1954 Vijayan graduated with a degree in English and began teaching at various colleges in Kerala until in 1958 he moved to Delhi. There he began to earn a living as a journalist and political cartoonist, publishing his cartoons on a freelance basis in numerous papers including »The Hindu« and »The Statesman«.

In 1969 O. V. Vijayan published his literary debut, »Khasakkinte Ithihasam« (»The Legends of Khasak«, 1994), which was written in Malayalam, the national language of Kerala. The touching portrayal of the village schoolteacher Ravi in the imaginary setting of Khasak was a significant departure from the realistic narrative style that characterizes his country's writing. Critics were moved to pronounce the beginnings of a new era. Henceforth, the history of modern literature in Kerala was to be divided into the pre and post-Khasak eras. Vijayan has continued to write novels, novellas, short stories and political essays, among them the novel »Dharmapuranam« (1985; »The Saga of Dharmapuri«, 1988), which he translated into English himself, and »Gurusagaram« (1987; »The Infinity of Grace«, 1996), which has received many awards and which he helped to translate.

With »The Saga of Dharmapuri«, Vijayan successfully came to the attention of the English-language public and press. The novel, which focuses on the suffering of the people of Dharmapuri under their tyrannical president, recounts how Siddharta – not the historic Buddha, but a messianic figure – ends their suffering. Using crude language and black humour, Vijayan describes the symbolic fight between the two antagonists. While some Indian critics reproached the novel for its »obscenity« and an »imperialist tendency«, others saw his style as a well-chosen vehicle for protest against the country's political situation.

The cartoonist Vijayan can also be heard in some of his novels. In his memoirs »A Cartoonist Remembers« (2002), he writes: »An indescribable sadness permeates the reality that I am supposed to describe, but nonetheless the prevailing superstition about my profession requires that I make people laugh.«

The Saga of Dharmapuri
Penguin, New Delhi, 1988
[Ü: O. V. Vijayan]
After the Hanging and Other Stories
Penguin, New Delhi, 1989
[Ü: O. V. Vijayan]
Pravacakanre vali
Current Books
Kottayam, 1993
The Legends of Khasak
Penguin, New Delhi, 1994
[Ü: O. V. Vijayan]
The Infinity of Grace
Penguin, New Delhi, 1996
[Ü: Ramesh Menon
O. V. Vijayan]
Selected Fiction
Penguin, New Delhi, 1999
[Ü: O. V. Vijayan]
Vijayan. A Cartoonist Remembers
Rupa & Co.
New Delhi, 2002

O. V. Vijayan wurde 1930 in Palakkad, im südindischen Bundesstaat Kerala, geboren. Als Sohn eines leitenden Polizeioffiziers der Malabar Spezialkräfte wuchs er in Kasernen auf. Wegen seiner schwachen Gesundheit begann seine schulische Ausbildung erst mit zwölf Jahren. 1954 schloss Vijayan ein Anglistikstudium ab und unterrichtete anschließend an verschiedenen Colleges in Kerala, bis er 1958 nach Delhi zog. Dort begann er, seinen Lebensunterhalt als Journalist und Zeichner politischer Cartoons zu verdienen, die er seit 1967 freischaffend in zahlreichen Zeitungen wie »The Hindu« und »The Statesman« veröffentlichte. 1969 erschien O. V. Vijayans Erzähldebüt »Khasakkinte Ithihasam« (engl. »The Legends of Khasak«, 1994), geschrieben in Keralas Landessprache Malayalam. Die einfühlsame Schilderung des Dorfschullehrers Ravi im imaginären Khasak wich in signifikanter Weise vom realistischen Erzählstil seiner Landsleute ab. Kritiker riefen daher den Beginn einer neuen Ära aus. Fortan wurde die Geschichte moderner Literatur in Kerala in eine prä- und eine post-Khasak-Ära eingeteilt. Seitdem hat Vijayan weitere Romane, Kurzgeschichten, Novellen und politische Essays geschrieben. Dazu zählen der von ihm selbst ins Englische übertragene Roman »Dharmapuranam« (1985; engl. »The Saga of Dharmapuri«, 1988) und das vielfach ausgezeichnete Werk »Gurusagaram« (1987; engl. »The Infinity of Grace«, 1996), an dessen Übersetzung er mitwirkte.

Mit »The Saga of Dharmapuri« stellte sich Vijayan erfolgreich der englischsprachigen Öffentlichkeit und Presse vor. Im Zentrum des Romans steht das Leiden des Volkes von Dharmapuri unter seinem tyrannischen Präsidenten, das durch Siddharta – nicht den historischen Buddha, sondern einer Messiasfigur – beendet wird. Vijayan beschreibt mit derber Sprache und schwarzem Humor den symbolischen Kampf der beiden Antagonisten. Einige indische Kritiker warfen dem Roman seine »Obszönität« und eine »imperialistische Tendenz« vor, während andere in diesem Stil die beste Möglichkeit zum Protest gegen die politische Situation des Landes sahen.

Aus seinen Romanen ist auch der Karikaturist Vijayan herauszuhören, der in seinen Memoiren »A Cartoonist Remembers« (2002) schreibt: »Eine unbeschreibliche Traurigkeit durchdringt die Realität, die ich darstellen soll, und dennoch verlangt es der herrschende Aberglaube meines Berufsstandes, dass ich die Leute zum Lachen bringe.«

dieter wellershoff

biography

Dieter Wellershoff was born in Neuss in 1925 and grew up in Grevenbroich in the lower Rhine region. In 1943, under the influence of war propaganda and while still a student, he voluntarily went to the front. Wellershoff was only able to work through the experience of the »bloody reality of the word ›battlefield‹« 50 years after the end of the war in his autobiographical book »Der Ernstfall« (1995). After the war Wellershoff studied German Language and Literature, Art History, and Psychology in Bonn. His dissertation on Gottfried Benn from the year 1952 is still considered a standard work for literary scholars. He was a member of the influential »Group 47« and in the 60's founded the »Kölner Schule des Neuen Realismus« (t: Cologne School for New Realism), which was inspired by representatives of the »nouveau novel« and supported a realistic approach to documentation literature. In 1966 he published his debut novel »Ein schöner Tag«. Since the 50's Dieter Wellershoff has worked as a freelance writer and critic, as a literary scholar at universities in Germany and abroad, and in addition as an editor at the publishing house Kiepenheuer & Witsch (1959 to 1981); all in all, he has become an influential figure in German literature. His own literary work, which comprises poems, stories, novels, radio plays, screenplays, essays on literature theory and, more recently, autobiographical texts is as wide ranging as it is comprehensive. He has received many renowned awards, including the Heinrich-Böll-Preis from the city of Cologne (1988). Two years ago he was presented with the Friedrich-Hölderlin-Preis and the Joseph-Breitbach-Preis for his life's work, with particular praise going to his most recent novel »Der Liebeswunsch« (2000) – a modern version of the »Wahlverwandtschaften« (»The Elective Affinities«).
The author approaches his subjects with an analytical eye, paying meticulous attention to even the tinyest details. The intense effect that unfolds in his novels is largely a result of the oppressively precise character descriptions – as Wellershoff puts it – as »beings capable of falling prey to illusion, who, in the search for the right life, tend to get caught up in the trap of their own imagination«. A search that – not only in the »quest for love« – will come to a fatal end since, in Wellershoff, life in a modern society, with its seemingly endless possibilities, reveals itself as an erotic competition that mostly generates losers. It is this idea of not living up to one's own desires that is again addressed in Wellershoff's current work. With his cultural-analytical book of essays »Der verstörte Eros« (2001), the author, who today lives in Cologne, presents a history of sublimated passions in literature from Goethe to Houellebecq, full of ideas and insights.

Ein schöner Tag
Fischer
Frankfurt a. M., 1981
Die Körper und die Träume
Kiepenheuer & Witsch
Köln, 1994
Das Kainsmal des Krieges
Landpresse
Weilerswist, 1998
Der Liebeswunsch
Kiepenheuer & Witsch
Köln, 2000
Die Schönheit des Schimpansen
Kiepenheuer & Witsch
Köln, 2000
Der verstörte Eros
Kiepenheuer & Witsch
Köln, 2001
Der Sieger nimmt alles
Goldmann, München, 2002

Hier meine Antwort auf Ihre Umfrage: "What makes the poet tick?" In diesem Fall das kleine Wort "Wie" oder die Vergleichbarkeit des Verschiedenen und seine Einheit im Ungefähren, die Sagbarkeit der Welt als ein Fächer von Metaphern –

Dieter Wellershoff

Dieter Wellershoff wurde 1925 in Neuss geboren. Seine Jugend verlebte er im niederrheinischen Grevenbroich, bis er sich 1943 unter dem Einfluss der Kriegspropaganda noch als Schüler freiwillig an die Front meldete. Die Erfahrung der »blutigen Wirklichkeit des Wortes »Schlachtfeld« konnte Wellershoff erst fünfzig Jahre nach Kriegsende in seinem autobiographischen Buch »Der Ernstfall« (1995) verarbeiten. Nach dem Krieg studierte Wellershoff Germanistik, Kunstgeschichte und Psychologie in Bonn. Seine Dissertation über Gottfried Benn aus dem Jahr 1952 gilt noch heute als literaturwissenschaftliches Standardwerk. Er war Mitglied der einflussreichen »Gruppe 47« und in den sechziger Jahren Begründer der »Kölner Schule des Neuen Realismus«, die angeregt von den Vertretern des »Nouveau Roman«, eine realistische Dokumentationsliteratur vertrat. 1966 erschien sein Debütroman »Ein schöner Tag«.

Seit den fünfziger Jahren ist Dieter Wellershoff als freier Schriftsteller und Kritiker, als Literaturwissenschaftler an Universitäten im In- und Ausland und nicht zuletzt als Lektor beim Verlag Kiepenheuer & Witsch (1959 bis 1981) tätig gewesen und zu einer prägenden Figur der deutschen Literaturlandschaft geworden. Sein eigenes literarisches Werk ist mit Gedichten, Erzählungen, Romanen, Hörspielen, Drehbüchern, literaturtheoretischen Essays und zuletzt autobiographischen Texten ebenso umfangreich wie vielseitig. Er erhielt mehrere renommierte Auszeichnungen, darunter den Heinrich-Böll-Preis der Stadt Köln (1988). Vor zwei Jahren wurde sein Lebenswerk unter besonderer Berücksichtigung seines jüngsten Romans »Der Liebeswunsch« (2000) – eine moderne Fassung der »Wahlverwandtschaften« – mit dem Friedrich-Hölderlin-Preis und dem Joseph-Breitbach-Preis gewürdigt.

Mit analytischem Blick, der akribisch bis zu den kleinsten Details vordringt, nähert sich der Autor seinen Sujets. Seine Romane entfalten ihre intensive Wirkung vor allem durch die beklemmend präzise Darstellung der Figuren als – wie Wellershoff es formulierte – »illusionsanfällige Wesen, die dazu neigen, auf der Suche nach dem richtigen Leben in die Falle der eigenen Phantasien zu gehen«. Eine Suche, die nicht nur im »Liebeswunsch« ein fatales Ende nimmt, denn das Leben in einer modernen Gesellschaft mit ihren scheinbar unendlich vielen Möglichkeiten entpuppt sich bei Wellershoff als erotischer Konkurrenzkampf, der vor allem Verlierer erzeugt. Es ist die Idee eines Scheiterns am eigenen Begehren, die auch Wellershoffs aktuelles Werk fortschreibt. Mit seinem kulturanalytischen Essayband »Der verstörte Eros« (2001) legte der heute in Köln lebende Autor eine geist- und kenntnisreiche Literaturgeschichte der sublimierten Leidenschaften von Goethe bis Houellebecq vor.

Wie Schnee im Kino
wie lautloser Schneefall
wie senkrecht fallende Schneeflocken
wie die Zeitansage im Telefon
wie ein leerer Bahnsteig
wie ein gefrorener Fluß
wie das kleine rote Auge eines Plattenspielers
    in einem verlassenen Zimmer
wie ein alter Mantel
    vergessen an einem Garderobenhaken
wie ein leerer Bahnsteig und ein leerer Zug
wie die Zeitansage und das kleine rote Auge
wie Schneefall
wie eine nur einen Spalt weit geöffnete Tür
wie eine Frau die sich selbst befriedigt
wie eine fremde Sprache in einem fremden Buch
wie ein verlassenes Zimmer
wie ein blindes Fenster in einem Treppenhaus
wie Brechreiz nach sinnlosen Gesprächen
wie das Knistern einer alten Schallplatte
wie Schneeflocken hinter einem blinden Fenster
wie Durst in der Nacht und Wassertrinken
wie ein langer Abschied
wie ein Gedanke der nie zur Vernunft kommt.

biyi bandele
alessandro baricco
lars saabye christensen
juan gustavo cobo borda
bora ćosić
nuruddin farah
raymond federman
aris fioretos
jonathan franzen
günter grass
lars gustafsson
mila haugová
zbyněk hejda
reinhard jirgl
walter kempowski
etgar keret
navid kermani
imre kertész
ko un
hanif kureishi
lee hochol
abdelwahab meddeb
lajos parti nagy
oskar pastior
ljudmila petruschewskaja
carlos ruiz zafón
boualem sansal
peter schneider
tilman spengler
shashi tharoor
ayu utami
martin walser
eliot weinberger
stefan ludmilla wieszner
leon de winter
jeanette winterson
saadi youssef
zhang jie

biyi bandele

biography

Biyi Bandele (actually Bandele-Thomas) was born in 1967 in northern Nigeria, a region which is largely Muslim. He stems from a family which belonged to the Yoruba tribe and converted to Christianity. He left his parents' house at age 14 to earn his living doing odd jobs, while also going to school. By then he had already started work on his first novel. He studied drama at the University of Ile-Ife from 1987 to 1990. With his theatre piece »Rain« he won first prize in a competition, a scholarship for a one-year stay in London. Bandele-Thomas remained in London to work as a freelance writer and has since written a rapid succession of texts: narrative prose, poetry, radio plays, screenplays, and theatre pieces. He has received various awards, including the London New Play Festival Award (1994) and has accepted invitations to go on reading tours, attend conferences, and see performances of his pieces in the US and Canada as well as in various countries in Africa, Asia, and Europe. Since 1993 he has primarily published his work under the name Biyi Bandele.

His first novel »The Man Who Came in from the Back of Beyond« was published in London in 1991 and in the same year in Germany under the title »Bozo David Hurensohn«; it depicts a shrill and realistic panorama of modern Nigeria. The novel's first-person narrator, Lakemfa, befriends his teacher who initially seems a bit odd. This teacher not only discloses details of his own past to Lakemfa, thereby triggering a series of bizarre events, but also gives him a manuscript to read. It is about Bozo, whose real name is David, but who is only called bastard by his father. Although at the end both stories prove themselves to be fiction, they trigger a process of change and maturity for Lakemfa. At the same time Bozo stands as a symbol for a country, which, following a war and a fatal oil boom, is in a state of upheaval. Daily school life, omnipresent violence also in the family, tension between urban bustle and rural life – Bandele transposes all of that in a language that is rich in imagery and more than just a little humorous. His elaborate narrative technique, wealth of language as well as his depth of imagination, which time and again adds suprising surrealistic twists to his plots, have repeatedly caused critics to draw parallels with representatives of magic realism, which include his fellow countryman Ben Okri. Bandele lives in London.

The Man Who Came in from the Back of Beyond
Heinemann, Oxford, 1991
Bozo David Hurensohn
dipa, Frankfurt a. M., 1991
[Ü: Gabriele Cenefels]
Kerosin Mangos
dipa, Frankfurt a. M., 1993
[Ü: Gabriele Cenefels]
Two Horsemen
Amber Lane Press
Oxford, 1994
The Street
Picador, London, 2000

Read Between the Signs

Television was a mythical dream-machine in Kafanchan, the small, dusty town in northern Nigeria where I was born in the late 1960s. It was rumoured to have been sighted in far-away Lagos. Not even Baba, my father, could convince me when he said he had seen this thing called television with his own eyes. For Baba, home was Abeokuta, the south-western town where he was born near Lagos. But for me and my siblings, home was Kafanchan and we knew no other. In Kafanchan, where most everyone worked for the railways, every child knew that education was the first word and the last in the struggle not to end up like their parents, stranded on the tracks of a dying, shambolic public transport system. And so the library was almost as popular as the football pitch. Every month, come payday, Baba would make a two-hour pilgrimage to Jos, the nearest big town, and would return with bags bulging with the latest Wole Soyinka play text, a new edition of "The Mill on the Floss", and Baba's especial favourites, what he called awawi – Yoruba for tittle-tattle, more properly translated as pulp fiction. It was an intoxicating brew of high and low culture. Then one night, TV came to Kafanchan. That is to say, precisely one set. Alhaji S, a building contractor and the wealthiest man in town had acquired a set with a 12-inch screen. Alhaji S, being a man of the people, set up the television not in his living room but in the spacious compound at the back of his house where we could all admire it. Within months, the TV bug had bitten virtually everyone in town. And it was on the freshly minted set that Baba had bought that I first, in a manner of speaking, went to the theatre. The play was John Osborne's "Look Back in Anger". I had encountered such inchoate and atavistic rage before – after all, I was

Biyi Bandele (eigentlich Bandele-Thomas), 1967 in Kafanchan im islamisch geprägten Norden Nigerias geboren, entstammt einer Familie, die dem Stamm der Yoruba angehörte und zum Christentum konvertierte. Im Alter von 14 Jahren verließ er sein Elternhaus, um neben dem Schulbesuch mit Gelegenheitsarbeiten seinen Lebensunterhalt zu verdienen. In dieser Zeit begann er bereits mit der Arbeit an seinem ersten Roman. Von 1987 bis 1990 studierte er an der Universität von Ile-Ife Theaterwissenschaft. Mit seinem Theaterstück »Rain« gewann er den ersten Preis bei einem Wettbewerb, ein Stipendium für einen einjährigen Aufenthalt in London. Bandele-Thomas blieb in London, um von nun an als freier Schriftsteller zu arbeiten, und schrieb seither in rascher Folge erzählende Prosa, Gedichte, Hörspiele, Drehbücher und Theaterstücke. Er erhielt verschiedene Auszeichnungen, u. a. den London New Play Festival Award (1994), und nahm Einladungen zu Lesereisen, Konferenzen und Aufführungen seiner Stücke in den USA, in Kanada sowie in verschiedenen Ländern Afrikas, Asiens und Europas wahr. Seit 1993 erscheinen seine Veröffentlichungen überwiegend unter dem Namen Biyi Bandele.

Sein erster Roman »The Man Who Came in from the Back of Beyond«, der 1991 in London veröffentlicht wurde und im selben Jahr in Deutschland unter dem Titel »Bozo David Hurensohn« erschien, entwirft ein grell-realistisches Panorama des modernen Nigeria. Der Ich-Erzähler des Romans, Lakemfa, freundet sich mit seinem zunächst kauzig erscheinenden Lehrer an. Dieser weiht ihn nicht nur in seine eigene Vergangenheit ein und wird damit Auslöser für abenteuerliche Verwicklungen, sondern gibt ihm auch ein Manuskript zu lesen, das von Bozo handelt, der eigentlich David heißt, von seinem Vater aber nur Hurensohn genannt wurde. Obwohl sich beide Geschichten am Ende als Fiktion erweisen, lösen sie einen Wandlungs- und Reifeprozess in Lakemfa aus. Zugleich steht Bozo stellvertretend für ein Land, das sich nach Krieg und fatalem Öl-Boom im Umbruch befindet. Schulalltag, allgegenwärtige Gewalt auch in der Familie, Spannungen zwischen städtischer Betriebsamkeit und ländlichen Lebenszusammenhängen – all das transponiert Bandele in eine bildreiche und nicht zuletzt humorvolle Sprache. Seine elaborierte Erzähltechnik, sein Sprachreichtum sowie seine ausufernde Phantasie, die seinen Plots immer wieder überraschende Wendungen ins Surreale verleiht, haben Kritiker wiederholt Vergleiche mit Vertretern des magischen Realismus, etwa seinem Landsmann Ben Okri, anstellen lassen. Bandele lebt in London.

growing up in a society that was still reeling from a 30-month civil war in which more than a million people had died. And so although I had yet to set foot outside Kafanchan, although I knew nothing about postwar British society, or the Angry Young Men when I met Jimmy Porter on the screen, I knew there was no need for introductions: I had known Jimmy all my life. I sometimes ask myself these days why that strange play made such a big impression on me that night over 20 years ago. I think it's because "Look Back in Anger" derives its power to startle or to repel, and its universality, not from the literal-realism of its narrative but from the sheer verve of Osborne's pathology of the human, his bloody-minded reverse-humanism. The veracity of the world he has created is poetic, not literal; he deals not in road signs but in symbols. Signs denote, they tell us how to get from A to B; symbols connote – they are external manifestations of energies within us that connect us to, or alienate us from, ourselves and our world. The complicity between an audience and the play it is watching, that willing suspension of disbelief, is grounded in this tacit agreement that theatre is essentially symbological. The infantile and insufferably self-obsessed fury expressed by Jimmy Porter no longer impresses me, but the lesson I learned watching "Look Back in Anger" has stayed with me. Great theatre is the telling of a truthful lie. It derives its universality not from catering to the lowest common denominator but by being specific and local. In the universe of the imagination to which we all belong, we may not always know where we are going, but we require no visas to go there and we need not worry about packing. The name of the place is home.

alessandro baricco

biography

Alessandro Baricco was born in Turin in 1958. After studying music and philosophy he worked for a time in advertising and as an opera critic for national Italian newspapers. In 1994 he had television success with the literary arts programme »Pickwick« and also published regular reports in the daily newspaper »La Repubblica«. In Turin, his home today, Baricco founded the private University of Creative Writing, »Scuola Holden«, in which numerous well-known authors and film-makers have given lectures. Baricco's books, a number of which have been filmed, have won several prizes, including the »Prix Médicis« (1991) and the Italian literary prize »Premio Viareggio« (1993).
Baricco's very first novel »Castelli di Rabbia« (1991) brings together many of the themes and narrative patterns that have made him an internationally successful writer. There is a suggestion of surrealism in the story of Rail, a glass-factory owner who continually sets off on journeys into the unknown and each time brings his dear wife, Jun, the same present. The setting is that of an imaginary 19th century and takes up the romantic motion of all embracing love.
Alessandro Baricco became known in German-speaking countries above all through his third book, the world bestseller »Silk« (1997), a mixture of parables on the theme of love, Far East mysticism and cleverly devised etudes based on language. In this book the author links a feature of Japanese literature, namely that which is not spoken, with the image of the ever-present return of what is the same, that »repetition of the past« which Gustave Flaubert narrates with such mastery in his book »Salammbô«. Here, once again, it is the 19th century in which Baricco sets his story: Hervé Joncourt, the hero of the novel, deals in silk worms and travels in search of a rare variety of this creature. Year in, year out his journey takes him to Japan, to the country of silk materials and the »Poetry of Longing«. There he falls for the charms of an indescribably beautiful woman who looks at him »with confusing intensity« but who at the same time remains unreachable. Torn from the monotony of his life up to that point, Joncourt becomes caught up in a labyrinth of imagination and longing. Not until his wife dies does he realise that it was only her he loved in that strangely beautiful woman.
Those meandering detours and repetitions, which Joncourt must undergo and which give the text its own rhythm, can be found in Baricco's most recent book »City«, published in 2000. Two outsiders, the gifted young Gould and the twenty-year-old Shatzy, conjure up their own imaginary world and so encounter all the preparterousness and presumptions of the »real« world. In numerous episodes Baricco criss-crosses times and landscapes, binding the strands of his story to motifs from comedy and advertising, along with film images and American myths. In this book Baricco has written a tribute to everyday dreams; it is a book about imagination and the power of friendship.

Hegels Seele oder die Kühe von Wisconsin
Piper, München, 2001
[Ü: Karin Krieger]
Land aus Glas
Piper, München, 2001
[Ü: Karin Krieger]
City
dtv, München, 2002
[Ü: Anja Nattefort]
Novecento
Piper, München, 2003
[Ü: Erika Cristiani]
Oceano Mare
Piper, München, 2003
[Ü: Erika Cristiani]
Seide
Piper, München, 2003
[Ü: Karin Krieger]
Ohne Blut
Hanser, München, 2003
[Ü: Anja Nattefort]

Alessandro Baricco, 1958 in Turin geboren, arbeitete nach dem Studium der Musikwissenschaft und Philosophie eine Zeitlang in der Werbebranche und schrieb Opernkritiken für überregionale italienische Zeitungen. 1994 feierte er mit dem populären Literaturmagazin »Pickwick« große Fernseherfolge, zudem veröffentlicht er regelmäßig Reportagen in der Tageszeitung »La Repubblica«. In Turin, wo Baricco lebt, gründete er die Privatuniversität »Scuola Holden« für kreatives Schreiben, in der zahlreiche bekannte Autoren und Filmemacher dozieren. Bariccos Bücher, von denen einige inzwischen verfilmt worden sind, wurden mehrfach ausgezeichnet, u. a. mit dem Prix Médicis (1991) oder dem italienischen Literaturpreis Premio Viareggio (1993).

Schon sein erster Roman »Castelli di Rabbia« (dt. »Land aus Glas«, 1999), der 1991 erschienen ist, vereint viele der Themen und erzählerischen Muster, die Alessandro Baricco international zu einem erfolgreichen Schriftsteller gemacht haben. Die surreal anmutende Geschichte des Glasfabrikanten Rail, der immer wieder zu Reisen ins Unbekannte aufbricht und seiner geliebten Frau Jun jedes Mal ein und dasselbe Geschenk mitbringt, ist in einem erfundenen 19. Jahrhundert angesiedelt und spielt mit den romantischen Ideen der allumfassenden Liebe. Im deutschsprachigen Raum wurde Alessandro Baricco vor allem durch sein drittes Buch, den Weltbestseller »Seide« aus dem Jahr 1996 bekannt, einer Melange aus Liebesparabel, fernöstlicher Mystik und ausgeklügelten Sprachetüden. Der Turiner Autor verbindet darin einen Topos der japanischen Literatur, das Unausgesprochene, mit der Vorstellung der ewigen Wiederkehr des Gleichen, jener »Wiederholung der Vergangenheit«, wie sie etwa Gustave Flaubert in seinem Roman »Salammbô« erzählerisch gemeistert hat. Erneut ist es das 19. Jahrhundert, in dem Baricco seine Geschichte spielen lässt: Hervé Joncourt, der Held des Romans, handelt mit Seidenraupen und reist, um eine besonders seltene Art dieser Tierchen zu kaufen, Jahr für Jahr nach Japan, in das Land der Seidenstoffe und der »Poesie der Sehnsucht«. Dort erliegt er dem Charme einer unsagbar schönen Frau, die ihn »mit verwirrender Intensität« anschaut und gleichwohl unerreichbar bleibt. Aus der Monotonie seines bisherigen Lebens gerissen, verfängt sich Joncourt im Labyrinth von Phantasie und Verlangen. Erst nach dem Tod seiner Gattin erkennt er, daß er nur sie in der fremden Schönen geliebt hat.

Jene mäandernden Umwege und Wiederholungen, die Joncourt durchleben muss und die dem Text einen eigenen Rhythmus verleihen, lassen sich auch in Bariccos jüngstem Buch »City« aus dem Jahr 2000 finden. Dort zaubern zwei Außenseiter, der hochbegabte Junge Gould und die zwanzigjährige Shatzy, ihre eigenen Phantasiewelten und unterlaufen so die Lächerlichkeiten und Zumutungen der »wirklichen« Welt. In einer Vielzahl von Episoden verschränkt er die Zeiten und Landschaften, versieht seine Erzählstränge mit Motiven aus Comic und Werbung, mit Filmbildern und amerikanischen Mythen. Eine Hommage an die Tagträume hat Baricco hier geschrieben, ein Buch über die Phantasie und die Kraft der Freundschaft.

lars saabye christensen

biography

Lars Saabye Christensen was born in Oslo, Norway in 1953. He has been a poet and author of books for young adults, detective stories, short stories, novels and screenplays since the 70's. It was his enthusiasm for rock music which made him take up writing. Inspired by his idols John Lennon and Jim Morrison, he wrote song lyrics and poetry. His first poetry collection »Historien om Gly« (t: Gly's Story), for which he won the Tarjei Vesaas Debutantpris award for young authors, was published in 1976. His first novel »Amatøren« (t: The Amateur) followed in 1977. With this work he created the prototype for all his characters, who are typified by a lack of overview over their own lives.

His literary breakthrough came with »Beatles« (1984), a novel about four young people in an Oslo suburb, which immediately became a bestseller. Lars Saabye Christensen is now one of Norway's best-known contemporary writers; his books have been translated into over 20 languages. His work inspires enthusiasm not only among his readers; it has also been awarded numerous prizes, including Norway's critics' prize. He won the renowned Nordic literary prize »Nordisk Räds Litteratur Pris« in 2002 for »Halvbroren« (2001; »The Half Brother«, 2003).

Lars Saabye Christensen's stories are artfully constructed and characterised by a both melancholy and humorous tone in their realistic narrative style. »Jubel« (1995) oscillates between Nordic laconicism, comedy and tragedy. It is the story of a musician who has not achieved the glittering career of a concert pianist he had hoped for, but whose destiny has instead brought him to a shabby hotel on the Lofoten islands to work as a piano player. Full of understanding for his absurd characters, Saabye Christensen also tells of losses and farewells, of biographies without climaxes, and of the realisation of one's own mediocrity in the short stories »Den misunnelige frisøren« (1997; t: The Jealous Hairdresser).

He has also gained recognition for his television-screenplay adaptations of Knut Hamsun's »August« trilogy, as a promoter of young Norwegian authors, and through musical readings with the band »Norsk Utflukt«. Lars Saabye Christensen lives in Oslo.

Der Joker sticht
Pettersson, Münster, 1995
[Ü: Christel Hildebrandt]
Yesterday
Goldmann, München, 1997
[Ü: Christel Hildebrandt]
Der eifersüchtige Friseur und andere Helden
Knaus, München, 1998
[Ü: Christel Hildebrandt]
Der Alleinunterhalter
Knaus, München, 1997
[Ü: Christel Hildebrandt]
Der falsche Tote
Goldmann, München, 2002
[Ü: Christel Hildebrandt]
Der Halbbruder
Goldmann, München, 2003
[Ü: Christel Hildebrandt]

Lars Saabye Christensen wurde 1953 in Oslo, Norwegen, geboren. Seit den siebziger Jahren ist er als Dichter und Autor von Jugendbüchern, Krimis, Erzählungen, Romanen und Drehbüchern tätig. Die Begeisterung für die Rockmusik der sechziger Jahre gab ihm den Anstoß zum Schreiben. Inspiriert von seinen Idolen John Lennon und Jim Morrison verfasste er Songtexte und Lyrik. 1976 erschien seine erste Gedichtsammlung »Historien om Gly« (Ü: Glys Geschichte), für die er den Tarjei Vesaas Debutantpris für junge Autoren erhielt. 1977 folgte sein erster Roman »Amatøren« (Ü: Der Amateur), mit dem er den Prototyp für alle seine Figuren schuf, für die der mangelnde Überblick über ihr eigenes Leben kennzeichnend ist.
Der literarische Durchbruch gelang ihm mit »Beatles« (1984; dt. »Yesterday«, 1989), einem Roman über vier Jugendliche in einem Vorort Oslos, der sofort zum Bestseller avancierte. Inzwischen ist Lars Saabye Christensen einer der bekanntesten zeitgenössischen Schriftsteller Norwegens, dessen Bücher in mehr als 20 Sprachen übersetzt wurden. Sein Werk begeistert nicht nur seine Leser, sondern wurde auch mit zahlreichen Preisen ausgezeichnet, u. a. mit dem Kritikerpreis Norwegens. 2002 erhielt er für »Halvbroren« (2001; dt. »Der Halbbruder«, 2003) den renommierten Nordischen Literaturpreis (Nordisk Räds Litteratur Pris).
Lars Saabye Christensens Geschichten sind kunstvoll konstruiert und in ihrer realistischen Erzählweise von einem ebenso humorvollen wie melancholischen Ton geprägt. Zwischen nordischer Lakonie, Komik und Tragik oszilliert »Jubel« (1995; dt. »Der Alleinunterhalter«, 1997), die Geschichte eines Musikers, dem die glanzvolle Karriere als Konzertpianist versagt bleibt und den das Schicksal stattdessen als Klavierspieler in ein schäbiges Hotel auf die Lofoten geführt hat. Voller Sympathie für seine skurrilen Figuren erzählt Saabye Christensen auch in den Erzählungen »Den misunnelige frisøren« (1997; dt. »Der eifersüchtige Friseur und andere Helden«, 1998) von Verlusten und Abschieden, von Biographien ohne Höhepunkte und vom Erkennen der eigenen Mittelmäßigkeit.
Bekannt wurde er außerdem durch seine Drehbuchadaptionen von Knut Hamsuns August-Trilogie für das Fernsehen, als Förderer junger norwegischer Autoren und durch vertonte Lesungen zusammen mit der Band »Norsk Utflukt«. Lars Saabye Christensen lebt in Oslo.

juan gustavo cobo borda

biography

Juan Gustavo Cobo Borda was born in the Colombian capital of Bogotá in 1948. After studying literature in Bogotá, he held several different posts in the Colombian cultural administration. In the 80's he was a cultural attaché in Buenos Aires. He returned to Bogotá in 1990 and worked in the cultural department of the foreign ministry – including as the culture-political advisor to the Colombian president – before going to Madrid as a cultural attaché. As of 1998 Cobo Borda was the Colombian ambassador to Athens, today he again lives in Bogotá.
Alongside his political career, Cobo Borda has made a remarkable contribution as a writer. His numerous critical essays are not only dedicated to other authors – like Borges and García Márquez – but to painting as well (»Mis Pintores«, 2002, t: My Painter). Between 1973 and 1984 he was publisher of the poetry magazine »Eco«. He has also published numerous anthologies (such as the »Antología de la poesía hispanoamericana«, 1985) and other works. As a member of the Colombian Academy for Language he was involved in the new edition of the »Diccionario de la Lengua Española« (t: Dictionary of the Spanish Language) – a project that he refers to as »another form of writing poetry.« Cobo Borda made his lyrical debut in 1974 with the collection »Consejos para sobrevivir« (t: Survival Advice), which was followed by more than a dozen further books of poetry. In his verse he is known for the pronounced use of irony, self-irony and humour, through which he describes and unveils situations. He is considered a member of the Nadaísmo group who, under the motto »nothingness or nothing«, hoped to modernise the old rhetoric of Colombian poetry through spontaneity, parody and radical negation. Three main topics emerge: the investigation into the world of young people, criticism of Colombian society, and the relationship between man and woman. His most recent publications include the book of poetry »La musa inclemente« (2001, t: The Merciless Muse), in which he reflects on the romantic passions. His use of language alternates between the colloquial and the literary; his tone is sometimes ironic, sometimes affectionate or despairing. Cobo Borda is extremely well read and both his poetry and essayistic work draw on this, yet he still knows how to articulate a wealth of ideas in a way that is formally concise. His work appears in numerous anthologies and has in part been translated into other languages.

Almanaque de versos
Editorial Oveja Negra
Bogotá, 1988
Poemas orientales y bogotanos
Universidad Nacional Autónoma de México
Mexiko, 1991
Furioso amor
El Áncora, Bogotá, 1997
No sabes con cuanto gusto te disfrutó, impúdica
Consejo Nacional para la Cultura y las Artes
Mexiko, 1997
La musa inclemente
Tusquets Editores
Barcelona, 2001
Mis Pintores
Villegas Editores
Bogotá, 2002

Juan Gustavo Cobo Borda wurde 1948 in der kolumbianischen Hauptstadt Bogotá geboren. Nach dem Studium der Literaturwissenschaft in Bogotá bekleidete er verschiedene Posten in der kolumbianischen Kulturverwaltung. In den achtziger Jahren war er Kulturattaché in Buenos Aires, kehrte 1990 nach Bogotá zurück und arbeitete in der Kulturabteilung des Außenministeriums – unter anderem als kulturpolitischer Berater des kolumbianischen Präsidenten –, bevor er wiederum als Kulturattaché nach Madrid ging. Cobo Borda, der ab 1998 Botschafter seines Landes in Athen war, lebt heute wieder in Bogotá.

Neben dieser politischen Karriere ist auch das publizistische Schaffen Cobo Bordas bemerkenswert. Seine zahlreichen kritischen Essays widmen sich nicht nur anderen Autoren – etwa Borges und García Márquez –, sondern auch der Malerei (2002; »Mis Pintores«, Ü: Meine Maler). Zwischen 1973 und 1984 gab er die Lyrikzeitschrift »Eco« heraus. Zudem ist er Herausgeber mehrerer Anthologien (z. B. »Antología de la poesía hispanoamericana«, 1985) und Werkausgaben. Als Mitglied der Kolumbianischen Akademie für Sprache war er an der Neuauflage des »Diccionario de la Lengua Española« (Ü: Wörterbuch der spanischen Sprache) beteiligt – ein Projekt, das er als »eine andere Form der Dichtung« bezeichnete.

Als Lyriker debütierte Cobo Borda 1974 mit der Sammlung »Consejos para sobrevivir« (Ü: Ratschläge zum Überleben), auf das über ein Dutzend weiterer Gedichtbände folgten. Charakteristische Stilmittel seiner Lyrik sind die ausgeprägte Ironie bzw. Selbstironie und der Humor. Mitunter wird er zur Gruppe des Nadaísmo gezählt, die unter dem Motto »Das Nichts oder nichts« angetreten war, die alte Rhetorik des kolumbianischen Lyrismus durch Spontaneität, parodistische Frivolität und radikale Negation zu modernisieren. Vor allem drei Themenkreise lassen sich ausmachen: die Auseinandersetzung mit der jugendlichen Erlebniswelt, die Kritik an der kolumbianischen Gesellschaft und das Verhältnis zwischen Mann und Frau. Zu seinen jüngsten Veröffentlichungen gehört der Gedichtband »La musa inclemente« (2001; Ü: Die unbarmherzige Muse), in dem er das Thema der amourösen Leidenschaften reflektiert. Der Sprachgebrauch schwankt dabei zwischen umgangssprachlich und literarisch, der Ton ist mal ironisch, mal zärtlich oder verzweifelt. Grundlage seiner Lyrik wie auch seines essayistischen Werks ist Cobo Bordas umfassende Belesenheit, wobei er jedoch die Gedankenfülle formaler Prägnanz unterzuordnen weiß. Seine Werke sind in zahlreichen Anthologien vertreten und wurden zum Teil in andere Sprachen übersetzt.

bora ćosić
biography

Bora Ćosić was born in Zagreb, Croatia, in 1932. In 1937 he moved to Belgrade to study philosophy. During the 50's he worked as an editor for various journals and translated from Russian (Mayakovsky, Khlebnikov). His first novel, »Kuca lopova« (House of Thieves), a surrealist confrontation with social reality in Yugoslavia, was published in 1956. Soon his name was on the blacklist which the state cultural authorities used to discourage national publishing houses from printing the works of certain authors. The stage version of his satirical novel, »Uloga moje porodice u svetskoj revoluciji« (»My Family's Role in the World Revolution«, 1997), written in 1969, was banned for many years.
In 1992 Ćosić left Belgrade in protest against the policies of the Serbian regime and settled in Rovinj, Istria. During his exile in Croatia, his country's declared enemy, he wrote »Dnevnik apatrida« (1993), which is filled with reflections on Proust and the Franco-Prussian War. He came to Berlin on a DAAD grant in 1995, and still lives here today. In 1999, when Nato troops were deployed in Kosovo, Ćosić demanded liberation for the Albanians as well as for the Serbs from Milosevic and »from themselves«, i.e., from »ethnic madness«. Ćosić has written more than thirty books, which have been translated into many European languages: German, English, French, Italian, Hungarian and Russian. Only a few have been translated into German. After a first satirical volume, »Wie unsere Klaviere repariert wurden«, in 1968, German publishers' interest in the author was not rekindled until the 90's. Since then German critics have acknowledged him as one of the wittiest and most outrageous contemporary authors. He owes this reputation largely to his novel »My Family's Role in the World Revolution«, which put him in the public eye in 1994, and which has since been labelled a »subversive classic« (Andreas Breitenstein, »NZZ«). Spanning the time from the German occupation to the establishment of the Tito regime, the vicious satire of this novel, in which historic and mundane events merge into a grotesque whole, results from the pseudo-naive perspective of the childlike first-person narrator. Although Ćosić bases this work, long celebrated as a cult book in Serbia, only implicitly on »The Tin Drum's« constructional principle, the playful treatment of Günther Grass and other role models such as Krleža, Musil, Dostoyevsky, Hamsun and Proust is conspicuously deliberate in other cases. This is evident in works such as »Musils Notizbuch«, »Ein zweites Treffen in Telgte«, »Geschichte Myschkins«, »Bergottes Witwe« and the fictional Autobiography of »Miroslav Krleža«. »Collaging existing material« is, according to the critic Karl-Markus Gauß, »a popular aesthetic principle«. This has also affected Ćosić's own work, which the author maintains is in a constant state of transformation and abounds in crossreferences. Ćosić's grandmother, for example, who has already been a figure of literature in »My Family's Role in the World Revolution«, becomes the wheelchair bound central character Suarda in the 1982 monologue novel »Bel Tempo«. Bora Ćosić has also been writing poetry for some years. His poetry volume »Die Toten« appeared in the DAAD publications list in 2001.

Wie unsere Klaviere repariert wurden
Suhrkamp
Frankfurt a. M., 1968
[Ü: Peter Urban]

Die Rolle meiner Familie in der Weltrevolution
Rowohlt, Reinbek, 1994
[Ü: Mirjana und Klaus Wittmann]

Musils Notizbuch
Droschl, Graz, 1994
[Ü: Barbara Antkowiak]

Bel Tempo: der Jahrhundertroman
Rowohlt, Berlin, 1998
[Ü: Irena Vrkljan und Benno Meyer-Welack]

Die Zollerklärung
Suhrkamp
Frankfurt a. M., 2001
[Ü: Katharina Wolf-Grießhaber]

Die Toten
DAAD, Berlin, 2001
[Ü: Irena Vrkljan und Benno Meyer-Wehlack]

Bora Ćosić wurde 1932 in Zagreb geboren. Ab 1937 lebte er in Belgrad, wo er nach seinem Schulabschluss Philosophie studierte. In den fünfziger Jahren arbeitete er als Redakteur für verschiedene Zeitschriften und als Übersetzer aus dem Russischen (Majakowski, Chlebnikow). 1956 erschien sein erster Roman »Kuca lopova« (Ü: Haus der Diebe), eine surrealistische Auseinandersetzung mit der gesellschaftlichen Wirklichkeit in Jugoslawien. Bald stand sein Name auf der »schwarzen Liste« der Autoren, von deren Publikation die staatliche Kulturbürokratie den einheimischen Verlagen abriet. Die Theaterfassung seines satirischen Romans »Die Rolle meiner Familie in der Weltrevolution« von 1969 zog ein mehrjähriges Publikationsverbot nach sich.
Aus Protest gegen den Kurs des serbischen Regimes verließ Ćosić 1992 Belgrad und ließ sich im istrischen Rovinj nieder. Während des Exils in Kroatien, dem offiziellen Feindesland Serbiens, entstand sein »Tagebuch eines Heimatlosen« (1993), das angefüllt ist mit Reflexionen über Proust und den deutsch-französischen Krieg. Ein Stipendium des DAAD führte ihn 1995 nach Berlin, wo er bis heute lebt. Als serbischer Autor im Exil plädierte Ćosić 1999 (anlässlich des Nato-Einsatzes im Kosovo) dafür, nicht nur die Albaner, sondern auch die Serben von Milosevic und »von sich selbst«, d. h. vom »völkischen Wahn« zu befreien.
Bora Ćosić hat über dreißig Bücher geschrieben, die in viele europäische Sprachen (u. a. ins Deutsche, Englische, Französische und Ungarische) übersetzt wurden. Nach der Veröffentlichung seines ersten Satire-Bands »Wie unsere Klaviere repariert wurden« (1968) interessierten sich deutsche Verlage erst wieder in den neunziger Jahren für den serbischen Schriftsteller. Seither wird er von der deutschen Kritik als einer der witzigsten und skurrilsten Autoren gefeiert. Diesen Ruf verdankt er insbesondere dem inzwischen zum »subversiven Klassiker« (Andreas Breitenstein, »NZZ«) avancierten Roman »Die Rolle meiner Familie in der Weltrevolution«, der 1994 in Deutschland erschien. Der satirisch-polemische Effekt dieser Familienchronik aus der Zeit von der deutschen Besatzung bis zur Etablierung des Tito-Regimes ergibt sich aus der scheinbar naiven Perspektive des kindlichen Ich-Erzählers, in der historische und alltägliche Ereignisse zu einem grotesken Gesamtbild verschwimmen. Orientiert sich Ćosić in diesem in Serbien als Kultbuch gefeierten Werk nur implizit an dem Konstruktionsprinzip der »Blechtrommel«, ist der spielerische Umgang mit Günter Grass und anderen Vorbildern, wie z.B. Krleža, Musil, Dostojewski, Hamsun oder Proust, in anderen Fällen programmatisch. Dies signalisieren Titel wie »Musils Notizbuch«, »Ein zweites Treffen in Telgte«, »Geschichte Myschkins«, »Bergottes Witwe« oder die fiktive Autobiographie »Miroslav Krleža« (1998). Die »Montage vorgefundenen Materials«, so der Kritiker Karl-Markus Gauß, ist bei Ćosić »ein bevorzugtes ästhetisches Prinzip«. Dies gilt auch innerhalb seines eigenen Werkes, das sich dem Autor zufolge in einem fortwährenden Prozess befindet und zahlreiche Querverbindungen aufweist. So entwickelte er etwa die an den Rollstuhl gefesselte Protagonistin Suarda im Monolog-Roman »Bel Tempo« von 1982 aus der Figur der Großmutter Ćosić', die schon in »Die Rolle meiner Familie in der Weltrevolution« literarisch verewigt wurde. Seit einigen Jahren schreibt Bora Ćosić auch Gedichte. Im Verlagsprogramm des DAAD erschien 2001 sein Gedichtband »Die Toten«.

nuruddin farah
biography

Nuruddin Farah was born in 1945 in Baidoa, Somalia. After having studied philosophy, sociology, and literature in India, where he also started work on his first literary compositions, he went to London initially to work at the theatre for two years. He did not however return to Somalia, as developments there meant he now had to fear reprisals from Siyad Barre's military regime. While abroad in the late 70's, he was indeed condemned to death. While in exile, guest professorships brought him to Africa, Italy, and the US, as well as to Germany, where as a DAAD scholarship holder he experienced the fall of the Wall. He currently lives in Cape Town.
Farah is considered one of Africa's most important authors and has received numerous international prizes. His novels, which are still banned in Somalia, have been translated into 17 languages. His mother and both great-grandfathers were traditional storytellers; even as a child he began to gain experience as a writer for the illiterate people of his village. His first works in the 60's were short stories and dramas. His narrative technique oscillates between the oral narrative tradition of Africa, which is rich in myth, and Western literature; his writing shows influences from Joyce and Grass but has its own unique experimental style, the reason for which may be attributable to Farah's multilingual background – Farah writes in English, but grew up with five languages. In his work he addresses Somalia's loss of identity, which he sees as the late effect of colonialism. Having been in exile for more than 25 years, he writes from the point of view of an outsider. In his novels, politics work as a foil against which the fate of his figures, primarily strong female characters, unfolds. His main work is divided into two trilogies. The first one focuses on the family unit as a safe refuge and as the antithesis to the threats of the dictatorship. The second trilogy, consisting of »Maps« (1986), »Gifts« (1993), and »Secrets« (1998), most of which came into being during the turmoil of the somalian civil war, takes the orphan as the central metaphor for the increasing distance from his country of origin. But in his poems he always returns to his native country. »Yesterday, Tomorrow: Voices from the Somali Diaspora« (2000), Farah's collection of refugee stories, will be published in German in September 2003 under the title »Yesterday/Tomorrow: Stimmen aus der somalischen Diaspora.«

Aus einer gekrümmten Rippe
Lamuv, Göttingen, 2000
[Ü: Gunter Böhnke]
Geheimnisse
Suhrkamp
Frankfurt a. M., 2000
[Ü: Eike Schönfeld]
Wie eine nackte Nadel
Suhrkamp
Frankfurt a. M., 2001
[Ü: Barbara Hillgen]
Vater Mensch
Frederking & Thaler
München, 2001
[Ü: Klaus Pemsel]
Duniyas Gaben
Suhrkamp
Frankfurt a. M., 2001
[Ü: Klaus Pemsel]
Bruder Zwilling
btb, München, 2002
[Ü: Martin Hielscher]
Tochter Frau
btb, München, 2003
[Ü: Klaus Pemsel]
Yesterday/Tomorrow: Stimmen aus der somalischen Diaspora
Suhrkamp
Frankfurt a. M., 2003

Nuruddin Farah wurde 1945 in Baidoa, Somalia, geboren. Nach dem Studium der Philosophie, Soziologie und Literatur in Indien, wo er auch mit seinen ersten literarischen Arbeiten begann, ging er nach London, um dort für zunächst zwei Jahre am Theater zu arbeiten.
Er kehrte jedoch nicht nach Somalia zurück, da er mittlerweile Repressalien vom Militärregime Siyad Barres befürchten musste. Tatsächlich wurde er Ende der siebziger Jahre in Abwesenheit zum Tode verurteilt. Im Exil führten ihn Gastprofessuren nach Afrika, Italien und die USA sowie nach Deutschland, wo er als DAAD-Stipendiat den Fall der Mauer erlebte. Gegenwärtig lebt er in Kapstadt.
Farah gilt als einer der bedeutendsten Autoren Afrikas und erhielt zahlreiche internationale Auszeichnungen. Seine Romane, in Somalia noch immer verboten, wurden in 17 Sprachen übersetzt. Seine Mutter sowie beide Urgroßväter waren traditionelle Erzähler, er selbst sammelte schon im Kindesalter Erfahrungen als Schreiber für die Analphabeten seines Dorfes. Seine ersten Arbeiten aus den sechziger Jahren waren Kurzgeschichten und Dramen.
Seine Erzählweise oszilliert zwischen der mythenreichen mündlichen Erzähltradition Afrikas und westlicher Literatur, sie zeigt Einflüsse von Joyce und Grass und neigt zu einem ganz eigenen experimentellen Stil, für den mitunter seine Multilingualität als Erklärung herangezogen wurde: Farah schreibt in englischer Sprache, ist aber mit fünf Sprachen aufgewachsen. In seinem Werk setzt er sich mit dem Identitätsverlust Somalias auseinander, den er als Spätfolge des Kolonialismus erachtet. Seit über 25 Jahren im Exil, schreibt er mit dem Blick des Außenseiters. Politik bildet in seinen Romanen eine Folie, vor der sich das Schicksal seiner Figuren, zumeist starke Frauencharaktere, abspielt. Sein Hauptwerk gliedert sich in zwei Trilogien. Die erste stellt die Familieneinheit als Hort der Geborgenheit und Gegenpol zu den Bedrohungen der Diktaturherrschaft ins Zentrum. Die zweite Trilogie, bestehend aus »Maps« (1986; dt. unter dem selben Titel 1992), »Gifts« (1993; dt. »Duniyas Gaben«, 2001) und »Secrets« (1998; dt. »Geheimnisse«, 2000), zum großen Teil während der Wirren des somalischen Bürgerkrieges entstanden, wählt das Waisenkind zur zentralen Metapher für die zunehmende Distanz zu seinem Herkunftsland. Dennoch kehrt er in seinen Geschichten immer wieder in seine Heimat zurück. Im September 2003 erscheint »Yesterday, Tomorrow: Voices from the Somali Diaspora« (2000), Farahs Sammlung von Flüchtlingsschicksalen, unter dem deutschen Titel »Yesterday/Tomorrow: Stimmen aus der somalischen Diaspora«.

raymond federman

biography

Raymond Federman is internationally considered one of the most influential representatives of postmodern literature. The French-American writer and literary scholar of Jewish descent was born in 1928 in Paris. However, he dates his »real« date of birth as July 16, 1942, the day when more than 12,000 people were arrested in Paris and deported to the concentration camps. Federman's parents and both of his sisters were murdered at Auschwitz. He himself survived because his mother hid him in a closet. Federman emigrated to the US in 1947, where he got by as a casual labourer and jazz saxophonist until he was drafted to the army in 1951; he served as a parachutist in Korea. In 1953 he was granted US citizenship. In 1954 he began to study Comparative Literature at Columbia University and concluded his studies in 1963 at UCLA with a doctoral dissertation on Samuel Beckett, with whom he became close friends. Since 1977, numerous guest professorships brought him to Europe, Africa and Asia.

Although his work encompasses books of poetry, volumes of essays, scholarly works, articles and translations, he considers himself primarily as a novelist. His experimental debut novel »Double or Nothing« was published in 1971; it later received numerous awards and immediately raised his international profile. The novel links the formal experiments of concrete poetry with epic prose and is considered one of the most important avantgarde works of the past century. His extensive, highly autobiographical work revolves around the sense of isolation and guilt felt by someone who survived by mere chance; this is also the case in »Take It or Leave It«, (1976) which he himself referred to as his most important book. In his Hamburger poetry lectures (1990), borrowing from Surrealism, he coined the term »surfiction« for the type of literature that exposes the fictitious nature of reality and is characterized by repetitions, digressions and personal reflections. In 2001 »Loose Shoes« was published, a journal-like book about his intellectual work, consisting of 365 experimental fragments and containing the programmatic motto against which the entirety of his work must be understood: »A novel is not so much about writing an adventure as it is about the adventure of writing.« Federman's work, which has in part been published bilingualy and translated into more than a dozen languages, has received numerous awards including the American Book Award (1986). He lives in San Diego.

Alles oder nichts
Eichborn
Frankfurt a. M., 1986
[Ü: Peter Torberg]
Die Stimme im Schrank/ The Voice in the Closet
Edition Michael Kellner
Hamburg, 1989
[Ü: Peter Torberg]
Now Then/Nun denn
Edition Isele
Eggingen, 1992
[Ü: Karin Graf]
Penner-Rap
Suhrkamp
Frankfurt a. M., 1998
[Ü: Peter Torberg]
Take It or Leave It
Rogner & Bernhard
Hamburg, 1998
[Ü: Peter Torberg]
Der Pelz meiner Tante Rachel
dtv, München, 2000
[Ü: Thomas Hartl]
Loose Shoes/ Offene Schuhe
Weidler, Berlin, 2002
[Ü: Martin Amdorfer]

Raymond Federman zählt international zu den einflussreichsten Vertretern der literarischen Postmoderne. Der franko-amerikanische Schriftsteller und Literaturwissenschaftler jüdischer Abstammung wurde 1928 in Paris geboren. Seine »wirkliche« Geburt datiert er jedoch auf den 16.7.1942, jenen Tag, an dem in Paris mehr als 12.000 Menschen verhaftet und in die Todeslager deportiert wurden. Federmans Eltern und beide Schwestern wurden in Auschwitz umgebracht, er selbst überlebte, weil seine Mutter ihn in einem Wandschrank verbarg. Federmann emigrierte 1947 in die USA, wo er sich als Gelegenheitsarbeiter und Jazz-Saxophonist durchschlug, bis er 1951 zur Armee eingezogen wurde und als Fallschirmspringer in Korea diente. 1953 erhielt er die amerikanische Staatsbürgerschaft. 1954 begann er das Studium der Vergleichenden Literaturwissenschaft an der Columbia University, das er 1963 an der UCLA mit einer Dissertation zu Samuel Beckett, mit dem er eng befreundet war, abschloss. Ab 1977 führten ihn zahlreiche Gastprofessuren nach Europa, Afrika und Asien.

Obwohl sein Werk Gedicht- und Essaybände, wissenschaftliche Arbeiten, Aufsätze und Übersetzungen umfasst, betrachtet er sich nach eigener Aussage in erster Linie als Romanschriftsteller. Sein 1971 erschienener experimenteller Debütroman »Double or Nothing« (dt. »Alles oder nichts«, 1971), der später mehrfach ausgezeichnet wurde und ihm sofort internationale Anerkennung brachte, verbindet die formalen Experimente der konkreten Poesie mit epischer Prosa und wird zu den wichtigsten avantgardistischen Werken des vorigen Jahrhunderts gerechnet. Sein umfangreiches, autobiographisch durchwirktes Werk kreist immer wieder um die Verlassenheit und das Schuldtrauma des zufällig Überlebenden, so auch in »Take It or Leave It« (1976, dt. 1998), das er selbst als sein wichtigstes Buch bezeichnet hat. In seinen Hamburger Poetik-Lektionen (1990) prägte er in Anlehnung an den Surrealismus den Begriff »Surfiction« für jene Art von Literatur, die die Fiktionalität der Wirklichkeit offenlegt und von Wiederholungen, Abschweifungen und Selbstreflexionen geprägt ist. 2001 erschien der Band »Loose Shoes« (dt. »Offene Schuhe«, 2002), eine aus 365 experimentellen Fragmenten bestehende, tagebuchartige Aufzeichnung seiner geistigen Arbeit, dem der programmatische Leitspruch vorangestellt ist, vor dessen Hintergrund sein ganzes Werk begriffen werden muss: »Ein Roman ist nicht so sehr das Schreiben eines Abenteuers als das Abenteuer des Schreibens.« Für sein Werk, das teils zweisprachig erschien und in mehr als ein Dutzend Sprachen übersetzt worden ist, erhielt Federman zahlreiche Auszeichnungen, unter anderem den American Book Award (1986). Er lebt in San Diego.

22-MAI-2003 15:48 VON:ILB 03027878685

The Reckless wanderer

Refusing all categorization
the Poet perplexes the experts
who cannot grasp
where he comes from

Born nowhere
but being everywhere
at the same time
he constantly arrives
and departs carrying
with him a bundle
of souvenirs tattooed
in his flesh
lest he forget

with effrontery
he abuses a language
unknown in the land
that lies between
here and elsewhere
between memory
and forgetfullness

He plays with words
that construct in spirals
a tale made of digressions
that cancel old souvenirs

But he fears nothing
because his infernal tale
is spiced with indifference
sweetened with laughter

Raymond Federman

aris fioretos

biography

Aris Fioretos was born in 1960 in Göteborg, to Greek and Austrian parents. He studied Comparative Literature at the University of Stockholm, the École des Hautes Études in Paris and Yale University. He has published essays and scholarly works on Hölderlin, Benjamin, and Celan, and he has also translated a number of writers, including Paul Auster, Friedrich Hölderlin and Vladimir Nabokov, into Swedish. In 1997, he was a writer-in-residence at the DAAD Künstlerprogramm in Berlin and in 2001, a Berlin Prize Fellow at the American Academy in Berlin. He has received numerous prizes, including the Swedish Academy's Karl Ragnar Gierow Prize (1994).
Fioretos has published fiction since 1991. His debut novel »Stockholm Noir« was published in 2000, and received several prizes. The German translation, which was published in the same year under the title »Die Seelensucherin«, was enthusiastically received by the critics. Fioretos not only brilliantly links various narrative levels, but also connects fictitious destinies with the real history of science. On winding routes, the reader accompanies a young Berliner on a three-day search for her father to Stockholm in the winter of 1925, gradually learning how her destiny is entwined with that of a self-styled Swedish »soul biologist«, who is convinced that he can locate the exact position of the soul in the human brain. Fioretos captures the 20's atmosphere in an evocative way. At the end, every detail, with its elaborate evidentiality proves itself indispensable for the novel as a whole. His second novel, entitled »Sanningen om Sasha Knisch« (t: The truth about Sasha Knisch), also takes Berlin of the 20's as its point of departure, using historical facts to interwine various types of narrative. What starts out as a love story about two people, turns, with the death of one of them, into a thriller, in which the saving truth is hidden in that which did not happen. Against the backdrop of a scientific conspiracy, Fioretos describes both the illicit and seductive nature of sexuality, offering a declaration of love to the powers of imagination that is as astute as it is comical. Reviewing »Die Seelensucherin«, German critic Hubert Winkels found that Fioretos achieved the highest task of literature, namely »to generate insight by using the means of poetry«. Currently, Aris Fioretos is cultural attaché at the Swedish Embassy in Berlin.

En bok om fantomer
Norstedt, Stockholm, 1991
Vanitasrutinerna
Norstedt, Stockholm, 1998
Die Seelensucherin
DuMont, Köln, 2000
[Ü: Paul Berf]
Die Wahrheit über Sascha Knisch
DuMont, Köln, 2003
[Ü: Paul Berf]
Mein schwarzer Schädel
DAAD, Berlin, 2003
[Ü: Paul Berf]
Der kritische Moment: Hölderlin, Benjamin, Celan
Suhrkamp
Frankfurt a. M.
erscheint 2004

LIEBESERKLÄRUNG AN FRÄULEIN UHR

Aris Fioretos

Kleiner psychischer Automatismus,
Was bringt mein Herz zum Klopfen
Wie ein kochendes Ei?
Ist es deine Stimme, deine Ruh,
Dein Sinn für Takt, dein Ton?
Du bist nur eine sehr kleine Göttin,
Ich weiß,
Kühl und elektrisch,
Mit einer Frekvenz
Wo es einem Puls gut ginge.
Leicht zu glauben,
Auch deine Atmung sei nur Illusion,
Kein Körper, keine Knochen,
Die Stimme bloß Passform
Für eine Passion.

Aris Fioretos wurde 1960 als Sohn griechisch-österreichischer Eltern in Göteborg, Schweden, geboren. Er studierte Vergleichende Literaturwissenschaften an der Universität Stockholm, an der École des Hautes Études in Paris und in Yale. Der habilitierte Literaturwissenschaftler publizierte Essays und wissenschaftliche Arbeiten – zu Hölderlin, Benjamin und Celan – und übersetzte u. a. Paul Auster, Friedrich Hölderlin und Vladimir Nabokov ins Schwedische. 1997 war er Gast des DAAD Künstlerprogramms in Berlin, 2001 Berlin Prize Fellow an der American Academy in Berlin. Für seine Arbeiten erhielt er zahlreiche Preise, u. a. den Karl Ragnar Gierow-Preis der Schwedischen Akademie (1994).
Seit 1991 hat Fioretos Kurzprosa veröffentlicht, sein Romandebüt »Stockholm Noir« erschien 2000 und wurde mehrfach ausgezeichnet. Die deutsche Übersetzung, die unter dem Titel »Die Seelensucherin« im selben Jahr erschien, wurde von der Kritik begeistert aufgenommen. Virtuos vernetzt Fioretos hier nicht nur verschiedene Erzählebenen, sondern auch reale Wissenschaftsgeschichte mit fiktiven Schicksalen. Auf verschlungenen Pfaden begleitet der Leser eine junge Berlinerin auf ihrer dreitägigen Suche nach dem Vater durch das winterliche Stockholm des Jahres 1925 und erfährt dabei, wie ihr Schicksal mit dem eines selbsternannten schwedischen »Seelenbiologen« verknüpft ist, der davon überzeugt ist, den Sitz der Seele im menschlichen Gehirn ausmachen zu können. Fioretos gelingt es auf suggestive Weise, die Atmosphäre der zwanziger Jahre einzufangen, wobei sich am Ende jedes Detail mit kunstvoller Selbstverständlichkeit als unverzichtbar für das Romanganze erweist. Auch sein zweiter Roman, »Sanningen om Sasha Knisch« (2002; dt. »Die Wahrheit über Sascha Knisch«, 2003), nimmt seinen Ausgang im Berlin der zwanziger Jahre und bedient sich historischer Fakten, um verschiedene Erzählmuster zu verbinden: Was als Liebesgeschichte zweier Menschen beginnt, schlägt mit dem Tod der Geliebten in einen Krimi um, bei dem die rettende Wahrheit sich in dem verbirgt, was nicht geschehen ist. Vor dem Hintergrund einer Verschwörung im Wissenschaftsmilieu erzählt Fioretos von den Verkleidungen und Verlockungen des Sexuellen und formuliert eine ebenso scharfsinnige wie komische Liebeserklärung an die Kraft der Einbildung. Hubert Winkels befand nach der Lektüre von »Die Seelensucherin«, Fioretos erreiche mit seinem Schreiben das, was höchste Aufgabe der Literatur sei, nämlich »mit poetischen Mitteln Erkenntnis zu zeugen«. Zur Zeit ist Aris Fioretos Botschaftsrat für kulturelle Fragen bei der Schwedischen Botschaft in Berlin.

Doch wissen wir beide, my Darling,
Der Augenblick
Läßt sich nicht ergreifen,
Sondern ergreift einen.
Und so ist es mit der Liebe.
Es gilt nur, nicht zu zögern,
Sein Herz zu öffnen.
So laß' mich meines öffnen,
Da die Gelegenheit sich nun bietet:
Wenn du in meinem Ohr bist,
Milde mechanische Muse,
Bin ich in deiner Gewalt.
Glaubst du mir nicht?
Mach' ein Herz nach,
Und du wirst sehen.

Aber nun muß ich auflegen.
So long,
Kleines elektrisches Kleinod,
So long.

Die weibliche Stimme der telephonischen Zeitansage trägt in Schweden den Namen „Fräulein Uhr". — Anmerkung des Übersetzers.

20.5.2003.

Aus dem Schwedischen von Paul Berf

jonathan franzen
biography

Jonathan Franzen was born in Western Springs, Illinois, in 1959 and grew up in a suburb of St. Louis, Missouri. He studied Literature in Philadelphia and in Berlin.
Franzen, who already started to write while at college, is the author of three novels and one collection of essays (»How to Be Alone«, 2002), which contains a revised version of his much discussed article from 1996 on the future and destiny of the novel (»Why bother?«). He writes for the »New Yorker« and »Harper's Magazine«.
With his third novel »The Corrections« (2001) Franzen impressively revived the genre of the social novel. Against the background of a turbulent, globalized world economy, he tells the story of how the Lambert family falls apart. While Alfred Lambert's character, whose life had been defined in terms of self-control and discipline, disintegrates as Parkinson's disease takes hold, his wife Enid becomes obsessed with celebrating the illusion of a happy life in a final Christmas together. Their three children try to »correct« their parents' image of life. But, as is stated in the book, »What made correction possible also doomed it« and while the next generation is confronted with its respective failure, the book closes with a more comprehensive correction: the collapse of the virtual boom on the financial markets. Franzen goes from the entrenched moral convictions of the 60's Midwest to present-day American cities with their technological obsession, their belief in effortless profit from a never-ending economic boom and their given norms of mental balance and sexual fulfillment. At the same time his narrative technique recalls the writing of the great realists of the 19th century. His language is ruthlessly exact yet at the same time compassionate in its humour and characterised by an unsentimental humaneness. This year the German translation of Franzen's first novel »The Twenty-Seventh City« (1988) will be published under the title »Die 27ste Stadt«. In this novel, S. Jammu, a young Indian woman from Bombay becomes chief of police in St. Louis. What starts out as another variation on the American dream develops in the course of the ensuing political conspiracy into a black comedy. Franzen combines realistic and fantastic elements, to brilliantly and cuttingly take stock of American society. Franzen has received various awards, including in 2001 the National Book Award for »The Corrections«. He lives in New York.

Strong Motion
Picador, New York, 2001
Die Korrekturen
Rowohlt, Reinbek, 2003
[Ü: Bettina Abarbanell]
Anleitung zum Einsamsein
Rowohlt, Reinbek, 2003
[Ü: Chris Hirte]
Die 27ste Stadt
Rowohlt, Reinbek, 2003
[Ü: Chris Hirte]

Jonathan Franzen wurde 1959 in Western Springs, Illinois, geboren und ist in einem Vorort von St. Louis, Missouri, aufgewachsen. Er studierte Literatur in Philadelphia und in Berlin. Franzen, der schon auf dem College zu schreiben begann, ist Autor von drei Romanen und einer Essaysammlung (»How to Be Alone«, 2002; dt. »Anleitung zum Einsamsein«, 2002), die eine revidierte Fassung seines vieldiskutierten Artikels von 1996 über Zukunft und Bestimmung des Romans enthält (»Why bother?«). Er schreibt für den »New Yorker« und »Harper's Magazine«.

Mit seinem dritten Roman »The Corrections« (2001, dt. »Die Korrekturen«, 2002) hat Franzen auf eindrucksvolle Weise das Genre des Gesellschaftsromans wiederbelebt. Er erzählt die Geschichte vom Auseinanderfallen der Familie Lambert vor dem Hintergrund einer entfesselten globalisierten Weltwirtschaft. Während sich Alfred Lamberts Persönlichkeit, die Zeit seines Lebens durch Selbstkontrolle und Disziplin charakterisiert war, im Verlauf der Parkinsonschen Krankheit auflöst, ist seine Frau Enid davon besessen, die Illusion eines geglückten Lebensentwurfes in einem letzten gemeinsamen Weihnachtsfest aufgehen zu lassen. Ihre drei Kinder versuchen indessen, diesen elterlichen Lebensentwurf zu »korrigieren«. Aber, wie es im Buch heißt, »was die Korrekturen möglich machte, vereitelte sie zugleich«, und während die nächste Generation mit ihrem jeweiligen Versagen konfrontiert ist, schließt das Buch mit einer umfassenderen Korrektur: dem Zusammenbruch des virtuellen Booms auf den Finanzmärkten. Franzen schlägt den Bogen von der in überkommenen Moralvorstellungen verhafteten Welt des mittleren Westens der sechziger Jahre bis in die Gegenwart der amerikanischen Großstädte mit ihrer Technik-Besessenheit, ihrem Glauben an mühelose Gewinne in einen niemals endenden Wirtschaftsboom und ihrem Imperativ der mentalen Ausgeglichenheit und sexuellen Erfülltheit. Zugleich erinnert seine Erzähltechnik an die der großen Realisten des 19. Jahrhunderts. Seine Sprache ist schonungslos genau, zugleich jedoch mitfühlend in ihrem Humor und von einer unsentimentalen Menschlichkeit geprägt. Franzens erster Roman »The Twenty-Seventh City« (1988) erscheint in diesem Jahr in deutscher Übersetzung unter dem Titel »Die 27ste Stadt«. Darin wird die junge Inderin S. Jammu aus Bombay zur Polizeifchefin von St. Louis ernannt. Was wie eine weitere Variation des amerikanischen Traums beginnt, entwickelt sich in der darauffolgenden politischen Konspiration zu einer schwarzen Komödie. Franzen verbindet realistische und phantastische Elemente zu einer brillanten und bissigen Bestandsaufnahme der amerikanischen Gesellschaft. Franzen erhielt verschiedene Auszeichnungen, u. a. 2001 den National Book Award für »The Corrections«. Er lebt in New York.

"A time-bomb of impatience with insipid questions."

günter grass

biography

Günter Grass was born in Danzig (now Gdansk) in 1927. He served on an anti-aircraft battery and as a tank gunner towards the end of the Second World War, eventually being wounded and captured by the U.S. Army. After his release he trained as a stonemason before studying graphic art and sculpture in Düsseldorf and Berlin, writing poetry and plays.

In 1955 he won a prize in a regional poetry competition. This success earned him his first reading for the Gruppe 47, an influential group of writers, and the publication of his first book of poems, prose and illustrations entitled »Die Vorzüge der Windhühner« in 1956.

In 1958 he was awarded the literary prize of the Gruppe 47 for the novel »The Tin Drum«, which was published in 1959 and established Grass on the global literary scene. This first volume of his so-called »Danzig Trilogy« of novels was followed by »Cat and Mouse« (1961) and »Dog Years« (1963). Although Grass also wrote dramas and poems, it was his prose with its autobiographical figures and narrators that drew most attention. His works are distinguished by the link between realism and absurd fantasy, a profound enjoyment of language games, jargon, and grotesque imagery.

The 60's saw Grass assuming an active role in politics, supporting the German Social Democrats on election campaigns and founding the Social Democratic Voters' Initiative. He continues to regularly express his critical views on political issues, most recently on the Iraq war in the spring of 2003. His writing also »lets the citizen in the writer have his say«, giving a political moralist's perspective on the history of Germany – whether the East Berlin worker's rebellion on June 17, 1953 in his drama »The Plebeians Rehearse the Uprising« (1966) or German reunification in the novel »Too Far Afield« (1995).

After receiving countless literary distinctions and honorary titles, Grass was awarded the Nobel Prize for Literature in 1999 for his life's work. He was cited in the official declaration as a writer »whose frolicsome black fables portray the forgotten face of history«. It was precisely this approach that is again featured in his latest novella, »Crabwalk« (2002), in which he portrays the sinking of the »Wilhelm Gustloff«, a former »Kraft durch Freude« cruise liner, in January 1945. His most recent publication is a book of poems entitled »Letzte Tänze« (2003). Grass lives near Lübeck.

Die Blechtrommel
Luchterhand
Darmstadt, 1959
Katz und Maus
Luchterhand
Darmstadt, 1961
Der Butt
Luchterhand
Darmstadt, 1977
Ein weites Feld
Steidl Verlag
Göttingen, 1995
Mein Jahrhundert
Steidl Verlag
Göttingen, 1999
Im Krebsgang
Steidl Verlag
Göttingen, 2002
Letzte Tänze
Steidl Verlag
Göttingen, 2003

Günter Grass wurde 1927 in Danzig geboren. Am Zweiten Weltkrieg nahm er als Luftwaffenhelfer und Panzersoldat teil, wurde verwundet und geriet in amerikanische Kriegsgefangenschaft. Nach seiner Freilassung absolvierte er eine Steinmetzlehre und studierte anschließend Graphik und Bildhauerei in Düsseldorf und Berlin, schrieb Gedichte und Theaterstücke.
1955 wurde er bei einem Lyrikwettbewerb des Süddeutschen Rundfunks ausgezeichnet. Dieser Erfolg bescherte ihm eine erste Lesung vor der Gruppe 47 und 1956 »Die Vorzüge der Windhühner«, seine erste Buchveröffentlichung mit Gedichten, Prosa und Zeichnungen. 1958 erhielt Grass den Preis der Gruppe 47 für den Roman »Die Blechtrommel«, der 1959 erschien und seinen weltweiten Ruhm als Schriftsteller begründete. Zusammen mit der Novelle »Katz und Maus« (1961) und dem Roman »Hundejahre« (1963) bildet er die »Danziger Trilogie«. Obgleich Grass auch Dramen und Gedichte geschrieben hat, fanden seine Prosawerke mit teils autobiographisch geprägten Figuren und Erzählern die größte Beachtung. Die Verbindung von Realismus und skurriler Phantasie, eine große Lust an Sprachspielen, Jargon und grotesken Bildern zeichnen seine Werke aus.
In den sechziger Jahren begann Grass, sich politisch zu engagieren, zog für die SPD in den Wahlkampf und gründete die Sozialdemokratische Wählerinitiative. Seitdem äußert er sich regelmäßig zu politischen Themen, so zuletzt zum Irak-Krieg im Frühjahr 2003. Auch in seinen literarischen Arbeiten lässt er »den Bürger im Schriftsteller zu Wort kommen« und reflektiert als politischer Moralist die Geschichte Deutschlands – seien es die Geschehnisse des 17. Juni 1953 in seinem Drama »Die Plebejer proben den Aufstand« (1966) oder die deutsche Wiedervereinigung in dem Roman »Ein weites Feld« (1995).
Neben zahlreichen literarischen Auszeichnungen und Ehrentiteln erhielt Grass 1999 den Literatur-Nobelpreis für sein Lebenswerk. Er habe, so die Schwedische Akademie, »in munterschwarzen Fabeln das vergessene Gesicht der Geschichte gezeichnet«. Ebendies gelang ihm auch in seiner jüngsten Novelle »Im Krebsgang« (2002), die den Untergang des ehemaligen »Kraft durch Freude«-Schiffs »Wilhelm Gustloff« im Januar 1945 erzählt. Zuletzt erschien der Gedichtband »Letzte Tänze« (2003). Grass lebt in der Nähe von Lübeck.

lars gustafsson

biography

Lars Gustafsson was born in Västerås, central Sweden, in 1936. He completed his philosophy studies at the University of Uppsala and Magdelen College, Oxford, in 1978 with a dissertation on »three extremists in the philosophy of language« (Friedrich Nietzsche, Alexander Bryan Johnson and Fritz Mauthner). He published his first novel, »Wegesrast. Ein Mysterienspiel in Prosa«, (t: Rest on the Way A Mystery Play in Prose), at the age of only 21. Gustafsson himself dates his actual debut from 1959, when »Letzte Tage und Tod des Dichters Brumberg« (t: Last Days and Death of the Poet Brumberg) appeared.
From 1960 Gustafsson was editor, and from 1965-1972 editor-in-chief, of the Swedish literary journal »Bonniers Litterära Magasin«. After this he travelled extensively and accepted various guest lectureships including in West Germany. The offer of a DAAD scholarship brought him to Berlin in 1972-73. Gustafsson had already made a name for himself internationally as a writer and academic when he decided to change his life dramatically in 1982 by emigrating to the US, remarrying and converting to Judaism.
He moved to Austin, Texas, and became an American citizen in 1983. He is now adjunct professor of Germanic Studies at the University of Texas.
His extensive work has won many awards, including the Prix Européen de l'essai Charles Veillon (1983), the Swedish Academy's Bellman Prize (1990) and the Swedish Pilot Prize (1996). Since 2000, he has been a member of the »Academy of Fine Arts« in Munich.
In Germany, Gustafsson first gained renown with his poetry during the 70's.
His poems focus on questions which he also tackles as a novelist and essayist. The search for identity, moral consciousness, the relationship between personal experience and self-awareness, juxtaposed with a philosophically founded scepticism towards language, are the main themes of his work.
Since the novel series »Die Risse in der Mauer« (t: The Cracks in the Wall), Gustafsson is regarded internationally as one of Scandinavia's best-known authors. Here the author uses crime motifs to present the fragility of a world view which relies on expressions such as »good« and »evil« and concepts of personal integrity. Yet the world is only out of joint for the hero of the first book »Die Sache mit dem Hund« (1994; t: The Thing About the Dog). The same incidents which make the ageing judge doubt himself and the world, driving him to despair, blend harmoniously into hairdresser Windy's trivial stream of chatter.
Lars Gustafsson is a master of the most varied literary forms. His most recent novel appearing in German »Blom und die zweite Magenta« (2001; Blom and the Second Magenta) is a thriller for young people. He recently published his poetry collection »En tid i Xanadu«.

Nachmittag eines Fliesenlegers
dtv, München, 1993
[Ü: Verena Reichel]
Das seltsame Tier aus dem Norden
dtv, München, 1995
[Ü: Verena Reichel]
Die Sache mit dem Hund
dtv, München, 1999
[Ü: Verena Reichel]
Der Tod eines Bienenzüchters
Fischer
Frankfurt a. M., 2001
[Ü: Verena Reichel]
Windy erzählt
dtv, München, 2003
[Ü: Verena Reichel]
Blom und die zweite Magenta
dtv, München, 2003
[Ü: Verena Reichel]
Auszug aus Xanadu
Hanser, München, 2003
[Ü: Verena Reichel
Hans Magnus
Enzensberger]

Lars Gustafsson wurde 1936 in Västerås, Mittelschweden, geboren. Sein Studium der Philosophie an der Universität Uppsala und dem Magdelen College in Oxford schloss er 1978 mit einer Dissertation über drei »sprachphilosophische Extremisten« (Friedrich Nietzsche, Alexander Bryan Johnson und Fritz Mauthner) ab. Bereits mit 21 Jahren veröffentlichte Gustafsson mit »Wegesrast. Ein Mysterienspiel in Prosa« seinen ersten Roman. Sein »eigentliches Debüt« datiert der Schriftsteller selbst allerdings erst auf 1959, dem Erscheinungsjahr des Romans »Letzte Tage und Tod des Dichters Brumberg«.
Ab 1960 war Gustafsson Redakteur, von 1965 bis 1972 Chefredakteur der schwedischen Literaturzeitschrift »Bonniers Litterära Magasin«. Danach unternahm er ausgiebige Reisen. An verschiedenen Universitäten, u. a. auch in West-Deutschland, hatte er Gastdozenturen inne. 1972/73 führte ihn ein Stipendium des DAAD nach Berlin. Gustafsson hatte sich bereits international als Schriftsteller und Wissenschaftler einen Namen gemacht, als er 1982 beschloss, sich in einen völlig neuen Rahmen zu begeben: Er siedelte in die USA über, heiratete wieder und konvertierte zum Judentum.
In Austin, Texas, unterrichtet der Autor seither als Adjunct Professor für Germanic Studies. Bereits 1983 nahm er die US-amerikanische Staatsbürgerschaft an. Für sein umfangreiches Werk erhielt der Autor unter anderem den europäischen Essay-Preis Charles Veillon (1983), den Bellman-Preis der Schwedischen Akademie (1990) und den schwedischen Pilot Prize (1996). Seit 2000 ist er Mitglied der Akademie der Schönen Künste in München.
In Deutschland wurde Gustafsson in den siebziger Jahren zuerst durch seine Lyrik bekannt. Sein Werk ist geprägt von der starken Wechselbeziehung zwischen Themen des Philosophen und Literaturwissenschaftlers Gustafsson und des Geschichtenerzählers bzw. Poeten. Die Suche nach Identität, das moralische Bewusstsein, die Beziehung zwischen persönlicher Erfahrung und Selbstreflexion sowie eine philosophisch untermauerte Sprachskepsis sind die Ausgangspunkte der Fragestellungen, die Gustafsson in seine Romane, Gedichte und Essays einbettet.
Seit der Romanreihe »Die Risse in der Mauer« zählt Gustafsson international zu den bekanntesten Schriftstellern Skandinaviens. Der Autor benutzt hier Motive aus Kriminalromanen, um die Zerbrechlichkeit einer Weltanschauung darzustellen, die auf Ausdrücken wie »gut«, »böse« oder der Vorstellung von persönlicher Integrität basiert. So muss dem Helden des ersten Buches »Die Sache mit dem Hund« (1994) die Welt zwangsläufig aus den Fugen geraten. Dieselben Ereignisse, die den alternden Konkursrichter an sich und der Welt zweifeln lassen und ihn in die Verzweiflung treiben, verschmelzen zugleich auf harmonische Weise mit dem trivialen Geplänkel des Friseurs Windy.
Lars Gustafsson ist ein Meister der verschiedensten literarischen Genres. So ist sein zuletzt auf Deutsch erschienener Roman »Blom und die zweite Magenta« (2001) eine Kriminalgeschichte für Jugendliche. Erst kürzlich erschien sein Lyrikband »En tid i Xanadu« (dt. »Auszug aus Xanadu«, 2003).

Good poets do not tick.

mila haugová

biography

The poet and translator Mila Haugová was born in Budapest, Hungary, in 1942 and raised in Slovakia. Daughter of a Hungarian mother and Slovakian father, she grew up speaking two languages.
Her father, an agricultural graduate, was imprisoned as a so-called »class enemy«, which consequently prevented the author from taking her chosen study path in Slovakian and German language and literature. From 1959 to 1964 she studied agriculture and then worked as an agronomist and thereafter as a teacher. She stopped teaching, and from 1986 to 1996 worked on the editorial staff of the literary magazine »Romboid«.
In the early 70's Haugová started to write her own poems, which she initially published in 1980 under the pseudonym Mila Srnková. But it is the book of poems »Premenlivý povrch« (1983, t: Changeable Surface(s)) that she regards as her true debut. From the start her verse has been characterised by themes related to naturalness and intimacy, particularly in the relationship between the sexes, but her poetic language – which grew increasingly radical – was not received well by mainstream literary critics. Starting in the early 80's, the author also began to make a name for herself as a translator of numerous poets, including Ingeborg Bachmann, Sylvia Plath, Sarah Kirsch, Friederike Mayröcker, Else Lasker-Schüler, Paul Celan and Georg Trakl. The breakthrough finally came for Haugová with the book of poems »Čisté dni« (1990, t: Pure Days), in which a female first-person narrator expresses herself in an uncompromising way; at the time such a stance was still unheard of in Slovakia. In addition to contributions to international poetry magazines and anthologies, Haugová has so far published 12 collections of poetry, which have been translated into English, French, Polish, Russian and German. To date, three poetry volumes have appeared in German, most recently the dual-language book »Atlas piesku/Sandatlas« (2001). Jaroslav Šrank praises the »cathartic openness« of Haugová's verse, which »in mapping mysterious gardens and wastelands [explores] the most basic and the most intimate questions of our existence«. Here, language is freed from its syntactic contexts, and through intertextual references to classical modern verse, polyvalent layers of meaning are opened.
Today Mila Haugová lives with her partner, the Austrian artist, BHX LOHMER, as a freelance writer in Bratislava and Zajacia Dolina Levice in Slovakia.

Nostalgia
Slovenský Spisovatel
Bratislava, 1993
Alfa Centauri
Drewo a Srd
Banská Bystrica, 1997
Kahlfrieren
BONsai-typART
Berlin, 1998
[Ü: Ursula Macht]
Das innere Gesicht
Edition Thanhäuser
Ottensheim a. d. Donau
1999
[Ü: Zdenka Becker]
Sandatlas
Edition Korrespondenzen
Wien, 2001
[Ü: Angela Repka]

Die Lyrikerin und Übersetzerin Mila Haugová wurde 1942 in Budapest, Ungarn, geboren und ist in der Slowakei aufgewachsen. Als Tochter einer Ungarin und eines Slowaken wurde sie zweisprachig erzogen.
Der Vater, ein Diplomlandwirt, wurde als sogenannter »Klassenfeind« inhaftiert, wodurch der Autorin das angestrebte Studium der slowakischen Sprache und Literatur und der Germanistik verwehrt war. Von 1959 bis 1964 studierte sie Landwirtschaft, danach arbeitete sie als Agronomin, später als Lehrerin. Sie gab den Schuldienst auf und begann 1986 ihre Arbeit in der Redaktion der Literaturzeitschrift »Romboid«, die sie bis 1996 fortsetzte. Anfang der siebziger Jahre begann Haugová eigene Gedichte zu schreiben, die sie 1980 unter dem Pseudonym Mila Srnková erstmals publizierte. Als ihr eigentliches Debüt sieht sie jedoch den Gedichtband »Premenlivý povrch« (1983, Ü: Veränderliche Oberfläche). Naturnähe und Intimität, besonders in der Beziehung der Geschlechter, prägten die Themen ihrer Lyrik von Anbeginn, wobei die zunehmende Radikalität ihrer poetischen Sprache bei der linientreuen Literaturkritik aneckte. Seit Anfang der achtziger Jahre kam eine neue Facette der literarischen Arbeit hinzu; so hat sich die Autorin als Übersetzerin zahlreicher Dichter, etwa von Ingeborg Bachmann, Sylvia Plath, Sarah Kirsch, Friederike Mayröcker, Else Lasker-Schüler, Paul Celan und Georg Trakl profiliert. Der Durchbruch gelang Haugová mit dem Gedichtband »Čisté dni« (1990, Ü: Reine Tage), in dem sich ein weibliches lyrisches Ich mit einer in der Slowakei bis dahin nicht gekannten Kompromisslosigkeit artikuliert. Neben Beiträgen für internationale Lyrikzeitschriften und Anthologien hat Haugová bislang zwölf Gedichtbände publiziert, die ins Englische, Französische, Polnische, Russische und Deutsche übertragen wurden. In deutscher Sprache sind bisher drei Gedichtbände von ihr erschienen, zuletzt der zweisprachige Band »Atlas piesku/Sandatlas« (2001). Jaroslav Šrank preist die »kathartische Offenheit« Haugovás Lyrik, die »im Kartographieren von geheimnisvollen Gärten und Wüsten die prinzipiellsten und intimsten Fragen unserer Existenz« auslotet. Die Sprache ist hier aus ihren syntagmatischen Zusammenhängen gelöst und durch intertextuelle Bezüge zur klassischen modernen Lyrik polyvalenten Sinnebenen geöffnet.
Mila Haugová lebt heute, gemeinsam mit ihrem Lebensgefährten, dem österreichischen Künstler BHX LOHMER, als freie Autorin in Bratislava und Zajacia Dolina Levice in der Slowakei.

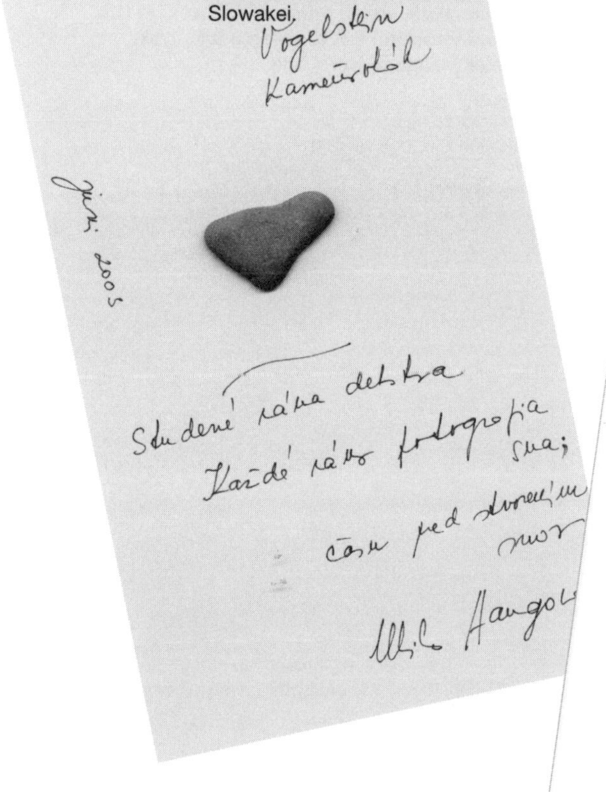

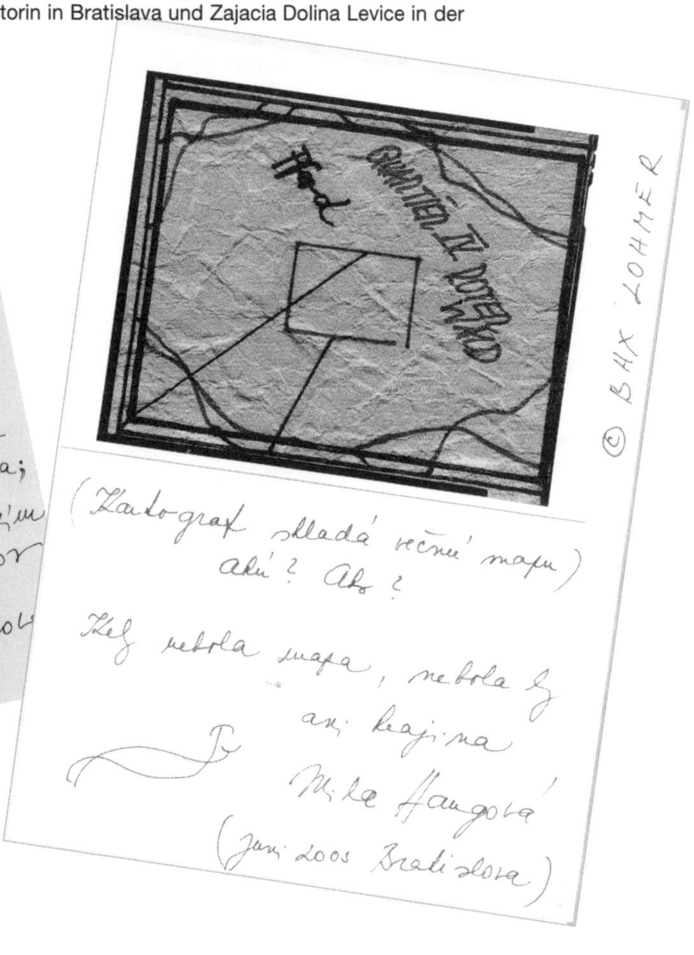

zbyněk hejda
biography

Zbyněk Hejda was born in Hradec Králové in the Czech Republic in 1930. After studying Philosophy and History at the Charles University in Prague, he worked from 1953 to 1958 as a historian and then for the city council of Prague until 1968. He lost his job as a publishing editor when he spoke out against the suppression of the Prague Spring uprising and, as one of the signatories of the »Charta 77«, had to work in a second-hand bookshop. Until 1989 he earned his living as a janitor.
Zbyněk Hejda has worked in the fields of literature and journalism since the late 50's. He was on the editorial staff of the nonconformist literary magazine »Tvář« and since 1985 has been co-publisher of the privately published magazine »Střední Evropa« (t: Central Europe). Zbyněk Hejda has published a total of six books of poetry of which only the first two, »Všechna slast« and »A tady všude muziky je plno« (t: And Everything Here Is Full of Music), could appear officially. Together with »Blízkosti smrti« (t: The Proximity of Death), which was published at the Samisdat, they comprise his first writing period, reflecting the dreary atmosphere of the 50's and 60's. The figures in this dead-end world spend their time between the cemetery and the bar, two central topics in Hejda's verse. Drunks, barmaids and evil bosses seem part of a waxwork exhibition of human misery. Critics loyal to the party line denounced his poems as »spiritualist« and »degenerate« – Hejda was banned from publication for more than 20 years.
The collection »Lady Felthamová«, first published at the Samisdat in 1979, draws together the central strands of a mysterious love story that recounts erotic memories and offers motifs of southern landscapes, which ardently takes up the paradoxical claim that »Bohemia lies at the sea.« In »Valse mélancolique« the author laconically takes stock of life. From an older person's perspective, abstract thoughts on transitoriness are deemed unacceptable. Instead, memories of the places where one spent one's childhood, of companions and the everyday marginalia that is only all too clearly taken note of, become the only comprehensible final certainties. These books, published in 2003 as German translations, are interspersed with very visual accounts of dreams, which as unconscious subtext ironically break with the fears and obsessions of the lyrical self.
In 1996 Hejda received the renowned Jaroslav Seifert Prize. Although awarded for »Valse mélancolique«, this award also applies to the entire work, which primarily focuses on two intersecting themes: death and eros. The poet and translator (of, to name a few, Trakl, Benn, Dickinson) lives in Prague and the Bohemian village of Horní Ves.

Všechna slast
Praha, Prag, 1964
Blízkosti smrti
KDM, Prag 1992
Básne
Torst, Prag, 1996
Lady Feltham
Valse mélancolique
Edition Korrespondenzen
Wien, 2002
[Ü: Christa Rothmeier]

Zbyněk Hejda wurde 1930 in Hradec Králové, Tschechien, geboren. Nach dem Studium der Philosophie und Geschichte an der Prager Karlsuniversität arbeitete er von 1953 bis 1958 als Historiker und danach bis 1968 in der Prager Stadtverwaltung. Seine Stelle als Verlagsredakteur verlor er durch den Protest gegen die Niederschlagung des Prager Frühlings, die darauf folgende Arbeit in einem Antiquariat durch die Unterzeichnung der »Charta 77«. Bis 1989 verdiente er seinen Lebensunterhalt als Hausmeister.
Literarisch und publizistisch ist Zbyněk Hejda seit der zweiten Hälfte der fünfziger Jahre tätig. Er gehörte zur Redaktion der nonkonformistischen Literaturzeitschrift »Tvář« und war seit 1985 als Mitherausgeber der Samisdatzeitschrift »Střední Evropa« (Ü: Mitteleuropa) tätig. Zbyněk Hejda veröffentlichte insgesamt sechs Gedichtbände, von denen nur die beiden ersten, »Všechna slast« (Ü: Alle Lust) und »A tady všude muziky je plno« (Ü: Und alles ist hier voller Musik), offiziell erscheinen konnten. Zusammen mit »Blízkosti smrti« (Ü: Nähe des Todes), der im Samisdat verlegt wurde, bilden sie einen ersten Werkabschnitt, der die triste Atmosphäre der fünfziger und sechziger Jahre reflektiert. Zwischen Friedhof und Wirtshaus, zwei zentralen Topoi in Hejdas Lyrik, tummeln sich die Gestalten einer maroden Welt: Betrunkene, Dirnen und Schinder bilden ein Panoptikum kreatürlicher Misere. Von der linientreuen Kritik wurden seine Gedichte als »spiritualistisch« und »entartet« gebrandmarkt – Hejda war mit einem mehr als zwanzigjährigen Publikationsverbot belegt.
Die Sammlung »Lady Felthamová«, 1979 erstmals im Samisdat verlegt, schildert am roten Faden einer verschlüsselten Liebesgeschichte erotische Reminiszenzen und führt Motive südlicher Landschaften an, die die paradoxe Behauptung, daß »Böhmen am Meer« läge, sehnsüchtig aufnehmen. In »Valse mélancolique« zieht der Autor eine lakonische Lebensbilanz. Aus der Altersperspektive werden abstrakte Gedanken zur Vergänglichkeit als unzulässig erkannt. Stattdessen werden Erinnerungen an die Orte der Kindheit, an Weggefährten und die mit überdeutlicher Schärfe wahrgenommenen alltäglichen Marginalien zu den einzig fassbaren und letzten Sicherheiten. Diese Bände, die in einer 2003 erschienenen deutschen Übersetzung vorliegen, sind durchsetzt von bildmächtigen Traumprotokollen, die als unbewusster Subtext die Ängste und Obsessionen des lyrischen Ich ironisch brechen.
1996 wurde Hejda der renommierte Jaroslav Seifert-Preis verliehen. Ausgesprochen für »Valse mélancolique«, galt diese Auszeichnung jedoch auch dem Gesamtwerk, das sich vor allem um zwei einander durchdringende Themenkreise – Tod und Eros – bewegt. Der Lyriker und Übersetzer (u. a. Trakl, Benn, Dickinson) lebt in Prag und dem böhmischen Dorf Horní Ves.

W. B. Yeats napsal, že ze sporu se sebou samými děláme básně. Jsou i někteří, kteří je dělají ze sporu se světem. Řekl bych, že to jsou spíše žurnalisté nebo kronikáři, i když píší ve verších.

Má osobní zkušenost je takováto: být básníkem se člověku přihodí; prostě se mu to stane. Zpočátku to, proč dělám básně, bylo mi skryto. A i dnes bych vlastně nejraději řekl: přihodilo se mi to.

Zbyněk Hejda

reinhard jirgl

biography

Reinhard Jirgl was born in East Berlin in 1953. He was raised by his grandparents in the Altmark. In 1964, at age 11, he returned to his parents in Berlin. After training as an electrician, he started studying electronics in 1971 at Berlin's Humboldt University. In 1975 he concluded his studies and worked at the Adlershofer Academy for three years. While there he started writing, something which he found more time for in 1978 when he accepted a position as lighting technician at the Volksbühne in East Berlin. By the time the Wall fell in 1989, Jirgl had completed six manuscripts, which, despite support from Heiner Müller, were not published in the GDR on the grounds that he was putting forth a »non-Marxist conception of history«. In 1990 Jirgl started to publish many works which were previously banned from publication as well as new works, including his debut novel »Mutter Vater Roman« (1990; t: Mother Father Novel), the novel »Abschied von den Feinden« (1995; t: Farewell to the Enemies), and the trilogy »Genealogie des Tötens« (2002; t: Genealogy of Killing), which is a collection of works from the 80's.

Jirgl's most recent novel »Die Unvollendeten« (2003; t: The Incomplete) is a family saga about four women, who in 1945 are driven out of the Sudetenland and have to find a new home in the Altmark. How the trauma of their expulsion influences their lives in the dramatic postwar years and the hard work that life in the GDR entails is told from the perspective of their descendent Reiner, who was born in 1953. Without pity, but not without feeling, in drastic scenes and monologues, the loss, the violent life, and the naïve and patient mentality of the women is described. As in previous works, Jirgl uses his own particular typography and orthography; for instance, »und« (and) is replaced with »u« or »&«; exclamation marks come before words and »einzeln« (solitary) might be spelled »1zeln«. These substitutions open up another semantic level, one in which the respective context is also physically visible in the text itself. In this way Jirgl, who is frequently compared to Arno Schmidt, can describe extremities in extreme ways and articulate his characters' dialogues in unpolished format, while at the same time keeping his reader's attention. For critic Iris Radisch the »dark and embittered sound« and »the historical distance, which enables the grandchild to accomplish what the son was unable to do« are the main reasons why »postwar Germany has never before been described as convincingly« as in this novel.

Jirgl has received numerous awards for his works, including the Alfred-Döblin-Preis (1993), the Literaturpreis der Stadt Marburg (1994) and the Joseph-Breitbach-Preis (1999). Since 1996 he has lived in Berlin, where he works as a freelance writer.

Mutter Vater Roman
Aufbau, Berlin, 1990
Im offenen Meer
Luchterhand
München, 1991
Abschied von den Feinden
dtv, München, 1998
Hundsnächte
dtv, München, 2001
Die atlantische Mauer
dtv, München, 2002
Genealogie des Tötens
dtv, München, 2002
Die Unvollendeten
Hanser, München, 2003

"What makes the poet tick?"

Reinhard Jirgl

La Poésie Tourette

Kein Money-Fest

*

Schreiben ist Angriff:
– Gegen die Recht-Winkligkeit gesellschaftlicher Verhältnisse;
– Gegen "die Poesie zu Fuß" (Hamsun): jene Schreibe, mit der man nichts riskiert;
– Gegen bilanzversiffte Koofmichs & Kassen-Wärter im politischen Rotstift-Milieu;
– Gegen DEN STAAT im Sprach-Leib.

Schreiben ist Angriff gegen die dümmste & mächtigste Form von STAAT's POLITIK, u Niemand kann sich entziehen: dem ALLTAG.....
Schreiben zu müssen, ist das Eingeständnis, wie !billig, selber schlecht leben zu können.

Reinhard Jirgl wurde 1953 in Ost-Berlin geboren. Die ersten elf Lebensjahre verbrachte er bei den Großeltern in der Altmark, bis er 1964 zu seinen Eltern nach Berlin zurückkehrte. Nach einer Ausbildung zum Elektromechaniker studierte er ab 1971 an der Berliner Humboldt-Universität Elektronik. 1975 schloss er sein Studium als Ingenieur ab und arbeitete für drei Jahre an der Adlershofer Akademie. Zeitgleich begann er mit dem Schreiben, für das er ab 1978 mehr Zeit fand, als er die Stelle eines Beleuchtungstechnikers an der Ost-Berliner Volksbühne annahm.

Bis zum Fall der Mauer 1989 hatte Jirgl sechs Manuskripte abgeschlossen, die trotz der Unterstützung durch Heiner Müller nicht in der DDR publiziert wurden, da ihnen eine »nicht-marxistische Geschichtsauffassung« vorgeworfen wurde. Seit 1990 hat Jirgl viele bis dato unveröffentlichte und neue Werke publiziert, darunter sein Debüt »Mutter Vater Roman« (1990), den Roman »Abschied von den Feinden« (1995) und die Trilogie »Genealogie des Tötens« (2002), die Arbeiten aus den achtziger Jahren versammelt.

Jirgls jüngster Roman »Die Unvollendeten« (2003) ist eine Familiensaga von vier Frauen, die 1945 aus dem Sudetenland vertrieben werden und in der Altmark eine neue Heimat finden müssen. Wie das Trauma der Vertreibung ihr Erleben der dramatischen Nachkriegsjahre und das arbeitsreiche Leben in der DDR bestimmt, wird aus der Perspektive des 1953 geborenen Nachkommen Reiner erzählt. Ohne Mitleid, aber nicht ohne Mitgefühl, werden in drastischen Szenen und Monologen die Verluste, das Leben inmitten von Gewalt und die naiv-duldsame Mentalität der Frauen geschildert. Jirgl verwendet dazu wie auch bei vorangegangenen Werken eine eigenwillige Typographie und Orthographie, bei der zum Beispiel »und« durch »u« oder »&« ersetzt wird, Ausrufezeichen vor Wörtern stehen und es nicht »einzeln« sondern »1zeln« heißen kann. Diese Substitutionen erschließen eine weitere semantische Ebene, indem der jeweilige Kontext auch in der Textphysis repräsentiert wird. Auf diese Weise kann Jirgl, der oft mit Arno Schmidt verglichen wurde, Extremes auf extreme Weise sowie Mündliches seiner Figuren ungeglättet wiedergeben und gleichzeitig die Aufmerksamkeit des Lesers wach halten. Für Iris Radisch sind vor allem der »dunkle und lebensbittere Sound« und »der historische Abstand, aus dem der Enkel vollbringt, was dem Sohn noch missglückte«, die Gründe dafür, dass »noch nie die deutsche Nachkriegszeit so überzeugend geschildert worden« sei wie in diesem Roman.

Jirgl erhielt für seine Werke zahlreiche Auszeichnungen, zu denen der Alfred-Döblin-Preis (1993), der Literaturpreis der Stadt Marburg (1994) und der Joseph-Breitbach-Preis (1999) gehören. Er lebt, seit 1996 als freier Schriftsteller, in Berlin.

Schreiben ist Solidarität. Deshalb darf Schreiben:

– Was dem gutbürgerlichen Gewissen in der Schrift peinlich & verstörend ist, wie die gewitterhaften Exaltationen des mit Tourette-Syndrom Begabten in einer vollbesetzten U-Bahn;

– Wirklichkeiten und Fiktion auf Kollisionskurs bringen. Aus dem Zusammenprall beider entsteht der Text.

– Poesie u Prosa vermischen. Ressort-"Denken" überlasse man Politikern & andern Kriminellen.

– Poesie darf Alles, nur 1 nicht: gebraucht werden.

J.

walter kempowski

biography

Walter Kempowski was born in Rostock, Germany, in 1929. He was forced to leave school and worked as an anti-aircraft auxiliary with the Hitler Youth. After the war, when he was an apprentice to a printer he ended up in in prison of US army in Wiesbaden. In 1948, on a visit to Rostock he was arrested on suspicion of espionage and received a 25 prison sentence in Bautzen but was granted an amnesty after eight years. It was during this time that Kempowski began writing: a diary-like prose in which he processed his experiences in prison.

In 1956 Kempowski left for the West where he eventually worked as a teacher in north Germany. His literary debut was »Im Block. Ein Haftbericht«, published in 1969, which recalls the years in prison in a single cell. However, his prose is not accusatory and written with cool detachment as a collage of remembrances. Interspersed with proverbs and colloquialisms, short narrative sections create a perspective which without any specific plot open one's view from the small scale to the larger scale, from the subjective personal time to objective history. While in solitary detention in Bautzen remembering is a survival strategy, he later re works the act of remembering into the basis for his writing and recreates the lost world of the past, very precisely, piece by piece, layer by layer: »The only time that really exists is time which has passed«. For Kempowski, being a writer means being a chronicler. On this basis he has produced a large literary oeuvre: novels, short stories, radio plays and non-fiction books. »Tadellöser & Wolff«, the author's second publication, helped him achieve his literary breakthrough in 1971 when he was awarded the Förderpreis des Lessingpreises der Stadt Hamburg. The story chronicles the life of a family, its theme is the confrontation of private experience within the family with political events during the Third Reich.

Between 1980 and 1991 Kempowski was a lecturer in Creative Writing at the University of Oldenburg. It was here that he founded the Archive for Contemporary Literature, in which he systematically collected documents from numerous private and public sources, above all material about the World War II. The emerging kaleidoscopic image of that period provided Kempowski with the material for his comprehensive work: »Das Echolot. Ein kollektives Tagebuch« (1993). As a collage of tens of thousands of documents »Das Echolot« develops the literary form of story telling through memories in a diary. After the years 1943 and 1945, the third part, which was published in 2002, focuses on the year of the attack on the Soviet Union: »Das Echolot. Barbarossa '41«.

Kempowski has been awarded, among numerous other prizes, the Konrad Adenauer Prize in 1994 and the Uwe Johnson Prize in 1995. In 2003 he published his novel »Letzte Grüße«. He is a member of the German P.E.N. and of the Free Academy of Arts in Hamburg. Walter Kempowski lives in Nartum, near Bremen.

Das Echolot: Januar und Februar 1943
Knaus, München, 1993
Bloomsday 1997
Knaus, München, 1997
Das Echolot: Winter 1945
Knaus, München, 1999
Alkor
Knaus, München, 2001
Tadellöser & Wolff
Goldmann, München, 2001
Das Echolot: Barbarossa '41
Knaus, München, 2002
Letzte Grüße
Knaus, München, 2003

Walter Kempowski wurde 1929 in Rostock geboren. Nachdem er, aus der Schule abkommandiert, als Flakhelfer bei der Hitlerjugend eingesetzt wurde und nach dem Krieg eine Lehre als Drucker angefangen hatte, kam er in eine Arbeitskompanie der U.S. Army in Wiesbaden.
Bei einem Besuch in Rostock wurde er 1948 wegen Spionageverdachts verhaftet und zu 25 Jahren Haft in Bautzen verurteilt, jedoch nach acht Jahren amnestiert. In dieser Zeit begann Kempowski zu schreiben: eine tagebuchartige Prosa, in der er die Erfahrungen der Haft aufarbeitete.
1956 in den Westen entlassen, holte Kempowski sein Abitur nach, studierte im Anschluss Pädagogik und arbeitete als Lehrer in Norddeutschland. Sein literarisches Debüt »Im Block. Ein Haftbericht« erschien 1969 und rekapituliert die Zeit von seiner Verhaftung bis zur Entlassung. In Einzelhaft, so Kempowski, könne man »schreien vor dem Nichtstun«. Dennoch ist seine Prosa bar jeder Anklage und aus kühler Distanz als Collage des Erinnerten verfasst. In einer Mischung aus Redensarten und Alltagssprache bilden kurze Erzählblöcke eine Perspektive, die ohne stringente Handlung den Blick vom Kleinen auf das Größere, von der subjektiven Privatzeit auf die objektive Geschichte eröffnet. War ihm das Erinnern in der Einzelhaft in Bautzen Überlebensstrategie, macht er es später, in der literarischen Verarbeitung, zum Prinzip und baut präzise, Stück um Stück, Schicht um Schicht, die verlorene Welt der Vergangenheit wieder auf: »Die einzige Zeit, die es wirklich gibt, ist die Vergangenheit.« Schriftsteller zu sein heißt für Walter Kempowski, Chronist zu sein.
Auf dieser Grundlage entstand ein umfangreiches literarisches Werk: Romane, Kurzgeschichten, Hörspiele und Sachbücher. »Tadellöser & Wolff«, die zweite Veröffentlichung des Autors, verhalf ihm 1971 mit dem Förderpreis des Lessingpreises der Stadt Hamburg zum literarischen Durchbruch. Das Buch ist eine literarische Familienchronik, die die Konfrontation des privaten Erlebens in der Familie mit den politischen Ereignissen im »Dritten Reich« zum Thema hat.
Zwischen 1980 und 1991 war Kempowski Lehrbeauftragter für »Fragen der Literaturproduktion« an der Universität Oldenburg. Dort gründete er das Zeithistorische Archiv, in dem er systematisch Dokumente aus unzähligen privaten und öffentlichen Quellen der jüngeren deutschen Vergangenheit sammelt, vor allem über die Zeit des Zweiten Weltkrieges. Das dabei entstehende kaleidoskopartige Bild jener Zeit verarbeitete Kempowski u. a. in seinem Monumentalwerk »Das Echolot. Ein kollektives Tagebuch« (1993). Als literarische Collage zehntausender Dokumente führt »Das Echolot« die Form der Erinnerungstagebücher konsequent fort. Nach der Beschäftigung mit den Jahren 1943 und 1945 hat sich der Autor nun im dritten Teil, der 2002 erschien, auch dem Jahr des Angriffs auf die Sowjetunion zugewandt: »Das Echolot. Barbarossa '41«.
Neben zahlreichen anderen Auszeichnungen wurde ihm 1994 der Konrad-Adenauer-Preis und 1995 der Uwe Johnson-Preis verliehen. 2003 veröffentlichte er den Roman »Letzte Grüße«. Er ist Mitglied des deutschen P.E.N. und der Freien Akademie der Künste in Hamburg. Walter Kempowski lebt in Nartum bei Bremen.

etgar keret

biography

Etgar Keret is an author and filmmaker who was born in Tel Aviv in 1967. He grew up in an unconventional family: His parents were Holocaust survivors, his sister extremely orthodox, his brother chairman of the Israeli movement to legalize marijuana. Keret began writing stories while serving in the army. He has since published several books of stories and one novel, and his books have been translated into German. Although the books are controversial in Israel, they are international bestsellers. His short films have received awards at international film festivals; he writes a column and a comic for newspapers in Jerusalem and Tel Aviv.

Keret belongs to a young generation of writers, who – unlike the major Israeli authors who were concerned with the existence and destiny of Israel – see, in a society that is increasingly falling apart, the end of all ideologies: »I often think that this country is like a bagel: many people are pushing their way around a centre, but there, where the ideology used to be, now there's only a hole. And we all stare into it spellbound.« The Palestinian conflict and the violence in the occupied territories, the religious tension, the militarism, and the generation problem only interest him to the extent that they play a role in everyday life. »If I want to move a person, I have to write about life. And it is not the case that in daily life the first thought that we have in the morning is that we should leave the occupied territories. It is rather, that somebody stole your car or that your girlfriend left you.«

The stories are told in a quick and forward manner; their tone is concise and laconic; they are not interested in being politically correct and combine poetry and brutality, comic elements and despair, everyday occurrences and the absurd. »Missing Kissinger« (1994) is about the mercilessness of the Ten Commandments, about the sobering insight that angels are just liars with wings; it is also about the use of foreign languages in the Third Reich and about making love. In episodes that are loosely linked together, the novel »Hakajtana schel Kneller« (1998; t: Pizzeria Kamikaze) describes a world which is already familiar to us from Keret's stories with their daily routines of regular work schedules and relationship problems, but with one difference: The figures in the novel are people who have committed suicide, who find one another in an unusually familiar beyond. In 2003 a new book of short stories will be published in German under the title »Mond im Sonderangebot«. Keret lives in Tel Aviv.

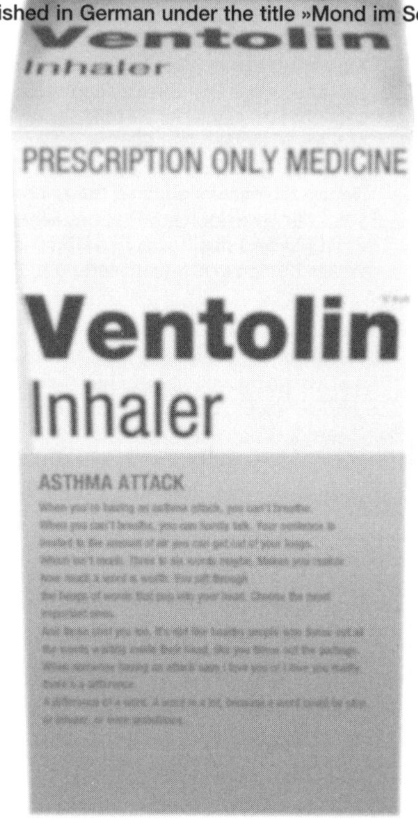

Lo banu lehenot
Keter, Jerusalem, 1996
Anîhû
Zmora-Bitan, Tel Aviv, 2002
Gaza Blues
Luchterhand
München, 2002
[Ü: Barbara Linner]
Pizzeria Kamikaze/ Der Busfahrer, der Gott sein wollte
Luchterhand
München, 2002
[Ü: Barbara Linner]
Mond im Sonderangebot
Luchterhand
München, 2003
[Ü: Barbara Linner]

Der 1967 in Tel Aviv geborene Autor und Filmemacher Etgar Keret wuchs in einer ungewöhnlichen Familie auf: die Eltern Überlebende des Holocaust, die Schwester ultra-orthodox, der Bruder Vorsitzender der israelischen Bewegung zur Legalisierung von Marihuana. Keret begann während des Militärdienstes, Geschichten zu schreiben. Mittlerweile hat er mehrere Erzählbände und einen Roman publiziert, die ins Deutsche übersetzt wurden und in Israel zwar umstritten, aber internationale Bestseller sind. Seine Kurzfilme wurden bei internationalen Filmfestivals ausgezeichnet, er ist Verfasser einer Kolumne und eines Comic für Zeitungen in Jerusalem und Tel Aviv.
Keret gehört einer jungen Generation von Literaten an, die – anders als die großen israelischen Autoren, denen es um die Existenz und Bestimmung Israels ging – in einer zunehmend auseinanderfallenden Gesellschaft das Ende aller Ideologien konstatiert: »Oft denke ich, dieses Land ist wie ein Bagel: Viele Leute drängen sich um ein Zentrum, aber da, wo früher die Ideologie war, ist nur noch ein Loch. Und wir alle starren gebannt hinein.« Der Palästinenserkonflikt und die Gewalt in den besetzten Gebieten, die religiöse Zerrissenheit, der Militarismus und das Generationenproblem interessieren ihn nur insofern, als sie das Alltägliche durchdringen. »Wenn ich einen Menschen bewegen will, muss ich doch vom Leben erzählen. Und der Alltag ist eben nicht so, dass der erste Gedanke morgens ist, dass wir die besetzten Gebiete verlassen sollten. Sondern, dass jemand dein Auto gestohlen oder deine Freundin dich verlassen hat.« Die Geschichten sind schnell und frech erzählt, ihr Ton ist knapp und lakonisch, sie scheren sich nicht um politische Korrektheit und vermischen Poesie und Brutalität, Komik und Verzweiflung, Alltägliches und Absurdes. In »Missing Kissinger« (1994; dt. »Gaza Blues«, 1996) geht es um die Gnadenlosigkeit der Zehn Gebote, um die ernüchternde Erkenntnis, dass Engel nur Lügenbolde mit Flügeln sind, und um den Nutzen von Fremdsprachen im Dritten Reich und beim Liebesakt. Der Roman »Hakajtana schel Kneller« (1998; dt. »Pizzeria Kamikaze«, 2000) schildert in lose miteinander verknüpften Episoden eine Welt, wie wir sie aus Kerets Erzählungen bereits zu kennen meinen mit ihrer Alltagsroutine aus geregelten Arbeitszeiten und Beziehungsproblemen – mit dem Unterschied allerdings, dass es sich bei den Figuren durchweg um Selbstmörder handelt, die sich in einem seltsam vertrauten Jenseits wiederfinden.
2003 erscheint in deutscher Übersetzung ein neuer Band mit Kurzgeschichten unter dem Titel »Mond im Sonderangebot«. Keret lebt in Tel Aviv.

ASTHMA ATTACK

When you're having an asthma attack, you can't breathe.

When you can't breathe, you can hardly talk. Your sentence is limited to the amount of air you can get out of your lungs. Which isn't much. Three to six words maybe. Makes you realize how much a word is worth. You sift through the heaps of words that pop into your head. Choose the most important ones. And those cost you too. It's not like healthy people who throw out all the words waiting inside their head, like you throw out the garbage. When someone having an attack says I LOVE YOU or I LOVE YOU MADLY, there's a difference. A difference of a word. A word is a lot, because a word could be stop, or inhaler, or even ambulance.

navid kermani
biography

Navid Kermani was born in Siegen in 1967, the fourth son of Iranian parents. After studying Drama, Philosophy and Islamic Studies in Cologne, Cairo and Bonn, he taught at the University of Bonn and worked as a literary and artistic director at the Schauspielhaus in Frankfurt and the Mülheimer Theatre an der Ruhr. His dissertation, an extensive analysis of the reception of the Koran, which he completed in 1997, was awarded the Ernst-Bloch-Förderpreis in 2000 and has already been reprinted in several editions.
His book entitled »Iran. Die Revolution der Kinder« (2001) (t: Iran – The Children's Revolution) is the product of reports and essays which he published on the country as a writer for the »Frankfurter Allgemeine Zeitung« from 1995 onwards. Also in 2001, Kermani surefootedly navigated »Ein Leben mit dem Islam« (t: A Life with Islam). It is the life story of the Egyptian scholar Nasr Hamid Abu Zaid, whose modern interpretation of the Koran not only earned him a reputation as a heretic, but also brought about the spectacular forced divorce from his wife. The phenomenon of suicide bombers is the topic of »Dynamit des Geistes. Martyrium, Islam und Nihilismus« (2002) (t: Dynamite of the Spirit – Martyrdom, Islam and Nihilism). »Schöner neuer Orient. Berichte von Städten und Kriegen (2003) (t: Beautiful New Orient – Reports of Cities and Wars) is a collection of six reports on Muslim regions which, due to extremism and violent conflict, have become the subject of international debate. The thoroughly positive reviews were underscored by the Israeli sociologist Natan Sznaider – for him it is »one of the most important books on globalization.«
With the intensity of his virtuosic literary style, which, in making regular reference to his own encounters and experiences, attests to the authenticity of his reports, Kermani has set the standard for the art of reportage and historiography. Kermani, who is a native Iranian and meanwhile a German citizen as well, is considered to be one of Germany's leading scholars on Islam. He is at once an expert on and critic of the Islamic world and one of its most important mediators. In addition he has made a name for himself as an author, essayist and literary critic. His recent book entitled »Buch der von Neil Young Getöteten« (t: The Book of Those Killed by Neil Young) is a homage to the Canadian musician and, at the same time, a narrative about life and death, also written for people who are unfamiliar with Neil Young. »Die Zeit« indentified a possible motive: »In the end this beautiful, intelligent little book is a homage to playing – on the stage of life.« For the past three years Kermani has held the post of Long-Term Fellow at the Berlin Wissenschaftskolleg (Institute for Advanced Study). In summer he returned to Cologne where he lives as a freelance writer with his wife and daughter. His next book will be published at the beginning of next year. It is called »40 Leben« (t: 40 Lives) and pursues the mysticism of everyday life in the form of forty narratives.

Gott ist schön
Beck, München, 1999
Iran
Beck, München, 2001
Nasr Hamid Abu Zaid: Ein Leben mit dem Islam
Herder, Freiburg i. Br., 2001
[Ü: Cherifa Magdi]
Das Buch der von Neil Young Getöteten
Ammann, Zürich, 2002
Dynamit des Geistes
Wallstein, Göttingen, 2002
Schöner neuer Orient
Beck, München, 2003

Navid Kermani wurde 1967 als vierter Sohn iranischer Eltern in Siegen geboren. Nach dem Studium der Islamwissenschaft, Theaterwissenschaft und Philosopie in Köln, Kairo und Bonn lehrte er an der Universität Bonn und war als Dramaturg am Schauspielhaus Frankfurt sowie am Mülheimer Theater an der Ruhr tätig. Seine Dissertation aus dem Jahr 1997, eine umfangreiche Rezeptionsanalyse des Koran, wurde im Jahr 2000 mit dem Ernst-Bloch-Förderpreis ausgezeichnet und erreichte schon mehrere Auflagen.
Aus Berichten und Reportagen, die er seit 1995 als Autor der »Frankfurter Allgemeinen Zeitung« über das Land veröffentlichte, ging sein Buch »Iran. Die Revolution der Kinder« (2001) hervor. Im selben Jahr führte Kermani behutsam durch »Ein Leben mit dem Islam«. Es ist die Lebensgeschichte des ägyptischen Gelehrten Nasr Hamid Abu Zaid, dem die moderne Auslegung des Koran nicht nur den Ruf eines Ketzers einbrachte, sondern auch die spektakuläre Zwangsscheidung von seiner Frau. Das Phänomen der Selbstmordattentäter ist Thema von »Dynamit des Geistes. Martyrium, Islam und Nihilismus« (2002). »Schöner neuer Orient. Berichte von Städten und Kriegen« (2003) versammelt sechs Reportagen über muslimische Regionen, die durch Extremismus und gewaltsame Konflikte in den Fokus der Weltöffentlichkeit geraten sind. Der israelische Soziologe Natan Sznaider unterstrich die durchgehend positiven Rezensionen – für ihn handelt es sich um »eines der wichtigsten Bücher über Globalisierung«.
Mit seinem virtuos verdichtenden literarischen Stil, der immer wieder in Exkursen von Begegnungen und Selbst-Erlebtem die Authentizität seiner Berichte herausstellt, hat Kermani für die Kunst der Reportage – sowie der Historiografie – Maßstäbe gesetzt. Kermani, iranischer und inzwischen auch deutscher Staatsbürger, gilt als einer der führenden Islamwissenschaftler Deutschlands. Als Kenner und Kritiker der islamischen Welt ist er zugleich einer ihrer wichtigsten Vermittler. Er ist zudem als Schriftsteller, Essayist und Literaturkritiker hervorgetreten. Zuletzt erschien sein »Buch der von Neil Young Getöteten« – eine Hommage auf den kanadischen Musiker und zugleich eine Erzählung über Leben und Tod im Allgemeinen. »Am Ende ist dieses schöne, kluge Büchlein ein großes Lob des Spielens – auf der Bühne und im Leben«, so die »Zeit«. In den vergangenen drei Jahren war Kermani Long Term Fellow am Berliner Wissenschaftskolleg. Im Sommer ist er nach Köln zurückgekehrt, wo er mit Frau und Tochter als freier Autor lebt. Anfang nächsten Jahres erscheint sein Buch »40 Leben«, das in Form von 40 Erzählungen der Mystik des Alltags nachgeht.

imre kertész

biography

Imre Kertész was born in Budapest, Hungary, in 1929. His parents were Jewish. At the age of 15, he was deported to Auschwitz and in 1945 freed from the Buchenwald concentration camp. After the war ended, Kertész worked in Communist Hungary as a journalist for the daily newspaper »Vilagosság« but lost his job when the paper took up the party's position. To earn a living, he wrote musicals and entertainment pieces. Starting in 1976 he also worked as a translator. He has translated Nietzsche, Freud, Wittgenstein, Hofmannsthal, Canetti, Josef Roth, Schnitzler and Tankred Dorst into Hungarian. Between 1960 and 1973 he wrote the Holocaust novel »Sorstalanság«, which was published in Hungary in 1975, but which first came to the public's attention in 1985. A new translation of the work was published in 1996 and helped Kertész, who in the meantime had also published numerous essays, stories and novels – like »A nyomkeresö« (1977), »Az angol lobogó« (1991; t: The English Flag) and the »Gályanapló« (1992; t: Galley Diary) – make his international breakthrough.

Kertész's writing focuses on his concentration camp experiences. In the highly autobiographical novel »Sorstalanság« (»Fateless«, 1992) Kertész describes in a deeply sensitive way and with rational distance, the suffering of a 15-year-old boy who is deported to a concentration camp and after his release has to face the people of Budapest and their lack of understanding. Together with the books »A kudarc« (1988; t: Fiasco) and »Kaddis a meg nem született gyermekért« (1990; »Kaddish for a Child Not Born«, 1992), this novel forms a »Trilogy of Fatelessness«. In »A kudarc«, Kertész tells the difficult story of how his first novel came into being and what a writer's life was like under the conditions of a Communist dictatorship. The novel »Kaddish for a Child Not Born« is about the lasting consequences of the Shoah. The monologue of a writer and Holocaust survivor, who after Auschwitz does not want to bring forth any new life, is presented in the form of a prayer of mourning.

In addition to various prizes, Kertész received a scholarship from the Institute for Advanced Study Berlin (Wissenschaftskolleg zu Berlin) for 2002, where he worked on his new novel »Felszámolás« (t: Liquidation), which is situated in Hungary at the time of the political change, and with which, as he himself says, he takes a last look at the Holocaust. In December 2002 Kertész received the Nobel Prize for Literature. The jury thereby acknowledged his work, »which is about the fragile experience of the individual in the face of the barbarisms of history.« Today he lives in Budapest and Berlin.

Kaddisch für ein nicht geborenes Kind
Rowohlt, Berlin, 1992
[Ü: György Buda
Kristin Schwamm]

Roman eines Schicksallosen
Rowohlt, Berlin, 1996
[Ü: Christina Viragh]

Ich - ein anderer
Rowohlt, Reinbek, 1999
[Ü: Ilma Rakusa]

Galeerentagebuch
Rowohlt, Reinbek, 1999
[Ü: Kristin Schwamm]

Fiasko
Rowohlt, Reinbek, 2001
[Ü: György Buda
Agnes Relle]

Die exilierte Sprache
Suhrkamp
Frankfurt a. M., 2003
[Ü: Kristin Schwamm]

Liquidation
Suhrkamp
Frankfurt a. M., 2003
[Ü: Christina Viragh]

Imre Kertész wurde 1929 in Budapest, Ungarn, als Sohn jüdischer Eltern geboren. Mit fünfzehn Jahren wurde er nach Auschwitz deportiert, 1945 aus dem KZ Buchenwald befreit. Nach Kriegsende war Kertész im kommunistischen Ungarn als Journalist bei der Tageszeitung »Vilagosság« tätig, verlor dann aber seine Stelle, als die Zeitung parteitreu wurde. Um sich seinen Lebensunterhalt zu sichern, schrieb er Musicals und Unterhaltungsstücke. Ab 1976 arbeitete er auch als Übersetzer. Er übertrug u. a. Nietzsche, Freud, Wittgenstein, Hofmannsthal, Canetti, Josef Roth, Schnitzler und Tankred Dorst ins Ungarische. Zwischen 1960 und 1973 verfasste er den Holocaust-Roman »Sorstalanság« (Ü: Schicksallosigkeit), der 1975 in Ungarn veröffentlicht wurde, dort aber erst 1985 Beachtung fand. Die 1996 publizierte Neuübersetzung (dt. »Roman eines Schicksallosen«) verhalf Kertész zum internationalen Durchbruch, der bis dahin in Ungarn, aber auch in Deutschland zahlreiche Essays, Erzählungen und Romane veröffentlicht hatte – so etwa »A nyomkeresö« (1977; dt. »Der Spurensucher«, 2002), »Az angol lobogó« (1991; dt. »Die englische Flagge«, 1999) oder das »Gályanapló« (1992; dt. »Galeerentagebuch«, 1993).
Kertész' Schreiben kreist um die Erfahrung des Todeslagers. Im autobiographisch geprägten »Roman eines Schicksallosen« schildert Kertész mit höchster Sensibilität und rationaler Distanz den Leidensweg eines fünfzehnjährigen Jungen, der ins KZ deportiert und nach seiner Befreiung mit dem Unverständnis der Menschen in Budapest konfrontiert wird. Dieser Roman bildet zusammen mit den Bänden »A kudarc« (1988; dt. »Fiasko«, 1999) und »Kaddis a meg nem született gyermekért« (1990; dt. »Kaddisch für ein nicht geborenes Kind«, 1992) eine »Trilogie der Schicksallosigkeit«. In »Fiasko« zeichnet Kertész die schwierige Entstehungsgeschichte des Romanerstlings und die Existenz eines Schriftstellers unter den Bedingungen der kommunistischen Diktatur nach. Im Roman »Kaddisch für ein nicht geborenes Kind« geht es um die bleibenden Folgen der Shoa. In Form eines Trauergebets gibt das Buch den Monolog eines Schriftstellers und Holocaust-Überlebenden wieder, der nach Auschwitz kein neues Leben mehr zeugen will. Neben diversen Auszeichnungen erhielt Kertész 2002 ein Stipendium am Wissenschaftskolleg in Berlin, wo er an seinem neuen Roman »Felszámolás« (dt. »Liquidation«, 2003) arbeitete, der im Ungarn zur Zeit der politischen Wende angesiedelt ist und mit dem er, wie er selbst sagt, einen letzten Blick auf den Holocaust werfe. Im Dezember 2002 wurde Kertész mit dem Nobelpreis für Literatur ausgezeichnet. Die Jury würdigte damit sein Werk, »das die zerbrechliche Erfahrung des Einzelnen gegenüber der barbarischen Geschichte behauptet«. Heute lebt er in Budapest und Berlin.

ko un

biography

Ko Un (real name Ko Un-t'ae) was born in Kunsan in what today is South Korea in 1933. His life is characterised by extreme biographical ruptures, which are closely connected to the history of his native country and which also surface in his work. During the Korean War he had to do compulsory labour service and attempted suicide for the first time. Influenced by these experiences, in 1952 he joined an order of Buddhist monks and started to write his first poems. After departure from the monastery and a period of artistic creativity, he became the director of a school from 1963 to 1967 and during this period began to write again. The verse he wrote at this time, for example, the collection of poems »Pian Gamsung« (1967, t: Beyond Feelings), is characterised by a sense of the transiance and insignificance of all life. After moving to Seoul in 1967, Ko Un was tortured by feelings of self-doubt and started to drink. In 1970 he again attempted suicide. The year 1973 saw the beginnings of his political involvement and marked the start of a new creative phase. He took an interest in the Korean democratization movement, and in the attempts at reunification with North Korea. In 1974 he was appointed secretary-general of the newly founded »Association for Korean Writers for the Realization of Freedom«, which led to spells in prison and maltreatment. Sentenced to death after the military coup of 1980, he was pardoned a few months later, but put under house arrest. While imprisoned he wrote a cycle of poems; the aim was to write a portrait of all of the people he had ever met in his life (»Maninbo«, started in 1986, t: Ten Thousand Lives). To date 15 books from the cycle have been published. His experience in the death cell leads to a final break from his nihilistic period of creativity. His marriage in 1983 and the birth of his daughter were followed by his most creative period, in which for example the collection »Junwon Sipyun« (t: Idyllic Psalms, 1986) came into being.

Ko Un is considered one of the most important Asian poets of the 20th century. His 100-plus publications, which have been translated into many languages, not only consist of books of poetry but also of novels, dramas, translations, biographies, essays, scholarly works and essays. Of his books of poetry »Die Sterne über dem Land der Väter« (1996; »Choguk-ui Byol,« 1984) and »Ein Tag voller Wind« (2002) are available in German. Since 1982 Ko Un has lived in Ansong, South Korea.

Maninbo
Ch'angjaksa, Seoul, 1986ff.
The Sound of my Waves
Cornell University
Ithaca, New York, 1993
[Ü: Anthony of Taizé
Young-Moo Kim]
Die Sterne über dem Land der Väter
Suhrkamp
Frankfurt a. M., 1996
[Ü: Woon-Jung Chei
Siegfried Schaarschmidt]
Sungan-ui Kott
Munhak Tongne
Seoul, 2001
Ein Tag voller Wind
Pendragon, Bielefeld, 2002
[Ü: Lim Jong-Dae
Jürgen Abel]

Ko Un (eigentlich Ko Un-t'ae) wurde 1933 in Kunsan, im heutigen Südkorea, geboren. Sein Leben ist von extremen biographischen Brüchen geprägt, die eng mit der Geschichte seines Heimatlandes verbunden sind und sich auch in seinem Werk niederschlagen.
Während des Koreakrieges zum Arbeitsdienst gezwungen, unternahm er seinen ersten Suizidversuch. Unter dem Eindruck dieser Erlebnisse trat er 1952 einem buddhistischen Mönchsorden bei und begann, seine ersten Gedichte zu schreiben. Nach seinem Austritt aus dem Kloster und einer künstlerischen Schaffenspause war er von 1963 bis 1967 Leiter einer Schule und begann mit dem Schreiben. Die Lyrik, die in dieser Zeit entstand, zum Beispiel die Gedichtsammlung »Pian Gamsung« (1967, Ü: Jenseits der Gefühle), ist von dem Gefühl der Vergänglichkeit und Sinnlosigkeit allen Lebens geprägt. Nach seinem Umzug nach Seoul 1967 begann Ko Un, von Selbstzweifeln gequält, zu trinken. 1970 unternahm er einen weiteren Selbstmordversuch. Das Jahr 1973 markiert mit dem Beginn des politischen Engagements eine neue Schaffensperiode, als er sich für die Demokratisierungsbewegung Koreas und die Bemühungen um Wiedervereinigung mit Nordkorea zu interessieren beginnt. Auf seine Ernennung zum Generalsekretär des 1974 neugegründeten »Verbands koreanischer Schriftsteller für die Verwirklichung der Freiheit« folgten immer wieder Gefängnisaufenthalte und Misshandlungen. Nach dem Militärputsch 1980 zum Tode verurteilt, wurde er Monate später begnadigt, jedoch mit Hausarrest belegt. Während seiner Haft entwarf er einen Gedichtzyklus, in dem er alle Menschen porträtieren wollte, die ihm in seinem Leben begegnet waren (»Maninbo«, ab 1986ff., Ü: Zehntausend Leben). Bislang sind von dem Zyklus 15 Bände erschienen. Die Erfahrung in der Todeszelle führt zu einer endgültigen Abkehr von seiner nihilistischen Schaffensperiode. Auf die Heirat 1983 und die Geburt der Tochter folgte seine kreativste Schaffensphase, in der z. B. die Sammlung »Junwon Sipyun« (Ü: Idyllische Psalmen, 1986) entstand.
Ko Un gehört zu den bedeutendsten asiatischen Dichtern des zwanzigsten Jahrhunderts. Seine inzwischen weit über 100 Veröffentlichungen, die in viele Sprachen übersetzt wurden, bestehen nicht nur aus Gedichtbänden, sondern auch aus Romanen, Dramen, Übersetzungen, Biographien, Essays, wissenschaftlichen Arbeiten und Aufsätzen. Auf Deutsch liegen von Ko Un die Gedichtbände »Die Sterne über dem Land der Väter« (1996; »Choguk-ui Byol«, 1984) und »Ein Tag voller Wind« (2002) vor. Ko Un lebt seit 1982 in Ansong, Südkorea.

hanif kureishi

biography

Hanif Kureishi was born in the London suburb of Bromley, Great Britain, in 1954. His mother was English, his father a Pakistani immigrant. He grew up belonging to no fixed cultural group, as is also the case for some of the heroes in his stories. Kureishi had already started to write novels as a teenager, but after graduating with a degree in philosophy, his initial success came as a dramatist at the Royal Court Theatre in London and as a script writer.
But it was his Oscar-nominated script for Stephan Frears' film »My Beautiful Laundrette« that brought him international recognition. The film tells the story of a young Pakistani, who, hungry for success, opens a lucrative laundrette with a white partner – a venture that, in Margaret Thatcher's Great Britain, is as unheard of as it is successful, a declaration of war against racial hatred and homophobia.
In Great Britain, Kureishi's first novel »The Buddha of Suburbia« received the renowned Whitbread Award in 1990. It is a satirical description of how the bisexual »Englishman« Karim Amir grows up between yoga and punk in London in the wild 70's. His second novel »The Black Album« again focuses on a young Pakistani who is drawn into the conflict between pop culture and Islamic fundamentalism – a subject that is still topical. Kureishi's stories are above all characterised by his keen eye for those facets of modern life that are enigmatic, yet at times somehow absurd in their banality.
The writer continues to be drawn to the big screen and he has even directed a film – the 1991 »London Kills Me«. »Intimacy«, a film by the French director Patrice Chéreau, is based on a short novel and stories by Kureishi and won the Golden Bear at the Berlin Film Festival in 2001. His most recent film »The Mother« was shown this year as part of the Directors Fortnight at the Film Festival in Cannes. Common to both works is the melancholy tone of former rebels as they increasingly ponder on the difficulties of growing older, an issue that is again explored in his most recent collection of prose. »The Body« (2002) tells the somewhat macabre story of an ageing writer who ends up losing his identity after having his brain transplanted into the body of a young man.
Hanif Kureishi lives in London.

Mein wunderbarer Waschsalon
Droemer Knaur
München, 1991
[Ü: Dinka Mrkowatschki]
Das schwarze Album
Droemer Knaur
München, 1997
[Ü: Bernhard Robben]
Der Buddha aus der Vorstadt
Droemer Knaur
München, 2001
[Ü: Bernhard Robben]
Intimacy
Rowohlt, Reinbek, 2001
[Ü: Leonie von Reppert-Bismarck
Bernhard Robben]
Dunkel wie der Tag
Rowohlt, Reinbek, 2002
[Ü: Bernhard Robben]
Gabriels Gabe
Kindler, Berlin, 2001
[Ü: Hans M. Herzog]
In fremder Haut
Kindler, Berlin, 2003
[Ü: Leonie von Reppert-Bismarck
Thomas Rütten]

Stories are everywhere, and they can be made from the simplest things. Preferably from the simplest things, as father would have said, if they are the right, the precise, the correct things, and if the chosen material is profitable, useful and sufficiently malleable. I say chosen, but if the writer is attentive the stories she needs to shape her urgent concerns will occur unbidden. There are certain ideas, like certain people, that the writer will be drawn to. She only has to wait and look. She cannot expect to know why this idea has been preferred to that until the story has been written, if then.
There is a sense – there has to be a sense – in which most writers do not entirely understand what they are doing. You suspect there might be something you can use. But you don't know what it is. You have to find out by beginning. And what you discover probably will not be what you originally imagined or hoped for. Some surprises can be discomfiting.

Hanif Kureishi wurde 1954 im Londoner Vorort Bromley, Großbritannien, geboren. Als Sohn einer Engländerin und eines pakistanischen Einwanderers ist er in einem kulturellen Zwischenraum aufgewachsen, in dem auch einige Helden seiner Geschichten angesiedelt sind. Kureishi begann schon als Teenager mit dem Schreiben von Romanen, war aber nach Abschluss seines Philosophiestudiums zunächst als Dramatiker am Royal Court Theatre in London und als Drehbuchautor erfolgreich. International bekannt geworden ist Kureishi 1985 durch sein für den Oscar nominiertes Skript für Stephen Frears Film »My Beautiful Laundrette« (dt. »Mein wunderbarer Waschsalon«, 1991). Der Film erzählt die Geschichte eines jungen, erfolgshungrigen Pakistani, der mit seinem weißen Freund einen gut gehenden Waschsalon eröffnet – im Großbritannien Margaret Thatchers eine ebenso unerhörte wie erfolgreiche Kampfansage an Rassenhass und Homophobie.
»The Buddha of Suburbia« (1990; dt. »Der Buddha aus der Vorstadt«, 1992), Kureishis erster Roman, erhielt in Großbritannien 1990 den renommierten Whitbread Award. Er schildert satirisch das Erwachsenwerden des bisexuellen »Englishman« Karim Amir zwischen Yoga und Punk im London der wilden siebziger Jahre. Im Zentrum seines zweiten Romans, »The Black Album« (1995; dt. »Das schwarze Album«, 1995), steht erneut ein junger Pakistani, der in den Konflikt zwischen Popkultur und islamischem Fundamentalismus gerät – ein Thema von anhaltender Aktualität. Dabei ist es vor allem der scharfe Blick für die schillernden, in ihrer Banalität zuweilen absurden Facetten des modernen Lebens, der die Geschichten Kureishis auszeichnet.
Immer wieder zieht es den Schriftsteller, der 1991 bei »London Kills Me« (dt. »London schafft alle«, 1991) selbst schon einmal Regie führte, zur Leinwand. »Intimacy«, ein Film des Franzosen Patrice Chéreau nach einem Kurzroman und Geschichten Kureishis, gewann den Goldenen Bär bei den Berliner Filmfestspielen 2001. Sein letzter Film »The Mother« wurde dieses Jahr im Rahmen der Directors Fortnight bei den Filmfestspielen in Cannes gezeigt. Gemeinsam ist beiden Werken der melancholische Ton des einstigen Rebellen, der zunehmend auch über die Schwierigkeiten des Älterwerdens nachdenkt. Eine Tendenz, die sich auch in seiner neuesten Prosasammlung fortschreibt. »The Body« (2002; dt. »In fremder Haut«, 2003) erzählt die fast schon mörderische Geschichte eines alternden Schriftstellers, der sein Gehirn in den Körper eines Jünglings versetzen lässt und darüber seine Identität verliert. Hanif Kureishi lebt in London.

But this useful ignorance, or tension with the unknown, can be fruitful, if not a little unreliable at times.

lee hochol

biography

Lee Hochol was born in 1932 not far from the port city of Wonsan in what today is North Korea. Shortly after the civil war started in 1950 he was drafted into the People's Army. As a prisoner of war, he met his more western South Korean countrymen for the first time; their life seemed freer and more independent. After his release he decided to remain in South Korea. When the war ended in July of 1953, he still did not return home. Today Lee Hochol lives as a writer in the vicinity of Seoul. Since 1997 he has been a guest professor at Kyongwon University which is also in Seoul. He has received many prizes for his essays, stories, and novels, including the Literature Prize of the Republic of Korea.
His experiences during the war, together with leaving his home and family at a young age, have had a lasting influence on Lee Hochol's creative output. His first work »Talhyang« (1955) is about the experiences he underwent at this time. His stories always focus on the lives of ordinary people; this is the case in the story »Tarajinun Saldul«, which was published in 1962 and received the prestigious Dongin Literature Prize. Since the 60's he has also been popular as an author of satirical works like the novel »Kongbok sahoe« (1968). Despite his literary success, Lee Hochol remained a social outsider for a long time, having made himself unpopular politically as a »leftist« and spokesperson for the ordinary people. He was politically persecuted in the 80's for his involvement in the democratisation movement and at times even arrested.
The highly autobiographical novel »Namnyok saram puknyok saram« is to date the only book by Lee Hochol available in German translation. He describes the despotism as well as the humaneness on both sides of the front through the eyes of an 18-year-old soldier in the People's Army, who during the civil war ends up in prison in South Korea. The author vigorously rejects the interpretation which has been made by some critics that the book is a condemnation of the North Korean system. What really interests Lee Hochol is that the two sister countries come to an understanding. He describes the consequences of the war and the division of Korea in a way that is neutral and free from ideological sharpness. The emphasis is not on the differences between the two states, but on the individual person and the question of how his or her life is influenced by political relations. Hence, at a time of wary reconciliation between North and South Korea, Hochol's work is being appreciated anew.

Menschen aus dem Norden, Menschen aus dem Süden
Pendragon, Bielefeld, 2002
[Ü: Ahn In-Kyoung Heidi Kang]

Lee Hochol, 1932 nahe der Hafenstadt Wonsan im heutigen Nordkorea geboren, wurde kurz nach Ausbruch des Bürgerkrieges 1950 zum Dienst in der Volksarmee eingezogen.
In Kriegsgefangenschaft begegnete er zum ersten Mal westlich geprägten Landsleuten aus dem Süden Koreas, deren Leben ihm freier und selbstbestimmter erschien. Er entschloss sich, nach seiner Freilassung in Südkorea zu bleiben, und kehrte auch nach dem Ende des Krieges im Juli 1953 nicht in seine Heimat zurück. Heute lebt Lee Hochol als Schriftsteller in der Nähe von Seoul. Seit 1997 ist er Gastprofessor an der dortigen Kyongwon Universität. Für seine Essays, Erzählungen und Romane wurde er mit zahlreichen Auszeichnungen geehrt, unter anderem mit dem Literaturpreis der Republik Korea.
Die Erfahrungen während des Krieges und die frühe Trennung von Heimat und Familie haben Lee Hochols künstlerisches Schaffen nachhaltig beeinflusst. In seinem Erstlingswerk »Talhyang« (1955; Ü: Fern der Heimat) verarbeitet er die Erlebnisse aus jener Zeit. Immer wieder steht das Leben einfacher Menschen im Zentrum seiner Geschichten, so etwa in der 1962 erschienenen Erzählung »Tarajinun Saldul« (Ü: Geschlagene Menschen), für die er den renommierten Dongin Literaturpreis erhielt. Aber auch als Autor satirischer Werke, wie dem Roman »Kongbok sahoe« (1968; Ü: Die Welt der Beamten), erlangte er seit den sechziger Jahren Popularität. Trotz des literarischen Erfolges blieb Lee Hochol lange ein gesellschaftlicher Außenseiter, da er sich als »Linker« und Fürsprecher der einfachen Menschen politisch unbeliebt machte. So wurde er in den achtziger Jahren wegen seines Engagements für die Demokratisierungsbewegung politisch verfolgt und zeitweise sogar inhaftiert.
Der autobiographisch geprägte Roman »Namnyok saram puknyok saram« (1996; dt. »Menschen aus dem Norden, Menschen aus dem Süden«, 2002) ist das bisher einzige Werk von Lee Hochol in deutscher Übersetzung. Aus der Perspektive eines 18-jährigen Volksarmisten, der während des Bürgerkriegs in südkoreanische Gefangenschaft gerät, werden Willkür, aber auch Humanität auf beiden Seiten der Front geschildert. Mit Nachdruck wies der Autor die Interpretation einiger Kritiker zurück, das Buch sei eine Verurteilung des nordkoreanischen Systems. Lee Hochol geht es vielmehr um eine Verständigung zwischen den beiden Brudervölkern. Unparteiisch und frei von ideologischer Schärfe beschreibt er die Folgen des Krieges und der Teilung Koreas. Nicht die Gegensätze beider Staaten stehen bei ihm im Vordergrund, sondern der individuelle Mensch und die Frage, wie sein Leben von den politischen Verhältnissen geprägt wird. In Zeiten vorsichtiger Annäherung zwischen Nord- und Südkorea erfährt das Werk Hochols wohl gerade deshalb eine neue Würdigung.

abdelwahab meddeb

biography

»I come from a family of Muslim theologians and academics in Tunis who belong to the theological tradition and I was present, during the fifties, at the unveiling of women in one of the strongholds of Islam, in the name of an ideology of westernisation and modernisation. It was for me a shock when the question of the veil and re-veiling of women in one of the strongholds of freedom and western culture, namely France, Paris, was raised again. I asked myself, what is happening here, where is the actual problem?« Abdelwahab Meddeb crosses frontiers in a way which is not often seen in current literature and he poses questions to which there are no easy answers, as in this interview with the magazine »Lettre International«. Born in Tunis in 1946, Meddeb is now a French national. Tunisia and France are equally close to him. But in his literary as in his academic work he is primarily concerned with the roots and history of Islam, its literature, its culture and the problematic integration of Muslim thought into the processes of modernity. And so, since September 11 his status has been raised as an expert on the kind of cultural exchange which is experienced by many as culture shock and understood by only a few. After studying art history and literature, Meddeb became editor for a short while at a large Parisian publishing company, before supervising, from 1974 to 1988, his own literary series at Editions Sindbad. Two of his novels which came out during those years were also translated into German. In »Talismano« (1979) the first person narrator in Paris imagines a stroll through Tunis, the town of his childhood, and recalls for the reader the diverse sensuousness of an Arabic medina. In »Phantasia« (1986) by contrast, the strolling narrator moves through the cityscape of Paris and links this with the city travels of Walter Benjamin. Since the 90's, Meddeb has dedicated himself increasingly to academic institutions. He has been invited as guest lecturer by universities and research centres in Geneva, Florence, Paris and Yale. He nevertheless spends most of his time as a freelance writer and journalist in Paris.

In his latest book, »La Maladie de l'Islam« (2002), he attempts to portray an exact analysis of the Islamic movement. On the one hand he contrasts the poetic tradition of the freethinkers and medieval mystics with that of a militant tradition of dogmatic thinkers and purist fanatics, and on the other hand he criticises the simplified thinking of the West which sees in Islam a deadly enemy. Meddeb places emphasis on a more detailed knowledge of tradition. Writers such as Ibn Arabi, Dante and Yehuda Halevi are for him models of a more humane world, whose philosophies touch upon one another rather than against one another.

Phantasia
Sindbad, Paris, 1986
Tombeau d'Ibn Arabi
Fata Morgana, Paris, 1987
Talismano
Wunderhorn
Heidelberg, 1993
[Ü: Hans Thill]
Blanches Traverses du passé
Fata Morgana
Montpellier, 1997
Aya
Wunderhorn
Heidelberg, 1998
[Ü: Hans Thill]
La metière des oiseaux
Fata Morgana
Montpellier, 2001
Die Krankheit des Islam
Wunderhorn
Heidelberg, 2002
[Ü: Hans Thill, Beate Thill]

»Ich stamme aus einer traditionellen Familie muslimischer Theologen und Gelehrter in Tunis, die der theologischen Tradition angehört, und ich habe in den fünfziger Jahren in einer der Hochburgen des Islam der Entschleierung der Frauen beigewohnt, im Namen einer Ideologie der Verwestlichung und der Modernität. Es war für mich wie ein Schock, als sich die Frage des Schleiers und der Wiederverschleierung der Frauen in einer der Hochburgen der Freiheit und der westlichen Kultur erneut stellte, nämlich in Frankreich, in Paris. Ich fragte mich, was geht hier vor, wo liegt das wirkliche Problem?« Abdelwahab Meddeb ist ein Grenzgänger, wie sie die aktuelle Literatur nur wenige kennt, und er stellt Fragen, auf die es keine leichten Antworten gibt – wie in diesem Interview mit dem Magazin »Lettre International«. 1946 in Tunis geboren, besitzt er heute die französische Staatsangehörigkeit. Tunesien und Frankreich sind ihm gleichermaßen vertraut. Aber in seinem belletristischen wie auch seinem wissenschaftlichen Werk beschäftigt er sich vorrangig mit den Wurzeln und der Geschichte des Islam, seinen Literaturen, seiner Kultur und der problematischen Integration muslimischen Denkens in den Prozess der Moderne. So ist er nach dem 11. September umso mehr zu einem vielgefragten Experten für den interkulturellen Austausch geworden, der von vielen als Kulturschock empfunden und nur von wenigen verstanden wird. Nach dem Studium der Kunstgeschichte und der Literaturwissenschaft war Meddeb für kurze Zeit Lektor in einem großen Pariser Verlag, bevor er bei den »Editions Sindbad« von 1974 bis 1988 seine eigene belletristische Reihe betreute. Zwei seiner in jenen Jahren entstandenen Romane sind auch ins Deutsche übersetzt worden. In »Talismano« (1979; dt. 1993) imaginiert ein Ich-Erzähler in Paris einen Streifzug durch Tunis, die Stadt seiner Kindheit, und vergegenwärtigt dem Leser die vielfältige Sinnlichkeit einer arabischen Medina. In »Phantasia« (1986; dt. »Aya«, 1998) hingegen bewegt sich der erzählende Flaneur durch die Stadtlandschaft von Paris und knüpft somit an die Stadtbegehungen Walter Benjamins an. Seit Anfang der neunziger Jahre widmet sich Meddeb zunehmend akademischen Belangen; so wurde er von Universitäten und Forschungszentren in Genf, Florenz, Paris und Yale zu Gastdozenturen eingeladen. Die meiste Zeit lebt er jedoch als freier Schriftsteller und Publizist in Paris.

In seinem neuesten Buch »La Maladie de l'Islam« (2002; dt. »Die Krankheit des Islam, 2002) versucht er, eine exakte Analyse der islamischen Bewegung zu geben. Auf der einen Seite kontrastiert er die poetische Tradition der Freidenker und mittelalterlichen Mystiker mit der militanten Tradition der Dogmatiker und fanatischen Puristen, auf der anderen Seite kritisiert er die vereinfachte Sichtweise des Westens, der den Islam als Todfeind betrachtet. Meddeb betont die Notwendigkeit einer genaueren Kenntnis der Tradition. Schriftsteller wie Ibn Arabi, Dante und Yehuda Halevi gelten ihm als Vordenker einer humaneren Welt, deren Philosophien sich ergänzen, anstatt miteinander zu kollidieren.

lajos parti nagy

biography

Lajos Parti Nagy was born in Szekszárd, Hungary in 1953. His father was an officer, so he grew up in various Hungarian cities. Although Parti Nagy studied Literature and History at the Pedagogical College in Pécs, he has never taught. In the 70's and 80's he lived in Pécs, where he worked as a librarian and from 1979 to 1986 as an editor for the literary magazine »Jelenkor«. Since 1986 he has lived in Budapest, where he works as a freelance writer and literary translator. He has translated works by Werner Schwab and Thomas Bernhard into Hungarian. In the early 90's he wrote articles for the literary magazine »Magyar Napló«. Until this time, his written output was solely poetic; he now also writes stories, novels, radio plays and dramas. In 1993 theatre critics awarded his first theatre piece »Ibusár« the title »Best Hungarian Drama«. Like »Mauzóleum« (1994) and his drama translations and adaptations, this piece is also frequently performed at Hungarian and international theatres.

Characteristic of Parti Nagy's writing is his obsessive way of dealing with colloquial Hungarian. Repetitions that initially »occur« unconsciously, work in the course of the text to make the material more clear. For Parti Nagy the colloquial language is a living reservoir and, rather than an impoverishment of the Hungarian language, he sees a »baroque turmoil« at work. In 1999 »Europink« a book of poetry written in four languages (including German) appeared. From 2001 to 2002 he lived in Berlin as a DAAD scholarship holder. His first German book publication is planned for next year. The allegorical story involving animals »Hősöm tere« (2000; t: My Hero's Square), written in the style of a satire by Swift, is told by a narrator and a consciousness independent of his person, which appears as the narrator's »hero«. This consciousness is imprisoned by his new neighbors, a »party of pigeons« formed for the sake of taking over power in the city. Parti Nagy has written a satirical finale on dictatorships of all colours.

Angyalstop
Magvető Könyvkiadó
Budapest, 1982
Csuklógyakorlat
Magvető Könyvkiadó
Budapest, 1986
Szódalovaglás
Jelenkor Kiadó, Pécs, 1990
Esti kréta
Jelenkor Kiadó, Pécs, 1995
Ibusár; Mauzóleum
Jelenkor, Pécs, 1996
Europink
Jelenkor; Lettre, Pécs, 1999
[Ü: Edit Baranyai
Kinga Dornacher]
Hősöm tere
Magvető Könyvkiadó
Budapest, 2001

Lajos Parti Nagy wurde 1953 in Szekszárd, Ungarn, geboren. Da sein Vater Berufsoffizier war, verbrachte er seine Kindheit in verschiedenen Städten Ungarns. Parti Nagy studierte zwar Literatur und Geschichte an der Pädagogischen Hochschule in Pécs, übte seinen Beruf jedoch nicht aus. In den siebziger und achtziger Jahren lebte er in Pécs, wo er als Bibliothekar und von 1979 bis 1986 als Redakteur der Literaturzeitschrift »Jelenkor« tätig war. Seit 1986 lebt er als freischaffender Schriftsteller und Übersetzer literarischer Werke in Budapest. Er übertrug u. a. Stücke von Werner Schwab und Thomas Bernhard ins Ungarische. Anfang der neunziger Jahre schrieb er Feuilletons für die Literaturzeitschrift »Magyar Napló«. Bis zu dieser Zeit verfasste er auf literarischem Gebiet ausschließlich Gedichte; seitdem schreibt er auch Erzählungen, Romane, Hörspiele und Dramen. 1993 wurde sein erstes Theaterstück »Ibusár« (dt. »Bahnstation Ibuschar«, 2003) von Theaterkritikern als bestes ungarisches Drama ausgezeichnet. Dieses Stück wird, genau wie »Mauzóleum« (1994) und seine Dramenübersetzungen und -bearbeitungen, oft an ungarischen und internationalen Theatern gespielt.
Kennzeichnend ist Parti Nagys obsessiver Umgang mit der ungarischen Alltagssprache. Immerwiederkehrende Wiederholungen, die zunächst unbewusst »passieren«, dienen im weiteren Fortgang des Textes der größtmöglichen Präzisierung. Die Umgangssprache ist ihm lebendiges Reservoir und anstatt einer Verarmung sieht er im Ungarischen eine »barocke Gärung« am Werk. 1999 erschien ein viersprachiger Gedichtband (u. a. auch auf Deutsch) unter dem Titel »Europink«. Von 2001 bis 2002 lebte er als Stipendiat des DAAD in Berlin. Im nächsten Jahr ist seine erste deutsche Buchveröffentlichung geplant. Der allegorische Tierroman »Hősöm tere« (2000; Ü: Heldenplatz), in der Tradition der Swiftschen Satiren verfasst, wird von einem Erzähler und einem von ihm abgespaltenen, unabhängigen Bewusstsein erzählt, das als »Held« des Erzählers auftritt. Es wird Gefangener seiner neuen Nachbarn, einer »Partei der Tauben«, die die Macht in der Stadt übernommen hat. Parti Nagy gelang mit diesem Buch ein satirischer Abgesang auf Diktaturen aller Couleur.

What makes the poet tick?
Ich weiß es nicht.
Ich sage es, und das ist es.
Vielleicht die Sprache.
Vielleicht das Spiel.
Vielleicht der Drang
zu wissen:
what makes the poet tick?

oskar pastior

biography

Oskar Pastior was born in Sibiu in the Transylvanian region of Romania in 1927. A member of the minority ethnic German community, he spent five years in a Soviet forced-labour camp after the end of the Second World War before being allowed to return home. From 1955 he studied German Language and Literature at the University of Bucharest, during which time he published his first poems. After graduating, he worked for the German language service of Romanian national radio. His first collection of poems, »Offne Worte«, was published in 1964. Despite winning literary awards in Romania, he felt confined by the »prefabricated and ideological language with its prescribed historical rules.« It was while studying in Vienna in 1968 that he emigrated to the West. He has since lived as a freelance writer and translator in Berlin. »Vom Sichersten ins Tausendste« (1969) was the first of many poetry books to be published in Germany.

In the poetically resonant parallel world of Pastior's writing, familiar language becomes alien and meaning is elevated to another dimension. The appeal of this surreal linguistic reality stems from a playful tendency to bend the rules. »He always perceived misconstruction, connotation, nonsense, wit and diversity as the true and genuine meaning of words,« Christoph Meckel once remarked about the linguistic pioneer. It comes as no surprise that Pastior is a member of OuLiPo (»Ouvroir de Littérature Potentielle«/ »Workshop for Potential Literature«), a group that has been working with revived and original writing techniques since its foundation in 1960.

Oskar Pastior is a master of lyrical forms, ranging from conventional writing in »Gedichtgedichte« (1973) to the creation of »sonetburger« (1983), from rummaging around in »Höricht« (1975) to exploring the potential of the anagram in »Anagrammgedichte« (1985). He played with the palindrome in »Kopfnuß Januskopf« (1990), invented the vocalise (»Vokalisen & Gimpelstifte«, 1992) and founded »Das Hören des Genitivs« (1997). His »o du roher iasmin«, published in 2002, comprised 43 variations on Charles Baudelaire's poem »Harmonie du soir«.

Oskar Pastior has won numerous awards for his works, among them the Aachener Walter-Hasenclever-Preis (2000) and the Wiener Erich-Fried-Preis (2002). The second volume of his collected works, »Jetzt kann man schreiben was man will«, was published in 2003 and comes before the first volume.

Lesungen mit Tinnitus
Hanser, München, 1986
Vokalisen & Gimpelstifte
Hanser, München, 1992
Eine kleine Kunstmaschine
Hanser, München, 1994
Das Unding an sich
Suhrkamp
Frankfurt a. M., 1994
Villanella & Pantum
Hanser, München, 2000
O du roher iasmin
Edition Urs Engeler, Weil am Rhein, 2002
Jetzt kann man schreiben was man will
Hanser, München, 2003

Oskar Pastior wurde 1927 in Hermannstadt (Sibiu)/Siebenbürgen, Rumänien, geboren. Kurz vor Kriegsende wurde er als Angehöriger der deutschen Minderheit in sowjetische Arbeitslager deportiert. Erst nach fünf Jahren Zwangsarbeit konnte er in seine Heimat zurückkehren. Ab 1955 studierte er Deutsche Sprache und Literatur an der Universität Bukarest, nebenher veröffentlichte er seine ersten Gedichte. Nach dem Studium arbeitete er als Redakteur für deutschsprachige Inland-Sendungen beim Rumänischen Rundfunk. 1964 erschien sein erster Gedichtband »Offne Worte«. Obwohl er in Rumänien für seine Dichtung ausgezeichnet wurde, fühlte er sich von der »Fertigbauteil- und Ideologiesprache mit verordneten historischen Gesetzmäßigkeiten« eingeengt. So nutzte er 1968 einen Studienaufenthalt in Wien, um in den Westen überzusiedeln. Seither lebt Oskar Pastior als freier Schriftsteller und Übersetzer in Berlin. »Vom Sichersten ins Tausendste« (1969) war der erste seiner zahlreichen Gedichtbände, die in Deutschland veröffentlicht wurden.

In der lautpoetischen Wunderwelt von Pastiors Lyrik wird die vertraute Sprache fremd und der Sinn changiert in neuen Dimensionen. Der Reiz dieser surrealen Sprachrealität liegt im spielerischen Umgang mit den Regeln. »Falschsinn, Nebensinn, Unsinn, Witz und Vielfalt wörtlicher Bedeutungen sind ihm von jeher wahr und wirklich erschienen«, wie Christoph Meckel einmal über Pastior bemerkte. Es verwundert nicht, dass der Sprachkünstler Pastior der Gruppe OuLiPo (»Ouvroir de Littérature Potentielle«/»Werkstatt für potentielle Literatur«) angehört, die sich seit 1960 mit reanimierten wie mit neu erfundenen Literaturtechniken beschäftigt.

Oskar Pastior ist ein Meister der lyrischen Formen. Mal schrieb er »Gedichtgedichte« (1973), mal kreierte er »sonetburger« (1983). Er stöberte im »Höricht« (1975) und forschte nach den Möglichkeiten des Anagramms (»Anagrammgedichte«, 1985). Er spielte mit dem Palindrom in »Kopfnuß Januskopf« (1990), erfand die Vokalise (»Vokalise & Gimpelstifte«, 1992) und ergründete »Das Hören des Genitivs« (1997). 2002 schuf er mit »o du roher iasmin« 43 Variationen von Charles Baudelaires Gedicht »Harmonie du soir«.

Oskar Pastior wurde für sein Schaffen mit zahlreichen Auszeichnungen gewürdigt, darunter mit dem Aachener Walter-Hasenclever-Preis (2000) und mit dem Wiener Erich-Fried-Preis (2002). Der zweite Band seiner Werkausgabe, »Jetzt kann man schreiben was man will«, erschien 2003.

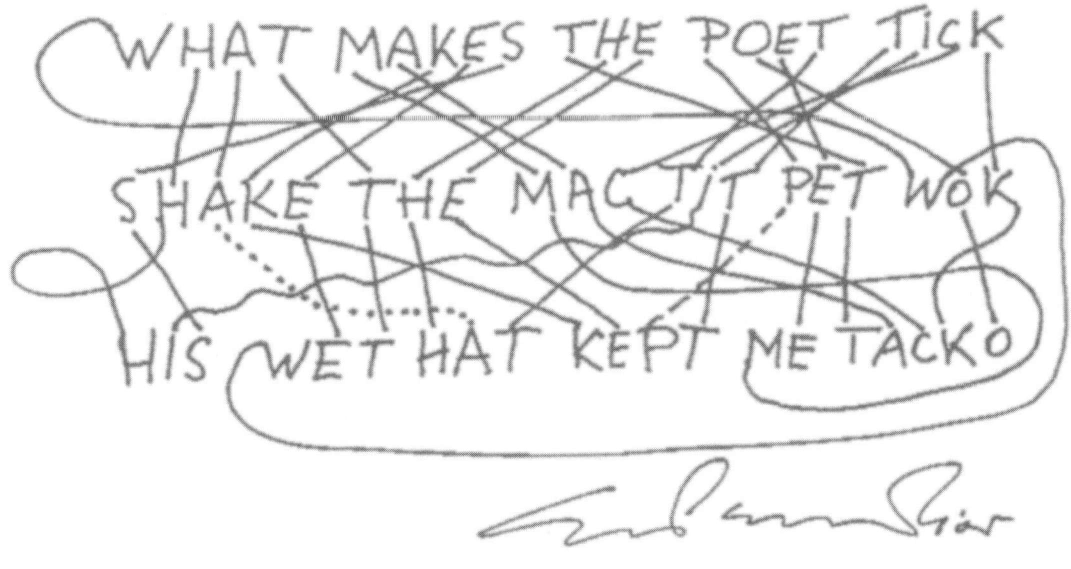

ljudmila petruschewskaja

biography

Ljudmila Petrushevskaya was born in Moscow in 1938. She comes from an intellectual family, which for several generations was subject to reprisals; this only stopped at the beginning of Perestroika. Petrushevskaya studied Journalism at Lomonossov University. From 1957 to 1973 she worked as a radio and television journalist. From 1974 to 1982, when she was not allowed to publish her works, she worked for the literary magazine »Nowyi Mir«.

She started writing her first prose pieces in 1963. Ruthlessly, and with documentary precision, her stories record the dark side of Soviet and post-Soviet reality. They are about fathers who have disappeared, alcoholic mothers, neglected children, the forgotten aged. They describe the daily fight to survive and the claustrophobic existence in cramped appartments. Petrushevskaya's prose is at times sober and laconic, but then becomes hectic, full of breaks, oblique metaphors, and repetitions. Closer explanations are provided afterwards or placed in brackets. As in Chekhov, with whom Petrushevskaya is frequently compared, in the characters' dialogues with their many layers of meaning, the tragic only bursts forth in brief allusions only to be immediately papered over by empty words and everyday chatter. Since the 70's Petrushevskaya has written more than 30 dramas. The one-act piece »Cinzano« (1973) is one of her best-known pieces. In the 90's she also wrote fairytales, which were published in Germany in the books »Der Mann, der wie eine Rose roch« (1993) and »Die neuen Abenteuer der schönen Helena« (1998). In her new narrative prose she is interested in the fantastic. In the book of stories »Der schwarze Mantel« (1999), she tells how in the country cottage of her deceased aunt a girl meets the ghost of the Russian poet Alexander Blok, and how a woman, whose son pretended to have committed suicide because he wanted to get hold of her savings, asks a dying alcoholic who looks like Christ for advice, so as to comfort herself in the end with the knowledge that her own suffering is relative.

Petrushevskaya's poems were never adorned with the heroic image of the worker and farmer as prescribed by the state and were for the most part censored. The stories and dramas were not published until the arrival of Perestroika. Today she is considered one of Russia's most important writers. She has received various prizes. In 1995 a five-volume set of her work was published in Russia. Petrushevskaya lives in Moscow.

Kommen Sie in die Küche
Henschel, Berlin, 1982
[Ü: Renate Landa]
Meine Zeit ist die Nacht
Rowohlt, Berlin, 1991
[Ü: Antje Leetz]
Der Mann, der wie eine Rose roch
Fischer
Frankfurt a. M., 1993
[Ü: Antje Leetz]
Der schwarze Mantel
Berlin Verlag, Berlin, 1999
[Ü: Antje Leetz]
Die neuen Abenteuer der schönen Helena
Piper, München, 2000
[Ü: Antje Leetz]

30/07/2003 12:13 +490337466991 SCHLOSS WIEPERSDORF S. 01

Побуждение может быть самое разное:
чьи-то слова, текст, музыка, вкус (знамени-
тые „эпифании" Марселя Пруста, вкус
пирожного „мадлен"); знакомое, но чужое
лицо, картина, кусок фильма, спектакль.
Приходилось писать прямо в зале или ухо-
дить, чтобы записать пришедший текст,
который как будто кто-то диктовал. Или
это случалось на улице, или в метро в толпе
Или в деревне на рассвете, когда мимо
окна гнали стадо и всходило солнце, как
желток в сыром белке. Текст приходил сразу
весь, надо было только потянуть за нитку,
чтобы клубок размотался. Потом я переста-

Ljudmila Petruschewskaja wurde 1938 in Moskau geboren. Sie entstammt einer Intellektuellenfamilie, die über mehrere Generationen, bis zum Beginn der Perestroika, Repressalien ausgesetzt war. Petruschewskaja absolvierte an der Lomonossow-Universität ein Journalistikstudium und arbeitete anschließend von 1957 bis 1973 als Rundfunk- und Fernsehjournalistin. In den Jahren 1974 bis 1982, als sie ihre Werke nicht veröffentlichen konnte, arbeitete sie bei der Literaturzeitschrift »Nowyi Mir«.

Ab 1963 schrieb sie ihre ersten Prosastücke. Ihre Erzählungen protokollieren schonungslos und mit dokumentarischer Genauigkeit die Schattenseiten sowjetischer und postsowjetischer Realität. Sie erzählen von verschwundenen Vätern und alkoholsüchtigen Müttern, von verwahrlosten Kindern und den vergessenen Alten. Sie beschreiben den Kampf ums Überleben im alltäglichen Organisieren und die klaustrophobische Enge in zu kleinen Wohnungen. Petruschewskajas Prosa ist zuweilen nüchtern und lakonisch, dann wieder gehetzt, voller Brüche, schiefer Metaphern und Wiederholungen. Nähere Erläuterungen werden nachgeschoben oder in Klammern gesetzt. Wie bei Tschechow, mit dem Petruschewskaja oft verglichen wird, blitzt in der mehrschichtigen Rede der Figuren das Tragische nur in kurzen Anspielungen auf, um sogleich wieder von leeren Worthülsen und Alltagsgeschwätz überdeckt zu werden. Seit den siebziger Jahren hat Petruschewskaja über 30 Dramen verfasst. Zu den bekanntesten Stücken gehört der Einakter »Cinzano« (1973, dt. 1989). Daneben entstanden in den neunziger Jahren auch Märchen, die in Deutschland in den Bänden »Der Mann, der wie eine Rose roch« (1993) und »Die neuen Abenteuer der schönen Helena« (1998) veröffentlicht wurden. Ihre neuere Erzählprosa weist einen Zug ins Phantastische auf.

In dem Erzählband »Der schwarze Mantel« (1999) trifft ein Mädchen den Geist des russischen Dichters Alexander Blok in der Datscha ihrer verstorbenen Tante, und eine Frau, deren Sohn Selbstmord vorgetäuscht hat, um an ihre Ersparnisse zu gelangen, befragt einen alkoholkranken Sterbenden, der christusähnliche Züge aufweist, um sich am Ende mit der Relativität ihres eigenen Elends zu trösten.

Petruschewskajas Geschichten deckten sich nicht mit dem von der Partei vorgegebenen heroischen Bild des Arbeiter- und Bauernstaates und unterlagen zum großen Teil der Zensur. Erst im Zuge der Perestroika konnten die Erzählungen und Dramen veröffentlicht werden. Heute zählt sie zu den bekanntesten Autorinnen Russlands. Sie wurde mit verschiedenen Preisen ausgezeichnet. 1995 erschien in Russland eine fünfbändige Werkausgabe. Petruschewskaja lebt in Moskau.

я записывать эти пришедшие тексты, так
как это уже шло легко, конвейером. Япон-
ские акварелисты, когда им становилось
легко рисовать, тут же меняли имя, мане
ру и даже руку – правую на левую. Я тоже
сменила „руку" – от прозы перешла к драме
как только стало легко, перешла к поэзии,
к сказке, потом вернулась к прозе. Сейчас
мое вдохновение – это ваш вопрос о вдохнове-
нии, я уже написала 11 страниц – посыла
ю вам кусочек...
Привет! Ваша Л. Петрушевска

carlos ruiz zafón

biography

Carlos Ruiz Zafón was born in Barcelona, Spain, in 1964. The close proximity of his parents' house to Gaudí's Sagrada Familia cathedral and the years he spent at the Gothic Jesuit school of Sarría made a lasting impression on the child's imagination. Even as a 10 year-old, he wrote Gothic tales which kept his schoolmates up all night – a talent which would later help him to achieve great success. After his student days, he worked in advertising for a few years, which he finally gave up so that he could thoroughly devote himself to literature.

In 1993 Ruiz Zafón received the Edebè Prize for his first novel »El príncipe de la niebla«. Against the historical background of the time after the Spanish Civil War, the author develops a novel which borrows from fantastic literature. Sunken ships, a mysterious sculpture garden, and a lighthouse keeper who refuses to tell what he knows are only some of the challenges that the young protagonist has to face together with his sister before the novel ends in a final confrontation with evil.

Ruiz Zafón's most recent novel »La sombra del viento« also takes place in the post-war years of the Franco regime. But this time the setting is the author's hometown, described in sombre, spine-chilling images. As a child, Daniel Sempere's father gives him the only existing copy of a mysterious book. Fascinated by the book's narrative world, the young reader spends years searching for the author Julián Carax. The more he inquires, the clearer it becomes that he is not the only one looking for the author. An agent from Franco's secret police and a mysterious man with a black leather mask also appear to take an active interest in the writer's whereabouts. The novel and the biography of its author mingle more and more with Daniel's life until it becomes clear that the person he is looking for is closer than he thought. The novel quickly became a bestseller in Spain and won best novel of the year in 2002. It has already been translated into 12 languages.

Carlos Ruiz Zafón has lived in Los Angeles since 1994. In addition to novels and screenplays, he writes for »El País« and »La Vanguardia«.

El palacio de la medianoche
Edebé, Barcelona, 1994
Las luces de septiembre
Edebé, Barcelona, 1995
Der Fürst des Nebels
dtv junior, München, 1996
[Ü: Ulrike Schuldes]
Marina
Edebé, Barcelona, 2003
Der Schatten des Windes
Insel, Frankfurt a. M. 2003
[Ü: Peter Schwaar]

Carlos Ruiz Zafón wurde 1964 in Barcelona, Spanien, geboren. Die unmittelbare Nähe seines Elternhauses zu Gaudís Sagrada Familia und die Jahre in der gotischen Jesuitenschule von Sarría hinterließen nachhaltige Spuren in der Phantasie des Kindes. Schon als Zehnjähriger schrieb er Schauergeschichten, mit denen er seine Klassenkameraden um den Schlaf brachte – ein Talent, dass ihm in späteren Jahren zu großem Erfolg verhelfen sollte. Nach der Schulzeit arbeitete er einige Jahre in der Werbebranche, der er jedoch schließlich den Rücken kehrte, um sich ganz der Literatur zu widmen.

Für seinen ersten Roman »El príncipe de la niebla« (dt. »Der Fürst des Nebels«, 1996) wurde Ruiz Zafón 1993 mit dem Edebè-Preis ausgezeichnet. Vor dem historischen Hintergrund der Zeit nach dem Spanischen Bürgerkrieg entwickelt der Autor einen Jugendroman, der immer wieder Anleihen bei der phantastischen Literatur nimmt. Versunkene Schiffe, ein mysteriöser Skulpturengarten und das Schweigen eines Leuchtturmwärters sind nur einige der Herausforderungen, denen sich der junge Protagonist gemeinsam mit seiner Schwester stellen muss, bevor es zur endgültigen Konfrontation mit dem Bösen kommt.

Ruiz Zafóns letzer Roman »La sombra del viento« (2001; dt. »Der Schatten des Windes«, 2003) spielt ebenfalls in den vom Franco-Regime bestimmten Nachkriegsjahren. Schauplatz ist diesmal jedoch die in düster-schaurigen Bildern beschriebene Heimatstadt des Autors. Erzählt wird die Geschichte von Daniel Sempere, der als Kind von seinem Vater das einzig noch existierende Exemplar eines geheimnisvollen Romans erhält. Fasziniert von der erzählerischen Welt begibt sich der Junge auf eine Jahre andauernde Suche nach dem Autor Julián Carax. Je mehr Nachforschungen er anstellt, desto deutlicher wird, dass er in seiner Suche nicht allein ist. Ein Agent aus Francos Geheimpolizei und ein mysteriöser Mann mit einer schwarzen Ledermaske scheinen sich ebenfalls lebhaft für den Verbleib des Schriftstellers zu interessieren. Mehr und mehr beginnen der Roman und die Biographie seines Verfassers sich mit Daniels Leben zu vermischen, bis schließlich klar wird, dass ihm der Gesuchte näher ist als gedacht. Der Roman wurde in Spanien schnell zu einem Bestseller und als bester Roman des Jahres 2002 ausgezeichnet. Er wurde bereits in zwölf Sprachen übersetzt. Carlos Ruiz Zafón lebt seit 1994 in Los Angeles und schreibt neben seinen Romanen und Drehbüchern als Autor für »El País« und »La Vanguardia«.

boualem sansal

biography

Boualem Sansal was born in Algeria in 1949 and started his career as a writer at the age of 50. Until that point the economist and engineer, who holds a doctoral degree, had focused on his work as a high-ranking official in the Algerian ministry of industry. But the assassination of President Boudiaf (1992), the death of a friend, and the ordeal of persecution in a homeland burdened with civil war inspired him to write about his country and in so doing enter into a state of inner exile. The outcome was that his debut novel »Le serment des barbares« was published in France, where it was praised by the press and received the Prix du Premier Roman. »Le Nouvel Observateur« celebrated the book as a »masterpiece«. The novel, now a film based on a screenplay by Jorge Sempruns, opens like a detective story: In the little Algerian city of Rouiba, two men of very different social standing – the wealthy and inviolable godfather of the region, Moh and the impoverished Bakour – are found murdered on the same day. When it becomes clear to the inspector in the Bakour case that the murders are related and that their background is politically charged, the story quickly turns into an examination of the state of affairs in the North African country. The inspector's investigations become a search for the roots of terrorist violence in present-day Algeria, amidst corruption, oppression and Islam.
In his novels Sansal draws the attention of Algerians, who have only existed as a nation since the independence of 1962, to potential paths for finding their own identity. Indeed, this would seem to be the idea encapsulated in the title of the novel »L'enfant fou de l'arbre creux« (t: The Mad Child from the Hollow Tree), which was published in 2000 and won the Michel Dard Literature Prize the following year. Sansal explains how the child, tied up in the courtyard of a prison, stands for the Algerian people in »this giant prison of Algeria. A childish people, blinded, held captive by lies. These people have reached a point where they neither know who they are, where they come from, nor what they want.«
In France, the former colonial power, Sansal is celebrated as a linguistic innovator because of his playful use of the French language. In Algeria on the other hand, due to the politically explosive topics of his satirical but at the same time poetic novels, he is perceived as a detriment to his country. Nevertheless he continues to reside with his wife and two adult daughters in his homeland and refuses to shield his identity by publishing under a pseudonym. The cheerfulness of Sansal's novels speaks for his faith in Algeria's future. His most recent work »Dis-moi le paradis« (2003; t: Tell Me about Paradise) represents a rough draft for such a future.

Das verrückte Kind aus dem hohlen Baum
Merlin, Gifkendorf, 2002
[Ü: Riek Walther]
Der Schwur der Barbaren
Merlin, Gifkendorf, 2003
[Ü: Regina Keil-Sagawe]
Dis-moi le paradis
Gallimard, Paris, 2003

Toutes les questions n'ont pas de réponses et c'est bien ainsi, la vie est avant tout un mystère qu'il fau préserver. Les réponses définitives, telles des verdicts sans appel, tarissent l'imagination, dessèchent l'intelligence. Mais alors pourquoi, précisément, revenant sans cesse sur cette ligne de front qui marque les limites du connu, sommes-nous toujours à vouloir tâtonner dans le vide, à sonder l'insondable, scruter l'invisible, entendre l'inaudible, dire l'indicible. Les réponses ne viennent jamais, au bout de nos mains le vide et le silence son des remparts inébranlables.
Nous serions comme ces d'alchimistes d'antan, vieux fous ou dangereux grigous, qui, pris par leur fièvre de Richesse et de Sapience, vont chercher dans ce que la nature a produit de plus vil, la pierre primitive, la pierre noire, informe et sans vie, la Pierre philosophale, la vérité de toutes les vérités. Sans doute. Ont-ils trouvé ? On ne le sait pas, sûrement que non, puisque nous, leurs lointains héritiers, sommes pauvres comme Job du côté de la vérité. De leur histoire, écrite en entier dans la marginalité et la démesure, nous restent des discours hermétiques, des axiomes sans effet, des catastrophes retentissantes, des rêves indéchiffrables.
Et d'ailleurs, qu'est-ce que la poésie ? Est-ce cet élan du cœur qui nous pousse à combler le vide qui nous enserre dans son effroi ou cet acte de raison qui nous conduit à édifier des théories apaisantes ? Nous ne finirons jamais de chercher qui de l'un ou de l'autre nous porte vers le rêve.

A côté des grands mystères, icebergs détachés de la banquise, vagabondent une infinité de mystères aux apparences faussement nonchalantes. Leur corps est immergé, on n'en voit que le bonnet, aussi les perçoit-on d'un œil tranquille. Le langage est de ceux-là mais il est le plus trompeur ; disponible à souhait, il se plie à tous les désirs, donnant autant aux riches qu'aux pauvres, aux tyrans qu'aux sages, aux illuminés qu'aux aveugles ; il parle avec la même facilité, dans tous les idiomes du monde, du connu et de l'inconnu, du bien et du mal, du beau et de l'affreux et il sait transcender le temps et l'espace comme un dieu, d'un seul mot. Et la lumière fut, mais aveugles nous sommes toujours ! En lui sont tous nos échecs et toutes nos aspirations, ceux et celles de nos ancêtres et les nôtres propres, plus fragiles

Der Algerier Boualem Sansal, geboren 1949, begann im Alter von fünfzig Jahren seine Karriere als Schriftsteller. Bis dahin hatte sich der promovierte Ökonom und Ingenieur auf seine Arbeit als hoher Beamter im algerischen Industrieministerium konzentriert. Das Attentat auf Präsident Boudiaf (1992), der Tod eines Freundes sowie die eigene Verfolgung in der bürgerkriegsbelasteten Heimat veranlassten ihn jedoch, sich in den neunziger Jahren mit dem Schreiben über sein Land ein inneres Exil zu schaffen. Sein Debüt »Le serment des barbares« (1999; dt. »Der Schwur der Barbaren«, 2003) erschien daher in Frankreich, wo es von der Presse gelobt und mit dem Prix du Premier Roman ausgezeichnet wurde. »Le Nouvel Observateur« feierte es als »Meisterwerk«. Der Roman, der mittlerweile nach einem Drehbuch Jorge Sempruns verfilmt wurde, beginnt zunächst wie ein Krimi. Im algerischen Städtchen Rouiba werden am selben Tag zwei Männer sehr unterschiedlichen Standes – der vermögende und unantastbare Pate der Region Moh sowie der mittellose Bakour – ermordet aufgefunden. Die Geschichte verwandelt sich allerdings schnell in eine Zustandsbeschreibung des nordafrikanischen Staates, als dem im Fall Bakour ermittelnden Kommissar klar wird, dass beide Morde zusammenhängen und einen politisch höchst brisanten Hintergrund haben. Seine Ermittlungen werden zur Suche nach den Wurzeln der terroristischen Gewalt im heutigen Algerien zwischen Korruption, Unterdrückung und Islamismus.
Sansal weist den Algeriern, die es als Nation erst seit der Unabhängigkeit von 1962 gibt, in seinen Romanen mögliche Wege zu einer eigenen Identität. Insbesondere der Titel des 2000 erschienenen Romans »L'enfant fou de l'arbre creux« (dt. »Das verrückte Kind aus dem hohlen Baum«, 2002), für den er 2001 den Michel Dard-Literaturpreis erhielt, hat diesbezüglich symbolischen Charakter: Das Kind, das im Hof eines Zuchthauses angebunden ist, steht laut Sansal für das algerische Volk in »diesem riesigen Gefängnis Algerien. Ein infantilisiertes Volk, verblendet, durch Lügen gefesselt. Es ist an einem Punkt angekommen, an dem es weder weiß, wer es ist, woher es kommt, noch was es will.«
In Frankreich, der ehemaligen Kolonialmacht, wird Sansal wegen seines spielerischen Umgangs mit dem Französischen als Spracherneuerer gefeiert. Aufgrund der politisch explosiven Themen seiner satirischen und zugleich poetischen Romane gilt er in Algerien hingegen als Nestbeschmutzer. Dennoch bleibt er mit seiner Frau und den zwei erwachsenen Töchtern weiterhin in seiner Heimat und veröffentlicht ohne den Schutz eines Pseudonyms. Die Heiterkeit seiner Romane spricht für Sansals Glauben an Algeriens Zukunft, für die sein jüngstes Werk »Dis-moi le paradis« (2003; Ü: Erzähl mir vom Paradies) einen ersten Entwurf darstellt.

parce que moins durcis par le temps, plus quelques-uns qui n'appartiennent à personne, venus des temps de avant la Genèse ou de l'espace, sur des météorites ou des soucoupes volantes. Il a sa magie qui n'est pas la nôtre. Et quand nous nous taisons, il parle en nous, doucement, intensément, puis plus vite jusqu'au délire. Les bruits du monde sont de son vocabulaire, nous en avons pris la phonétique mais nous en ignorons le sens. Au-delà des apparences, le langage se parle à lui-même. Il s'invente et se construit à notre insu. A part les enfants qui dans leur berceau capitonné babillent librement et parlent aux anges, en dehors de tout langage établi, qui peut jamais se targuer d'avoir inventé un seul mot ? Et pourtant, ils sont là et nous faisons comme s'ils étaient nôtres de toute éternité. L'usufruitier finit infailliblement par se croire l'héritier légitime si personne ne vient le traîner en justice.
Alors, de quoi parle le poète et d'où prend-il son inspiration ? Cet homme paradoxal, et un peu fou, dit le silence avec des mots, de la musique et l'emphase. Comment le comprendre ?
Baudelaire, le plus marginal d'entre eux disait dans un de ces délires dont il avait le secret :
« Qui aimes-tu donc le plus, o étranger ? Ton père, ta mère, tes frères ou tes sœurs ? Je n'ai ni père, ni mère, ni frères, ni sœurs. Ton pays ? J'ignore sous quelle latitude il se trouve. L'or ? Je le hais autant vous haïssez Dieu. Et qu'aimes-tu donc, ô énigmatique étranger ? J'aime les nuages… les merveilleux nuages qui passent… là-bas… dans le ciel ».

What makes the poet tick ? Mais bien sûr que nous ne le savons pas. Tant qu'il y aura des poètes, nous ne saurons jamais d'où vient la poésie. Ces gens-là ne vivent pas comme nous, au jour le jour, ils vivent dans une éternelle expectative. Les poèmes se cueillent au petit matin après que la nuit se soit passée en question ou en prière.
Mais toutes les nuits ne s'achèvent pas le matin. Il en est qui ne voient jamais le lever du jour.
Nous sommes le 10 juin 2003, 21 jours après le séisme qui, à vingt heures, à l'heure du dîner, a fait d'une sympathique station balnéaire, Boumerdès, ma ville, mon refuge, un immense champ de ruines. C'est la poésie de la vie, brutale, sanglante, incompréhensible, définitive.
Boualem Sansal

peter schneider
biography

Peter Schneider was born in Lübeck in 1940 and grew up in Freiburg, where he began his studies in German, history and philosophy. He completed his education in Berlin, where he lives today. His political ambitions developed as early as 1965, when he wrote speeches for SPD politicians engaged in the Bundestag election campaign. Schneider quickly found a role as one of the key activists in the 1968 students movement. He has written short stories, novels, scripts and commentaries. In addition, he has written essays and speeches that have tackled, with incisive argument, the political and ideological questions of his time. Since 1985 he has taught as a guest lecturer at American universities, including at Stanford and at Princeton.
Peter Schneider's texts are a mixture of politics and literature. In his story »Lenz«, written in 1973, he presents a very critical no-holds-barred analysis of the 1968 movement. Schneider's »Lenz« is similar to Büchner's »Lenz« insofar as both works portray destruction directly resulting from the individual's desire for freedom. The Lenz of the late sixties agitates intensively using posters and texts, he takes part in demonstrations and sit ins, only to feel the pointlessness of it all when his girlfriend leaves him – after an uninspiring journey through Italy he abandons his theories in favour of a liberative form of self analysis, with particular emphasis on his physical self and his relationship to it. »Paarungen« – his first novel, published in 1992 – is an in depth critical discussion between the main character Eduard, who is a molecular biologist, and his friends; the central theme of their heated discussion focuses on the faded illusions of the '68 movement. This protagonist, having become part of that society against which he formerly rebelled, tries to test his utopian ethic of twenty years before, in the context of his newly formed status. Schneider's latest publication, »Das Fest der Missverständnisse« (2003) is a compilation of old and new short stories. In these, Schneider is concerned with the moment in which the mind goes blank, as in the case of Burk, who has committed himself to the history of medicine in the Third Reich. In a language which is succinct and delusively light the author describes how Burk's preoccupation evolves into an obsession which will finally cost him his sanity.

Lenz
Rotbuch, Berlin, 1973
Der Mauerspringer
Luchterhand
Neuwied, 1982
Vati
Luchterhand
Neuwied, 1987
Paarungen
Rowohlt, Berlin, 1992
Eduards Heimkehr
Rowohlt, Berlin, 1999
Das Fest der Missverständnisse
Rowohlt, Reinbek, 2003

Peter Schneider wurde 1940 in Lübeck geboren und wuchs in Freiburg auf, wo er sein Studium der Germanistik, Geschichte und Philosophie aufnahm. Er beendete seine Ausbildung in Berlin, seinem heutigen Wohnort. Schon früh entwickelte er politische Ambitionen. Im Bundestagswahlkampf von 1965 etwa schrieb er Reden für SPD-Politiker. In kurzer Zeit avancierte Schneider zu einem der Wortführer der 68er-Bewegung. Er hat Erzählungen, Romane, Drehbücher und Reportagen geschrieben sowie Essays und Reden, die in pointierter Weise zu den politischen und ideologischen Fragen seiner Zeit Stellung bezogen. Seit 1985 unterrichtet er als Gastdozent an amerikanischen Universitäten, unter anderem Stanford und Princeton.

Peter Schneiders Texte vermischen Politik und Literatur. Seine Erzählung »Lenz« aus dem Jahr 1973 hinterfragt in ihrer ruppigen Tektonik die Postulate der 68er-Bewegung. Schneiders »Lenz« ist ein Wiedergänger des Büchnerschen »Lenz«, der einst am eigenen Freiheitsdrang zerbrach. Der Lenz der späten sechziger Jahre hat intensiv mit Plakaten und Texten agitiert, hat an Demonstrationen und Sit-Ins teilgenommen. Als ihn unerwartet seine Freundin verlässt, erscheint ihm sein bisheriges Leben sinnlos. Nach einer gleichsam purgatorischen Reise quer durch Italien verwirft er die kopflastigen Theoreme und findet ein neues, befreites Verhältnis zu sich selbst – was vor allem heißt: zu seinem Körper und zur eigenen Wahrnehmung.

»Paarungen«, Schneiders erster Roman (1992), ist eine präzise Auseinandersetzung mit den verblassten Vorstellungen der Studentenbewegung von 1968. Alle Reflexionsstränge gehen von jener Kneipe aus, in der die Hauptfigur Eduard Gespräche mit Freunden führt. Der Protagonist, ein Molekularbiologe, ist längst Teil jener Gesellschaft, gegen die er einmal aufbegehrt hat, und so erprobt er, was nach zwanzig Jahren von den linken Utopien übrig geblieben ist.

Schneiders neuester Erzählband »Das Fest der Missverständnisse« (2003) versammelt eine Auswahl alter und neuer Texte. In einer lapidaren, trügerisch leichten Sprache werden hier jene Augenblicke festgehalten, in denen der Verstand aussetzt und in denen sich das Leben als »Fest der Missverständnisse« erweist. So etwa im Falle Burks, der sich der Erforschung der nationalsozialistischen Medizingeschichte verschrieben hat, sie zur Obsession werden lässt und an ihr zerbricht (»Skizze eines Enthüllers«).

tilman spengler

biography

Tilman Spengler was born in Oberhausen in 1947. He studied Sinology, Political Science and Modern History in Heidelberg, Taipeh and Munich. After completing his doctoral studies, he initially worked as a research assistant at the Max Planck Institute for Social Sciences in Starnberg. In the early 80's he taught and did research at the Academy of Sciences in Peking and at the Wissenschaftskolleg (Institute for Advanced Study) in Berlin.

In addition to his academic work, he has written reports and essays for »Die Zeit«, »Geo« and »Die Woche«. Since 1980 he has been co-publisher of the »Kursbuch«. Not only has Spengler worked as a writer, essayist and freelance journalist, he has also been active as a screenplay writer, documentary film maker (»Bitter Balkan«, 1999), and as a speech writer for the former minister of culture Michael Naumann as well as for Chancellor Gerhard Schröder. In 1999 Spengler was the town chronicler in Mainz and in 2003 received the Ernst-Hoferichter-Preis for his work.

In 1991 he published his first novel »Lenins Hirn« which was very well received and has to date been translated into 21 languages. The novel draws on historical facts and focuses on the Berliner neurologist Prof. Dr. Oskar Vogt (1870–1959), who using Lenin's brain, wants to produce physical proof of genius.

China, pictures, and portraits of China are taken as the subjects for »Der Maler von Peking« (1996) and »Die Stirn, die Augen, der Mund« (1999). Here Spengler combines his knowledge of Sinology with a joy for telling stories, thereby bringing to life two different epochs of China. He has a knack for irony and for mixing facts with fiction, which is also what makes his most recent book such a good read. »Meine Gesellschaft. Kursbuch eines Unfertigen« (2001) is an autobiographical kaleidoscope of sorts, in which anecdote and fact, real and unreal are juxtaposed over 62 sections. Tilman Spengler takes the reader on a trip through his world – it's motto: »certain facts are true, because one can only tell them like that and not differently.« Tilman Spengler lives in Ambach at Lake Starnberg and in Berlin.

Lenins Hirn
Rowohlt, Reinbek, 1991
Die Stirn, die Augen, der Mund
Rowohlt, Berlin,1999
Die neuen Eliten
Rowohlt, Berlin, 2000
Moskau-Berlin
Berlin Verlag, Berlin, 2001
Meine Gesellschaft
Berlin Verlag, Berlin, 2001
Das Glück wartet draußen vor der Stadt
Berliner Taschenbuch-Verlag Berlin, 2002
Wenn Männer sich verheben
Rowohlt, Reinbek, 2002

Tilman Spengler wurde 1947 in Oberhausen geboren. In Heidelberg, Taipeh und München studierte er Sinologie, Politologie und Neuere Geschichte. Nach seiner Promotion war er zunächst wissenschaftlicher Mitarbeiter am Max-Planck-Institut für Sozialwissenschaften in Starnberg. Anfang der achtziger Jahre folgten Forschungs- und Lehraufenthalte an der Akademie der Wissenschaften in Peking und am Wissenschaftskolleg in Berlin.
Neben seiner akademischen Tätigkeit schrieb er Reportagen und Essays für »Die Zeit«, »Geo« und »Die Woche«. Seit 1980 ist er Mitherausgeber des »Kursbuch«. Spengler arbeitete nicht nur als Schriftsteller, Essayist und freier Journalist, sondern auch als Drehbuchautor, Dokumentarfilmer (»Bitter Balkan«, 1999) sowie als Redenschreiber für den ehemaligen Kulturminister Michael Naumann und Bundeskanzler Gerhard Schröder. Spengler war 1999 Stadtschreiber von Mainz und wurde 2003 mit dem Ernst-Hoferichter-Preis für sein Schaffen ausgezeichnet.
1991 gelang ihm mit »Lenins Hirn« sein erster, viel beachteter Roman, der bisher in 21 Sprachen übersetzt wurde. Im Mittelpunkt der auf historischen Tatsachen beruhenden Romanbiographie steht der Berliner Nervenarzt Prof. Dr. Oskar Vogt (1870 - 1959), der anhand von Lenins Gehirn einen physiologischen Beweis für Genialität erbringen wollte. Um China, Bilder und Chinabilder geht es augenzwinkernd in »Der Maler von Peking« (1996) und »Die Stirn, die Augen, der Mund« (1999). Spengler vereint hier sein sinologisches Wissen mit seiner Freude am Fabulieren und lässt dadurch zwei unterschiedliche Epochen Chinas lebendig werden. Sein bevorzugter künstlerischer Kniff ist neben der Ironie die Vermischung von Fakten und Fiktionen. Dadurch wird auch sein letztes Buch zum Leseerlebnis. »Meine Gesellschaft. Kursbuch eines Unfertigen« (2001) ist eine Art autobiographisches Kaleidoskop, in dem sich Anekdoten und Tatsachen, Erlebtes und Erfundenes in 62 Abschnitten aneinanderreihen. Tilman Spengler nimmt seine Leser mit auf eine Reise durch seine Welt – frei nach dem Motto »bestimmte Sachverhalte sind wahr, weil man sie nur so und nicht anders erzählen kann«. Tilman Spengler lebt in Ambach am Starnberger See und in Berlin.

What makes the poet tick?

Ich bin froh, daß ich es nicht weiß!

shashi tharoor

biography

The Indian writer and diplomat Shashi Tharoor was born in 1956 in London; at the time his father worked for the English-language Indian newspaper »The Statesman«.
Tharoor studied in India and in the US, where at age 22 he received a doctorate in law and diplomacy. He then worked for the United Nations. In the early 80's, at the time of the crisis with the Vietnamese »boat people«, he was in charge of the UN refugee office in Singapore and later coordinated measures to secure peace in the former Yugoslavia. From 1997 to 1998 he was the assistant to UN Secretary General Kofi Annan; in 2002 Annan appointed him Under Secretary-General for Communications and Public Information at the UN.
Tharoor, who initially saw his diplomatic work as a passing thing, today describes writing and the UN as two equally important aspects of his responses to the world: »Without either, a part of my psyche would wither on the vine.« He continually takes new approaches to one central topic: his native country, India. While he remains faithful to this one topic, he works with a variety of literary genres and in addition to novels, he writes newspaper articles, short stories, non-fiction and scholarly works. »The Great Indian Novel« (1989) is a modern ironic adaptation of the 2000-year-old national epic, the »Mahabharata«, and is narrated from a 20th-century viewpoint. »Show Business« (1992) – filmed in 1994 under the title »Bollywood« – is a satire on the Indian film industry. He has received numerous awards for his works.
Set against the background of religious tensions in India, Tharoor's most recent novel »Riot – A Love Story« (2001) is about an American and a married government official who have a secret love affair. After riots between Hindus and Muslims at a procession, the woman is found stabbed. In this book, as in his non-fiction book »India – From Midnight to Millennium« (1997), Tharoor does without a general narrative perspective; instead he brilliantly combines fictitious newspaper articles, diary entries, letters, and fragments from conversations into a collage, which not only leaves it up to the reader to decide which truth he or she would like to follow, but also makes it clear that the Indian reality with its long and varied history and its current pluralisms and conflicts is too complex to be reduced to a simple formula: »Whatever one might say about India – the opposite is also true«, says Tharoor. Today he lives in New York.

Reasons of State
Vikas Pub House
New Delhi, 1982
The Five-Dollar Smile
Viking, New Delhi, 1990
Show Business
Picador, London, 1994
Der große Roman Indiens
Claassen, Hildesheim, 1995
[Ü: Anke Kreutzer]
Indien
Insel, Frankfurt a. M., 2000
[Ü: Max Looser]
Aufruhr
Insel, Frankfurt a. M., 2002
[Ü: Anke Kreutzer]

Der indische Schriftsteller und Diplomat Shashi Tharoor wurde 1956 in London geboren, als sein Vater dort für die englischsprachige indische Zeitung »The Statesman« tätig war. Tharoor studierte in Indien und in den Vereinigten Staaten, wo er mit 22 Jahren in Jura promovierte und anschließend in den Dienst der Vereinten Nationen trat. Während der Krise um die vietnamesischen »Boat People« in den siebziger Jahren leitete er das Büro des UN-Flüchtlingswerks in Singapur und koordinierte später friedenssichernde Maßnahmen im früheren Jugoslawien. Von 1997 bis 1998 war er Assistent von UNO-Generalsekretär Kofi Annan, 2002 wurde er von diesem zum Stellvertretenden Leiter der Abteilung für Öffentlichkeitsarbeit der UNO ernannt.
Tharoor, der seine diplomatische Tätigkeit zunächst nur als vorübergehend betrachtete, bezeichnet Schreiben und seine Arbeit für die UNO als zwei gleichermaßen wichtige Aspekte seines Lebens: »Wenn ich das eine oder das andere aufgeben müsste, würde ein Teil meiner Seele sterben.« Sein Werk befasst sich mit einem zentralen Gegenstand, seiner Heimat Indien. So treu er sich diesem Thema bleibt, so unterschiedlich sind die literarischen Gattungen, in die er es kleidet: Neben Romanen verfasst er Zeitungsartikel, Kurzgeschichten, Sachbücher und wissenschaftliche Arbeiten. »The Great Indian Novel« (1989; dt. »Der große Roman Indiens«, 1995) ist eine moderne ironisierende Adaption des 2000 Jahre alten Nationalepos »Mahabharata« – erzählt aus Sicht des 20. Jahrhunderts. »Showbusiness« (1992) – 1994 unter dem Titel »Bollywood« verfilmt – ist eine Satire auf die indische Filmindustrie. Für seine Arbeiten erhielt er zahlreiche Auszeichnungen.
Tharoors jüngster Roman »Riot. A Love Story« (2001; dt. »Aufruhr. Eine Liebesgeschichte«, 2002) erzählt vor dem Hintergrund religiöser Spannungen die Geschichte der heimlichen Liebe zwischen einer Amerikanerin und einem verheirateten Regierungsbeamten. Nach Ausschreitungen zwischen Hindus und Muslimen bei einer Prozession wird die Frau erstochen aufgefunden. Wie schon in seinem Sachbuch »India. From Midnight to Millenium« (1997; dt. »Indien. Zwischen Mythos und Moderne«, 2000) verzichtet Tharoor auch hier auf eine durchgängige Erzählperspektive. Statt dessen verknüpft er virtuos fiktive Zeitungsartikel, Tagebucheinträge, Briefe und Gesprächsaufzeichnungen zu einer Collage, die dem Leser nicht nur überlässt, welcher Wahrheit er folgen möchte, sondern auch deutlich macht, dass die indische Realität mit ihrer langen und wechselvollen Geschichte und ihren gegenwärtigen Pluralismen und Konflikten weit komplexer ist, als dass sie sich auf eine einfache Formel bringen ließe: »Was immer man über Indien sagt – das Gegenteil ist auch richtig«, sagt Tharoor. Er lebt heute in New York.

What makes the poet tick?
The same thing that makes a clock
tick:
the inexorable march of time,
which punctuates all creation,
and one day places a full stop
at the end of all creativity.

ayu utami

biography

Ayu Utami was born in Bogor near the Indonesian capital of Jakarta in 1968. She is one of the most prominent representatives of a new generation of Indonesian writers, who, even before the end of the Suharto regime, were already openly adressing the social and cultural conflicts of the island state, and today accompany the transition to democracy with a critical voice. While still studying Russian language and literature at the Universitas Indonesia in Jakarta, Utami began publishing reports and essays in various newspapers. As cofounder of a union of freelance journalists, which was declared illegal by the government, she was banned from practising her occupation in 1994 and some of her colleagues were arrested. She continued her journalistic work underground, which included the anonymous publication of a black book on corruption in the Suharto regime.

With her debut novel »Saman« (1998) Ayu Utami achieved more than just her breakthrough as a writer – in her native country the book was printed many times and was celebrated as a literary sensation. »Saman« was published only a few weeks before General Suharto was deprived of power and its publication was also a sign of the approaching political change. The author treats social taboos in an open way, thereby breaking with Indonesian literature to date. Utami writes freely about love and sexuality and thematises the difficult relationship between Muslims and Christians as well as the hatred of the Chinese minority. Her novel focuses on the story of a Catholic priest, who, through his advocacy work for oppressed small farmers, joins the Indonesian resistance, falls in love in the process, gives up the priesthood and emigrates to New York. At the same time one reads about the fate of a group of young women, who self-consciously make decisions about their lives and renounce traditional gender roles.

Utami's prose is lively and modern and as such reflects the richness of Indonesian oral tradition. The author masterfully switches between various narrative perspectives, locations and time scales, links dream sequences and old myths with descriptions of the political and societal relations in Indonesia in the 90's. »Saman« is the first in a cycle of novels, the second part of which was published in 2001 under the title »Larung«. Both of her novels have been published in Dutch. In 1998 »Saman« was awarded the prize for best Indonesian novel; in 2000 Ayu Utami received the renowned Prins Claus Prijs from the Dutch government. Today Ayu Utami lives in Jakarta and since 1998 has been copublisher of the culture magazine »Kalam«.

Saman
KPG, Jakarta, 2001
Larung
KPG, Jakarta, 2001
Larung
Breda, De Geus, 2001
[Ü: Maya Sutedja-Liem
Monique Soesman]
Samans missie
De Geus, Breda, 2001
[Ü: Maya Sutedja-Liem
Monique Soesman]

Ayu Utami wurde 1968 in Bogor, nahe der indonesischen Hauptstadt Jakarta, geboren. Sie gehört zu den prominentesten Vertretern einer neuen Generation indonesischer Schriftsteller, die sich schon vor dem Ende der Suharto-Herrschaft offen mit den sozialen und kulturellen Konflikten des Inselstaates auseinandersetzte und heute den Aufbruch in die Demokratie mit kritischer Stimme begleitet. Bereits während ihres Studiums der Russischen Sprache und Literatur an der Universitas Indonesia in Jakarta begann Utami Reportagen und Essays in verschiedenen Zeitschriften zu publizieren. Als Mitbegründerin einer Vereinigung unabhängiger Journalisten, die von der Regierung für illegal erklärt wurde, belegte man sie 1994 mit einem Berufsverbot und verhaftete einige ihrer Kollegen. Im Untergrund führte sie ihre journalistische Arbeit fort, unter anderem als anonyme Verfasserin eines Schwarzbuchs über die Korruption des Suharto-Regimes.

Mit ihrem Debütroman »Saman« (1998) gelang Ayu Utami nicht nur der Durchbruch als Schriftstellerin, das Buch erreichte in ihrer Heimat Höchstauflagen und wurde als literarische Sensation gefeiert. »Saman« erschien nur wenige Wochen vor der Entmachtung General Suhartos, gleichsam als Vorbote des politischen Wandels. Die Offenheit, mit der die junge Autorin gesellschaftliche Tabus behandelte, stellte einen Bruch mit der bisherigen indonesischen Literatur dar: Utami schrieb freizügig über Liebe und Sexualität, thematisierte das schwierige Verhältnis zwischen Muslimen und Christen sowie den Hass auf die chinesische Minderheit. Im Zentrum ihres Romans steht die Geschichte eines katholischen Priesters, der über sein Engagement für unterdrückte Kleinbauern zum indonesischen Widerstand stößt, sich dabei verliebt, sein Priesteramt aufgibt und nach New York emigriert. Gleichzeitig wird das Schicksal einer Gruppe junger Frauen erzählt, die selbstbewusst über ihr Leben bestimmen und sich den traditionellen Rollenzuweisungen verweigern.

Utami schreibt in einer lebendigen und modernen Prosa, in der sich auch die reiche indonesische Tradition der mündlichen Überlieferung widerspiegelt. Virtuos wechselt die Autorin zwischen verschiedenen Erzählperspektiven, Schauplätzen und Zeitebenen, verknüpft Traumsequenzen und alte Mythen mit Schilderungen der politischen und gesellschaftlichen Verhältnisse im Indonesien der neunziger Jahre. »Saman« bildet den Anfang eines Romanzyklus, dessen zweiter Teil unter dem Titel »Larung« 2001 erschien. Ihre beiden Romane erschienen in niederländischer Übersetzung. 1998 wurde »Saman« als bester indonesischer Roman ausgezeichnet, im Jahr 2000 erhielt Ayu Utami den renommierten Prins Claus Prijs der Niederländischen Regierung. Ayu Utami lebt heute in Jakarta und ist seit 1998 Mitherausgeberin des Kulturmagazins »Kalam«.

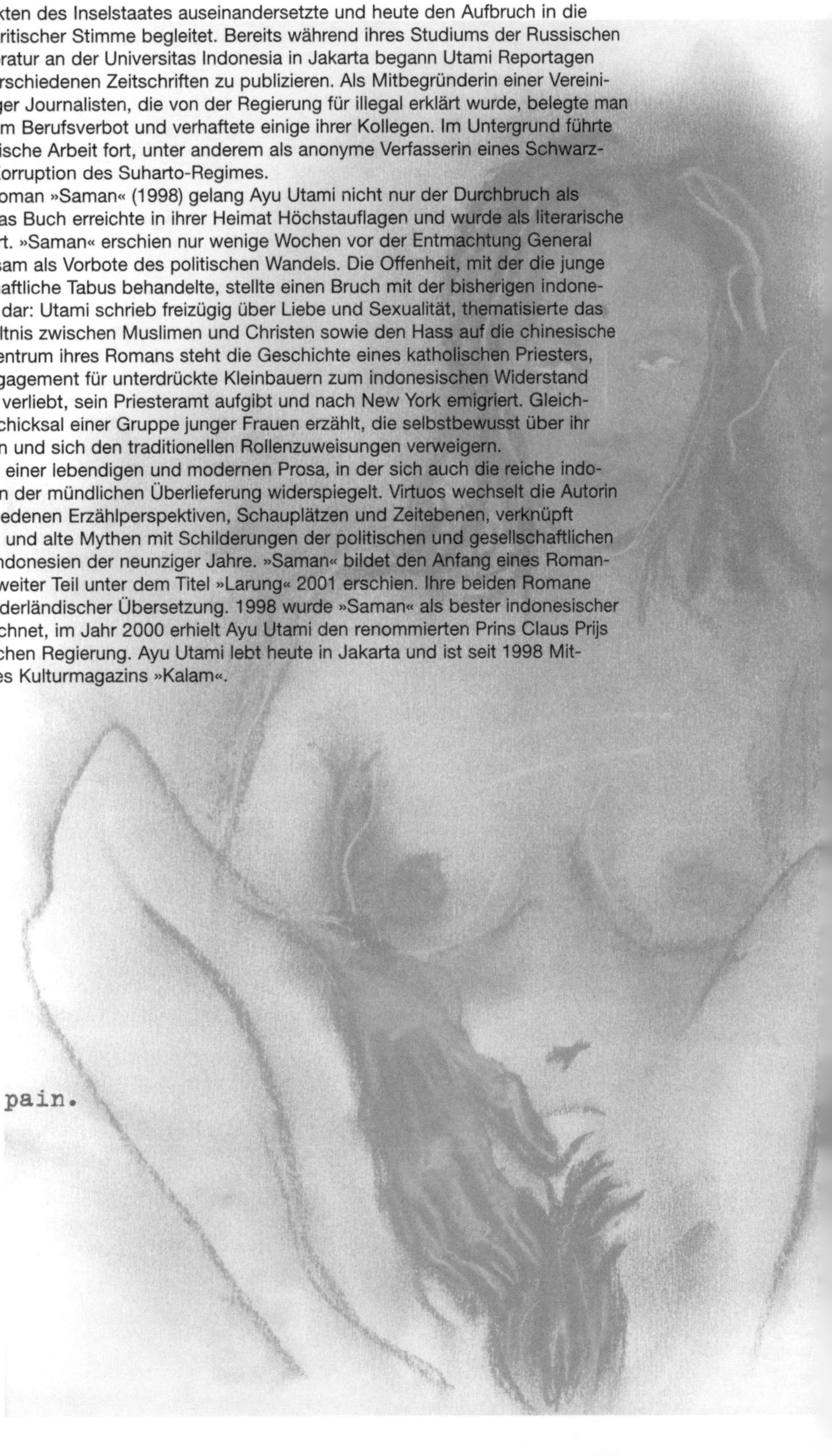

What makes the poet tick?

Tears and pain.

martin walser
biography

Martin Walser was born in Wasserburg on Lake Constance in 1927. He composed his first poems at the age of twelve. He studied literature, history and philosophy in Regensburg and Tübingen, where he wrote his doctorate on Franz Kafka in 1951. From 1949 to 1957, Walser worked as a reporter, director and radio playwright for the Süddeutscher Rundfunk regional radio station. He was a member of the Gruppe 47 from 1953 onwards, winning the literary group's prize for one of his first short stories »Templones Ende« (t: Templone's End) in 1955. He received the Herman Hesse Prize for his first novel »Ehen in Phillipsburg« (1957, t: Marriages in Phillipsburg). His work consists of prose, theatre plays, screenplays, radio plays and translations, as well as a great number of essays, speeches and lectures. One critic described the author's book »Ein fliehendes Pferd« (1978, t: A Fleeing Horse) as »a show-piece of German prose«. It tells the story of the teacher Halm, a typical Walser anti-hero, who retreats to an unexciting corner of Lake Constance, because he believes he can only hold out in a state of the greatest possible lethargy. Walser describes himself as a »literary expert on identity damage«. His mostly middle-class protagonists, characters plagued by identity problems and feelings of inferiority, are characterised by inner monologues in few sentences, their weaknesses are portrayed through irony, with empathy but without mercy. He often leads his protagonist through several novels, for example the character of Anselm Kristlein in the trilogy »Halbzeit« (1960, t: Half-Time), »Einhorn« (1966, t: Unicorn) and »Der Sturz« (1973, t: The Fall). In 1985 a collection of short texts, »Meßmers Gedanken« (t: Meßmer's Thoughts), was published. His latest novel »Meßmers Reisen« (2003, t: Meßmer's Travels) starts where this book left off. Walser was awarded the Peace Prize of the German Booksellers for his novel »Ein springender Brunnen« (1998, t: A Springing Fountain), in which the author recounts his youth in Wasserburg during the Third Reich. His acceptance speech, in which he criticised »the instrumentalisation of Auschwitz« as a »moralising cudgel«, caused reactions accusing him of »anti-Semitism«. The intensity of the resulting »Walser Bubis debate«, as of the later reactions to his novel »Tod eines Kritikers« (2002, t: Death of A Critic), marks out the arbitrary and indistinct intellectual and moral nature of the discussion of Germany's past. Walser, who has always expressed controversial opinions on subjects of general interest alongside his literary activities, is one of the most significant authors of German post-war literature and has received countless prizes for his literary work, among them the Georg Büchner Prize in 1981. He has also been awarded the Ordre pour le Mérite and named Officier de L'ordre des Arts et des Lettres. Martin Walser lives in Überlingen on Lake Constance.

Vormittag eines Schriftstellers
Suhrkamp
Frankfurt a. M., 1996

Finks Krieg
Suhrkamp
Frankfurt a. M., 1998

Die Verteidigung der Kindheit
Suhrkamp
Frankfurt a. M., 2002

Ohne einander
Suhrkamp
Frankfurt a. M., 2002

Ein springender Brunnen
Suhrkamp
Frankfurt a. M., 2002

Tod eines Kritikers
Suhrkamp
Frankfurt a. M., 2002

Meßmers Reisen
Suhrkamp
Frankfurt a. M., 2003

Martin Walser wurde 1927 in Wasserburg am Bodensee geboren. Mit zwölf Jahren verfasste er erste Gedichte. Er studierte Literaturwissenschaft, Geschichte und Philosophie in Regensburg und in Tübingen, wo er 1951 mit einer Arbeit über Franz Kafka promovierte. 1949 bis 1957 arbeitete Walser beim Süddeutschen Rundfunk als Reporter, Regisseur und Hörspielautor. Seit 1953 gehörte er der Gruppe 47 an, deren Preis er 1955 für eine seiner ersten Erzählungen, »Templones Ende«, erhielt. Für seinen ersten Roman »Ehen in Phillipsburg« (1957) erhielt er den Herman-Hesse-Preis. Seine Arbeit umfasst neben Prosawerken auch Theaterstücke, Drehbücher, Hörspiele und Übersetzungen sowie eine Vielzahl von Aufsätzen, Reden und Vorlesungen. »Ein Glanzstück deutscher Prosa«, so ein Kritiker, gelang dem Autor 1978 mit dem Band »Ein fliehendes Pferd«. Walser schildert hier die Geschichte des Studienrates Halm, eines typisch Walserschen Antihelden, der sich in einen ereignisarmen Winkel am Bodensee zurückzieht, weil er glaubt, nur in einem Zustand größtmöglicher Lethargie ausharren zu können. Walser bezeichnet sich selbst als »literarischen Experten für Identitätsbeschädigung«. Seine meist aus der Mittelschicht stammenden Protagonisten, von Identitätsproblemen und Minderwertigkeitsgefühlen geplagte Figuren, werden mit inneren Monologen in wenigen Sätzen charakterisiert, ihre Schwächen mittels Ironie so einfühlsam wie gnadenlos dargestellt. Mit Vorliebe führt er seine Protagonisten durch mehrere Romane, so etwa die Figur des Anselm Kristlein in der Trilogie »Halbzeit« (1960), »Einhorn« (1966) und »Der Sturz« (1973). 1985 erschien »Meßmers Gedanken«, eine Sammlung kurzer Texte, an die sein neuestes Buch, »Meßmers Reisen« (2003), anknüpft. Für den 1998 erschienenen Roman »Ein springender Brunnen«, in dem der Autor seiner Jugend in Wasserburg während des Dritten Reiches nachspürt, erhielt Walser den Friedenspreis des Deutschen Buchhandels. Auf seine Dankesrede, in der er »die Instrumentalisierung von Auschwitz« als »Moralkeule« kritisierte, reagierten einige Stimmen mit dem Vorwurf des »Antisemitismus«. Die daraus resultierende »Walser-Bubis-Debatte«, wie auch die späteren Reaktionen auf den 2002 erschienenen Roman »Tod eines Kritikers«, markieren in ihrer Heftigkeit die intellektuellen und moralischen Beliebigkeiten und Unschärfen in der Auseinandersetzung mit der deutschen Vergangenheit. Walser, der neben seiner literarischen Tätigkeit auch immer wieder kontrovers zu öffentlichen Themen Stellung bezogen hat, zählt zu den bedeutendsten Autoren der deutschen Nachkriegsliteratur und hat für sein literarisches Werk zahlreiche Preise erhalten, darunter 1981 den Georg-Büchner-Preis. Außerdem wurde er mit dem Orden »Pour le mérite« ausgezeichnet und zum Officier de L'ordre des Arts et des Lettres ernannt. Martin Walser lebt in Überlingen am Bodensee.

eliot weinberger
biography

Eliot Weinberger was born in 1949 in New York City, where he still lives. At age 19, he published his first book, a translated volume of poetry by the later Nobel prizewinner Octavio Paz. Since 1970 Weinberger has translated numerous authors from the Spanish (including Octavio Paz, Jorge Luis Borges, and Vicente Huidobro) as well as from the Chinese (Bei Dao). He has edited anthologies of American and classical Chinese poetry, and in 1999 received the prize of the National Book Critics Circle for his edition of Borges' »Selected Non-Fictions«. In 1986 with »Works on Paper« he published his first book of essays. Six books are now available in English, including »Karmic Traces« (2000) as well as a collection of recent political writings entitled »9/12« (2003). For the support he has given to Hispanic literature in the US, he was the first to receive the P.E.N./Kolovakos Award in 1992. In 2000 he was the first US writer to be honoured with the Order of the Aztec Eagle from the Mexican government. He is prominently featured in the »Visitor's Guide to Iceland«. His work has been translated into some twenty languages. In Germany, he regularly appears in »Lettre International« and a selection of his essays (»Kaskaden«) was published in 2003.

»He has seemingly read, read about, or seen firsthand practically everything on planet Earth«, writes the »Multicultural Review« about Eliot Weinberger. And indeed there do not appear to be any limits to the essayist's subject matter – his texts are dedicated to the love life of guppies and naked mole rats, MTV and Icelandic sagas, saints and poets, precolonial India and the civil war in Rwanda. Even formally he uses the full scope of what he sees as the unlimited potential of the genre, and many of his texts, while strictly »non-fiction«, are closer to prose poetry or narrative than traditional essays. Although at first glance these texts appear to be very heterogeneous, there is nothing random about them. The political reality of our time together with literature are what constitute our world, which Weinberger discovers anew. There is one criteria that his essays must always fulfill: »I never make things up«, says Weinberger, referring to the verifiability of all of the seemingly fantastic details. »His work« writes the »Times Literary Supplement«, »makes you sit up in your seat.«

Nineteen Ways of Looking at Wang Wei
Moyer Bell
Mount Kisco, 1987

The Collected Poems of Octavio Paz (Ed.)
New Directions
New York, 1987

Outside Stories
New Directions
New York, 1992

Karmic Traces
New Directions
New York, 2002

9/12: New York After
Prickly Paradigm Press
Chicago, 2003

Kaskaden
Suhrkamp
Frankfurt a. M., 2003
[Ü: Peter Torberg]

The New Directions Anthology of Classical Chinese Poetry (Ed.)
New Directions
New York, 2003

Eliot Weinberger wurde 1949 in New York City geboren, wo er auch heute lebt. Bereits mit 19 Jahren veröffentlichte er seinen ersten Band mit Übersetzungen von Gedichten des späteren Nobelpreisträgers Octavio Paz. Seit 1970 folgten zahlreiche Übersetzungen aus dem Spanischen (u. a. Octavio Paz, Jorge Luis Borges, Vicente Huidobro) sowie aus dem Chinesischen (Bei Dao). Er edierte Anthologien amerikanischer und chinesischer Lyrik und wurde 1999 für seine Ausgabe der »Selected Non-Fictions« von Borges mit dem Preis des National Book Critics Circle ausgezeichnet. Mit »Works on Paper« erschien 1986 sein erster Band mit Essays. Inzwischen liegen auf Englisch sechs Bände vor, darunter »Karmic Traces« (2000) sowie unter dem Titel »9/12« (2003) eine Sammlung aktueller politischer Texte.
Für seinen Beitrag zur Förderung hispanischer Literatur in den USA erhielt er 1992 als erster Preisträger den P.E.N./Kolovakos Award. 2000 zeichnete ihn die mexikanische Regierung als ersten US-amerikanischen Schriftsteller mit dem Order of the Aztec Eagle aus. Hervorgehoben wird er außerdem im »Visitor's Guide to Iceland«. Sein Werk wurde in rund zwanzig Sprachen übersetzt. In Deutschland schreibt er regelmäßig in »Lettre International«, eine Auswahl seiner Essays erschien 2003 unter dem Titel »Kaskaden«.
»Er hat ganz offenbar praktisch alles auf dem Planeten Erde gelesen, darüber gelesen oder mit eigenen Augen gesehen«, schreibt die »Multicultural Review« über Eliot Weinberger. Und tatsächlich scheint es für den Essayisten keine thematischen Grenzen zu geben – seine Texte widmen sich dem Liebesleben von Guppies und Nacktmullen, MTV und isländischen Sagen, Heiligen und Dichtern, dem präkolonialen Indien und dem bürgerkriegserschütterten Ruanda. Auch formal nutzt er das in seinen Augen unbegrenzte Potential der Gattung in seiner ganzen Breite aus. So ähneln viele seiner Texte eher Prosagedichten oder Erzählungen als traditionellen Essays – auch wenn sie keineswegs fiktiv sind. Doch obgleich diese Texte auf den ersten Blick äußerst heterogen anmuten, wirken sie doch niemals beliebig. Immer stehen die politische Realität unserer Zeit und die Literatur hinter dieser Welt, die Weinberger neu entdeckt. Und immer müssen seine Essays einem Maßstab genügen: »Ich erfinde nie etwas«, behauptet Weinberger und verweist damit auf die Nachprüfbarkeit aller noch so phantastisch erscheinenden Details. »Sein Werk«, so das »Times Literary Supplement«, »verändert die Sicht auf die Dinge.«

What Makes the Poet a Tick?

A tick is very small, the size of a single letter in a book. Who would notice? Its survival is dependent on a chance encounter with a host brushing past the leaves or grass. It wanders a body anonymously, searching for its place, and when it settles, it maintains its obscurity by emitting an anaesthetic so its host won't feel the impending bite. It cuts the skin with the pincers of its chelicerao and inserts the scary, serrated prong of its hypostome. From its midgut it injects a complex saliva with vasodilators to keep the veins and capillaries open, a whole family of anticoagulants to keep the blood flowing, agents to subdue threatening immune responses, and a kind of moisture-resistant glue to remain attached. It injects saliva, draws blood, injects saliva, draws blood, and grows fat, the size of a single letter in a chapter title. In its saliva are tens of thousands of bacteria; among them, the spirals of borrelia burgdorferi that induce facial paralysis, arthritis in the joints and numbness in the extremities, heartbeat irregularities leading to dizziness and fainting, perpetual sleepiness, and an inability to concentrate or to remember. When it has eaten, the tick drops off. The nourishment allows it to produce the hundreds of eggs it lays in the ground.

stefan ludmilla wieszner

biography

Stefan Ludmilla Wieszner was born in Wilhelmshaven, Germany in 1964. He became a sailor at the age of 19. After four years at sea he decided to study philosophy, theatre and Comparative Literature in Munich, Vienna and Berlin. He wrote his first plays as a student. During the following »theatre journeyman's years« he worked as a director's assistant at various notable European theatres such as the Vienna Burgtheater, the Munich Kammerspiele, the Deutsches Theater in Berlin and the Théâtre Odéon de L'Europe in Paris. In 1994 he founded and ran a free ensemble in Berlin, the »Theater unter den Leichen« (Theatre under the Corpses), with which he staged his own plays including »Testament Firmament« (1996), a play about financial difficulties and cravings for recognition. He worked as a theatre critic, freelance journalist and artistic director. He was awarded a number of grants to carry out creative work in international artistic networks towards the end of the 90's, for example at the Akademie Schloss Solitude in Stuttgart, at the Villa Mont Noir in France and in the Japanese artists' village Akiyoshidai. Wieszner mixes German dialects and sociolects with foreign languages, blurring communication and perception by exposing pigeonhole thinking and typical role patterns. Over twenty of his plays have appeared to date, partly in French translation. He is now just as well known for his literary texts as he is for his dramatic work. He writes novels, short stories and poems. A collection of poems written during his stay in Japan has been published under the title »Südlich von Hagi« (2002; t: South of Hagi). In his poetic texts a certain tension also unfolds from the use of apparently incompatible elements. »They seem both modern and from times gone by because, while the thoughts written into them are very contemporary, they do not shy away from intense words and intense feelings.« (Joachim Satorius). Inspired by natural images similar to those of classical Japanese poetry, Wieszner pursues lonely channels of thought and asks existential questions such as »Let yourself go, but where to?« Stefan Ludmilla Wieszner currently lives and works as a freelance author, journalist and director in Berlin.

Stefan Ludmilla Wieszner wurde 1964 in Wilhelmshaven geboren. Im Alter von 19 Jahren fuhr er zunächst zur See. Nach vier Jahren Seefahrt entschied er sich für ein Studium der Philosophie, Theaterwissenschaft und Vergleichenden Literaturwissenschaften in München, Wien und Berlin. Neben dem Studium verfasste er erste Theaterstücke. Während der folgenden »Theater- und Wanderjahre« war er Regieassistent an verschiedenen namhaften Bühnen Europas, u. a. am Wiener Burgtheater, den Münchner Kammerspielen, am Deutschen Theater in Berlin sowie am Théâtre Odéon de L'Europe in Paris. 1994 gründete und leitete er ein freies Ensemble in Berlin, das »Theater unter den Leichen«, mit dem er seine eigenen Texte inszenierte, darunter »Testament Firmament« (1996), ein Stück über Finanznöte und Geltungssüchte. Er war als Theaterkritiker, freier Journalist und Dramaturg tätig. Eine Reihe von Stipendien ermöglichte ihm zum Ende der neunziger Jahre die kreative Arbeit in internationalen künstlerischen Netzwerken, beispielsweise an der Akademie Schloss Solitude in Stuttgart, an der Villa Mont Noir in Frankreich und im japanischen Künstlerdorf Akiyoshidai.
Wieszner mixt deutsche Dialekte und Soziolekte mit Fremdsprachen, irritiert Kommunikation und Wahrnehmung, indem er Schubladendenken und typische Rollenmuster sprengt. Bisher sind mehr als zwanzig seiner Theaterstücke erschienen, die zum Teil in französischer Übersetzung vorliegen. Inzwischen ist er ebenso bekannt für seine literarischen Texte wie für seine Inszenierungen. Er schreibt Romane, Kurzgeschichten und Gedichte. Unter dem Titel »Südlich von Hagi« (2002) wurden Gedichte veröffentlicht, die während seines Aufenthaltes in Japan entstanden sind. Auch in seinen poetischen Texten entfaltet sich aus Elementen, die unvereinbar scheinen, eine besondere Spannung. »Sie muten zugleich modern und aus vergangenen Zeiten an, weil das in ihnen eingeschriebene Denken ganz zeitgenössisch ist, sie aber vor den großen Worten und den großen Gefühlen nicht zurückscheuen.« (Joachim Satorius). Inspiriert von Naturbildern ähnlich denen der klassischen japanischen Dichtung, folgt Wieszner einsamen Gedankenströmen und stellt existentielle Fragen wie »Sich gehen lassen, aber wohin?« Stefan Ludmilla Wieszner lebt und arbeitet derzeit als freier Autor, Journalist und Regisseur in Berlin.

leon de winter

biography

Leon de Winter was born in s'Hertogenbosch, Holland, in 1954. His Jewish parents were the only members of their family to survive the Holocaust. Leon de Winter started writing at the age of twelve, as a reaction to his father's early death. Central themes of his work have since been farewells, mourning, loss and death. He confronts his fear of personal tragedies in his storytelling. »I imagine the worst and then I create a ritual, the ritual of writing, to control it and to protect reality.« After finishing school he trained at Bavaria Film studios in Munich and subsequently studied at the film academy in Amsterdam.
He has been a freelance writer since 1976. He retained his ties to the film world, working as a film-maker, script writer and producer.
De Winter's love of cinema also comes across in his novels. His storytelling relies on various techniques of film narration. He has a good feeling for plots and settings, and is a master of polished dialogue. He is not afraid of momentous feelings. His plot structures are as complex as they are dramatically perfect, his characters alive and multi-faceted. One of de Winter's best-known novels is »Leo Kaplan« (1986, published in Germany in 2001). Parallel and simultaneously contrary to his own biography, in this novel the author invents his own alter ego, a writer suffering from writer's block. The character of Hoffman in »Hoffman's honger« (1990; t: Hoffman's Hunger) is also a tragic hero searching for a way to cope with the blows dealt by fate.
In 1999 de Winter set up the film production company Pleswin, with the idea of making European material attractive for the US market. In 2000 the film »The Hollywood Sign« was adapted from his novel »De Hemel van Hollywood« (1997; t: Heaven over Hollywood) and directed by Sönke Wortmann. A film adaptation of »SuperTex« (directed by Jan Schütte) will be released in 2003. To date there are screen versions of six of his novels. Leon de Winter also writes theatre plays, reports and short stories. He regularly comments on political subjects in essays and newspaper articles, e.g. on European unification, the Israeli-Palestinian situation and the war in Iraq.
In 2002 he received the WELT prize for literature for his life's work. His tenth novel »God's Gym« (2002) was published in Germany in Spring 2003 under the title »Malibu«. Leon de Winter lives with his wife, the writer Jessica Durlacher, and children in Amsterdam and Los Angeles.

Hoffmanns Hunger
Diogenes, Zürich, 1995
[Ü: Sibylle Mulot]
Zionoco
Diogenes, Zürich, 1997
[Ü: Hanni Ehlers]
Solokows Universum
Diogenes, Zürich, 1999
[Ü: Sibylle Mulot]
Der Himmel von Hollywood
Diogenes, Zürich, 2000
[Ü: Hanni Ehlers]
Leo Kaplan
Diogenes, Zürich, 2001
[Ü: Hanni Ehlers]
Malibu
Diogenes, Zürich, 2003
[Ü: Hanni Ehlers]

Leon de Winter wurde 1954 in s'Hertogenbosch, Niederlande, geboren. Er stammt aus einer jüdischen Familie, deren Angehörige Opfer des Holocaust wurden. Nur seine Eltern überlebten. Leon de Winter begann im Alter von 12 Jahren mit dem Schreiben als Reaktion auf den frühen Tod seines Vaters. Zentrale Themen sind für ihn seither Abschied, Trauer, Verlust und Tod. »Ich stelle mir das Schlimmste vor, und dann mache ich ein Ritual, das Ritual des Schreibens, um das zu kontrollieren und die Wirklichkeit zu schützen.« Nach der Schule folgte eine Ausbildung bei der Bavaria Film in München, anschließend studierte er an der Filmakademie in Amsterdam. Seit 1976 arbeitet er als freier Schriftsteller. Dem Film blieb er verbunden: als Filmemacher, Drehbuchautor und Produzent.

Auch in seinen Romanen ist de Winters Leidenschaft für den Film spürbar. Seine Erzählweise stützt sich auf diverse filmisch-narrative Techniken. Er besitzt ein großes Gespür für Plots und Settings und ist ein Meister der geschliffenen Dialoge. Die Handlungsstränge sind ebenso komplex wie dramaturgisch perfekt angelegt, die Figuren wirken lebendig in ihrer Vielschichtigkeit.

Zu de Winters bekanntesten Romanen zählt »Leo Kaplan« (1986, dt. 2001). Parallel und gleichzeitig konträr zur eigenen Biographie erfindet der Autor hier sein alter ego, einen Schriftsteller, der an seiner Schreibblockade leidet. Auch die Figur Hoffman in »Hoffman's honger« (1990; dt. »Hoffmans Hunger«, 1994) ist ein tragischer Held auf der Suche nach einem Ausweg, wie er die Schicksalsschläge des Lebens ertragen kann.

1999 gründete de Winter die Filmproduktionsfirma Pleswin mit der Idee, europäische Stoffe für den amerikanischen Markt attraktiv zu machen. 2000 entstand »The Hollywood Sign« nach seinem Roman »De Hemel van Hollywood« (1997; dt. »Der Himmel von Hollywood«, 1998) unter der Regie von Sönke Wortmann. Eine Adaption von »SuperTex« (Regie: Jan Schütte) kommt 2003 in die Kinos. Bisher sind sechs seiner Romane verfilmt worden.

Leon de Winter schreibt auch Theaterstücke, Reportagen und Erzählungen. In Essays und Zeitungsartikeln äußert er sich regelmäßig zu politischen Themen, z. B. zum vereinten Europa, zur israelisch-palästinensischen Situation sowie zum Irak-Krieg.

2002 wurde ihm für sein Gesamtwerk der WELT-Literaturpreis verliehen. Sein zehnter Roman »God's Gym« (2002) erschien im Frühjahr 2003 auf deutsch unter dem Titel »Malibu«. Leon de Winter lebt mit seiner Frau, der Schriftstellerin Jessica Durlacher, und seinen Kindern in Amsterdam und Los Angeles.

jeanette winterson

biography

Jeanette Winterson was born in Manchester, Great Britain, in 1959. She grew up in nearby Accrington as the adopted daughter of a working-class couple, who belonged to the Whitsun movement and raised her with missionary zeal. While still at school, Winterson already began to distance herself from her parents' mindset. When, as a result of her first lesbian relationship, she was excluded from the community, she left home and attended St. Catherine's College in Oxford, financing her studies by doing odd jobs. In 1981 she graduated with a degree in English. Today Winterson lives in London.

In her debut novel of 1985 »Oranges Are Not the Only Fruit«, there are clear traces of irony and satire in Winterson's telling of the story of her childhood and youth. The novel received the renowned Whitbread Award and was filmed as a television series by the BBC in 1990. The novel »Oranges« is the first in what became a loose cycle of successful and in part prizewinning stories on love and other passions. In 1992 she became known internationally with her novel »Written on the Body«, which has been translated into 16 languages. Winterson has also written short stories, essays and screenplays, as well as the children's book »The King of Capri« (2001), which will be published in Germany in 2003 under the title »Der König von Capri«.

A simple and unusually light language characterises Winterson's work, which despite an occasionally almost careless undertone is able to communicate a wealth of feelings. With her humorous and witty stories that thrive on the experimental and are seldom governed by the limits of time and space, the author is reminiscent of Virginia Woolf. And like Woolf, whose works she edited anew together with her partner Margaret Reynolds, Winterson also breaks with traditional gender roles – not lastly through the emphasis she places on homoerotic relationships.

In »The Powerbook«, with which Winterson completed her prose cycle in 2000, cyberspace has become the playground for her literary fantasy. Taking a modern love triangle as the framework for her story, she explores the freedoms and dangers of the virtual cosmos.

Auf den Körper geschrieben
Fischer
Frankfurt a. M., 1992
[Ü: Stephanie Schaffer-de Vries]
Das Geschlecht der Kirsche
Fischer
Frankfurt a. M., 1993
[Ü: Brigitte Walitzek]
Kunst und Lügen
Berlin Verlag, Berlin, 1995
[Ü: Brigitte Walitzek]
In dieser Welt und anderswo
Berlin Verlag, Berlin, 2000
[Ü: Monika Schmalz]
Verlangen
BvT, Berlin, 2002
[Ü: Bettina Runge]
Orangen sind nicht die einzige Frucht
BvT, Berlin, 2002
[Ü: Brigitte Walitzek]
Das Powerbook
BvT, Berlin, 2003
[Ü: Monika Schmalz]

Jeanette Winterson wurde 1959 in Manchester, Großbritannien, geboren. Im nahegelegenen Accrington wuchs sie als Adoptivtochter eines Arbeiterpaars auf, das der Pfingstbewegung angehörte und sie mit missionarischem Eifer erzog. Winterson begann jedoch schon in ihrer Schulzeit, sich innerlich von den Vorstellungen ihrer Eltern zu distanzieren. Als sie wegen einer ersten lesbischen Beziehung aus der Gemeinde ausgeschlossen wurde, riss sie von zu Hause aus und ermöglichte sich mit Gelegenheitsarbeiten ein Anglistik-Studium am St. Catherine's College in Oxford, das sie 1981 abschloss. Winterson lebt heute in London.

In ihrem Debüt »Oranges Are Not the Only Fruit« von 1985 (dt. »Orangen sind nicht die einzige Frucht«, 1993) erzählt Winterson auf zum Teil ironische und satirisch überzogene Weise die Geschichte ihrer eigenen Kindheit und Jugend. Der Roman wurde mit dem renommierten Whitbread Award ausgezeichnet und 1990 von der BBC als Fernsehserie verfilmt. Die »Orangen« bilden den Auftakt zu einem losen Zyklus von zum Teil preisgekrönten Erzählungen über Liebe und andere Leidenschaften, an dem die Autorin seither erfolgreich gearbeitet hat. International machte sie dabei 1992 mit ihrem Roman »Written on the Body« (dt. »Auf den Körper geschrieben«, 1993) von sich reden, der in sechzehn Sprachen übersetzt wurde. Darüber hinaus hat Winterson Kurzgeschichten, Essays und Drehbücher verfasst sowie das Kinderbuch »The King of Capri« (2001), das 2003 unter dem Titel »Der König von Capri« auf Deutsch erscheint.

Charakteristisch für Wintersons Werke ist eine weitgehend schmuck- und schwerelose Sprache, die es trotz eines bisweilen fast saloppen Untertons vermag, große Gefühle zu vermitteln. Mit ihren humorvollen, geistreichen und von immenser Experimentierfreude geprägten Geschichten, die vor den Grenzen von Zeit und Raum nur selten Halt machen, erinnert die Autorin an Virginia Woolf. Und wie Woolf, deren Werke sie zusammen mit ihrer Lebensgefährtin Margaret Reynolds neu ediert hat, löst auch sie sich von den traditionellen Geschlechterrollen – nicht zuletzt durch die Betonung homoerotischer Beziehungen.

In »The Powerbook« (dt. »Das Powerbook«, 2001), mit dem Jeanette Winterson im Jahr 2000 ihren Prosazyklus vollendet hat, ist es der Cyberspace, der zum Schauplatz der schriftstellerischen Phantasie wird. Im Rahmen einer modernen Dreiecksgeschichte lotet sie hier die Freiheiten und Gefahren im virtuellen Kosmos aus.

saadi youssef

biography

The poet Saadi Youssef was born in the vicinity of Basra, Iraq, in 1934. In 1948, the year in which the state of Israel was founded, young intellectuals broke with classical Arabic literary tradition and introduced free verse into Arabic poetry. This new style spread, unstoppable like the desert winds, and influenced the ensuing generation of writers, which also included Youssef.
He studied Arabic literature in Bagdad. He later had to leave the country repeatedly due to his political involvement – a fate he shared with the majority of Iraq's intellectuals. In the late 70's when Saddam Hussein came to power, Saadi Youssef left Bagdad for good. Today, after years of exile in various countries, he lives in London.
Youssef was influenced by the most important poets of the »free verse« movement, the Iraqis Badr Shakir as-Sayyab and Abdalwahab al-Bayati, who wanted to give poetry a strong position at the phalanx of the progressive, revolutionary powers. In the 50's and 60's Youssef wrote political poetry and, like Mahmud Darwish and Amal Dunqul, could claim to be a people's poet. He sympathized with the anti-imperialist movement, which at the time convened as socialist and communist parties.
In the second half of the 70's he stopped writing political verse. His poems became increasingly like a Zen-Koan: full of secrets and yet so simple. Like in the children's game »I spy with my little eye…« he speaks about things of an apparently everyday nature and in doing so, gets at the things behind the things.
Youssef's language, which is characterised by lyrical realism, is stunningly authentic and direct. As a translator into Arabic of works by Oktay Rifat, Melih Cevdet Anday, Garcia Lorca, Jannis Ritsos, Walt Whitman and above all Konstantin Kavafis, he feels a close connection to these poets of world literature. Saadi Youssef is an artist who – given no choice – has taken to the seas and not once cast anchor in his native country. Perpetual longing accompanies him on his travels, the topic of exile and migration is omnipresent: »The pole lost its guiding star – but my distant home still awaits me.«
Today Saadi Youssef speaks, shortly after the end of the Iraq War, in a forthright way about the political future: »We must still, it seems to me, brace ourselves for a possible series of shock waves in the aftermath of the recent seismic upheavals in Iraq.« What makes his poetry so fascinating is that despite the oppressive political reality, it is surprisingly light.

What makes the poet tick?

Surprising …

Often the term "surprising" is associated with poetry and what poetry evokes. The expression has arrested my attention for a long time and made me recall a verse of al-Muraqqish the Younger:

They were adorned with sappires, set gems and gilt
With onyx of Zufar and twinned pearls

The women of al-Muraqqish the Younger, those adorned beauties, how did they stand out for us in their glorious halo of art? The women of Saint-John Perse and Rilke, how did they reach us?
Al-Muraqqish al-Asghar said nothing more than naming things. They were things we know, but the poet placed them in front of us in such a way as to see them for the first time. He granted us color and form. He provided us with delightful touches and wide-open eyes, and he invited us through touching and seeing to enter into an imaginative universe which we would have never been able to enter without him, without that surprise pouring in front of us like colored rain.
The senses, therefore, are the targets of the poet's spell. They are addressed because they receive; and because imaginative and

Afkar Bi-Sawt Hadi
Dar al-Farabi, Beirut, 1972
Tahta gidariyyati Fa'iq Hasan
Dar al-Farabi, Beirut, 1974
Hanat al-qird al-mufakkir
Dar al-nahar, Beirut, 1997
Loin du premier ciel
Actes Sud, Paris, 1999
[Ü: Abdellatif Laâbi]
Without an alphabet, without a face
Graywolf Press
Saint Paul, 2002
[Ü: Khaled Mattawa]

Der Dichter Saadi Youssef wurde 1934 in der Nähe von Basra, Irak, geboren. Im Jahr der israelischen Staatsgründung 1948 brachen junge Literaten mit der klassischen arabischen Dichtungstradition und führten den »free verse« in die arabische Literatur ein. Unaufhaltsam wie der Wüstenwind verbreitete sich dieser neue Stil und prägte die folgende Dichtergeneration, der auch Youssef angehört.
Er studierte arabische Literatur in Bagdad. Später musste er aufgrund seines politischen Engagements wiederholt das Land verlassen – ein Schicksal, das er mit der Mehrheit der irakischen Intelligenzia teilte. Ende der siebziger Jahre, als Saddam Hussein an die Macht kam, verließ Saadi Youssef Bagdad endgültig. Heute lebt er, nach jahrelanger Odyssee durch arabische Exilorte, in London.
Geprägt wurde Youssef von den bedeutendsten Lyrikern der »free verse« Bewegung, den Irakern Badr Shakir as-Sayyab und Abdalwahab al-Bayati, die der Dichtung eine starke Position in der Phalanx der progressiven, revolutionären Kräfte geben wollten. Youssefs Gedichte waren in den fünfziger und sechziger Jahren von politischem Engagement gezeichnet; wie Mahmud Darwish oder Amal Dunqul vertrat er den Anspruch, als Dichter für das Volk einzutreten. Er stand der anti-imperialistischen Bewegung nahe, die sich seinerzeit in sozialistischen und kommunistischen Parteien sammelte.
In der zweiten Hälfte der siebziger Jahre wandte er sich von der politischen Dichtung ab. Immer mehr glichen seine Verse einem Zen-Koan: voller Geheimnis und doch so einfach. Wie im Kinderspiel »Ich sehe was, was du nicht siehst« spricht er über scheinbar Alltägliches und meint damit die Dinge hinter den Dingen.
Youssefs von lyrischem Realismus gekennzeichnete Sprache ist verblüffend authentisch und direkt. Als Übersetzer der Werke von Oktay Rifat, Melih Cevdet Anday, Garcia Lorca, Jannis Ritsos, Walt Whitman und vor allem Konstantin Kavafis ins Arabische fühlt er sich diesen Dichtern der Weltliteratur stark verbunden. Saadi Youssef ist ein Künstler, der – zwangsläufig – die Meere bereist, ohne den Anker in seiner Heimat je gelichtet zu haben. Ständige Sehnsucht begleitet ihn auf seinen Reisen, das Thema von Exil und Migration ist allgegenwärtig: »der Pol hat den Leitstern verloren – doch mein fernes Zuhause wartet noch immer auf mich.«
Saadi Youssef spricht heute, kurz nach Ende des Irakkriegs, mit schonungsloser Einsicht über die politische Zukunft: »Mir scheint, wir müssen uns auf eine mögliche Serie von Druckwellen gefasst machen, die in der Folge des letzten Bebens im Irak auf uns zukommen.« Was seine Dichtung so faszinierend macht, ist, dass sie trotz der erdrückenden politischen Realität von einer erstaunlichen Leichtigkeit ist.

isionary elements go first through the senses
nd then continue their trajectory towards
he subsequent artistic operation ; that is the
econd half of the operation which is related
o the reader – the reader who will pick
p the elements and rearrange them after
is inclination and level.
Where, then, is the surprise in this?
think the surprise is in the elements of
eality and the things selected by the poet-
he raw material (the elements and the
hings) addresses the senses by alluding and
ot through declarations ; that is, the
elationship between the person and the
orld is returned to its beginning, to its
tarting point, to its sudden truth.
n the table in front of me there is a paper,
matchbox, an ashtray and a cigarette.
here are four things in front of me, and
t is up to me to play. These four things
have their familiar conventional order.

You forget the paper ; you light the cigarette with a match stick ; you smoke, then you put the cigarette in the ashtray. This is what we do daily. but it is up to me to play, to change the familiar conventional order, to make my poem diverge, differ and at the same time I must conserve the keys for me and the reader my keys are the things. Thus I shall take out a cigarette from its pack and light it with a match stick, but I shall not put it, lit, in the ashtray. I shall bring in the paper in the scene and put the lit cigarette on the paper, leaving things to interact outside the familiar context.
I leave them to interact in the alchemy of poetry.

Saadi Yousef
London 18.05.03

zhang jie
biography

Zhang Jie was born in Peking, China in 1937. She was the daughter of an elementary school teacher and grew up without a father. Contrary to her hopes, she was assigned a degree-course place in Planning Studies rather than Literature at the People's University of Peking. After concluding her studies in 1960, she worked for almost 20 years at the ministry of industry for mechanical engineering. Because she was the daughter of a »right winger«, she was forced to participate in re-educational measures at a special school from 1969 to 1972. It was at this time that she also began to write. Only after the Cultural Revolution (1966–67) did she publish her first story »Die Musik der Wälder« (1978), which won the national prize for best short story. In 1979 she received the national literature prize for »Wer hat mehr vom Leben«. In the same year she became a member of the Chinese Association of Writers. In 1980 she joined the Chinese Communist Party. She has worked as a freelance writer since 1982. In the same year her novel »Schwere Flügel« appeared in the German translation. In 1984 for »Die Voraussetzungen sind noch nicht reif« she received the literature prize of the renowned magazine »Beijing wenxue«. In 1985 she participated in the »Horizonte-Festival« in Berlin and in 1987 received a scholarship to write and reside in Vienna for six months. Thereafter she traveled extensively in Europe and held numerous readings. For »Zwei Liebeserzählungen« she received the Malaparte Literature Prize.

In her stories the author reflects on the radical changes brought about by modernization, and especially on how life has changed for women in her country. Characteristic of the way her writing has developed is the change from the gentle lyrical voice of her first stories to a cruder tone, which even sounds satirical when thematizing the various manifestations of the phenomenon of power. Her most recent publication was the novel »Abschied von der Mutter«, which is about the last months Zhang Jies spent with her mother. The author herself calls the novel »a love story between mother and daughter,« – at the same time it is a critical mirror image of the social changes in China. The author is one of her country's best-known writers. Today she lives in Peking and works for the »Chinese Writers' Association«.

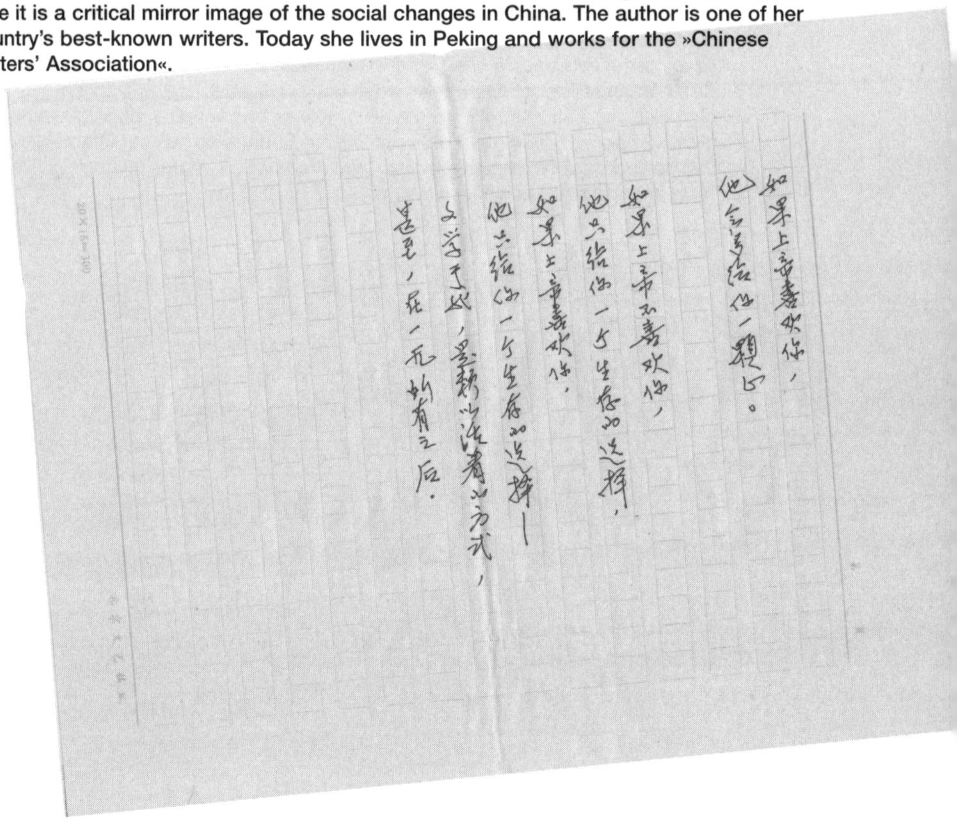

如果上帝喜欢你，
他会给你一颗心。
如果上帝不喜欢你，
他只给你一个生存的选择，
如果上帝喜欢你，
他只给你一个生存的选择——
文学于我，是赖以活着的方式，
甚至，死，[illegible]有之后.

Schwere Flügel
Aufbau, Berlin, 1982
[Ü: Michael Kahn-Ackermann]
Solange nichts passiert, geschieht auch nichts
dtv, München, 1989
[Ü: Michael Kahn-Ackermann]
Zwei Liebeserzählungen
Fischer
Frankfurt a. M., 1990
[Ü: Claudia Magiera]
Abschied von der Mutter
Unionsverlag, Zürich, 2000
[Ü: Eva Müller]

Zhang Jie wurde 1937 in Peking, China, geboren. Sie wuchs ohne den Vater bei ihrer Mutter, einer Volksschullehrerin, auf und wurde entgegen ihrer Hoffnung auf ein Studium der Literatur, dem Studium der Planungswissenschaften an der Volksuniversität Peking zugeteilt. Nach dem Abschluss 1960 arbeitete sie fast zwanzig Jahre lang im Industrieministerium für Maschinenbau. Als Tochter eines »Rechten« musste sie sich von 1969 bis 1972 an einer Kaderschule Umerziehungsmaßnahmen beugen. In diesen Zeitraum fällt auch der Beginn ihres Schreibens. Erst lange nach der Kulturrevolution (1966-67), nämlich 1978, veröffentlichte sie ihre erste Erzählung »Die Musik der Wälder«, mit der sie den nationalen Preis für die beste Kurzgeschichte erhielt. 1979 folgte der Staatliche Literaturpreis für »Wer hat mehr vom Leben«. Im gleichen Jahr wurde sie Mitglied des chinesischen Schriftstellerverbandes. 1980 trat sie in die Kommunistische Partei Chinas ein. Seit 1982 ist sie freiberuflich tätig. Im gleichen Jahr erschien ihr Roman »Schwere Flügel« in deutscher Sprache. Für »Die Voraussetzungen sind noch nicht reif« wurde sie 1984 erneut ausgezeichnet, diesmal mit dem Literaturpreis der renommierten Zeitschrift »Beijing wenxue«. 1985 erhielt sie den wichtigsten chinesischen Literaturpreis, den Mao-Dun-Preis. Im selben Jahr nahm sie am »Horizonte-Festival« in Berlin teil. 1987 erhielt sie ein Stipendium für einen sechsmonatigen Schreibaufenthalt in Wien. Sie unternahm danach größere Reisen und Lesungen in ganz Europa. Das folgende Buch »Zwei Liebeserzählungen« (dt. 1987) wurde mit dem Malaparte-Literaturpreis ausgezeichnet. In ihren Geschichten reflektiert die Autorin die Umwälzungen der Modernisierung und besonders die veränderte Lebenssituation der Frauen in ihrem Land. Kennzeichnend für ihre literarische Entwicklung ist der Wechsel von einer sanften lyrischen Stimmung der ersten Erzählungen hin zu einem raueren Ton, der das Phänomen der Macht in seinen unterschiedlichen Erscheinungsformen auch in satirischem Tonfall thematisiert, z. B. in »Solange nichts passiert, geschieht auch nichts« (dt. 1987). Zuletzt erschien ihr Tatsachenroman »Abschied von der Mutter« (dt. 2000). Der Roman erzählt von den letzten gemeinsamen Monaten Zhang Jies mit ihrer Mutter. Die Autorin selbst nennt den Roman »eine Liebesgeschichte zwischen Mutter und Tochter«, die zugleich ein kritischer Spiegel des sozialen Wandels in China ist. Die Autorin gehört zu den bekanntesten Schriftstellerinnen ihres Landes. Sie lebt heute in Peking und arbeitet für die »Chinese Writers' Association«.

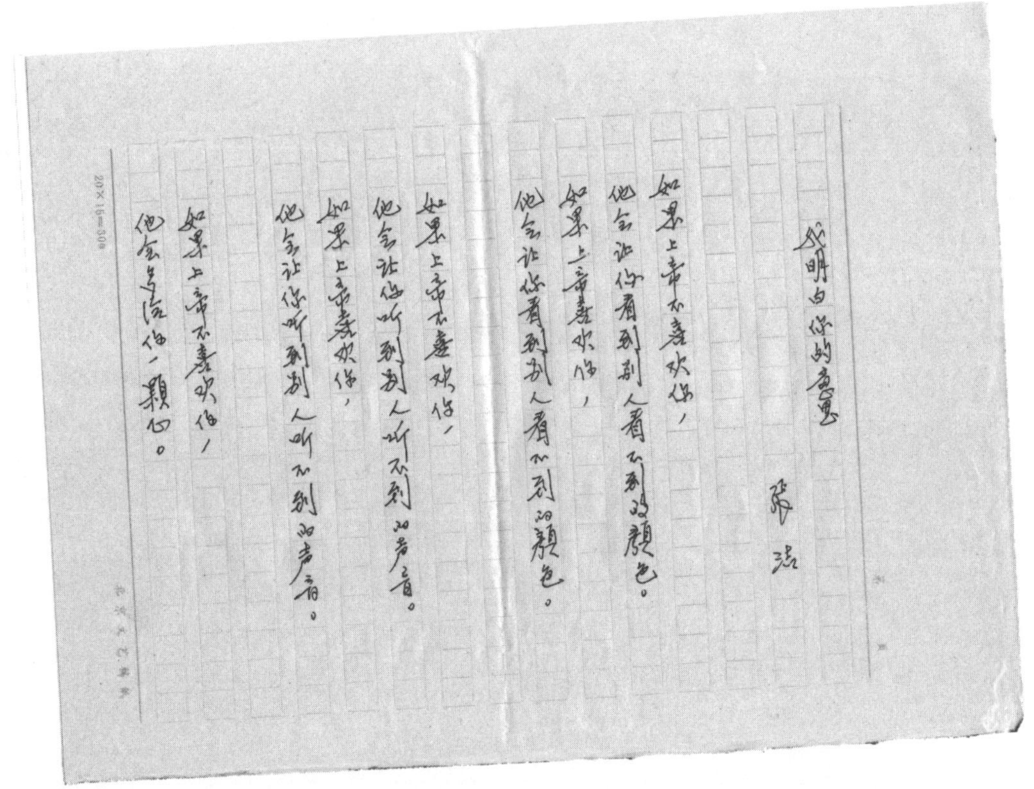
我明白你的意思

张洁

如果上帝不喜欢你，
他会让你看到别人看不到的颜色。
如果上帝喜欢你，
他会让你看到别人看不到的颜色。
如果上帝不喜欢你，
他会让你听到别人听不到的声音。
如果上帝喜欢你，
他会让你听到别人听不到的声音。
如果上帝不喜欢你，
他会给你一颗心。

samhita arni
azouz begag
jeanne benameur
melvin burgess
carolyn coman
miro gavran
klaus hagerup
heinz janisch
desa muck
veronica murguía
roberto piumini
notaila rashed
matthew sweeney
annika thor
eugene trivizas

samhita arni

biography

Samhita Arni, the daughter of a diplomat, was born in Madras, India, in 1984, and grew up in India, Indonesia, Pakistan and Thailand. Making lasting friendships was difficult, not only because her family was constantly moving, but also because of the tense political relations between Pakistan and India, which made carefree relationships with her classmates in Karachi, Pakistan almost impossible. Exclusion and antagonism were characteristic of her daily life as an Indian in Pakistan. Instead of meeting other children, Samhita Arni began reading Greek myths and occidental tales, most notably the innumerable versions of the two Indian national epic stories. Almost every child in India knows the stories of the Mahabharata and the Ramayana – be it from oral narrative, comic books or movies. The Mahabharata is considered the more significant and extensive, as well as the older of the two epics. It is a complex religious, philosophical and simultaneously literary work, which tells the tale of a feud between two related ruling families, of rival princes, humiliated princesses and all-powerful gods. One of its most famous stories is the Bhagavad-Gita, which has inspired the likes of Goethe, Nietzsche and Hesse.
When Samhita Arni returned to India at the age of eight, she used her remaining school holidays to start putting her own version of the famous epic into writing on pieces of paper, in notepads and in her diary. Following the suggestion of a publisher, she completed the collection of texts and pictures a few years later. »The Mahabharata. A Child's View« was published in two volumes in 1996 – the result of an encounter between ancient subject matter and an Indian girl living in the present.
Samhita Arni »feel[s] that the real message of the Mahabharata has to do with war. It tells us that war is futile«. It is with this in mind that she rewrote the epic. The omissions and the decision to add particular episodes lie in a deep understanding of the characters and the overall plot. Thus Arni's serious and simple language and the alternately beautiful and grotesque characters complement each other in a unique way.
In 1999 the German translation was published in the children's book series BAOBAB and, like the original, was accompanied by a dictionary and a family tree of the characters and gods. Samhita Arni's debut has already been translated into numerous languages and has received multiple awards, including from the German Academy for Children's and Young Adults' Literature Volkach, and the first prize in the National Level Art Competition in Thailand. The author is studying film and religious studies in Massachusetts, USA.

What makes the poet tick?

Das Mahâbhârata. Von einem Mädchen erzählt (ab 8) Nagel & Kimche Zürich, 1999 [Ü: Heike Brandt]

The source of the poet's ability, in my opinion, is the same as that of the artist, the composer, the writer, or even – in modern terms – the sensitive film-maker, the intelligent cartoonist. This isn't a unique observation, many of us – some of us who consider ourselves belonging to that broad category called artists, or those of us who appreciate art; (most of the human population belongs one way or the other to one of the above categories) – have pondered on the origin of a masterpiece; the spring of imagination that directed the artist. Or say, even a computer game or programme that crosses the boundaries of the familiar, can be the subject of such thoughts. Then – is it imagination that makes the poet tick? Perhaps, but familiar and common subjects have been rendered poetic by the master craftsman. Is it the ability to convey in unique and original terms, something common to human experience? Maybe, or maybe not. Is it the aesthetic quality of the product? Possibly, but then there is a lot of bad, or rather 'unappreciated', art, literature and poetry out there – whose creators

Samhita Arni wurde 1984 in Madras, Indien, geboren und wuchs als Tochter eines Diplomaten in Indien, Indonesien, Pakistan und Thailand auf. Dauerhafte Freundschaften zu schließen, war für die heranwachsende Autorin nicht nur wegen des stetigen Reisens ihrer Familie schwierig. Die angespannten politischen Verhältnisse zwischen Indien und Pakistan bestimmten ihren Aufenthalt in Karachi, Pakistan, und machten einen unbeschwerten Umgang mit Klassenkameraden beinahe unmöglich. Zurückweisung und Feindseligkeit prägten ihren Lebensalltag als Inderin in Pakistan. Anstatt sich mit anderen Kindern zu treffen, begann Samhita Arni griechische Mythen und abendländische Märchen, vor allem aber die zahllosen Versionen der beiden indischen Nationalepen zu lesen. Fast jedes Kind in Indien kennt die Geschichten des Mahâbhârata und des Ramâyâna – ob aus Nacherzählungen, Comicheften oder Verfilmungen. Das Mahâbhârata gilt als das bedeutendere, umfangreichere und ältere der beiden Epen. Es ist ein komplexes religiöses, philosophisches und zugleich literarisches Werk, das vom Streit zweier verwandter Herrscherfamilien erzählt, von verfeindeten Prinzen, gedemütigten Prinzessinnen und allmächtigen Göttern. Zu seinen berühmtesten Erzählungen gehört die Bhagavadgita, die schon Goethe, Nietzsche und Hesse inspirierte.
Als sie im Alter von acht Jahren nach Indien zurückkehrte, nutzte Samhita Arni die verbleibende Ferienzeit, indem sie ihre eigene Fassung des berühmten Epos schrittweise auf Zetteln, in Notizbüchern und ihrem Tagebuch aufzuzeichnen begann. Auf Anregung einer Verlegerin vervollständigte sie die Sammlung von Texten und Bildern einige Jahre später. 1996 erschien »The Mahâbhâratha. A Child's View« in zwei Bänden – entstanden aus der Begegnung eines indischen Mädchens von heute mit einem uralten Stoff.
Für Samhita Arni »hat die wirkliche Aussage des Mahâbhârata etwas mit Krieg zu tun. Sie besagt, dass Krieg sinnlos ist.« In diesem Verständnis hat sie das Epos neu verfasst. Ihre Kürzungen und die Entscheidung, bestimmte Episoden hinzuzufügen, wurzeln in einem tiefen Gespür für die Figuren und den Gesamtzusammenhang. Dabei ergänzen sich Arnis ernste und karge Sprache und die abwechselnd schönen und grotesken Figuren auf einzigartige Weise.
1999 erschien die deutsche Übersetzung in der Kinderbuchreihe BAOBAB, wie das Original ergänzt um ein Wörterbuch und einen Stammbaum der Figuren und Gottheiten. Samhita Arnis Debüt wurde bereits in mehrere Sprachen übersetzt und vielfach ausgezeichnet, u. a. 1999 von der Deutschen Akademie für Kinder- und Jugendliteratur Volkach sowie mit dem ersten Preis der National Level Art Competition in Thailand. Die Autorin studiert Film- und Religionswissenschaften in Massachusetts, USA.

deem themselves poets or artists - and is fair to repudiate their claims to the artistic simply because of the lack of appreciation? Is it simply the ability to create, as Joyce suggested? Maybe it is all of these things, and maybe it is none of them.
Part of the difficulty in answering this question lies in what one considers poetry - what sets it apart from other arts, if such an exclusive definition can be arrived at. In this modern age when formerly rock-hard conventions are thrown to the winds, and conformity eschewed, I'd (personally, not being able to consider myself 'rightfully' a poet or artist) prefer to think of poetry as a sort of human quality. There are moments of the day that appear poetic, certain objects in a particular mix of light and shadow achieve the poetic, shadings of thought and emotion that verge on the poetic. The poetic - as such - is something that is universal to the human species - it isn't the sole property of one caste, occupation or priesthood who achieve their position by ability or inclination. So what is poetry? If someone can tell me, perhaps I can arrive at a more decisive conclusion.

azouz begag

biography

Azouz Begag, the son of an Algerian »guestworker«, was born in 1957 in Villeurbanne, near Lyon. He has a PhD in economics and is currently working as a sociologist in Paris and Lyon. Alongside his academic research, which focuses on the mobility and identity of immigrants, he has published highly acclaimed novels for children, young people and adults. His literary work has been well received by critics and the public in France and Germany and is often an integral part of regional studies curricula used for French classes in schools.

In 1986 Begag became the best-known representative of »littérature beure« with the publication of his first, autobiographically inclined novel, »Le gône du chaâba«, in which he describes a boy's childhood in a »slum-like« suburb of Lyon. In the eighties, literary texts, theatre plays and musical pieces written by »Beurs«, young people of North African origin who grew up in France, articulated the outlook on life shared by this second generation of immigrants, whose integration still poses a contentious problem in contemporary French society. Begag's first novel focuses on belonging to two cultures and the double identity that results from an affiliation to a distant, unknown homeland and a new, unfamiliar country. The author colourfully depicts the »guestworker« child Azouz's efforts to be accepted in his own country. The adolescent Azouz has to fight against the isolation, which he experiences on the one hand on account of his intelligence, causing him to distance himself from the milieu of his illiterate parents and their Arabic family traditions, and on the other hand because his fellow pupils constantly make him aware of the stigma related to his North African origin. Begag by no means places emphasis »on pity and sentimentality, but rather on the subversive power of humour, by exposing comic and exact detail« (»Neue Zürcher Zeitung«). »Le gône du chaâba« was awarded many prizes including the French journalists' prize, Prix du meilleur roman in 1986. The film, directed by Christophe Ruggia, was shown at the Berlinale in 1998.

The politically active author views his writing, journalism and academic work as building blocks for a Franco-Maghrebian identity, and as a medium which can be used to mediate between the political elite in France and the reality in the immigrant quarters. In the sequel »Béni ou le paradis privé«, which was published in France in 1989, the emphasis is placed even more strongly on everyday racism in France, which begins long before the first steps to open violence are taken. The author lives in Paris.

Les voleurs d'écritures
(ab 10)
Seuil, Paris, 1990

Aber die Erde ist rund
(ab 10)
Beltz & Gelberg
Weinheim, 1993
[Ü: Ruth Subjetzki]

Quand on est mort, c'est pour toute la vie
Gallimard, Paris, 1994

Azouz, der Junge vom Stadtrand
(ab 10)
Nagel & Kimche
Zürich, 1998
[Ü: Regina Keil]

Fast überall
(ab 12)
Nagel & Kimche
Zürich, 2000
[Ü: Regina Keil]

Le passeport
Seuil, Paris, 2000

Le théorème de Mamadou
(ab 8)
Seuil, Paris, 2002

Azouz Begag wurde 1957 als Sohn eines algerischen Gastarbeiters bei Lyon geboren. Er promovierte in Wirtschaftswissenschaften und arbeitet heute als Soziologe in Paris und Lyon. Neben wissenschaftlichen Studien, in denen sich Begag mit der Mobilität und Identität von Immigranten beschäftigt, hat er vielbeachtete Romane für Kinder, Jugendliche und Erwachsene veröffentlicht. Seine literarischen Werke fanden sowohl in Frankreich als auch in Deutschland große Resonanz bei Kritik und Publikum und sind oft Bestandteil von Landeskundedossiers für den Französisch-Unterricht in der Schule.
1986 avancierte Begag mit seinem ersten – autobiographisch gefärbten – Jugendroman »Le gône du chaâba« (dt. »Azouz, der Junge vom Stadtrand«, 1998), in dem er dessen Kindheit in einer »slumartigen« Lyoner Vorstadtsiedlung beschreibt, zum bekanntesten Vertreter der »littérature beure«. In literarischen Texten, Theater- und Musikstücken der in Frankreich aufgewachsenen Jugendlichen nordafrikanischer Herkunft, der »Beurs«, artikulierte sich in den achtziger Jahren das Lebensgefühl dieser zweiten Einwanderergeneration, deren Integration noch immer ein »brennendes« Problem der französischen Gesellschaft darstellt. Begag thematisiert die Zugehörigkeit zu zwei Kulturen und die doppelte Identität zwischen einer fernen, unbekannten Heimat und einem neuen, wenig vertrauten Land. Anschaulich schildert der Autor die Mühen des »Gastarbeiter«-Kindes Azouz, im eigenen Land anzukommen. Der heranwachsende Azouz hat mit der Isolation zu kämpfen, die er erleidet, weil er sich einerseits durch seine Intelligenz dem Milieu seiner Eltern, die Analphabeten sind, sowie den arabischen Familiensitten entfremdet und er andererseits durch seine Mitschüler immer wieder das Stigma seiner nordafrikanischen Abstammung zu spüren bekommt. Dabei setzt Begag »nicht auf Mitleid und Larmoyanz, sondern auf die subversive Kraft des Humors, auf entlarvende Komik und Detailtreue« (»Neue Zürcher Zeitung«). »Le gône du chaâba« wurde mit zahlreichen Preisen ausgezeichnet, u. a. 1986 mit dem französischen Journalistenpreis »Prix du meilleur roman«. Die Verfilmung des Regisseurs Christophe Ruggia wurde 1998 auf der Berlinale präsentiert.
Der politisch engagierte Autor versteht seine schriftstellerische, journalistische und wissenschaftliche Arbeit als Bausteine einer franko-maghrebinischen Identität und als Möglichkeit, zwischen den politischen Eliten in Frankreich und der Realität in den Immigrantenvierteln zu vermitteln. In seinem Fortsetzungsroman »Béni ou le paradis privé« (dt. »Fast überall«, 2000), der 1989 in Frankreich erschien, richtet er den Fokus noch stärker auf den alltäglichen Rassismus in Frankreich, der nicht erst beginnt, wenn offen gehetzt und zur Gewalt geschritten wird. Der Autor lebt in Paris.

jeanne benameur

biography

Jeanne Benameur, the fourth child of an Italian mother and a Tunisian father, was born in Algeria in 1952 and grew up in the French coastal town of La Rochelle. Benameur began writing at the age of seven. After studies in Poitiers and a few years of teaching, her debut novel for adolescents »Samira des Quatre-Routes« was published in 1992. She was awarded the Grand Prix des Jeunes Lecteurs for the book in 1993. Since then she has published numerous books for young adults, of which two have also been translated into German.

»Quitte ta mère« (1998) is a touching tale about the adventure of growing up. Jeanne Benameur writes about thirteen year-old Bastien's decision to leave his single mother when, during his holidays, he notices that his ageing grandfather needs him more urgently. With the inner eye, she examines his current situation, which also changes because of Anne, whom he meets during his vacation. In a simple yet non-pathetic way, she documents the maturing process of her young protagonist and makes his thoughts, feelings, insecurities and fears transparent.

In the award-winning »Si même les arbres meurent« from 2000, the author dares to tackle a topic that is difficult not only for young people: the loss of a loved one. »With crystal clear, memorable sentences and deeply intense images Jeanne Benameur portrays the harmonious psycho-transference of the two siblings, who have become half-orphaned« (»Bulletin für Jugend& Literatur«). She sketches Mathieu and Celine's slow and painful parting from their father, who is lying in a coma after an accident in the mountains. Cautiously the author concedes insight into the secret dream world to which the two children flee and where their father is the unconquerable Native-American chieftain Big Eagle. The author interprets the existential experience of illness and death as full of magic. Her text breathes with metaphors and creates space to make one's own associations. »Si même les arbres meurent« was awarded the Prix Jeunes Lecteurs de Brives 2001, amongst others.

In recent years, Jeanne Benameur has also dedicated herself to adult literature. Her novel »Les Demeurées« was published in 2000 and was awarded the Prix UNICEF (2001). But the author does not plan on making a choice between adult and young people's literature. Jeanne Benameur, who also writes poems and plays, does not distinguish between genres. Her objective is to write »real« texts for readers of different ages. Jeanne Benameur has settled in Paris as a freelance writer.

Ce qui me met en route pour écrire, c'est l'émotion. Une émotion forte venue de ma vie ou de celle des autres dans le monde. Il faut qu'elle m'imprègne longtemps.

Souvent je ne peux pas clairement la nommer. Je n'en connais pas l'exacte forme.

J'en éprouve juste l'intensité Suffisante pour me mettre en écriture.

Le texte qui s'écrira alors sculptera sa forme. Je la découvrirai complètement quand j'aurai fini d'écrire.

Samira des Quatre-Routes
Flammarion, Paris, 1992
Les Demeurées
Denoël, Paris, 2000
Un jour mes princes sont venus
Denoël, Paris, 2001
Hinter dem Hafen das Meer
(ab 12)
Patmos, Düsseldorf, 2002
[Ü: Rosemarie Griebel-Kruip]
Großer Adler schläft nur
(ab 12)
Patmos, Düsseldorf, 2002
[Ü: Rosemarie Griebel-Kruip]
Ça t'apprendra à vivre
(ab 12)
Denoël, Paris, 2003

Jeanne Benameur wurde 1952 als viertes Kind einer italienischen Mutter und eines tunesischen Vaters in Algerien geboren und wuchs in der französischen Küstenstadt La Rochelle auf. Benameur begann bereits im Alter von sieben Jahren zu schreiben. Nach ihrem Literaturstudium in Poitiers und einigen Berufsjahren als Lehrerin erschien 1992 ihr Debütroman »Samira des Quatre-Routes«, ein Roman für Heranwachsende, für den sie 1993 mit dem Grand Prix des Jeunes Lecteurs ausgezeichnet wurde. Seitdem hat sie zahlreiche Jugendbücher veröffentlicht, von denen zwei auch in deutscher Übersetzung vorliegen.
»Quitte ta mère« (dt. »Hinter dem Hafen das Meer«, 2002) von 1998 ist die berührende Erzählung vom Abenteuer erwachsen zu werden. Jeanne Benameur erzählt von der Lebensentscheidung des dreizehnjährigen Bastien, seine alleinerziehende Mutter zu verlassen, als er während eines Ferienaufenthalts spürt, dass sein alternder Großvater ihn dringender braucht. Mit dem inneren Auge durchleuchtet sie Bastiens Lebenssituation, die sich auch durch Anne verändert, die er während seines Ferienaufenthalts kennenlernt. Schlicht und unpathetisch dokumentiert sie den Reifungsprozess ihres jugendlichen Protagonisten und macht dessen Gedanken, Gefühle, Unsicherheiten und Ängste transparent.
Im preisgekrönten »Si même les arbres meurent« (dt. »Großer Adler schläft nur«, 2002) aus dem Jahr 2000 wagt sich die Autorin an ein nicht nur für Jugendliche schwieriges Thema: den Verlust eines geliebten Menschen. »Mit kristallklaren, einprägsamen Sätzen und Bildern von großer Intensität zeichnet Jeanne Benameur ein stimmiges Psychogramm zweier Geschwister, die zu Halbwaisen werden« (»Bulletin für Jugend&Literatur«). Sie skizziert den langsamen und schmerzhaften Abschied der Geschwister Mathieu und Celine von ihrem Vater, der nach einem Unfall im Koma liegt. Behutsam gewährt die Autorin Einblick in die geheime Traumwelt, in die sich die beiden Kinder flüchten und in der ihr Vater der unbesiegbare Indianerhäuptling Großer Adler ist. Die Autorin interpretiert die existentielle Erfahrung von Krankheit und Tod voller Magie. Ihr Text atmet durch seine Metaphern und schafft Raum für eigene Assoziationen. »Si même les arbres meurent« wurde u. a. 2001 mit dem Prix Jeunes Lecteurs de Brives prämiert.
In den letzten Jahren hat sich Jeanne Benameur verstärkt auch der Erwachsenenliteratur gewidmet. Ihr Roman »Les Demeurées« erschien 2000 und wurde 2001 mit dem Prix UNICEF (2001) ausgezeichnet. Eine Entscheidung zwischen Jugendbuch und Erwachsenenliteratur aber wird es für die Autorin nicht geben. Jeanne Benameur, die auch Gedichte und Theaterstücke verfasst, trennt nicht zwischen den Genres. Ihr Anliegen ist es, »wahre Texte« für Leser verschiedener Altersstufen zu schreiben. Benameur hat sich als freie Schriftstellerin in Paris niedergelassen.

Chaque texte est pour moi cette expérience renouvelée. A chaque texte, je m'approche un peu plus de territoires que je ne connaissais pas précisément à l'intérieur de moi. De tout être humain, puisque nous sommes semblables.

Des mots sont là pour donner forme à ce qui ne se nomme pas. Il y faut beaucoup de silence. Alors, le souffle.

C'est cette aventure qui me fait écrire.

melvin burgess
biography

Melvin Burgess was born in London, Great Britain in 1954 and is one of the most prolific and most widely discussed British authors of young people's fiction. He grew up in Sussex and Surrey, moved to Bristol after he had finished school and later to London and spent fifteen years experimenting with writing. He completed a training course in journalism and had numerous casual jobs before publishing his first book for young adults »The Cry of the Wolf«, which was immediately nominated for the Carnegie Medal (1991).
Melvin Burgess writes challenging novels for young people. Honestly, relentlessly and humorously he tackles sensitive topics. His literature offers no easy answers. He leaves his readers agitated and responsible for making their own verdicts and decisions. His style remains close to the adolescents about whom and for whom he writes. His gripping and fast tales are both entertainment and a warning, for example his socio-realistic novel for young adults »Junk« (1996) with which Burgess became known as a Brit-Pop author in Germany in 1999. In 1997, the remarkable story about homeless, drug-addicted youths in Bristol was awarded the Guardian Children's Fiction Award and the Carnegie Medal. In an open yet sensitive way, Burgess captures the way of life of Gemma and Tar who run away from home, become junkies and nearly lose control of their lives. No less shocking and persuasive is Burgess' Shakespearian, utopian, fantastical novel »Bloodtide« (1999), which is based on the Icelandic Völsungen saga and tells a tale of love and betrayal, deceit, revenge and the pitfalls of hubris.
While his books have won numerous awards and are read eagerly by youths, critics and adult readers do not infrequently react to his openness with skeptisism. He himself points out that there is not enough literature for older youths which tackles their questions – questions that they find important and exciting. In his novel for teenagers »Lady. My life as a Bitch«, published in 2001, he tells the story of the phantasmagoric dual identity of a seventeen year-old who is turned into a dog and who starts to exploit her newly won freedom, while simultaneously reflecting self-critically on her previous life as a human. The offensive depiction of sexuality provided much food for discussion. Burgess views his novel as »a comic allegory about sex and life – and all the important, darker issues that some people can't handle teenagers reading about.«
Burgess' latest publication is his novel for young adults »Doing It«. This »Burgess« also encourages us to reconsider the genre »young people's literature«. »The Ghost behind the Wall« and »Billy Elliot«, the novel adapted for the film by Stephen Daldry, are two of his books for younger readers and are just as warm-heartedly and vividly told as his novels for young adults. The author lives with his family in Manchester.

Die letzten Wölfe
(ab 14)
Rowohlt, Reinbek, 1993
Junk
(ab 16)
Fischer
Frankfurt a. M., 1999
[Ü: Heike Brandt]
Schlachten
(ab 14)
Carlsen, Hamburg, 2000
[Ü: Heike Brandt]
Billy Elliot
(ab 11)
Ravensburger
Ravensburg, 2001
[Ü: Heike Brandt]
Das Geheimnis im Schacht
. (ab 11)
Carlsen, Hamburg, 2003
[Ü: Heike Brandt]
Hundsfrau
(ab 14)
Carlsen, Hamburg, 2003
[Ü: Heike Brandt]
Doing it
(ab 16)
Andersen Press
London, 2003

Melvin Burgess wurde 1954 in London, Großbritannien, geboren und ist einer der profiliertesten und meistdiskutierten britischen Jugendbuchautoren. Aufgewachsen in Sussex und Surrey, zog er nach seinem Schulabschluss nach Bristol, später nach London, und widmete sich fünfzehn Jahre lang auf experimentelle Weise dem Schreiben. Er absolvierte eine Journalistenausbildung und nahm Gelegenheitsjobs an, bevor 1990 mit »The Cry of the Wolf« (dt. »Die letzten Wölfe«, 1993) sein erstes Jugendbuch publiziert und sogleich für die Carnegie Medal (1991) nominiert wurde.

Melvin Burgess schreibt herausfordernde Romane für junge Menschen. Ehrlich, schonungslos und humorvoll greift er heikle Themen auf. Seine Literatur bietet keine einfachen Antworten. Sie lässt seine Leser aufgewühlt zurück, aber doch versehen mit Anhaltspunkten dafür, eigene Urteile und Entscheidungen zu treffen. In seinem Erzählstil bleibt Burgess den Heranwachsenden nahe, über die und für die er schreibt. Seine fesselnden und temporeichen Romane sind Unterhaltung und Warnung zugleich, so auch sein »sozialrealistischer« Jugendroman »Junk« (1996), mit dem Burgess 1999 als Brit-Pop-Autor in Deutschland bekannt wurde. Bereits 1997 wurde die bemerkenswerte Geschichte um drogenabhängige und heimatlose Jugendliche in Bristol mit dem Guardian Children's Fiction Award und der Carnegie Medal ausgezeichnet. Offen und sensibel fängt Burgess das Lebensgefühl von Gemma und Tar ein, die von Zuhause abhauen, zu Junkies werden und die Kontrolle über ihr Leben zu verlieren drohen. Nicht minder schockierend und überzeugend ist Burgess' shakespearehafter, utopisch-phantastischer Jugendroman »Bloodtide« von 1999 (dt. »Schlachten«, 2000), der auf der isländischen Völsungen-Saga basiert und von Liebe und Verrat, Täuschung, Rache und den Fallstricken menschlicher Hybris erzählt.

Vielfach ausgezeichnet und von seinen jugendlichen Lesern begeistert gelesen, begegnen Kritik und erwachsene Leser Burgess' Offenheit nicht selten skeptisch. Er selbst weist darauf hin, dass es nicht genügend Literatur für ältere Jugendliche gebe, in der ihre Fragen aufgegriffen werden – Fragen, die für sie wichtig und aufregend sind. In seinem 2001 erschienenen Jugendroman »Lady. My Life as a Bitch« (dt. »Hundsfrau«, 2003) erzählt er von der phantastischen Doppelidentität einer Siebzehnjährigen, die in einen Hund verwandelt wird und ihre neu gewonnene Freiheit auszuleben beginnt, aber auch ihre Lebenssituation als Mensch selbstkritisch reflektiert. Die offensive Darstellung von Sexualität hat für Diskussionen gesorgt. Burgess sieht seinen Roman als »ein humorvolles Gleichnis über die Sexualität und das Leben – und all' die wichtigen und schwierigen Aspekte des Lebens, über die sich viele Erwachsene mit ihren heranwachsenden Kindern nicht austauschen wollen«.

Zuletzt erschien Burgess' Jugendroman »Doing it« (2003). Auch dieser »Burgess« regt an, das Genre »Jugendbuch« neu zu überdenken. Mit »The Ghost behind the Wall« (dt. »Das Geheimnis im Schacht«, 2003) und »Billy Elliot« (dt. »Billy Elliot. I will dance«, 2001), dem Roman zum Film von Stephen Daldry, legte er Bücher für jüngere Leser vor – ebenso warmherzig und plastisch erzählt wie seine Romane für junge Erwachsene. Der Autor lebt mit seiner Familie in Manchester.

What makes the poet tick?

I have no idea, none whatsoever – but I do believe that anyone who becomes interested in anything is a poet in their own way.

Melvin Burgess

carolyn coman

biography

»All I ever really wanted to do was write my own books«, says Carolyn Coman. That she began writing for children and young adults was more of a coincidence: »I found out that I write for children and teens by accident, only after I'd written stories and a novel that were about (and from the point of view of) children.« Her teachers had an especially strong influence on her, persuading her to reflect on what she was reading and writing and thus, from an early age, she nurtured her gift of careful observation and her ability to put feelings into words. Coman, who was born in Evanston, Illinois in 1951, and who studied at Hampshire College in Amherst, Massachusetts, had always felt the need to work with books. For many years she worked as a bookbinder and then as an editor at an educational publisher. In 1993 she drew attention to herself as an author with the publication of her debut novel »Tell me Everything«. Since then, she has been writing for adolescents and young adults. In 1995 »What Jamie Saw« followed, a forceful book about fear and the retrieval of trust and wellbeing, told from the point of view of nine year-old Jamie, whose mother has to flee from her violent partner with Jamie and his little sister.

With much empathy and courage, Carolyn Coman writes about painful upheavals experienced while growing up as an adolescent. This is also the case in her latest novel for young adults »Many Stones« (2000), which will be published in 2004 in German translation and which tells the tale of sixteen year-old Berry Morgan and her father. On a trip to South Africa, both of them try to work through their mutual past. Carolyn Coman specialises in writing between the lines, with a psychological depth that delicately depicts her characters. Her texts deal with extreme situations and borderline experiences – violence, death, alienation, speechlessness – which go so far as to intrude on daily (family) life. »I am very interested in how people (especially young people) respond to, and figure out, the complications of their lives. I am interested in the emotional journeys that involve moving out of the darkness and into the light.«

Coman's novels have received many awards, for example »What Jamie Saw« was awarded the John Newbery Honor Award (1996) and »Many Stones« the Michael L. Printz Honor Award (2001). Both books were nominated for the National Book Award. Besides her work as an author, Carolyn Coman teaches in the Writing for Children Programme at Vermont College, and is a freelance editor for Front Street Books. She is married to publisher Stephen Roxburgh, and the mother of two children. Carolyn Coman lives in Sout Hampton, New Hampshire and Ashville, North Carolina.

Nur ein einziges Zeichen
(ab 12)
Fischer
Frankfurt a. M., 1998
[Ü: Bernhard Regen]

Bee and Jacky
Front Street
Asheville/North Carolina
1998

In sicherer Ferne
(ab 12)
Sauerländer
Aarau; Frankfurt a. M.
Salzburg, 1999
[Ü: Cornelia Krutz-Arnold]

Many Stones
(ab 14)
Front Street
Asheville/North Carolina
2000

»Bücher zu schreiben war genau das, was ich wirklich immer tun wollte«, sagt Carolyn Coman. Dass sie dies für Kinder und Jugendliche tut, ist eher ein Produkt des Zufalls: »Erst als ich ganz beiläufig bemerkte, dass ich Geschichten und Romane über und aus der Sicht von Kindern und Jugendlichen geschrieben hatte, stellte ich fest, dass ich auch für junge Leser schreibe.« Vor allem von ihren Lehrern beeinflusst, die sie dazu anhielten, über Gelesenes und Geschriebenes nachzudenken, schulte sie früh ihre genaue Beobachtungsgabe und ihre Fähigkeit, Gefühle behutsam in Worte zu kleiden. Coman, die 1951 in Evanston, Illinois, geboren wurde und am Hampshire College in Amherst, Massachusetts, studierte, war es schon früh ein Bedürfnis, mit Büchern umzugehen, und arbeitete viele Jahre als Buchbinderin und Lektorin in einem Schulbuchverlag. 1993 schließlich machte sie mit ihrem Debütroman »Tell Me Everything« (dt. »Nur ein einziges Zeichen, 1998) erstmals als Autorin auf sich aufmerksam. Seither schreibt sie für Jugendliche und junge Erwachsene. 1995 folgte »What Jamie Saw« (dt. »In sicherer Ferne«, 1999), ein eindringliches Buch über Angst und das Wiederfinden von Zutrauen und Geborgenheit, erzählt aus der Perspektive des neunjährigen Jamie, dessen Mutter mit ihm und seiner kleinen Schwester vor ihrem gewaltbereiten Lebensgefährten fliehen muss.
Einfühlsam und mutig schreibt Carolyn Coman über schmerzhafte Umbrüche im jugendlichen Erwachsenwerden. So auch in ihrem aktuellen Jugendroman »Many Stones« (2000), der 2004 in deutscher Übersetzung erscheinen wird und von der schwierigen Annäherung der sechzehnjährigen Berry Morgan und ihres Vaters erzählt. Auf einer Reise nach Südafrika versuchen beide, ihre gemeinsame Vergangenheit aufzuarbeiten. Carolyn Coman ist Spezialistin für Zwischentöne, psychologische Tiefe und feinfühlige Darstellung von Charakteren. In ihren Texten beschäftigt sie sich mit extremen Situationen und Grenzerfahrungen – Gewalt, Tod, Entfremdung, Sprachlosigkeit –, die auch vor dem alltäglichen (Familien-) Leben nicht Halt machen. »Mich interessiert, wie Menschen, insbesondere junge Menschen, Problemen begegnen und Lösungen suchen. Ich bin interessiert am Seelenleben junger Menschen und daran, wie sie von der Schattenseite des Lebens ins Licht zurückfinden.« Comans Romane wurden mit einer Vielzahl an Auszeichnungen bedacht, so beispielsweise »What Jamie Saw« mit dem John Newbery Honor Award (1996) und »Many Stones« mit dem Michael L. Printz Honor Award (2001). Beide Bücher waren für den National Book Award nominiert. Neben ihrer schriftstellerischen Arbeit ist Carolyn Coman Dozentin am Vermont College im Writing for Children-Programm und freiberufliche Lektorin bei Front Street Books. Sie ist verheiratet mit dem Verleger Stephen Roxburgh und Mutter von zwei Kindern. Carolyn Coman lebt in South Hampton, New Hampshire und Ashville, North Carolina.

What makes a poet tick?

not knowing – and dying to!

miro gavran

biography

Miro Gavran was born in Zagreb, Croatia in 1961 and is one of the most prolific authors of his generation. After he received his degree from the Academy for Theatre, Film and Television, he at first worked as a dramatist between 1986 and 1992 and later as artistic director at the renowned Teatar & TD. For the last ten years, Miro Gavran's main profession has been writing and he has become the most widely translated contemporary Croatian playwright. In 1983 he made his debut with »Kreontova Antigona« (»Kreon's Antigone«). Since then he has produced more than 30 plays, which have been staged at Croatian as well as international theatres. He celebrated one of his greatest successes in 1999 with the premiere of his play »Kraljevi i konjušari« (»Royalty and Rogues«) at the Eugene O'Neill Theatre Centre in Waterford, USA.
His credibility as an author has been confirmed by the excellent response he received from critics and readers alike for his six novels and seven books for children and young adults. His novel »Judita« (2001) was nominated for the International Dublin Literary Award 2003. »Sretni Dani« (1994; »Happy Days«), the amusing and warmheartedly told story about two eleven year-olds, who wish for a »real« family and who use little tricks to coax their single parents into falling in love, was awarded the Mato-Lovrak Prize in 1995. In 1996 Gavran's short story for young adults »Pokušaj zaboraviti« (t: Try to forget) about seventeen year-old Anita, who moves to Zagreb with her parents to be able to gain distance from a rape, was published. The silent wish to forget the past is not fullfilled at first. But when she meets her new classmate Daniel, it looks as if her life is about to change. Gavran mirrors the psyche of his young protagonists in an unusual way: while Daniel writes letters to his best friend, in which he reveals his affection for Anita, Anita recordes her mixed emotions in her diary. Gavran's »Zaboravljeni sin« (1989; t: The Forgotten Son) will be published in German in 2004 titled »Der vergessene Sohn oder Der Engel von Omorina«. In a realistic yet moving way, he tells the story of mentally disabled Mislav, who after having spent years in an institution finally returns to his family. In the form of diary entries, the twenty year-old reports on the initial shame felt by his parents, class prejudices and his fondness for a young woman. »Zaboravljeni sin« was included on the IBBY Honour List 2002 as a book for young adults.
Miro Gavran's work has been translated into seventeen languages and has been awarded many prizes, including the European Time International Literary Award for the Best Central European Writer of the Year 1999. In the autumn of 2002, he founded the GAVRAN theatre with his wife, the actress Mladena Gavran in Zagreb, where he lives.

Pokušaj zaboraviti
Znanje, Zagreb, 1996
Sretni Dani
Mozaik Knjiga, Zagreb, 2000
Judita
Mozaik Knjiga, Zagreb, 2001
Svasta u mojoj glavi
Mozaik Knjiga, Zagreb, 2002
Der vergessene Sohn oder der Engel von Omorina
Knaus/Bertelsmann
München, erscheint 2004

Miro Gavran wurde 1961 in Zagreb, Kroatien, geboren und ist einer der profiliertesten kroatischen Autoren seiner Generation. Nach seinem Studium an der Akademie für Theater, Film und Fernsehen in Zagreb arbeitete er von 1986 bis 1992 zuerst als Dramaturg, später als künstlerischer Direktor am renommierten Teatar &TD. Seit zehn Jahren schreibt Miro Gavran hauptberuflich und avancierte zum meistübersetzten kroatischen Dramatiker der Gegenwart. Er debütierte 1983 mit »Kreontova Antigona«. Seither hat er mehr als dreißig Theaterstücke vorgelegt, die an nationalen wie internationalen Bühnen inszeniert wurden. Einen seiner größten Erfolge feierte er 1999 mit der Uraufführung seines Schauspiels »Kraljevi i konjušari« am Eugene O'Neill Theater Center in Waterford, USA.

Mit sechs Romanen und sieben Kinder- und Jugendbüchern fand Miro Gavran auch als Erzähler große Resonanz bei Kritik wie Lesern. Sein Roman »Judita« (2001) wurde für den International Impac Dublin Literary Award 2003 nominiert. »Sretni Dani« (1994), die amüsante und warmherzig erzählte Geschichte über zwei elfjährige Klassenkameraden, die sich eine »richtige« Familie wünschen und mit kleinen Tricks eine Liebesbeziehung zwischen ihren alleinlebenden Eltern stiften, wurde 1995 mit dem Mato Lovrak-Preis prämiert. 1996 erschien Gavrans Kurzroman für Jugendliche »Pokušaj zaboraviti« über die siebzehnjährige Anita, die mit ihren Eltern nach Zagreb umzieht, um Abstand von einer Vergewaltigung zu gewinnen. Die stille Hoffnung, das Geschehene vergessen zu können, wird zunächst enttäuscht. Die Begegnung mit ihrem neuen Klassenkameraden Daniel beginnt ihr Leben jedoch abermals zu verändern. Gavran spiegelt das Seelenleben seiner jugendlichen Protagonisten auf ganz ungewöhnliche Art und Weise: Während Daniel Briefe an seinen besten Freund schreibt und darin seine Zuneigung zu Anita preisgibt, hält Anita ihre wechselnden Gefühle in ihrem Tagebuch fest. Unter dem Titel »Der vergessene Sohn oder der Engel von Omorina« wird 2004 Gavrans Roman »Zaboravljeni sin« (1989) erscheinen. Lebendig und bewegend erzählt er darin die Geschichte des lernbehinderten Mislav, der nach Jahren im Heim zu seiner Familie zurückkehrt. In Form von Tagebuchnotizen berichtet der Zwanzigjährige von der anfänglichen Scham seiner Eltern und Geschwister, von den Vorurteilen seiner Umgebung und seiner liebevollen Zuneigung zu einer jungen Frau. »Zaboravljeni sin« wurde als Jugendbuch auf die IBBY-Honour-List 2002 aufgenommen.

Miro Gavrans Werk wurde in siebzehn Sprachen übersetzt und u. a. 1999 mit dem Central European Time International Literary Award als Best Central European Writer of the Year ausgezeichnet. Mit seiner Ehefrau, der Schauspielerin Mladena Gavran, gründete der Autor im Herbst 2002 das GAVRAN Theater in Zagreb, wo er auch lebt.

29-JUL-2003 13:48 VON:ILB 03027878685 AN:49 30 7813925 S.001/001

WHAT MAKES THE POET TICK?

When I want to understand the world, then I read.
When I want the world to understand me, then I write.

Miro Gavran

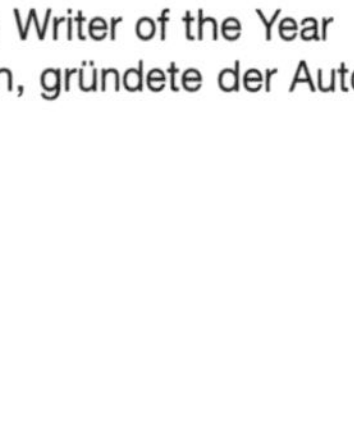

klaus hagerup
biography

Klaus Hagerup was born in Oslo, Norway in 1946 and grew up in a family of authors. He decided to become an actor and partly funded his education with his poetry collection, »Silk tenker jeg på dere«, with which he made his debut in 1969. In the following years he worked as an actor, director, playwright and translator. In the eighties, writing increasingly took on a larger and larger role in his professional life. Today, Hagerup is considered one of the most important authors in Norway; he writes novels, theatre plays and radio plays, most of which target young adults. In a sensitive and humorous way, he writes about early puberty, finding oneself, friendship and the turbulent complexities of being in love for the first time. He does not write about the big leap into the well-defined world of adults, but about the many small, quaint and disproportionately more important developments. In doing so, he contrives to expose his protagonists to hysterically funny dialogues and hilarious scenes.

In his novel for young adults »Høyere en himmelen« (1990), the author tells the tale of twelve year-old Mari, who does not like herself very much and finds just about everything quite daft, until she meets the wacky yet impressive teacher Miss Kjoer. The novel was awarded Sonja Hagemanns barnebokpris (1990) and the IBBY Certificate of Honour for Writing. Hagerup became hugely popular with the publication, in 1993, of the children's mystery »Bibbi Bokkens magiske bibliotek«, which he co-wrote with Jostein Gaarder, the author of »Sophie's World«. His international breakthrough came in 1994 with the publication of »Markus og Diana og lyset fra Sirius«, the first book of four about the antihero, Markus Simonsen, who is afraid of everything, but most of all of girls. His last book about Markus, »Markus og Sigmund« will be published in Norway in autumn 2003. In an affectionate, charming and yet always respectfully distant manner, Hagerup depicts the daily fears of a completely normal teenager and his first steps into the wide world of love, which are sometimes delightful and sometimes painful, but always instructive.

Klaus Hagerup's versatile work has been widely translated and has received numerous awards, while two of his books for young adults have been filmed. In recent years, he has produced just as highly acclaimed books for adults, including »Herremannen« (2000). His current work, »Kaninen synger i mørket« (2001), which will be published in the German translation in 2004, proves that he has also remained faithful to his younger readers. In his version of the »Alice in Wonderland« motif, Else goes on a fantastical journey, where she meets rabbits in shorts and other curious creatures. Klaus Hagerup lives in Gressvik, Norway.

Tiefer als der Ozean
(ab 12)
Sauerländer
Aarau; Frankfurt a. M.
Salzburg, 1995
[Ü: Gabriele Haefs]

Markus und Diana
(ab 12)
Sauerländer
Aarau; Frankfurt a. M.
Salzburg, 1997
[Ü: Gabriele Haefs]

Küss mich – oder ich verlieb mich in dich!
(ab 12)
Carlsen, Hamburg, 2001
[Ü: Gabriele Haefs]

Verliebt zwischen Ecke und Elfmeter
(ab 12)
Sauerländer
Aarau; Frankfurt a. M.
Salzburg, 2001
[Ü: Gabriele Haefs]

Die Kaninchen singen im Dunkeln
Hanser
München, erscheint 2004
[Ü: Gabriele Haefs]

klaus hagerup

Klaus Hagerup wurde 1946 in Oslo, Norwegen, geboren und wuchs in einer Literatenfamilie auf. Er entschied sich, Schauspieler zu werden, und finanzierte seine Ausbildung u. a. mit dem Gedichtband »Slik tenker jeg på dere«, mit dem er 1969 debütierte. In den Folgejahren arbeitete er als Bühnendarsteller, Regisseur, Dramatiker und Übersetzer. Mehr und mehr rückte in den achtziger Jahren das Schreiben in den Mittelpunkt seines beruflichen Schaffens. Heute gehört Hagerup zu den wichtigsten Literaten Norwegens und verfasst Romane, Theaterstücke und Hörspiele für ein größtenteils jugendliches Publikum. Empfindsam und humoristisch schreibt er über die frühe Phase der Pubertät, vom Sich-Finden, von Freundschaft und den turbulenten Verwicklungen der ersten Liebe. Er erzählt nicht vom großen Sprung in die abgeklärte Erwachsenenwelt, sondern von den vielen kleinen, wunderlichen und ungleich wichtigeren Entwicklungsschritten. Dabei versteht er es, seinen Helden urkomische Dialoge und wahnwitzige Szenen auf den Leib zu schreiben.

In seinem Jugendroman »Høyere enn himmelen« (dt. »Tiefer als der Ozean«, 1995) erzählt der Autor von der zwölfjährigen Mari, die sich selbst nicht besonders mag und alles irgendwie doof findet, bis sie die etwas schrullige und zugleich imponierende Lehrerin Fräulein Kjoer kennenlernt. Der Roman wurde mit dem Sonja-Hagemann-Preis (1990) und dem IBBY Certificate of Honour for Writing prämiert. Große Popularität brachte Hagerup 1993 der Kinderkrimi »Bibbi Bokkens magiske bibliotek« (dt. »Bibbi Bokkens magische Bibliothek«, 2001), den er zusammen mit dem Autor von »Sofies Welt«, Jostein Gaarder, verfasste. Der internationale Durchbruch gelang ihm 1994 mit »Markus og Diana og lyset fra Sirius« (dt. »Markus und Diana«, 1997), dem ersten Band seiner vierteiligen Buchserie um den Antihelden Markus Simonsen, der sich vor Gott und der Welt, vor allem aber vor den Mädchen fürchtet. Sein aktuelles Buch der »Markus«-Serie, »Markus und Sigmund«, erscheint im Herbst 2003 in Norwegen. Liebevoll, charmant und stets in respektvoller Distanz schildert Hagerup die Alltagsangst eines ganz normalen Teenagers und dessen erste Gehversuche im weiten Feld der Liebe, die manchmal schön und manchmal schmerzhaft, immer aber lehrreich sind.

Klaus Hagerups vielseitiges Werk wurde mehrfach übersetzt und ausgezeichnet, zwei seiner Jugendbücher erfolgreich verfilmt. In den letzten Jahren hat er u. a. mit »Herremannen« (2000) auch vielbeachtete Romane für Erwachsene vorgelegt. Mit seinem aktuellen Werk »Kaninene synger i mørket« (2001), das 2004 in deutscher Übersetzung erscheint, ist er aber seinen jungen Lesern treu geblieben. In seiner Fassung des »Alice im Wunderland«-Motivs begibt sich Else auf eine phantastische Reise, auf der sie neben Kaninchen in kurzen Hosen allerhand sonderbaren Gestalten begegnet. Klaus Hagerup lebt in Gressvik, Norwegen.

What makes me tick
is the memory of my childhood,
and the urg to live life
one more time.

heinz janisch

biography

Heinz Janisch was born in Güssing, in the Austrian state of Burgenland and studied German literature and journalism at the University of Vienna. Since 1982 he has been working as a freelancer for ORF-radio and is the editor-in-charge of the series »Menschenbilder«. Since the publication of his first children's book »Mario, der Tagmaler« (1989; t: Mario the Daypainter), he has produced a number of picture books, poetry collections and stories for children and adults.

Heinz Janisch is capable of bestowing his texts with a lyric note and of carrying the magic of poetry into the world of children's literature. The tone of his language, the surprising turnarounds, and the ability to lyrically bring figures and objects to life make Heinz Janisch inimitable and unmistakable (»1001 Buch«). »Ich schenk Dir einen Ton aus meinem Saxofon« (t: I'll Give You a Tone from my Saxophone) – a collection of whimsical tales and pleasurable verses for children over the age of seven – was a big success. The individual texts encapsulate themes that are close to both adults and children: the self, the home, grandparents, animals, love, hopes and dreams. In Janisch's texts, familiar things and events mutate, gain new contours, an unusual strangeness: a house has a headache and moves to the country, a cactus shaves and makes its way to the sea, and a frog wants to travel to Africa in a Jaguar. Sensitively and fleet-footedly, the author traces the meanings of words, revealing a quiet observer and a carefree day-dreamer. The effect which grows from his texts and Linda Wolfsgruber's insistent black and white illustrations is sometimes comic, sometimes tragic, sometimes thought-provoking and sometimes high-spirited. »Yesterday my house was drunk! Stood there and stumbled and mumbled and growled / and sang very loudly!« In his picture book about the resolute »Prinzessin auf dem Kürbis« (1998; t: Princess on the Pumpkin) he depicts a new image of a princess, which no longer has anything to do with the princess and the pea. Using magical pictures, also illustrated by Linda Wolfsgruber, his picture book fluctuates between a fairytale tone and the fresh and cheeky comments of the emancipated princess. In his tragicomic story about a bird, the author uses a fine sense of humour and a great deal of empathy to unfold the psychosis of the little bird Sigmund, who, after falling from his nest, can only croak »Zack bumm!«. Illustrated by Helga Bansch, it tells the tale of Sigmund's healing on the big grass-green »reflecting sofa«, which belongs to the old and white hare Carl Gustav. His latest publication »Schenk mir Flügel« (2003; t: Give Me Wings) is a picture book for all ages.

Heinz Janisch has already received numerous awards for his children's books, including the Österreichischer Kinder- und Jugendbuchpreis (1998, 1999, 2001) as well as the Kinderbuchpreis der Stadt Wien several times. He is a member of the Grazer Autorenversammlung and lives in Vienna and in Burgenland.

Die Prinzessin auf dem Kürbis
(ab 5)
Gabriel, Wien, 1998
[Ill: Linda Wolfsgruber]

Ich schenk dir einen Ton aus meinem Saxofon
(ab 7)
Jungbrunnen, Wien, 1999
[Ill: Linda Wolfsgruber]

Zack bumm
(ab 4)
Jungbrunnen, Wien, 2000
[Ill: Helga Bansch]

Die Reise zu den Fliegenden Inseln
(ab 10)
Jungbrunnen, Wien, 2001

Her mit den Prinzen!
(ab 3)
Betz, Wien, 2002
[Ill: Birgit Antoni]

Schenk mir Flügel
(Bilderbuch für jedes Alter)
NP, St. Pölten, 2003
[Ill: Selda Marlin Soganci]

the silence

Heinz Janisch wurde 1960 in Güssing im österreichischen Burgenland geboren und studierte Germanistik und Publizistik an der Universität Wien. Seit 1982 ist er freier Mitarbeiter des ORF-Hörfunks und leitet heute als verantwortlicher Redakteur die Reihe »Menschenbilder«. Seit der Veröffentlichung seines ersten Kinderbuchs »Mario, der Tagmaler« (1989) hat er eine Vielzahl von Bilderbüchern, Gedichtbänden und Erzählungen für Kinder und Erwachsene vorgelegt.

Heinz Janisch versteht es, seinen Texten eine lyrische Note zu verleihen und den Zauber der Poesie in die Welt der Kinderliteratur zu tragen. In der Färbung seiner Sprache, in den überraschenden Wendungen und der Fähigkeit, Figuren und Gegenstände lyrisch zum Leben zu erwecken, darin ist Heinz Janisch unnachahmlich, unverkennbar (»1001 Buch«). Zu einem großen Erfolg wurde »Ich schenk dir einen Ton aus meinem Saxofon« (1999) – eine Sammlung von skurrilen Geschichten und vergnüglichen Versen für Kinder ab sieben Jahre. Die einzelnen Texte kreisen um Themen, die Erwachsenen und Kindern gleichermaßen nahe sind: um das Ich, das Zuhause, um die Großeltern, um Tiere, um Liebe, um Wünsche und Träume. Vertraute Dinge und Ereignisse verändern sich in Janisch' Texten, erhalten eine neue Kontur, eine merkwürdige Fremdheit: Ein Haus hat Kopfweh und zieht aufs Land, ein Kaktus rasiert sich und fährt zum Meer und ein Frosch will im Jaguar nach Afrika reisen. Sensibel und leichtfüßig spürt der Autor der Bedeutung von Worten nach, zeigt sich als stiller Beobachter und heiterer Tagträumer. Was aus seinen Texten und den eindrücklichen Schwarzweiß-Illustrationen Linda Wolfsgrubers erwächst, ist mal komisch, mal traurig, mal nachdenklich oder voller Übermut: »Gestern war mein Haus betrunken! Stand da und wankte und schwankte und grölte/und sang ganz laut!« In seinem Bilderbuch über die resolute »Prinzessin auf dem Kürbis« (1998) zeichnet er ein neues Prinzessinnenbild, das nichts mehr mit der zimperlichen Prinzessin auf der Erbse zu tun hat. Mit magischen Bildern, ebenfalls von Linda Wolfsgruber illustriert, changiert sein Bilderbuch zwischen einem märchenhaften Ton und den frisch-frechen Aussagen der emanzipierten Prinzessin. Mit feinem Humor und großem Einfühlungsvermögen entfaltet der Autor in seiner tragikomischen Vogelgeschichte »Zack bumm!« (2000) die Psychose des kleinen Vogels Sigmund, der nach einem Sturz aus seinem Nest nur noch »Zack bumm!« krächzt. Illustriert von Helga Bansch erzählt er von Sigmunds Heilung auf dem großen, grasgrünen »Nachdenksofa« des alten weißen Hasen Carl Gustav. Zuletzt erschien »Schenk mir Flügel« (2003), ein Bilderbuch für jedes Alter.

Heinz Janisch wurde für seine Kinderbücher bereits mehrfach ausgezeichnet, darunter dreimal mit dem Österreichischen Kinder- und Jugendbuchpreis (1998, 1999, 2001) sowie mehrmals mit dem Kinderbuchpreis der Stadt Wien. Er ist Mitglied der Grazer Autorenversammlung und lebt in Wien und im Burgenland.

Die Stille ist ja ein schöner Lärm.
Wenn man lange genug in diesen Lärm
hineingehört hat, beginnt man zu
sprechen.

desa muck

biography

Desa Muck was born in Ljubljana in 1955 and is one of Slovenia's most versatile authors for children and young people. Her novels, textbooks and radio plays have received many awards and have been widely translated. Many of her books belong to the set texts for the children's reading competition »Bralna značka«. Before Desa Muck made writing her main profession, she worked as a technical illustrator, a carer for mentally handicapped children, an actress and a presenter and she published 150 »dime novels«. She attracted a great deal of attention with the parallel publication of her two books for young people, »Pod milim nebom« and the good-humoured textbook »Blazno resno o seksu« (1999), and she soon advanced into the ranks of the most popular children's and young people's literature authors in her country.
With a keen grasp of adolescents' perception of their surroundings, their thoughts and their language, Muck uses her novels to tackle the problems with which teenagers are often confronted: school, friendship, love, sexuality and questions about which path to follow in life. In her five part »Deadly Serious« series she uses stories, amusing quizzes and scientific explanations to address themes such as sexuality, behaviour, drugs and the media. She always finds the right tone to understandingly and humorously mirror young people's view of reality with all its follies, disappointments, challenges and obstacles. In doing so she picks up on young readers' questions, and offers them encouraging solutions without patronising them. For Susi, in »Lažniva Suzi« (1997), it is so important to be popular amongst her new classmates that she starts telling lies. When her invented stories are uncovered, she has to cope with a lot of harassment until her participation in a theatre group allows her to accept herself the way she is. »Lažniva Suzi« was awarded the Večernica-Prize (1997), which is awarded annually to the best Slovenian book for young adults. Recently, the author has also been writing for younger readers. Her children's book series for beginners »Anica«, which includes six books to date, was awarded the prize »My favourite book« in 2003, which is chosen by children from all over Slovenia. Having published over 300 newspaper columns, Desa Muck also belongs to the most widely read columnists in Slovenia. Since 1985 she has also been working in television and radio, has adapted Roald Dahl's »Mathilda« for theatre and in 2000 she was the leading actress in the TV series »Bolnišnica na Robu«. The author lives in Mokronog with her three daughters.

Pod milim nebom
Hermagoras/Mohorjeva
Klagenfurt; Ljubljana; Wien
1996
[Ill: Zvonko Čoh]
Wahnsinnig ernst über Sex
(ab 11)
Hermagoras/Mohorjeva
Klagenfurt; Ljubljana; Wien
1999
[Ü: Marica Kulnik]
[Ill: Bernhard Čarre]
Soma Doma
(ab 12)
Mladinska knjiga
Ljubljana, 2001
[Ill: Sebastijan Čamagajevac]
Anica in grozovitež
(ab 7)
Mladinska knjiga
Ljubljana, 2001
[Ill: Ana Košir]
Lažniva Suzi
(ab 12)
Mladinska knjiga
Ljubljana, 2001
Welche Farbe hat die Welt?
Hermagoras/Mohorjeva
Klagenfurt; Ljubljana
Wien 2003
[Ü: Tamara Kapus]
[Ill: Branka Schwarz]

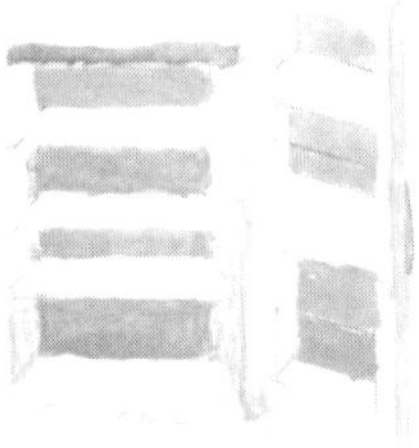

← 1.

The refrigerator when it is empty

↑ 3.

The home I wish to have

← 2.

The annoying editor

Desa Muck wurde 1955 in Ljubljana geboren und ist eine der vielseitigsten Kinder- und Jugendbuchautorinnen Sloweniens. Ihre Romane, Sachbücher und Hörspiele wurden mehrfach ausgezeichnet und übersetzt. Viele ihrer Bücher gehören zur Pflichtlektüre des Kinderlesewettbewerbs »Bralna značka«. Bevor Desa Muck das Schreiben ganz zu ihrem Beruf machte, arbeitete sie als technische Zeichnerin, Pflegerin geistig behinderter Kinder, Schauspielerin und Moderatorin und veröffentlichte 150 »Groschenromane«. Mit zwei parallel publizierten Jugendbüchern – dem Roman »Pod milim nebom« (Ü: Unter freiem Himmel) und dem heiteren Sachbuch »Blazno resno o seksu« (dt. »Wahnsinnig ernst über Sex«, 1999) – machte sie 1993 auf sich aufmerksam und avancierte dann zu einer der populärsten Kinder- und Jugendbuchautorinnen ihres Landes.

Mit großem Gespür für die Lebenswelt, Gedanken und Sprache heranwachsender Jugendlicher behandelt Muck in ihren Jugendromanen Themen, mit denen sich Teenager auseinandersetzen: Schule, Freundschaft, Liebe, Sexualität und die Frage, wie man sich in der Welt zurechtfinden kann. In ihrer fünfteiligen »Wahnsinnig ernst«-Serie führt sie mit Geschichten, lustigen Fragespielen und wissenschaftlichen Erklärungen an Themen wie Sexualität, Benehmen, Drogen und Medien heran. Stets findet sie den richtigen Ton, die Lebenswirklichkeit junger Menschen mit all ihren Verrücktheiten, Enttäuschungen, Herausforderungen und Stolpersteinen verständnis- und humorvoll zu spiegeln. Dabei greift sie die Fragen junger Leser auf und legt ihnen Problemlösungen aufmunternd ans Herz, ohne sie zu bevormunden. Der »aufgedrehten« Susi in »Lažniva Suzi« (1997; Ü: Die verlogene Susi) ist es so wichtig, bei ihren neuen Klassenkameraden beliebt zu sein, dass sie dafür lügt. Als ihre erfundenen Geschichten »auffliegen«, muss sie viel einstecken, bis sie durch ihr Mitwirken bei einer Theatergruppe sich selber anzunehmen beginnt. »Lažniva Suzi« wurde u. a. mit dem Večernica-Preis (1997) ausgezeichnet, der alljährlich für das beste Jugendbuch Sloweniens vergeben wird.

Seit einigen Jahren schreibt die Autorin auch für jüngere Leser. Ihre Kinderbuchserie für Erstleser »Anica«, in der bisher sechs Titel erschienen sind, wurde 2003 mit dem Preis »Mein liebstes Buch« ausgezeichnet, das Kinder aus ganz Slowenien auswählen. Mit mehr als 300 veröffentlichten Zeitungskolumnen gehört Desa Muck außerdem zu den meist gelesenen Kolumnistinnen Sloweniens. Zudem arbeitet sie seit 1985 als TV- und Radio-Szenaristin, adaptierte Roald Dahls »Mathilda« für das Theater und spielte 2000 in der TV-Serie »Bolnišnica na Robu« die weibliche Hauptrolle. Die Autorin lebt mit ihren drei Töchtern in Mokronog.

↑ 4.

My three daughters who are always in need of something

5. →

Someone invisible on the top of the hill who tells me stories

verónica murguía

biography

Verónica Murguía was born in Mexico City in 1960. She began studying history before deciding to pursue an art degree. For a number of years, she worked as an aerobics teacher, a banana-bread baker as well as a radio talk-show host. Today she works as a freelance writer in Mexico City, teaches at the Escuela de Sociedad General de Escritores de Mexico and writes the column »Las rayas de la cebra« for the daily newspaper »La Jornada« – about her love-hate relationship with the big city jungle she calls home. Murguía has published seven illustrated children's books, two novels for young adults and a short-story collection for adults »El ángel de Nicolás« in 2003. Right at the beginning of her career, she was awarded the Juan de la Cabada Prize for her children's book »Historia y aventuras de Taté el mago« (1990).

Her first book for young adults was published in German in 2001. »Auliya« (1999) is a fantastical fairy-tale for ambitious readers, which stands in the tradition of Arabic prose. It tells the tale of a paralysed Bedouin girl, who grows up ridiculed by the members of her nomadic tribe and develops curious characteristics. It is a dying stranger on his deathbed, who finally manages to open Auliya's heart and to free her magical abilities. After his death, the girl decides to leave her unloved home behind and complete Abu al-Jakum's journey to the ocean. »Auliya« narrates this wonderful journey with impressive authenticity, during which the peculiar young girls turns into a »magical« woman. Murguía's language is poetic, adorned with foreign terms and interlaced with the motif of loss and recovery. »Auliya« was nominated for the Rattenfänger Literaturpreis (2002). Carlos Fuentes praised the novel as »a magical and noble book«. No less fantastical is the Mexican's second book for young adults »El fuego verde« (1999), which was published in German in 2003. Once again the author turns to a time long gone and a far-away culture. She says, »I write to live in another time amongst other people.« The story begins as a classical medieval novel and develops into a magical tale about thirteen year-old Luned, who lives in the forests of Brocelandia. She goes to the city with the travelling storyteller Demne, where she learns to read and write. Repelled by the many people, the cold city walls and the exclusion of the poor and sick, she decides to return to her village. On her way home, she meets the elf Alder, whom she follows to the kingdom of elves, fairies and goblins. Finally, Luned will have to decide whether her home is in the forest, amongst the elves and forever in the realm of Fairy where everyone is immortal, or to go back to Demne, to the world of men, where everybody, sooner or later, gets old and dies.

Historia y aventuras de Taté el mago
Institutio Nacional de Bellas Artes
Mexiko, 1990
El guardián de los gatos
Eco/Conaculta
Mexiko, 1990
Mors Repentina
Verdehalago, Mexiko, 2001
Auliya
(ab 14)
Nagel & Kimche
Zürich, 2001
[Ü: Ilse Layer]
Das grüne Feuer
(ab 10)
Nagel & Kimche
Zürich, 2003
[Ü: Ilse Layer]
El ángel de Nicolás
Ediciones Era, Mexiko, 2003

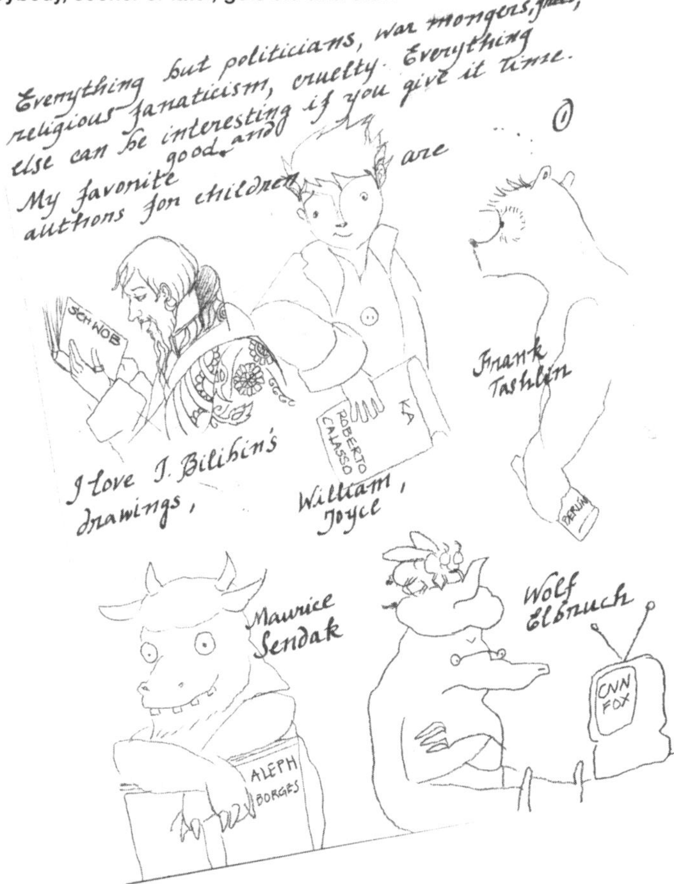

Verónica Murguía wurde 1960 in Mexiko-Stadt geboren. Sie studierte einige Semester Geschichte, bevor sie ein Kunststudium aufnahm. Mehrere Jahre arbeitete sie als Aerobiclehrerin, Bananenbrotbäckerin sowie als Moderatorin einer Radiotalkshow. Heute lebt sie als freie Schriftstellerin in Mexiko-Stadt, unterrichtet an der Schule der Sociedad General de Escritores de Mexico und schreibt für die Tageszeitung »La Jornada« die Kolumne »Las rayas de la cebra« – eine »Hassliebeserklärung« an den heimatlichen Großstadtdschungel. Murguía hat sieben illustrierte Kinderbücher, zwei Jugendromane und die 2003 erschienene Kurzgeschichten-Sammlung für Erwachsene »El ángel de Nicolás« veröffentlicht. Gleich zu Beginn ihrer Laufbahn wurde sie für ihr Kinderbuch »Historia y aventuras de Taté el mago« (1990) mit dem Juan de la Cabada-Preis ausgezeichnet.
Seit 2001 liegt ihr erstes Jugendbuch in deutscher Sprache vor. »Auliya. Eine magische Reise durch die Wüste« (1999) ist ein phantastisches Märchen für anspruchsvolle Leser, das in der Tradition der arabischen Prosadichtung steht. Es erzählt die Geschichte eines lahmen Beduinenmädchens, das verspottet in einem Nomadenstamm heranwächst und sonderbare Eigenarten entwickelt. Erst ein im Sterben liegender Fremder vermag es, Auliyas Herz zu öffnen und ihre magischen Fähigkeiten freizusetzen. Nach seinem Tod beschließt das Mädchen, die ungeliebte Heimat hinter sich zu lassen und Abu al-Jakums Reise zum Meer zu vollenden. »Auliya« berichtet mit beeindruckender Authentizität von dieser wunderbaren Reise, die das seltsame Kind in eine »zauberhafte« Frau verwandelt. Murguías Sprache ist poetisch, verziert mit fremdländischen Begriffen und durchflochten vom Motiv des Verlustes und des Wiederfindens. »Auliya« stand auf der Auswahlliste zum Rattenfänger-Literaturpreis (2002). Carlos Fuentes lobte den Roman als »ein magisches und edles Buch«.
Nicht minder phantastisch ist das zweite Jugendbuch der Mexikanerin, »Das grüne Feuer« (»El fuego verde«, 1999), das 2003 in deutscher Sprache erschienen ist. Wiederum versetzt sich die Autorin in eine ferne Zeit und fremde Kultur. Sie sagt: »Ich schreibe, um in anderer Zeit und unter anderen Menschen zu leben.« Was wie ein klassischer Mittelalterroman beginnt, entwickelt sich bald zu einer magischen Erzählung über die dreizehnjährige Luned, die in den Wäldern Brocelandias lebt. Mit dem fahrenden Geschichtenerzähler Demne geht sie in die Stadt, wo sie Lesen und Schreiben lernt. Von den vielen Menschen, den kalten Stadtmauern und der Ausgrenzung der Armen und Kranken abgeschreckt, entschließt sie sich, in ihr Dorf zurückzukehren. Auf ihrem Heimweg begegnet sie dem Elf Erle, dem sie ins Reich der Elfen, Feen und Kobolde folgt. Letztlich wird sich Luned entscheiden müssen, ob ihr Zuhause im Märchenreich der Elfen im Wald ist oder ob sie zurückkehrt zu Demne ins Reich der Menschen, wo jeder, früher oder später, alt wird und stirbt.

Van Allsburg ... but the list could go on
and on. I love many writers -
Jorge Luis Borges is very close to my heart.
Bach's music. Shakespeare, to whom I
owe my deep love for English.
The french historian Georges Duby.
Gothic cathedrals.
So ... There are many things.
But cats I love the best.
Cats, daughter, my husband,
good food, sunny and crisp
days, B movies. Baroque Spanish
Poetry. Caravaggio - Bosch.
Joseph Brodsky - Roberto Calasso -
Teaching my classes. Lifting weights
(ew!) Those things and many
others. Life makes me tick.
Verónica Murguía

roberto piumini

biography

Roberto Piumini was born in Edolo, near Brescia, Italy in 1947 and is considered the most important contemporary Italian author for children and young adults. He studied education and then worked for a few years as a teacher, actor and puppeteer, before he found his way into writing. In the meantime he has published many novels for children, young adults and adults, theatre plays, poems, fables, fairy tales and ballads, screenplays, television and radio texts, song lyrics and opera librettos.

Although he had already been immensely popular in Italy for a number of years, »Matti e il nonno« (1993; »Mattie and Grandpa«) was the first of six books to be published in Germany in 1994. In it, Piumini describes the fictitious walk that a seven year-old takes with his dying grandfather. As in classical fairy tales, during their mutual journey they have to make decisions, overcome tests of courage and adventure and they have to draw lessons from their experiences. With unobtrusive implicitness, Piumini narrates about loving, saying-goodbye, the ability-to-let-go and not-being-forgotten. In picturesque yet clear language he writes – as the dedication in the book emphasises – »for all those, who talk to children«. »Matti e il nonno« was nominated for the Deutscher Jugendliteraturpreis (1995).

One of the most important pieces in his literary work is his poetic tale »Il stralisco«, published in 1993. Without using complicated words and depicted with poignantly delicate narrative images, Piumini tells a meditative story about our perception of the world, to which death also belongs. With each individual stroke of his brush, the painter Sakumat makes the world come alive on the walls of the palace, within which the fatally ill Madurer is confined. The critics praised Piumini's small, gentle story about friendship and the life-giving potential of art as a »gift for one's own life« (»Die Zeit«).

Light-footedly and without pointing fingers, Piumini's stories seem to be carried on a completely different breeze. The fascination lies in the astounding mixture of adventure, worldly wisdom, fantasy and the beauty of his language. Thus he follows in the footsteps of Gianni Rodari (1920-1980), who freed Italian children's and juvenile literature from its »childishness« and patronisation. Piumini realises the importance of inventing fascinating narrative panoramas and giving his texts multilayered depth. This is also the case in his novel for young adults »Motu-Iti. L'isola dei gabbiani« (1997), for which he was awarded the Rattenfänger Literaturpreis in 1998. His story about the just and prudent chieftain Tou-Ema, who is the ruler on the famous Easter Island, is an »impressive yet simultaneously thought-provoking book about power and its misuse« (»Süddeutsche Zeitung«).

Roberto Piumini's highly acclaimed books have already been translated into eleven languages. His most recent publications were his novel for adults »L'ultima volta che venne il vento« (2002) and his children's book »Rosaspina« (2003). The author lives in Milan and in Buonconvento, near Siena.

Matti und der Großvater
(ab 7)
Hanser
München, 1994
[Ü: Maria Fehringer]
[Ill: Quint Buchholz]

Motu-Iti
Die Insel der Möwen
(ab 11)
Hanser
München, 1997
[Ü: Maria Fehringer]
[Ill: Günter Mattei]

Eine Welt für Madurer
(ab 10)
Hanser
München, 1999
[Ü: Maria Fehringer]

Der Diener
der bösen Geister
(ab 11)
Hanser
München, 2001
[Ü: Maria Fehringer]

L'ultima volta che
venne il vento
Nino Aragno, Turin, 2002

Rosaspina
Fabbri Editori
Mailand, 2003
[Ill: Serena Riglietti]

Roberto Piumini wurde 1947 in Edolo bei Brescia, Italien, geboren und gilt als der bedeutendste italienische Kinder- und Jugendbuchautor der Gegenwart. Der studierte Pädagoge arbeitete einige Jahre als Lehrer, Schauspieler und Puppenspieler, bevor er zur Schriftstellerei fand. Inzwischen hat er in seiner Heimat eine Vielzahl von Romanen für Kinder, Jugendliche und Erwachsene, Theaterstücke, Gedichte, Fabeln, Märchen und Balladen, Drehbücher, Fernseh- und Radiotexte, Liedtexte und Opernlibretti veröffentlicht.
Während er in Italien schon seit vielen Jahren außerordentliche Popularität genießt, wurde 1994 mit »Matti und der Großvater« (»Mattia e il nonno«, 1993) sein erstes von bisher sechs Büchern in deutscher Sprache veröffentlicht. Darin schildert Piumini den fiktiven Spaziergang des siebenjährigen Matti mit seinem sterbenden Großvater. Wie im klassischen Märchen haben sie auf ihrem gemeinsamen Weg Entscheidungen zu treffen, Mutproben und Abenteuer zu bestehen sowie Lehren aus ihren Erlebnissen zu ziehen. Mit unaufdringlicher Selbstverständlichkeit erzählt Piumini vom Lieb-Haben, Abschied-Nehmen, Loslassen-Können und Nicht-Vergessen-Werden. In ebenso bildhafter wie klarer Sprache schreibt er – wie die Widmung des Buches betont – »für alle, die mit Kindern reden«. »Matti und der Großvater« wurde für den Deutschen Jugendliteraturpreis (1995) nominiert.
Eines der zentralen Werke im literarischen Schaffen Piuminis ist seine poetische Erzählung »Il stralisco« von 1993 (dt., »Eine Welt für Madurer«, 1999). Ohne große Worte und in ergreifend zarte Sprachbilder gefasst, erzählt Piumini eine meditative Geschichte über die Wahrnehmung der Welt, zu der auch der Tod gehört. Pinselstrich für Pinselstrich lässt der Maler Sakumat die Welt für den todkranken Madurer auf Palastwänden lebendig werden. Die Kritik lobte Piuminis kleine, federleichte Erzählung über Freundschaft und die lebensstiftende Kraft der Kunst als ein »Geschenk für das eigene Leben« (»Die Zeit«).
Leichtfüßig und ohne erhobenen Zeigefinger kommen Piuminis Geschichten daher, getragen von einem ganz eigenen Atem. Ihre Faszination beziehen sie aus der verblüffenden Mischung von Abenteuer, Lebensweisheit, Phantasie und Schönheit der Sprache. Damit steht er in der Nachfolge Gianni Rodaris (1920-1980), der die italienische Kinder- und Jugendliteratur von seiner »Kindlichkeit« und jeglichem Pädagogisieren befreite. Piumini versteht es, faszinierende Erzählpanoramen zu entwerfen und seinen Texten eine vielschichtige Tiefe zu verleihen, so auch in seinem Jugendroman »Motu-Iti. L'isola die gabbiani« (»Motu-Iti. Die Insel der Möwen«, 1997), für den er 1998 mit dem Rattenfänger Literaturpreis ausgezeichnet wurde. Seine Geschichte um den gerechten und besonnenen Häuptling Tou-Ema, der auf der berühmten Osterinsel regiert, ist ein »eindrucksvolles und zugleich nachdenkliches Buch über Macht und ihren Missbrauch« (»Süddeutsche Zeitung«).
Roberto Piuminis vielfach preisgekrönten Bücher wurden bereits in elf Sprachen übersetzt. Zuletzt erschienen sein Erwachsenenroman »L'ultima volta che venne il vento« (2002) und sein Kinderbuch »Rosaspina« (2003). Der Autor lebt in Mailand und in Buonconvento bei Siena.

What makes the poet tick?
What makes the poet be ticked?
If "tick", as my vocabulary first says,
is a "tic-tac", a "*ticchettio*", an "instant",
it is the first tick, I suppose,
the one in which the poet was born
as a corporal soul, a sensitive man,
sliding with relative pain
from his *mater dolorosa*: the sense
of being no more in a liquid, warm, safe,
but in a dry, empty, icy space,
like a sole sole in a big-self-bang.
If "tick" is, second meaning,
a "*zecca*", a sucking insect,
it's a matter, I guess, of sweet blood of poets.
If it is a "*guanciale*" or something,
it refers to the insolent idleness
of the only poet I know:
because it's a rather romantic lie
that poetry's uninterruptedly in rest,
and often would our fellow prefere
to rest, instead of sinking to the knees
chasing reserved images
in deep aromatic pounds. If it is
"*pagare a credito*" it alludes, I suppose,
to the eternal poverty of poets:
about which no more will be said.

notaila rashed

biography

Notaila Ibrahim Rashed, known as Mama Lobna, was born in 1934 in Cairo, Egypt, and is known as the pioneer of Egyptian children's literature. She has not only written numerous children's books and books for young adults, short stories and contributions for diverse children's magazines, radio and television shows for children and young people in the whole Arabic speaking region, but has also campaigned ambitiously for, and has had a profound influence on, the promotion of Egyptian children's and young people's literature. From its first publication in 1956 until 2002 she worked for the renowned Arabic children's magazine »Samir«. In 1965 she founded the children's book section of the publishing house Darel-Hilal in Cairo, where she worked as a publisher for five years. She is a member of the High Committee of the Cairo International Festival for Children's Film, and of the Child and Young People Committee of the Alexandria Library.

Notaila Rashed began writing for children and young people while she was a student at Cairo University. Her first short stories were broadcast on the radio in 1953. A number of broadcastings of her children's and young people's programmes for radio and television followed. One of her most famous books is »The Diary of Yasser Family«, which was published in 1979 in two parts. It includes the story »The Doll« which was used as the model for the first, and to date the only, children's film produced by the Egyptian National Council of Culture. In 1979 she also published »Abou Keer and Abou Seer«, a »modern« adaptation of the story from »A thousand and one nights« about a good neighbour and an evil neighbour. In her work, Rashed tries to combine the literary-cultural traditions of ancient and »modern« Egypt. She wants her texts to provide children all around the world with an authentic portrayal of life in contemporary Egypt: »The world knew Pharaonic Egypt; and Egypt in the early Arab and Islamic epochs; but 20th century Egypt is not familiarly known to the same extent.«

Besides her work as an author, Rashed has also translated children's classics into Arabic, including Andersen's »The Emperor's New Clothes«, Wilde's »The Happy Prince« and Swell's »Black Beauty«. She takes part in international congresses on children's and young people's literature, as well as in congresses on children's film, TV and radio. Her socioliterary commitment has been highly acclaimed. In 1978 she was awarded the State Award for Children's Literature. In 1995 she received the State Award for Children's Journalism and in 2002 the Medal of the Council of the Ministry of Culture. The author has three children and four grandsons and lives in Cairo.

Abou Keer and Abou Seer
Dar-el-Hilal, 1979
The Green Island Camp
Dar-el-Hilal, 1979
The Diary of Yasser Family 1 u. 2
Rosa-el-Youssef, 1979 f.
Hurrah for Life
Information Service of Egypt, 1980
[Ü: Dr. Nihad Selaiha]
Tomorrow I will sing again
Dar-el-Maaref, 2002

What makes the poet tick?

Oh great God...
what a nice question?!!
It is a very simple one, which
makes it very difficult to answer.
So, Notaila, why not give it a try...

يا إلهي...
يا له من سؤال جميل.. سهل وبسيط.. ومن هنا
تكمن صعوبة الإجابة..
من أين البداية يا إلهي؟!
ما منبع الوحي يا رب؟!
هل من تأمل الجمال في الكون؟ من صحبة الحياة لحظة
ميلاد الكائنة الصغيرة: طفل، كتكوت، قطة.. قرد.. أسد..
دودة قز؟!
الشروق.. الغروب.. منظر شجرة ملكة الليل عندما
تتمايل بحركة النسيم بعد غروب الشمس، وتعطر الهواء...

Notaila Ibrahim Rashed, bekannt als Mama Lobna, wurde 1934 in Kairo, Ägypten, geboren und gilt als Pionierin der ägyptischen Kinder- und Jugendliteratur. Sie hat nicht nur zahlreiche Kinder- und Jugendbücher sowie Kurzgeschichten und Beiträge für diverse Kindermagazine, Radio- und Fernsehsendungen für Kinder und Jugendliche in der gesamten arabischsprachigen Welt geschrieben, sondern sich ebenso visionär und einflussreich für die Förderung ägyptischer Kinder- und Jugendliteratur eingesetzt. Von 1956 bis 2002 leitete sie das weit verbreitete arabische Kindermagazin »Samir«. 1965 gründete sie die Kinderbuchsparte des Verlagshauses Dar-el-Hilal in Kairo. Sie ist Mitglied des High Committee of Cairo International Festival for Children's Film und des Child and Juvenile Committee of Alexandria Library.
Notaila Rashed begann während ihres Studiums an der Cairo University für Kinder und Jugendliche zu schreiben. Bereits 1953 wurden ihre ersten Kurzgeschichten im Radio ausgestrahlt. Eine Vielzahl von Radio- und Fernsehausstrahlungen ihrer Kinder- und Jugendprogramme sollte folgen. Zu ihren bekanntesten Büchern gehört »The Diary of Yasser Family«, das ab 1979 in zwei Teilen erschien. Darin enthalten ist die Geschichte »The Doll«, die als Vorlage für den ersten und bisher einzigen vom ägyptischen National Council of Culture produzierten Kinderfilm diente. Ebenfalls 1979 legte sie mit »Abou Keer and Abou Seer« eine »moderne« Adaption der Geschichte um einen guten und einen bösen Nachbarn aus »Tausendundeiner Nacht« vor. In ihrer Arbeit geht es Rashed vor allem um die Verbindung der literarisch-kulturellen Tradition des Alten und des »neuen« Ägyptens. Mit ihren Texten möchte sie Kindern und Jugendlichen in aller Welt ein authentisches Bild vom Leben im heutigen Ägypten vermitteln. »Vor allem das Ägypten des Pharaonenzeitalters und das der frühen arabischen und islamischen Epoche ist über die Grenzen des Landes bekannt und berühmt. Mit dem Ägypten des 20. Jahrhunderts jedoch sind die Menschen außerhalb des Landes noch immer viel weniger vertraut.«
Neben ihrer schriftstellerischen Arbeit übersetzte Rashed Kinderbuchklassiker ins Arabische, u. a. Andersens »Des Kaisers neue Kleider«, Wildes »Der glückliche Prinz« und Swells »Black Beauty«. Sie nimmt an internationalen Kongressen zur Kinder- und Jugendliteratur sowie zu Kinderfilm-, Fernseh- und Radioproduktionen teil. Ihr literarisch-gesellschaftliches Engagement wurde vielfach gewürdigt. Bereits 1978 wurde Notaila Rashed mit den State Award for Children's Literature ausgezeichnet. 1995 erhielt sie den State Award for Children's Journalism, 2002 die Golden Medal of the Council of Ministry of Culture. Die Autorin hat drei Kinder und vier Enkelkinder. Sie lebt in Kairo.

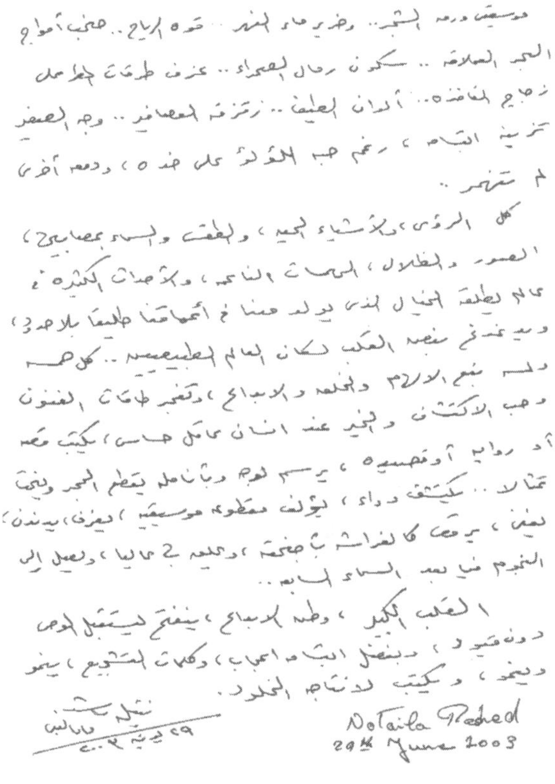

matthew sweeney

biography

Matthew Sweeney, poet, novelist and publisher, was born in County Donegal, Ireland in 1952 and lived in London for many years. He studied English and German in London and in Freiburg, placing special emphasis on 19th and 20th century German literature. He has published a large number of poetry collections for adults, including »Blue Shoes« (1989), »Cacti« (1992), »The Bridal Suite« (1997) and »A Smell of Fish« (2000). In 2002 a selection of his poems from ten volumes and from his twenty years of work as a poet was published as »Selected Poems«, Matthew Sweeney's literary work also includes poems and stories for younger readers. »The Flying Spring Onion« (1992), »Fatso in the Red Suit« (1995) and »Up on the Roof: New and selected Poems«(2001) are all highly acclaimed poetry collections for children. His stories for children include »The Chinese Dressing-Gown«(1987) and »The Snow Vulture«(1992).
In Sweeney's poetry, the world lies open and visible. His texts are persistently profound and full of forceful realism. His poems make the enigmatic, irreconcilable, unbelievable and endless things in life visible. Furthermore, his language is full of elegance and lightness, as in his highly praised novel »Fox«, published in 2002, an exciting and simultaneously thought-provoking story about growing up and the gift of friendship. Sweeney tells the tale of eleven year-old Gerard, who moves to another town and his difficulties in adapting to his new life. Suspended from school for a week because of a fight, he patrols his new surroundings with curious eyes and encounters a homeless man and his unusual companion, a tame fox. As time goes by, a band of affection and trust is formed. the closer Gerard gets to Mr. Black and the more he discovers about him, the more stability he finds in his own new life and gains the attention and encouragement that his busy parents cannot give him. In his novel Matthew Sweeney cautiously examines the themes that concern children at the age of the protagonist: problems at school, bullying by classmates, feeling misunderstood or friendship. The author shows his young readers how important it is to respect others, to carry responsibility, to show initiative and to gain trust of and for one's self and one's fellow human-beings. »Fox« is »an often lyrical but unsentimental account of friendship and loss« (»The Times«) – written in short, insistent chapters and authentically illustrated by Christopher Corr. The novel has been nominated for the CBI/Bisto Award, one of the most important Irish awards and has been published in German.
Matthew Sweeney's poetry has received numerous awards, including the Cholmondeley Award (1987) and the Arts Council of England Writers Award (1999) and has already been published in Slovakia, Latvia, Mexico, Romania and the Netherlands. In 2002 his latest poetry collection, titled »Sanctuary«, will be published. Currently, the author lives and writes in Berlin and Romania.

The Chinese Dressing-Gown
Raven Arts Press
Dublin, 1987
The Snow Vulture
Faber and Faber
London, 1992
The Flying Spring Onion
(ab 8)
Faber and Faber
London, 1992
Fatso in the Red Suit
(ab 8)
Faber and Faber
London, 1995
Up On The Roof
(ab 8)
Faber and Faber
London, 2001
Selected Poems
Cape, London, 2002
Fuchs
(ab 10)
Berlin Verlag, Berlin, 2003
[Ü: Cornelia Krutz-Arnold]
[Ill: Christopher Corr]

Matthew Sweeney, Lyriker, Erzähler und Herausgeber, wurde 1952 in County Donegal, Irland, geboren und lebte viele Jahre in London. Dort und in Freiburg studierte er Englisch und Deutsch und befasste sich intensiv mit der deutschsprachigen Literatur des 19. und 20. Jahrhunderts. Er hat zahlreiche Lyrikbände für Erwachsene veröffentlicht, darunter »Blue Shoes« (1989), »Cacti« (1992), »The Bridal Suite« (1997) und »A Smell of Fish« (2000). 2002 erschien eine Auswahl seiner Gedichte aus zehn Bänden und zwanzig Jahren dichterischer Arbeit in »Selected Poems«. Matthew Sweeneys literarisches Schaffen umfasst auch Gedichte und Erzählungen für jüngere Leser. Mit »The Flying Spring Onion« (1992), »Fatso in the Red Suit« (1995) und »Up on the Roof: New and Selected Poems« (2001) legte er vielbeachtete Gedichtbände für Kinder vor. Zu seinen Erzählungen für Kinder gehören »The Chinese Dressing-Gown« (1987) und »The Snow Vulture« (1992).

In Sweeneys Lyrik liegt die Welt offen und macht sie sichtbar. Seine Texte sind von bezwingendem Realismus und eindringlicher Prägnanz. Seine Gedichte geben den enigmatischen, unversöhnlichen, unglaublichen und endlosen Dingen des Lebens Sichtbarkeit. Dabei ist Sweeneys Sprache von großer Eleganz und Leichtigkeit, so auch in seinem 2002 erschienenen, vielgelobten Roman »Fox«, einer spannenden und zugleich nachdenklichen Geschichte über das Erwachsenwerden und das Geschenk der Freundschaft. Sweeney erzählt von dem elfjährigen Gerard, der in eine fremde Stadt zieht und sich nur schwer in sein neues Leben einfinden kann. Wegen einer Rauferei für eine Woche von der Schule verwiesen, durchstreift er mit neugierigen Augen seine neue Umgebung und begegnet dabei einem obdachlosen Mann und dessen seltsamen Weggefährten, einem zahmen Fuchs. Nach und nach entsteht ein Band der Zuneigung und des Vertrauens. Je näher Gerard dem obdachlosen Mr. Black kommt, je mehr er über ihn erfährt, desto mehr findet auch er selbst Halt in seinem neuen Leben, und er erhält die Aufmerksamkeit und Ermutigung, die ihm seine beschäftigten Eltern nicht geben können. Matthew Sweeney geht in seinem Roman behutsam auf die Themen ein, die Kinder im Alter des Protagonisten beschäftigen: Probleme in der Schule, Hänseleien durch Mitschüler, Sich-Unverstanden-Fühlen oder Freundschaft. Der Autor zeigt seinen jugendlichen Lesern, wie wichtig es ist, Respekt zu üben, Sorge zu tragen, Initiative zu zeigen und Vertrauen zu gewinnen – zu sich selbst und den Mitmenschen. »Fox« ist ein »poetisches, aber unsentimentales Buch über Freundschaft und Verlust« (»The Times«) – geschrieben in kurzen, eindringlichen und von Christopher Corr authentisch illustrierten Kapiteln. Der Roman ist für den CBI/Bisto Award, eine der wichtigsten Auszeichnungen Irlands, nominiert und in deutscher Sprache erschienen.

Matthew Sweeneys dichterisches Werk wurde mehrfach ausgezeichnet, u. a. mit dem Cholmondeley Award (1987) und dem Arts Council of England Writers' Award (1999) und bereits in der Slowakei, in Lettland, Mexiko, Rumänien und den Niederlanden veröffentlicht. 2004 erscheint sein neuester Gedichtband unter dem Titel »Sanctuary«. Der Autor lebt und schreibt derzeit in Berlin und Rumänien.

annika thor

biography

Annika Thor was born to Jewish parents in Gothenburg, Sweden in 1950. Originally educated as a librarian, she made a name for herself in her homeland as a film and TV critic, before she devoted herself solely to the writing of children's and young people's books, theatre plays, and screenplays for film and television. Annika Thor is now one of the best known Swedish authors for children and young adults. Her novels have been translated into various languages and have been awarded many prizes.
Her debut novel »En ö i havet« (1996) was received with much enthusiasm by critics and readers alike. In 1996 it was nominated for the most prestigious literature prize in Sweden, the August Prize, and was awarded the Deutscher Jugendliteraturpreis. »En ö i havet« is the first of four novels, in which the author tells the story of two Jewish sisters, Steffi and Nelli, who are sent into exile in Sweden by their parents in Vienna, in order to protect them from persecution by the National Socialists. The tetralogy follows the two girls through their adolescence and depicts their sometimes difficult, sometimes untroubled daily life as refugee children. By telling the story from the point of view of the protagonists, human vices and virtues are made both realistic and comprehensible.
The publication of her novel »Sanning eller konsekvens« in 1997 coincided with the release of the award-winning film by Christina Olofson, for which Annika Thor wrote the screenplay. The novel was awarded the August Prize and is one of the most important literary contributions on the topic of bullying of school children. Written from the point of view of twelve year-old Nora, who is afraid that she has lost her best friend to her classmate Fanny, and who on no account wants to »hang out« with unpopular Karin, the novel tells a tale of peer pressure, fear of exclusion and the cruelties of daily life at school. Annika Thor creates a sensitive, didactic piece of writing, which calls upon us to treat fellow humans with respect – and to take responsibility for our own actions, without a hint of patronising.
Annika Thor's first children's book »Rött hjärta blå fjäril« (2002), a charming love story about the primary school children Alva and Love, has just been published in German.
As a script writer, she recently adapted her tetralogy about Steffi and Nelli into a TV series, which will be broadcast on Swedish television in December 2003. The author lives in Stockholm.

Eine Insel im Meer
(ab 12)
Carlsen, Hamburg, 1998
[Ü: Angelika Kutsch]
Eine Bank am Seerosenteich
(ab 12)
Carlsen, Hamburg, 1999
[Ü: Angelika Kutsch]
Ich hätte Nein sagen können
(ab 11)
Beltz und Gelberg
Weinheim, 2000
[Ü: Angelika Kutsch]
In der Tiefe des Meeres
(ab 12)
Carlsen, Hamburg, 2000
[Ü: Angelika Kutsch]
Offenes Meer
(ab 12)
Carlsen, Hamburg, 2000
[Ü: Angelika Kutsch]
Ein rotes Herz, ein blauer Schmetterling
Carlsen, Hamburg, 2003
[Ü: Angelika Kutsch]
[Ill: Heike Vogel]
Pirr i magen klump i halsen
Bonnier Carlsen
Stockholm, 2003

```
Von: Annika Thor
Gesendet: Freitag, 16. Mai 2003 18:16
An: miriam.moellers@literaturfestival.com
Betreff: Re: ilb 2003: What makes the poet tick?

So for me, the only possibility is to answer very simply, the first thing
that comes into my mind:

REAL LIFE.

Best wishes,

Annika
```

Annika Thor wurde 1950 als Kind jüdischer Eltern in Göteborg, Schweden, geboren. In ihrer Heimat machte sich die gelernte Bibliothekarin zunächst als Film- und Fernsehkritikerin einen Namen, bevor sie sich ganz dem Schreiben von Kinder- und Jugendbüchern, Theaterstücken, Film- und TV-Drehbüchern widmete. Inzwischen gehört Annika Thor zu den bekanntesten schwedischen Kinder- und Jugendbuchautorinnen. Ihre Romane wurden in verschiedene Sprachen übersetzt und vielfach ausgezeichnet.

Schon ihr Debüt »En ö i havet« von 1996 (dt. »Eine Insel im Meer«, 1998) wurde von Kritik und Leserschaft begeistert aufgenommen. Der Jugendroman wurde 1996 für den höchsten Literaturpreis Schwedens, den Augustpriset, nominiert und 1999 mit dem Deutschen Jugendliteraturpreis ausgezeichnet. »Eine Insel im Meer« ist der erste von vier Romanen, in denen die Autorin die Geschichte der jüdischen Schwestern Steffi und Nelli erzählt, die 1939 von ihren Eltern aus Wien ins schwedische Exil geschickt werden, um sie vor der Verfolgung durch die Nationalsozialisten zu schützen. In ihrer Tetralogie folgt sie den beiden Mädchen durch ihre Jugendjahre und schildert den manchmal schwierigen, manchmal unbeschwerten Alltag der Flüchtlingskinder. Indem sie aus der Sicht ihrer Protagonistinnen erzählt, werden menschliche Tugenden und Bösartigkeiten gleichermaßen lebendig und verständlich. Zeitgleich mit der preisgekrönten Verfilmung von Christina Olofson, für die Annika Thor das ebenfalls prämierte Drehbuch schrieb, erschien 1997 ihr Roman »Sanning eller konsekvens« (dt. »Ich hätte Nein sagen können«,1998), der in Schweden mit dem Augustpriset prämiert wurde und einen der wichtigsten literarischen Beiträge zum Thema Mobbing unter Schülern darstellt. Aus der Perspektive der zwölfjährigen Nora, die fürchtet, ihre beste Freundin an Fanny und ihre Clique verloren zu haben und sich auf keinen Fall mit der unbeliebten Karin »abgeben« möchte, erzählt die Autorin von Gruppenzwang, Angst vor Ausgrenzung und den Boshaftigkeiten des Schulalltags. Annika Thor entwickelt ein einfühlsames, niemals anbiederndes Lehrstück, das ohne jede Schulmeisterlichkeit dazu auffordert, Mitmenschen mit Respekt zu behandeln und die Verantwortung für das eigene Handeln zu übernehmen.

Annika Thors erstes Kinderbuch »Rött hjärta blå fjäril« (2002), die charmante Liebesgeschichte der Grundschüler Alva und Love, ist soeben in deutscher Übersetzung erschienen. Als Drehbuchautorin adaptierte sie kürzlich ihre Tetralogie über Steffi und Nelli, die als Vierteiler im Dezember 2003 im schwedischen Fernsehen ausgestrahlt wird. Die Autorin lebt in Stockholm.

Real Life.

eugene trivizas

biography

Eugene Trivizas, author of more than 100 children's books, was born in Athens, Greece in 1946, and is one of the most important contemporary Greek authors for children. He received his LLB degree in Athens, followed by a BSc in politics and economics. The following year he received an LLM degree in comparative criminal law and procedure from the University of London, where he was also awarded his PhD in criminology in 1979. He is currently Professor of criminology and criminal justice at the University of Reading, Great Britain. For more than thirty years, he has been involved with almost all genres of literature: fairytales, poetry, stories, humorous historical texts, opera librettos, children's theatre, comics and educational software.

Trivizas' picture book »Ta tría mikrá lykákia« (t: The three little wolves and the big bad pig), published in 1993, became an international bestseller, after his adaptation of the classical fairytale had lain around on his desk for years, because no publisher was willing to publish a book in which the wolf is not evil, but good. Modernised into a work as entertaining as it is profound, it has been translated into seventeen languages and has been incorporated into the Heinemann collection of the ten best classic picture books ever published. In September 2003 a miniature and pop-up celebratory edition of the book will be published. Trivizas' surrealistic humour and his creative use of language are unique.

A charming teller of fairytales, Trivizas must be taken seriously in his unseriousness, in his infectious enthusiasm for the limitless, invented, improbable, and the phantasmagoric, for beauty and tragedy in the world. Behind his stories' fabulous and humorous »masks«, serious social issues are concealed. His novel »Hé teleftaía mávri gáta« (t: The Last Black Cat), which was published in 2001, is the story of a ruthless hunt in a society full of prejudice and superstition, and a plea for an end to exclusion, persecution and cruelty – persistently portrayed from the perspective of an animal protagonist, »the last black cat«.

»Ta 88 dolmadákia« is an extraordinary work; this »interactive« book animates young readers to make their own decisions about the story's order of events. His latest publications include the Olympic novel »Despina kai to peristeri« (2001; t: Despina and the dove), which has been published by the Organising Committee for the Olympic Games Athens 2004, and »Ena helidoni gia tin Europi« (2003; t: A Swallow over Europe) – an as yet unparalleled book project for children about European integration.

Eugene Trivizas has received the most prestigious Greek awards and a large number of international honours. In 1997, he won a spectacular court case against Coca Cola, who wanted to register the term »Fruitopia« in Greece as a trademark for soft drinks. Trivizas' homonymic work »Frutopia« had namely already existed as a successful TV series and theatre play, and the title of a comic series since 1985. Trivizas' works have been adapted for theatre, TV and radio, have become required reading in Greek and American schools, and have been translated into many languages. The author lives in Reading and Athens.

Die drei kleinen Wölfe und das große böse Schwein
(ab 6)
Sauerländer, Aarau, 1993
[Ü: Rolf Inhauser]
[Ill: Helen Oxenbury]

Ta 88 dolmadákia
Kalentis, Athen, 1997
[Ill: Rania Varvaki]

Hé teleftaía mávri gáta
Ellinika Grammata
Athen, 2001
[Ill: Stephan West]

Poios ékane pipí sto Misisipí
Ellinika Grammata
Athen, 2001
Ill: Kely Matathia Kovo

Despina und die Taube
Ellinika Grammata
Athen, 2001
[Ü: Doris Wille]
[Ill: Maro Alexandrou
Spyros Gousis
Kapatsoulia]

Eine Schwalbe für Europa
Griechisches
Außenministerium
2003
[Ü: Doris Wille]
[Ill: Rania Varvaki]

Eugene Trivizas, Autor von mehr als 100 Kinderbüchern, wurde 1946 in Athen, Griechenland, geboren und ist einer der bedeutendsten griechischen Kinderbuchautoren der Gegenwart. Er studierte Jura, Politik- und Wirtschaftswissenschaften in Athen, ist promovierter Jurist und Professor für Kriminologie und Vergleichendes Strafrecht an der Universität Reading, Großbritannien. Seit mehr als dreißig Jahren befasst er sich mit nahezu allen Gattungen der Literatur: Märchen, Dichtung, Erzählung, humoristische Geschichtsschreibung, Opernlibretti, Kindertheater, Comics und Lernsoftware.
Trivizas' Bilderbuch »Ta tría mikrá lykákia« von 1993 (dt. »Die drei kleinen Wölfe und das große böse Schwein«, 1993) wurde zu einem internationalen Bestseller, nachdem die Bearbeitung des klassischen Märchens jahrelang auf seinem Schreibtisch liegen blieb, weil kein Verlag ein Buch drucken wollte, in dem der Wolf nicht der Böse, sondern der Gute ist.
Zu einem ebenso unterhaltsamen wie tiefsinnigen Werk modernisiert, wurde es in siebzehn Sprachen übersetzt und in die Heinemann-Sammlung der zehn besten klassischen Bilderbücher aller Zeiten aufgenommen. Im Herbst 2003 erscheint eine Festausgabe in sieben Sprachen als Pop-up-Buch. Unverwechselbar sind Trivizas' surrealistischer Humor und der kreative Umgang mit Sprache. Trivizas ist ein charmanter Märchenerzähler, den man in seinem Un-Ernst ernst nehmen muss, in seiner mitreißenden Begeisterung für das Grenzenlose, Erfundene, Unwahrscheinliche, Traumhafte, für das Wunderschöne und Traurige der Welt. Hinter der märchenhaften und humorvollen »Maske« seiner Texte verbergen sich ernsthafte gesellschaftliche Themen. Sein 2001 erschienener Roman »Hé teleftaia mavri gata« (Ü: Die letzte schwarze Katze) ist die Geschichte einer erbarmungslosen Jagd in einer Gesellschaft voller Vorurteile und Aberglaube und ein Plädoyer gegen Ausgrenzung, Verfolgung und Grausamkeit – eindringlich portraitiert aus der Perspektive eines »tierischen« Protagonisten, der »letzten schwarzen Katze«. Ein außergewöhnliches Buch ist »Ta 88 dolmadákia« (Ü: Die achtundachtzig Weinblätterrollen). Es handelt sich um ein »interaktives« Buch, das seine jugendlichen Leser animiert, selbst Entscheidungen über den weiteren Handlungsablauf zu treffen. Zu Trivizas' aktuellsten Veröffentlichungen gehören der Olympiaroman »Despina kai to peristeri« (dt. »Despina und die Taube«, 2001), der vom Organisationskomitee der Olympischen Spiele Athen 2004 herausgegeben wurde, und »Ena helidoni gia tin Europi« (dt. »Eine Schwalbe für Europa«, 2003) – ein bisher einmaliges Buchprojekt für Kinder über das Zusammenwachsen Europas.
Eugene Trivizas wurde mit den bedeutendsten Auszeichnungen Griechenlands und einer Vielzahl internationaler Ehrungen bedacht. 1997 konnte er einen spektakulären Prozess gegen den Coca-Cola-Konzern gewinnen, der in Griechenland den Begriff »Fruitopia« zur Bezeichnung eines Soft-Drinks verwenden wollte. Schon 1985 war Trivizas' klanggleiches Werk »Frutopia« erschienen, das als Fernsehserie und Theaterstück Erfolge feierte und Titel einer vielbändigen Comicserie ist. Trivizas' Werke wurden für das Theater, Fernsehen und Radio adaptiert, unter die Lesebücher griechischer und amerikanischer Schulen aufgenommen und in zahlreiche Sprachen übersetzt. Der Autor lebt in Reading und Athen.

What makes the poet tick

Quite insignificant and neglected objects make me tick and become sources of inspiration., items such as a burned matchstick , a striped drinking straw , a cherry stalk , a milk bottle top , a sugar cube, a puff ball, or a cinnamon stick. There is magic in the ordinary, there is enchantment in what passes mostly unnoticed.

The other day as was checking in at Heathrow airport, I noticed again a list of forbidden items, objects that you are not allowed to take with you in the airplane. The list included cutlery, catapults, toy guns, scissors and knitting needles! I decided to write a series of stories of such confiscated items each one having its one tale to tell. The knitting needles of an old lady talking to the catapult of a naughty boy and the scissor reminiscing his days of glory at the hand of an haute coiffure hairdresser or perhaps sharing his dream of cutting the string and setting free marionettes

katerína angeláki-rooke
jorgi jatromanolakis
ioanna karystiani
menis koumandareas
dimosthenis kourtovik
nikos panajotopoulos
jorgos skambardonis
ersi sotiropoulos
soti triantafillou
charis vlavianos

katerína angeláki-rooke

biography

Katerína Angeláki-Rooke was born in Athens in 1939. She studied foreign languages in Athens, France and Switzerland, and concluded her studies with a diploma in translation and interpretation for English, French and Russian.
Angeláki-Rooke emerged as a forerunner to the second generation of post-war poets (the so-called »sceptical generation«). She iconoclastically addressed familiar mythological subjects and symbols, questioning their conventional content. Following her works in the 60s – »Liki kai sinnefa« (1963; t: Wolves and Clouds), »Piimata 63-69« (1971; t: Poems 63-69) – her poetry began to focus on what would later become the defining theme of her very personal material: the description of the physicality of feeling. Limbs, organs and features of the body become lexical and sensual sounding boards for the poet's consciousness. The world with which this consciousness engages in dialogue is a cold, wintery landscape that – far from being sombre – leads to a comprehension of solitude as being peaceful and dignified. Loneliness is understood rather as a more profound, ontological state of existence. This stance, unusual in Greek poetry, is expressed in the collections »Magdalini, to megalo thilastiko« (1974; t: Magdalena, the Large Mammal) and »Ta skorpia chartia tis Pinelopis« (1977; t: Penelope's Scattered Papers) and above all in »O thriamvos tis statheris apolias« (1978; t: The Triumph of Continual Loss), »Enantios erotas« (1982; t: Adverse Love) and »I mnistires« (1984; t: The Prostitute's Client).
In Angeláki-Rooke's more recent works »Epilogos aeras« (1990; t: Epilogue Wind), »Lipiu« (1995; t: Land of Mourning) and »Orea erimos i sarka« (1996; t: Beautiful Wasteland, Flesh), greater emphasis is laid on the narrative element. There are direct autobiographical references. The tone is new and the voice seems to be conducting a muted dialogue with death.
Poems by Katerína Angeláki-Rooke have been translated into more than 10 languages. A few poems have appeared in German translation in the anthologies »Und ich, die nur wollte, ich« (1992; t: And I, Who Only Wanted, I) and »Unter dem Gewicht der Wörter« (1999; t: Under the Weight of Words). She has translated a number of works herself, both prose and poetry, from English, French and Russian into Greek. The poet lives in Athens.

Liki kai sinnefa
Zarvanos, Athen, 1963
Piimata
Ermias, Athen, 1971
Enantios erotas
Kedros, Athen, 1982
I mnistires
Kedros, Athen, 1984
Epilogos aeras
Kedros, Athen, 1990
Adia fisi
Kedros, Athen, 1993
Orea erimos i sarka
Kastaniotis, Athen, 1996

Katerína Angeláki-Rooke wurde 1939 in Athen geboren. Sie studierte Fremdsprachen in Athen, Frankreich und der Schweiz und schloss mit einem Diplom als Übersetzerin und Dolmetscherin für Englisch, Französisch und Russisch ab.
Angeláki-Rooke trat als Vorreiterin der zweiten Dichtergeneration nach dem Krieg (der sogenannten »Generation der Skepsis«) in Erscheinung, indem sie sich bilderstürmerisch mit bekannten mythologischen Motiven und Symbolen auseinandersetzte und deren konventionelle Inhalte infrage stellte. Nach den Arbeiten der sechziger Jahre – »Liki kai sinnefa« (1963; Ü: Wölfe und Wolken), »Piimata 63-69« (1971; Ü: Gedichte 63-69) – konzentrierte sie sich in ihrer Dichtung auf das, was ihr ganz persönliches Erkennungsmerkmal werden sollte: die Beschreibung der Körperlichkeit der Gefühle. Gliedmaßen, Organe und Merkmale des Körpers werden auf buchstäbliche und sinnliche Weise zu Resonanzböden des Bewusstseins der Dichterin. Die Welt, mit der dieses Bewusstsein im Dialog steht, ist eine kalte, winterliche Landschaft, die jedoch – weit davon entfernt, düster zu sein – zu einer ruhigen und würdevollen Annahme der Einsamkeit zu führen scheint. Einsamkeit wird hier als tieferes, ontologisches Wesen des Daseins begriffen. Diese Haltung, ungewöhnlich in der griechischen Dichtung, findet ihren Ausdruck in den Sammlungen »Magdalini, to megalo thilastiko« (1974; Ü: Magdalena, das große Säugetier), »Ta skorpia chartia tis Pinelopis« (1977; Ü: Die verstreuten Papiere der Penelope) und vor allem in »O thriamvos tis statheris apolias« (1978; Ü: Der Triumph des stetigen Verlustes), »Enantios erotas« (1982; Ü: Widrige Liebe) und »I mnistires« (1984; Ü: Die Freier).
In den neueren Arbeiten Angeláki-Rookes »Epilogos aeras«, (1990; Ü: Nachwort Wind), »Lipiu« (1995; Ü: Trauerland) und »Orea erimos i sarka« (1996; Ü: Schöne Wüste, das Fleisch) kommt hingegen das erzählerische Element stärker zum Tragen, es gibt direkte autobiographische Bezüge. Neu ist der Ton eines wie mit gedämpfter Stimme geführten Dialoges mit dem Tod.
Gedichte von Katerína Angeláki-Rooke sind in mehr als zehn Sprachen übersetzt worden. In deutscher Übersetzung liegen einige Gedichte in den Anthologien »Und ich, die nur wollte, ich« (1992) und »Unter dem Gewicht der Wörter« (1999) vor. Sie selbst hat eine Vielzahl von Werken, sowohl Lyrik als auch Prosa, aus dem Englischen, Französischen und Russischen ins Griechische übertragen. Die Dichterin lebt in Athen.

FROM : ANGHELAKI-ROOKE PHONE NO. : P0

What makes the tic
of the Poetics?

The tic of the heart
the tic of the clock
the tic of the walking stick
the tic of the nail into your final case
into the case of oblivion.

Katerina Anghelaki-Rooke

jorgi jatromanolakis

biography

Jorgi Jatromanolakis was born in Saros on the island of Crete in 1940. He studied Classical Philology in Athens and then began his postgraduate studies at King's College London, where he completed a doctorate degree. He initially worked as a high school teacher. Since 1975 he has been teaching at the University of Athens, where today, after a guest professorship at Harvard University from 1979 to 1980, he lectures in Classical Philology.

Jatromanolakis published his first prose texts in the seventies. His literary breakthrough came in 1982 with the novel »Istoría« (»A History of a Vendetta«, 1991) for which he received the Greek national award and the Nikos Kasantzakis Award. Two novels followed: »Anofelés diíjima« (1993; »A Report of a Murder«, 1995) and »Erotikón« (1995; »Eroticon«, 2001). His most recent novel to date, »Stin kiláda ton Athinón« (2000; t: In the Valley of Athens), has yet to be translated into German. Jatromanolakis also writes poems and scientific texts on Classical Philology and New Greek Literature.

In »A Report of a Murder« two physicists are shot by a graduate student during a seminar on the island of Crete. The assailant then flees to the mountains and commits suicide. His corpse is discovered by a shepherd months later. In formal terms the text is arranged as a scientific report by an anonymous narrator who attempts to reconstruct the murders on the basis of newspaper articles, autopsy reports, photographs and evidence gathered at the scene of the crime. However, out of the mysterious and inexplicable nature of the acts, emerges the mythical strength of ancient legends, which still seem to be present in the holy mountains of Crete.

Jorgi Jatromanolakis's books are characterised by their complexity and rigid adherence to form. The modern, sometimes not easily accessible language of his texts is animated and enriched by stylistic elements from Greek literary traditions. »If the first sentence of a crime thriller already reveals the identity of the assailant, then the author must be aiming at something other than nail-biting suspense«, wrote Ulrich M. Schmid on »A Report of a Murder«. It is not the sequence of events that forms the actual core of Jatromanolakis's stories, but rather an investigation into narrative perspective and the search for moral categories of judgment. The fact that many of his works are set in Greece does not but also provides the background encompassed within the inseperatability of the characters from the environs in which they live. Their history, tradition and myths have become part of their personality.

A very personal translation
of Homer's Odyssey, book 1. line 1-10
by Jorgi Jatromanolakis

Limonario
Kalvos, Athen, 1974
I arravoniastikia
Kedros, Athen, 1979
O sacharenios erastis
Stigmi, Athen, 1984
Der Schlaf der Rinder
Bruckner & Thunker
Köln, 1996
[Ü: Norbert Hauser]
Bericht von einem vorbestimmten Mord
DuMont, Köln, 1998
[Ü: Norbert Hauser]
Erotikon
DuMont, Köln, 2001
[Ü: Norbert Hauser]
Elinas kleos
Agra, Athen, 2002

My dearest Muse,
you see, I am too old to clearly recall places, things and persons, so kindly, would you please help me a bit? My requests will not be too great, or too absurd; at

Jorgi Jatromanolakis wurde 1940 in Saros auf Kreta geboren. Er studierte Klassische Philologie in Athen, anschließend begann er ein Postgraduiertenstudium am King's College in London, das er mit dem Doktortitel abschloss. Zunächst arbeitete er als Gymnasiallehrer. Seit 1975 unterrichtet er an der Universität Athen, wo er heute, nach einer Gastprofessur an der Harvard University von 1979 bis 1980, als Professor für Klassische Philologie tätig ist. Seine ersten Prosatexte veröffentlichte Jatromanolakis in den siebziger Jahren. Der literarische Durchbruch gelang ihm 1982 mit dem Roman »Istoría« (dt. »Der Schlaf der Rinder«, 1996), für den er den Griechischen Staatspreis und den Nikos-Kasantzakis-Preis erhielt. Seither erschienen die Romane »Anofelés diíjima« (1993; dt. »Bericht von einem vorbestimmten Mord«, 1998) und »Erotikón« (1995; dt. »Erotikon«, 2001). Sein bislang letzter Roman »Stin kiláda ton Athinón« (2000; Ü: Im Tal von Athen) wurde noch nicht ins Deutsche übersetzt. Daneben schreibt Jatromanolakis Gedichte sowie wissenschaftliche Texte zur Klassischen Philologie und zur neugriechischen Literatur.

Im »Bericht von einem vorbestimmten Mord« werden während eines Seminars auf Kreta zwei Physiker von einem Doktoranden niedergeschossen, der daraufhin in die Berge flieht und Selbstmord begeht. Erst Monate später wird seine Leiche von einem Hirten entdeckt. Formal ist der Text als wissenschaftlicher Bericht eines anonym bleibenden Erzählers gestaltet, der anhand von Zeitungsartikeln, Obduktionsberichten, Fotos und Ortsbegehungen die Morde zu rekonstruieren versucht. Im Geheimnisvollen und Unerklärlichen der Taten tritt jedoch die mythische Kraft antiker Sagen hervor, die in den heiligen Bergen Kretas noch gegenwärtig zu sein scheint.

Jorgi Jatromanolakis' Bücher zeichnen sich durch ihre Vielschichtigkeit und eine große Formstrenge aus. Die moderne, bisweilen schwer zugängliche Sprache seiner Texte wird durch Stilelemente aus den Traditionen der griechischen Literatur bereichert und belebt. »Wenn schon der erste Satz eines Krimis die Identität des Täters preisgibt, muss der Autor anderes im Sinn haben als spannende Unterhaltung«, schrieb Ulrich M. Schmid über den »Bericht von einem vorbestimmten Mord«. Nicht der Handlungsablauf bildet den eigentlichen Kern von Jatromanolakis' Geschichten, vielmehr geht es um den Blickwinkel des Erzählers und die Suche nach moralischen Kategorien der Bewertung. Dass viele seiner Werke in Griechenland spielen, dient nicht nur der Erzeugung eines bestimmten regionalen Kolorits. Die Figuren, die der Autor entwirft, sind untrennbar mit dem Ort verbunden, an dem sie leben. Dessen Geschichte, Tradition und Mythen sind Teil ihrer Persönlichkeit geworden.

least, not as great and absurd of those of that blind old poet. That old chap asked your help just once, but he demanded a lot: "give me this, give that. Tell me about that man, tell me about his travels, about the people he met, especially the women, the cities that he leveled, et cetera, et cetera". He was so eager to learn from you all the personal, very personal, data of this man, and you, you silly girl, were so kind, so generous to him. Why?

Why did you offer him so much information about a man who was absolutely corrupt; a thief, a killer, a liar, a cunning, tricky man, a destroyer? He left behind his naive wife, yes, a naive, stupid wife, Penelope by name. Do you know that? Do you know that he even abandoned his little son? He left his comrades to die. OK. At least I am pleased that those stupid men died; they died because they ate some crazy cows on the isle of Sun. Certainly whoever consumes meat of crazy cows deserves to die. But that Ulysses, he was not a kind person. So why, my Muse, did you give all this information to that poet? Anyway. It's my turn now. My time has come. So please, my little Muse, can you visit me one of these days? But, please, don't be too late. I have already made a list of my requests; they are not many, just a few. About some people, about some facts (I don't care if these facts are really accurate, OK?), about some places. That's all.

From the heaven where you are, my sweety Muse, give me your help.

ioanna karystiani

biography

Ioanna Karystiani was born in Chania, Crete, in 1952. After studying law, she initially made a name for herself as a cartoonist and screenplay writer. It was not until the 90's that she decided to publish prose. She made her debut in 1995 with the collection of stories »I kyria Kataki«, which was quickly followed by her first novel »Mikra Anglia«, published in Germany in 2001 under the title »Die Frauen von Andros« (t: The Women of Andros), and then by her most recent work »Koustoumi sto choma«. In addition to her literary work, Karystiani is also intensely involved in film. In the summer of 2002 she worked on the production of her screenplay »The Brides« with Martin Scorcese in Athens and Crete. Ioanna Karystiani's work has earned her widespread recognition; she received the Greek state prize for literature and the prize of the Athenian Academy for her first novel, and the Diavaso literature prize for her second. She is married to the renowned film director Pantelis Voulgaris, has two children and lives in Athens and on the island of Andros.

Karystiani writes about the small, seemingly only circumstantial details in the lives of her characters. It was the photos of drowned sailors in the Kafenions and in people's homes on Andros that provided the impetus for researching the stories behind the pictures and describing the world of the women whose lives centre more than ever on the men after they have died. »Die Frauen von Andros« is a family story, which alternates between the confines of island life and the expanse of the ocean. As the »Neue Züricher Zeitung« has aptly written, »Karystiani avoids any inconsequentialities that could detract from the substance of her writing, above all those that one-sidedly identify with a character. In her writing, perspectives continuously change to create a panorama of life on Andros that seems all the more natural because the author portrays many protagonists without exhaustively focusing on just one.«

The situation is similar for the women of Crete, who make public the death of family members killed in a feud by wearing the victims' black shirts. In »Schattenhochzeit« (t: Shadow Wedding) Karystiani tells the story of the distinguished scholar Kyriakos Roussias, who has remained away from his native Crete for almost 30 years and suddenly has to face his cousin of the same name, his alter ego – and his father's murderer.

The author formulates questions concerning the dialectics of the civilising processes central to her work as follows: »How can one deal with forgetting? How can one kill? Why do we avoid an encounter with our actual self? Why is reconciliation more difficult than confrontation?«

I kyria Kataki
Kastaniotis, Athen, 1995
Die Frauen von Andros
Suhrkamp
Frankfurt a. M., 2001
[Ü: Norbert Hauser]
Schattenhochzeit
Suhrkamp
Frankfurt a. M., 2003
[Ü: Michaela Prinzinger]

Ioanna Karystiani wurde 1952 in Chania, Kreta, geboren und machte sich nach dem Jura-Studium zunächst als Cartoonistin und Drehbuchautorin einen Namen. Erst in den neunziger Jahren entschloss sie sich, Prosatexte zu veröffentlichen. Den Anfang machte 1995 ein Erzählband »I kyria Kataki« (Ü: Frau Kataki), bald darauf folgte ihr erster Roman »Mikra Anglia«, auf deutsch 2001 unter dem Titel »Die Frauen von Andros« erschienen, sowie zuletzt »Koustoumi sto choma« (dt. »Schattenhochzeit«, 2003). Neben ihrer literarischen Arbeit beschäftigt sich Karystiani weiterhin intensiv mit dem Film; so arbeitete sie beispielsweise im Sommer 2002 mit Martin Scorcese an der Realisierung ihres Drehbuchs »The Brides« in Athen und auf Kreta. Ioanna Karystianis Werk wurde vielfach ausgezeichnet – so erhielt sie den Griechischen Staatspreis für Literatur für ihren ersten und den Preis der Athener Akademie sowie den Diavaso-Literaturpreis für ihren zweiten Roman. Sie ist mit dem renommierten Filmregisseur Pantelis Voulgaris verheiratet, hat zwei Kinder und lebt in Athen und auf Andros.
Karystiani nimmt sich der kleinen, nur scheinbar nebensächlichen Details im Leben ihrer Figuren an. So waren die Erinnerungsfotos der ertrunkenen Seemänner in den Kafenions und Privathäusern auf Andros der Auslöser, nach den Geschichten hinter den Bildern zu forschen und die Welt der Frauen zu schildern, in deren Leben die Männer die größte Präsenz erst entwickeln, wenn sie zu Tode kommen. Treffend formulierte die »NZZ« über »Die Frauen von Andros«, eine Familiengeschichte, die zwischen der Enge der Inselheimat und der Weite der Ozeane hin- und herwechselt: »Karystiani vermeidet alle Untiefen, die ihren Stoff zur Kolportage machen könnten, vor allem die der einseitigen Identifikation mit einer Figur. Fortwährend nimmt sie wechselnde Perspektiven ein und erschafft damit ein Panorama andriotischen Lebens, das umso natürlicher wirkt, als die Autorin von vielen Protagonisten erzählt, ohne auch nur von einem einzigen erschöpfend zu berichten.«
Ähnlich ergeht es den kretischen Frauen, die die schwarzen Hemden der Familienmitglieder tragen, die auf einen Fehdetoten verweisen. In »Schattenhochzeit« beschreibt Karystiani die Geschichte von Kyriakos Roussias, einem hochdekorierten Wissenschaftler und seit fast dreißig Jahren seiner kretischen Heimat ferngeblieben, der plötzlich seinem gleichnamigen Cousin und alter ego gegenübersteht, dem Mörder seines Vaters.
Die Fragen der Dialektik der zivilisatorischen Prozesse, die für das Werk der Autorin zentral sind, formuliert sie selbst folgendermaßen: »Wie hält man das Vergessen aus? Wie erhebt sich eine Hand zum Töten? Warum weichen wir der Begegnung mit unserem tatsächlichen Ich aus? Warum ist Versöhnung schwieriger als Feindschaft?«

menis koumandareas

biography

Menis Koumandareas was born in Athens in 1931. He began to write at a young age, but first earned his living working for insurance and shipping agencies. In 1962 his first publication, the book of stories »Ta michanákia«, marked the start of an extensive and award-winning prose oeuvre, which has been translated into six European languages.
In 1972 the author, who has also distinguished himself as a translator of writers including Poe, Hemingway, and Faulkner, received a scholarship from the DAAD in Berlin.
Koumandareas is considered the leading representative of social realism in Greek prose. His stories primarily take place in his hometown of Athens, which the author has only ever left reluctantly and then for only short periods of time. His themes are the boys without hope, the failures on the periphery of a cruel middle class society. His language is direct and precise, but his realistic narrative style also contains lyrical and elegiac elements. With his works Koumandareas not only speaks out against the regressive petty bourgeoisie, but also against all forms of state despotism, which during the years of the Greek military dictatorship from 1967 to 1974 caused serious problems for the author. Together with his chronicles »To arménisma« that were published in 1966, the co-author of the »18 Texts«, which Greek writers wrote out of protest against the conformity enforced by the colonels, has been cited in a court of law more than once, but was finally cleared of the accusation of obscenity. His debut novel »Viotechnía jalikón« which was influenced by his impressions from this time was published a year after the fall of the dictatorship and received the first Greek state prize (1976) granted after the end of the junta.
The novel »O oräos lochagós« that was published in 1982 is also about Greece in the 60's. At the Frankfurt Book Fair in 2001 it received the newly established Blue Book Prize created to support Greek literature and was translated into German. It tells of the subtle homoerotic encounter between an aging judge and a young captain, who at the Administrative Court wants to sue for his promotion. The scenery in the novel is hazy and, in its repressive and threatening qualities, recalls Kafka's »The Trial«. Against this background the insistent captain increasingly falls apart, thereby becoming a symbol of a youth that passes without having been lived.

Ta michanákia
Fexis, Athen, 1962
I kyria Koula
Kedros, Athen, 1978
Glasfabrik
Erpf, Bern, 1985
[Ü: Norbert Hauser]
I fanela me to enia
Kedros, Athen, 1986
Der schöne Hauptmann
FVA, Frankfurt a. M., 2001
[Ü: Luna Gertrud Steiner]
Dio fores Ellinas
Kedros, Athen, 2001
Mein fantastischer Frisiersalon
Hainholz, Göttingen, 2002
[Ü: Luna Gertrud Steiner]

Menis Koumandareas wurde 1931 in Athen geboren. Er begann schon früh zu schreiben, verdiente seinen Lebensunterhalt aber zunächst bei Versicherungsagenturen und Reedereien. Seine erste Veröffentlichung, der Erzählband »Ta michanákia« (Ü: Die Mofas), wurde 1962 zum Ausgangspunkt für ein umfangreiches und vielfach prämiertes Prosaœuvre, das in sechs europäische Sprachen übersetzt worden ist. 1972 erhielt der Grieche, der sich auch als Übersetzer von Autoren wie Poe, Hemingway oder Faulkner hervorgetan hat, ein Stipendium des DAAD Berlin.
Koumandareas gilt als der führende Vertreter des sozialen Realismus in der griechischen Prosa. Den szenischen Hintergrund seiner Geschichten bildet meist Athen, die Heimatstadt, die der Autor stets ungern und nur für kurze Zeit verlassen hat. Sein Thema sind die Jungen ohne Hoffnung, die Scheiternden am Rande einer verrohten bürgerlichen Gesellschaft. Seine Sprache ist schlicht und präzise, seine realistische Erzählweise lässt jedoch auch lyrische und elegische Elemente anklingen.
Koumandareas bezieht mit seinen Werken nicht nur Stellung gegen das regressive Kleinbürgertum, sondern auch gegen jede Form staatlicher Willkür, was ihm in den Jahren der griechischen Militärdiktatur von 1967 bis 1974 erhebliche Schwierigkeiten eingebracht hat. Der Mitverfasser der »18 Texte«, mit denen sich griechische Schriftsteller gegen die Gleichschaltung durch die Obristen verwahrten, wurde im Zusammenhang mit seinen 1966 erschienenen Chroniken »To arménisma« (Ü: Der Segeltörn) mehrfach vor Gericht zitiert, schließlich aber vom Vorwurf der Obszönität freigesprochen. Sein unter den Eindrücken jener Zeit entstandenes Romandebüt »Viotechnía jalikón« (dt. »Glasfabrik«, 1985) erschien ein Jahr nach dem Sturz der Diktatoren und wurde mit dem ersten nach dem Ende der Junta verliehenen Griechischen Staatspreis (1976) ausgezeichnet.
Mit dem Griechenland der sechziger Jahre beschäftigt sich auch der 1982 erschienene Roman »O oräos lochagós« (dt. »Der schöne Hauptmann«), der im Rahmen der Frankfurter Buchmesse 2001 mit dem neu geschaffenen Blue Book Preis zur Förderung griechischer Literatur ausgezeichnet und ins Deutsche übersetzt wurde. Er erzählt von der subtil homoerotisch angelegten Begegnung eines alternden Richters mit einem jungen Hauptmann, der vor dem Verwaltungsgericht seine Beförderung einklagen will. Der Roman entwirft eine diffuse, in ihrer Repressivität und Bedrohlichkeit an Kafkas »Prozess« erinnernde Szenerie, vor der der beharrliche Hauptmann zusehends zerfällt und so zum Symbol für eine Jugend wird, die vergeht, ohne je gelebt worden zu sein.

dimosthenis kourtovik

biography

Dimosthenis Kourtovik was born in Athens in 1948. He studied biology in his native city and in Germany, where he also worked as a director, playwright and actor at the Greek Theatre in Stuttgart. In 1986 he concluded his doctoral studies at the University of Wroclaw, Poland, with a dissertation on the origin of Human Sexuality. In the 90's he taught human sexuality and behavioural studies at the University of Crete. Kourtovik made a name for himself as a feature writer, in particular with his literary criticism. He writes for the most important newspapers in his country, including the Athenian newspaper »Ta Nea« as well as for a few foreign papers. In addition, he has translated more than 60 novels from eight different languages into Greek. With his translation of Peter Hoeg's bestseller »Miss Smilla's Sense of Snow«, he helped raise the profile of the detective story genre in Greece. Since 1979 he has published stories, novels, essays and aphorisms, as well as in 1995 the lexicon »Griechische Schriftsteller der Gegenwart«. It is the first reference book on post-war Greek literature to be made available in German and to feature detailed commentary on the life and work of modern Greek authors. Kourtovik's work is characterised by a demythicisation of the cultural tradition and present-day reality in Greece. His debut »Tris chiliades chiliometra« (1980; t: 3,000 Kilometers) is about Greek expatriates in Germany and tells stories that are a far cry from the usual clichés associated with migrant workers; »O teleutaios seismos« (1985) and »To elliniko fthinoporo tis Eva-Anita Bengtson« (1987), a parody of a detective story, also testify to this. Kourtovik's most recent novel »I nostalgia ton drakon« (2000) is narrated by Professor Drakas, Director of the Athenian Museum for Early History, who had been tortured by the Greek junta for sympathizing with the Communists. He has to travel through Europe with the daughter of his former torturer to recover a mummy that was stolen from his museum. The search for the »Ibykus« mummy becomes an odyssey through European history, but also an excursion through literary genres from the epistolary novel to the gothic novel to the thriller. Today Dimosthenis Kourtovik lives in Athens.

Tris chiliades chiliometra
Kalvos, Athen, 1980
O teleutaios seismos
Eolos, Athen, 1985
Der griechische Herbst der Eva-Anita Bengtson
Dialogos,Wannweil,1989
[Ü: Gaby Wurster]
I skoni tu galaxia
Estia, Athen, 1991
Antilexiko ellinikis christomathias
Tramakia
Thessaloniki, 1994
Griechische Schriftsteller der Gegenwart
Romiosini, Köln, 2000
Die Mumie des Ibykus
Reclam Leipzig
Leipzig, 2002
[Ü: Gaby Wurster]

Dimosthenis Kourtovik wurde 1948 in Athen geboren. Er studierte Biologie in seiner Heimatstadt und in Deutschland, wo er auch als Regisseur, Stückeschreiber und Schauspieler an der Griechischen Theaterbühne Stuttgart tätig war. 1986 promovierte er an der Universität Wrocław, Polen, mit einer Dissertation über die Entstehung der menschlichen Sexualität. In den neunziger Jahren unterrichtete er an der Universität Kreta Sexualkunde und Verhaltenslehre. Kourtovik hat sich als Feuilletonist, insbesondere als Literaturkritiker, einen Namen gemacht. Er schreibt für die wichtigsten Zeitungen seines Landes, u. a. für die Athener Zeitung »Ta Nea« sowie für einige Zeitungen im Ausland. Überdies hat er über 60 Romane aus acht Sprachen ins Griechische übertragen. Mit seiner Übersetzung von Peter Høegs Bestseller »Fräulein Smillas Gespür für Schnee« trug er zur Anerkennung des Krimi-Genres in Griechenland bei. Seit 1979 hat er Erzählungen, Romane, Essays, Aphorismen sowie das 1995 erschienene Lexikon »Griechische Schriftsteller der Gegenwart« (dt. 2000) veröffentlicht. Es ist das erste in deutscher Sprache vorliegende Handbuch der modernen griechischen Literatur ab 1945, das ausführlich auf Leben und Werk griechischer Autoren eingeht. Kourtoviks Werk ist geprägt von einer Demythisierung der kulturellen Tradition und der heutigen Wirklichkeit Griechenlands. Sein Debüt »Tris chiliades chiliometra« (1980; Ü: Dreitausend Kilometer), ein Band, dessen Erzählungen von den griechischen Auswanderern in Deutschland fernab aller Klischees des Gastarbeiters berichtet, und auch die folgenden Romane »O teleutaios seismos« (1985; Ü: Das letzte Erdbeben) sowie »To elliniko fthinoporo tis Eva-Anita Bengtson« (1987; dt. »Der griechische Herbst der Eva-Anita Bengtson«, 1989), eine Krimiparodie, zeugen davon. Kourtoviks jüngster Roman »I nostalgia ton drakon« (2000; dt. »Die Mumie des Ibykus«, 2002) erzählt von Professor Drakas, Leiter des Athener Museums für Frühgeschichte, der aufgrund seiner Nähe zu den Kommunisten von der griechischen Junta gefoltert wurde. Nun muss er mit der Tochter seines einstigen Folterers durch Europa reisen, um eine Mumie, die aus seinem Museum gestohlen wurde, wiederzufinden. Die Suche nach der Mumie »Ibykus« wird zu einer Odyssee durch die europäische Geschichte, aber auch zu einem Streifzug durch literarische Genres, vom Briefroman über die Gothic Novel bis zum Thriller. Heute lebt Dimosthenis Kourtovik in Athen.

Gemäss einem vulgär weisen Spruch, so kräftig man auch schüttelt,
der letzte Tropfen fällt immer in die Unterhose.
Der Tick der Poeti(c)k ist der unrealisierbare Wunsch des Dichters,
den letzten Tropfen seiner Not doch dorthin abzuwerfen,
wohin er gehören sollte:
in die Kloake, die alle menschlichen Leiden wegträgt.

nikos panajotopoulos

biography

The Greek author Nikos Panajotopoulos was born in Athens in 1963. While studying engineering, he was also involved in the theatre. After a brief phase as an arts journalist, he started to work as a script writer for television and feature films; he also teaches at a film school in Athens. In 1996, at the Thessaloniki Film Festival, he received the screenplay prize for the film »Apontes«. Since 1997 his volume of stories and two novels have also earned him a name as a prose writer.

In his books, Panajotopoulos, who is influenced by American film and literature, speculates on the influence modern science and technology have on our culture. He uses the genre of science fiction, which has hither to received little attention in Greek literature, as a means for discussing contemporary social problems. In the age of globalisation, his heroe's identities cannot really be defined in terms of location anymore; neither do they belong to a particular nation. The central theme in his stories is the irreconcilable tension between the inner and the outer worlds of the characters. Faced with incidents of an abrupt and scientifically »measurable« nature, i.e. sickness or death, the characters confront their emotional limits and their day-to-day rhythm breaks down.

In the novel »O Ziggy apo ton Marfan – To imerologio enos exogiinou«, a sick 12-year-old boy attempts to deal with his parents' conflict-laden separation. The boy reinterprets his feelings of alienation vis-à-vis his family and environment in terms of an extraterrestrial existence on a rough and inhospitable planet – which simultaneously has a comic and tragic effect. Panajotopoulos' second novel »To gonidio tis amfivolias« (1999), which was published in Germany under the title »Die Erfindung des Zweifels« (2002), is a utopian satire about using genetic engineering as proof of someone's artistic talents. The hero, an author of the old school, experiences all the highs and lows of a writer's existence in an imagined future where the result of a gene test is the singular factor deciding the fate of an artist's career. The work, whose fictive authorship is cleverly made into a mystery, is a parable on the fear of the post-enlightened age in the face of uncertainty. The discontent regarding the present is intensified in a vicious caricature of a future literary business, where the genetic code makes all doubts, talent searches and literary criticism superfluous. Panajotopoulos' novel is characterised by a sober prose and, with its sharp irony, has delighted both critics and public alike. The author lives and works in Athens.

What makes the poet tick?
Well, it could be something that he sees,
Let's say, a magic mountains peak;
Or, it could be just a feeling,
Let's say, that he's homesick;
or, even more, a sad eyed lady
gazing at the sea, while he
stands behind her on the deck,
staring at her, feeling seasick

I enochi ton ilikon
Polis, Athen, 1997
O Ziggy apo ton Marfan – To imerologio enos exogiinou
Polis, Athen, 1998
Die Erfindung des Zweifels
Reclam, Leipzig, 2002
[Ü: Ulf-Dieter Klemm]

Der griechische Autor Nikos Panajotopoulos wurde 1963 in Athen geboren. Während seines Studiums der Ingenieurwissenschaften beschäftigte er sich auch mit dem Theater. Nach einer kurzen Phase als Kulturjournalist arbeitet er heute als Drehbuchautor für Fernseh- und Kinofilme und unterrichtet an einer Filmschule in Athen. 1996 erhielt er beim Filmfestival von Thessaloniki den Drehbuchpreis für den Spielfilm »Apontes« (»Die Abwesenden«). Seit 1997 hat er sich mit einem Erzählband und zwei Romanen auch als Prosaschriftsteller einen Namen gemacht.
Panajotopoulos, der vom amerikanischen Film und von amerikanischer Literatur geprägt ist, spekuliert in seinen Büchern über den Einfluss moderner Wissenschaft und Technologie auf unsere Kultur. Das Science-Fiction-Genre, in der griechischen Literatur bisher kaum beachtet, dient ihm dabei als Spielfeld zur Erörterung aktueller Gesellschaftsprobleme. Im Zeitalter der Globalisierung haben seine Helden fast keine ortsgebundene Identität mehr und gehören keiner bestimmten Nation an. Zentrales Thema seiner Geschichten ist die unüberbrückbare Spannung zwischen Innen- und Außenwelt der Figuren. Durch jäh eintretende, wissenschaftlich »messbare« Ereignisse, wie z. B. Krankheit und Tod, stoßen sie an ihre emotionalen Grenzen und werden aus den Bahnen des Alltäglichen gerissen. In dem Roman »O Ziggy apo ton Marfan – To imerologio enos exogiinou« (1998; Ü: Ziggy vom Marfan – Tagebuch eines Außerirdischen) versucht ein kranker zwölfjähriger Junge mit der konfliktreichen Trennung seiner Eltern umzugehen. Sein Gefühl der Entfremdung gegenüber Familie und Umwelt deutet er in eine außerirdische Existenz auf einem rauen und ungastlichen Planeten um – was gleichzeitig komisch und tragisch wirkt. Panajotopoulos' zweiter Roman »To gonidio tis amfivolias« (1999), der in Deutschland unter dem Titel »Die Erfindung des Zweifels« (2002) erschien, ist eine utopische Satire über die Nutzung der Gentechnik zum Nachweis von künstlerischer Begabung. Der Held, ein Autor der alten Schule, durchläuft alle Höhen und Tiefen einer Schriftstellerexistenz in einer imaginierten Zukunft, in der nur noch das Ergebnis eines Gentests über die Karriere eines Künstlers entscheidet. Bei dem Werk, dessen fiktive Autorschaft geschickt verrätselt wird, handelt es sich um eine Parabel über die Angst des post-aufgeklärten Zeitalters vor jeder Unklarheit. Das Unbehagen an der Gegenwart wird hier zur bissigen Karikatur eines künftigen Literaturbetriebs gesteigert, in dem der genetische Code jeden Zweifel, alle Talentsuche und Literaturkritik überflüssig macht. Panajotopoulos' Roman ist in einer nüchternen Prosa gehalten und begeisterte mit seiner scharfen Ironie Kritiker und Publikum gleichermaßen. Der Autor lebt und arbeitet in Athen.

It could be less than that, of course,
let's say, a wall's red brick
–perhaps a brick that is too thick–
or, an erected prick,
a sounding clock's tick,
the first day of the week,
an ass he wants to kick,
a hopeless rhyme like this
–a rhyme that is too weak,
making this poem sound
like nothing but a cheap trick...

It could as well be just a fleeting thought
let's say, that God is simply the invention of a freak,
who came up with this as he was standing by a creek,
after having some beers,
desperately seeking for a place to take a leak;
or, to make it simple, as a fleeting thought should be,
that life is nothing but a kick,
a playful pick on universe's cheek...

jorgos skambardonis
biography

Jorgos Skambardonis was born in Thessaloniki in northern Greece in 1953. After studying French literature, he worked as a freelance journalist for the press, radio and television; he also wrote screenplays and worked for and published various literary magazines. He is currently editor-in-chief of the culture magazine »Panselinos« in Thessaloniki. Skambardonis first made his debut as a writer in 1989. He primarily writes short prose, which is what he became known for. Most of the stories with their dense atmospheres are situated in the author's hometown, in Thessaloniki, and its surroundings. With stories that feature strange, solitary heroes and that frequently cross into imaginary zones – into memories, dreams, and the supernatural – Skambardonis is considered a modern representative of poetic realism in the tradition of Alexandros Papadiamantis. The sudden switch to the imaginary often leads back not only to his protagonists' pasts, but also to a half-forgotten folk tradition, whose traces have largely been washed away by modern urban life – a topic which permanently interests the author. In 1993 in his native country he received the state literature prize for prose. A selection of his stories was published in 1998 in German translation under the title »Der Staatsanwalt im Nebel«.
Skambardonis's novels are clearly influenced by his short prose writing: In »Gernáo epityxós« the woman tells of the bitterness of an insignificant life that passed without leaving any real trace and does so as if she is sitting before a camera. Brief flashbacks form a fragmentary image of an existence and surprise the reader with lurid transgressions of reality that work like psychological dashes for the exit. The author rewrote the book as a theatre piece and its performance was a great success. In his second novel »Ouzeri Tsitsanis« (2001), with an almost film-like technique, Skambardonis paints an oppressive portrait of Thessaloniki at the time of the German occupation and the persecution of the Jews. At the same time he takes a look at the life of the great Rembetiko artist Vassilis Tsitsanis and at Greece's traditional subculture. The apparently carefree creativity of the musician acts as a counterweight to a life that was at this time otherwise characterised by fear, hunger, persecution and death. The novel's plot is a reduced one; the dialogue and character-filled text is composed of heterogeneous sequences, which also contain documentary material and surreal moments and which live solely from the mood.

Mati fosforo, koumanto gero
Ianos, Thessaloniki, 1989
I stenopos ton ifasmaton
Kastaniotis, Athen, 1992
Pali kentaei o stratigos
Kastaniotis, Athen, 1996
Der Staatsanwalt im Nebel
Romiosini, Köln, 1998
[Ü: Renate Sack
Nelly Weber]
I psicha tis metalavias – Akriani lorida
Kastaniotis, Athen, 1998
Gernáo epityxós
Kedros, Athen, 2000
Ouzeri Tsitsanis
Kedros, Athen, 2001

Jorgos Skambardonis wurde 1953 im nordgriechischen Thessaloniki geboren. Nach dem Studium der Französischen Literatur arbeitete er als freier Journalist für Presse, Rundfunk und Fernsehen, verfasste Drehbücher und war als Mitarbeiter und Herausgeber verschiedener Literaturzeitschriften tätig. Derzeit ist er in Thessaloniki Chefredakteur des Kulturmagazins »Panselinos«.

Als Schriftsteller debütierte Skambardonis erst 1989. Er wurde vor allem durch seine Kurzprosa bekannt, die den größten Teil seines Werkes ausmacht. Die meisten der atmosphärisch dichten Erzählungen sind in der Heimat des Autors angesiedelt, in Thessaloniki und seiner weiteren Umgebung. Mit den eigenbrötlerischen, skurrilen Helden seiner Geschichten und dem häufigen Wechsel in imaginäre Bereiche – in Erinnerung, Traum oder Übersinnliches – gilt Skambardonis als moderner Vertreter eines poetischen Realismus in der Nachfolge von Alexandros Papadiamantis. Der Schwenk ins Imaginäre führt oft nicht nur in die Vergangenheit seiner Protagonisten, sondern auch in eine halb vergessene Volkstradition, deren Spuren das moderne urbane Leben weitgehend weggespült hat – ein Thema, das den Autor nachhaltig beschäftigt. 1993 wurde er in seiner Heimat mit dem Griechischen Staatspreis ausgezeichnet. Eine Auswahl seiner Erzählungen erschien 1998 unter dem Titel »Der Staatsanwalt im Nebel« in deutscher Übersetzung.

Einflüsse der Kurzprosa lassen sich auch in Skambardonis' Romanen ausmachen: Wie vor einer Kamera sitzend, erzählt eine Frau in »Gernáo epityxós« (2000; Ü: Ich altere erfolgreich) von der Bitterkeit eines unbedeutenden Lebens, das vorüberging, ohne wirkliche Spuren zu hinterlassen. Ausschnittartige Rückblenden fügen sich zum fragmentarischen Bild einer Existenz zusammen und überraschen durch grelle Realitätsüberschreitungen, die wie psychische Fluchtbewegungen wirken. Das Buch wurde vom Autor zum Theaterstück umgeschrieben und mit großem Erfolg aufgeführt. In seinem zweiten Roman, »Ouzeri Tsitsanis« (2001; Ü: Die Tsitsanis-Taverne), zeichnet Skambardonis mit nahezu filmischer Technik ein beklemmendes Bild Thessalonikis in den Jahren der deutschen Besatzung und Judenverfolgung. Gleichzeitig wird ein Blick auf das Leben des großen Rembetiko-Künstlers Vassilis Tsitsanis und die volkstümliche Subkultur Griechenlands geworfen. Die scheinbar unbekümmerte Kreativität des Musikers bildet eine Gegenwelt zum übrigen Leben in jener Zeit, die von Angst, Hunger, Verfolgung und Tod bestimmt war. Auch dieser Roman zeichnet sich durch eine reduzierte Handlungsführung aus: Skambardonis setzt den dialog- und personenreichen Text aus heterogenen Sequenzen zusammen, die auch dokumentarisches Material und surrealistische Momente enthalten und ganz aus der Stimmung leben.

ersi sotiropoulos

biography

The writer Ersi Sotiropoulos belongs to the avant-garde of the Greek literary world. She was born in Patras in 1953, studied philosophy and cultural anthropology in Florence and went on to work in the Greek embassy in Rome. She published her debut novel »I fársa« (t: The Trick) in 1982, in which she describes life in a strict patriarchal society. The novel centres around two women who make anonymous telephone calls to arbitrary men and expose them, as representatives of their sex, to public ridicule on behalf of the whole male world. Readers and critics gave the book an enthusiastic reception.

Since her successful debut, Sotiropoulos, who also writes columns and screenplays, has published further novels, short story collections and poetry in her home country. So far only her fifth novel »Zig-Zag stis Nerantzies« has been published in German translation, as »Bittere Orangen« in 1999. In 2000 the original text became the first Greek work of prose to receive the country's two most important literary awards: the Greek state prize for literature and the prize of the literature magazine »Diavaso«.

»Zig-Zag stis Nerantzies« traces the fortunes of a group of young people, whose destinies follow winding paths to become interlinked. They include the mysteriously ill Lia, her unemployed brother Sid, the strange male nurse Sotiris and the dreamy girl Nina. When Lia feels badly treated by her nurse in an Athens hospital she asks her brother to teach him a lesson. Sid then steals into the life of the lone wolf Sotiris. However, an unusual friendship arises between the two men, contrary to Lia's plan. Sid is pulled in to a grotesque murder plot by the nurse, with which he intends to get rid of the twelve year-old Nina, who knows an embarrassing secret. For Nina, one of the most moving characters in the novel, writing is the only way for her to articulate herself and to be able to escape the »idiots and zombies«. Sotiropoulos's novel, whose original title means literally »Zigzag under the Seville Oranges«, thrives on its obscure black humour and passion for the absurd. The author describes life in a society between tradition and modernity using precise and unsentimental language, and tells of the search for love and closeness as well as of the impossibility of sharing one's feelings. Continually changing perspectives emphasize the isolation of Sotiropoulos's heroes. The author lives in Athens.

Milo + Thanatos + ... + ...
Plethron, Athen, 1980
Diakopes choris ptoma
Akmon, Athen, 1980
Eortastiko triimero sta Jannena
Nefeli, Athen, 1982
I farsa
Kedros, Athen, 1982
Mexiko
Kedros, Athen, 1988
O zestos kiklos
Ellinika Grammata
Athen, 2000
Bittere Orangen
dtv, München, 2001
[Ü: Doris Wille]

Die Schriftstellerin Ersi Sotiropoulos gehört zur Avantgarde der griechischen Literaturszene. Sie wurde 1953 in Patras geboren, studierte in Florenz Philosophie und Kulturelle Anthropologie und arbeitete anschließend in der Griechischen Botschaft in Rom. 1982 debütierte sie mit dem Roman »I fársa« (Ü: Der Streich), in dem sie das Leben in einer streng patriarchalen Gesellschaft beschreibt. Im Zentrum stehen zwei Frauen, die anonym fremde Männer anrufen, um sie stellvertretend für die gesamte Männerwelt der Lächerlichkeit preiszugeben. Publikum und Kritik nahmen das Buch mit Begeisterung auf.
Seit ihrem erfolgreichen Erstling hat Sotiropoulos, die auch Kolumnen und Drehbüche schreibt, in ihrer Heimat weitere Romane, Erzählbände und Gedichte veröffentlicht. In deutscher Übersetzung liegt bislang nur ihr fünfter Roman »Bittere Orangen« vor, der 1999 erschien. Als erstes griechisches Prosawerk erhielt das Buch im Jahr 2000 die beiden bedeutendsten literarischen Auszeichnungen des Landes: den Griechischen Staatspreis für Literatur und den Preis der Literaturzeitschrift »Diavaso«.
»Bittere Orangen« handelt von einer Gruppe junger Menschen, deren Schicksale über verschlungene Pfade miteinander verbunden sind. Zu ihnen gehören die mysteriös erkrankte Lia, ihr arbeitsloser Bruder Sid, der sonderbare Krankenpfleger Sotiris und das verträumte Mädchen Nina. Als sich Lia in einem Athener Krankenhaus von ihrem Pfleger schlecht behandelt fühlt, bittet sie ihren Bruder, diesem einen Denkzettel zu verpassen. Sid schleicht sich daraufhin in das Leben des Eigenbrötlers Sotiris ein. Aber anders als geplant, entsteht zwischen beiden Männern eine eigenartige Freundschaft. So wird Sid in einen grotesken Mordplan des Krankenpflegers hineingezogen, mit dem dieser die zwölfjährige Nina aus dem Weg räumen will, da sie ein peinliches Geheimnis kennt. Für das Mädchen Nina, eine der ergreifendsten Figuren des Romans, bleibt nur das Schreiben, um sich artikulieren und von den »Idioten und Scheintoten« abheben zu können. Sotiropoulos' Roman, dessen Originaltitel wörtlich »Zickzack unter den Pomeranzenbäumen« bedeutet, lebt von seinem schrägen, schwarzen Humor und einem Hang zum Absurden. Mit ihrer präzisen und unsentimentalen Sprache beschreibt die Autorin das Leben in einer Gesellschaft zwischen Tradition und Moderne und erzählt von der Suche nach Nähe und Liebe sowie von der Unmöglichkeit, sich dem Anderen mitzuteilen. Ein ständiger Perspektivwechsel verdeutlicht die Isolation von Sotiropoulos' Helden. Die Autorin lebt in Athen.

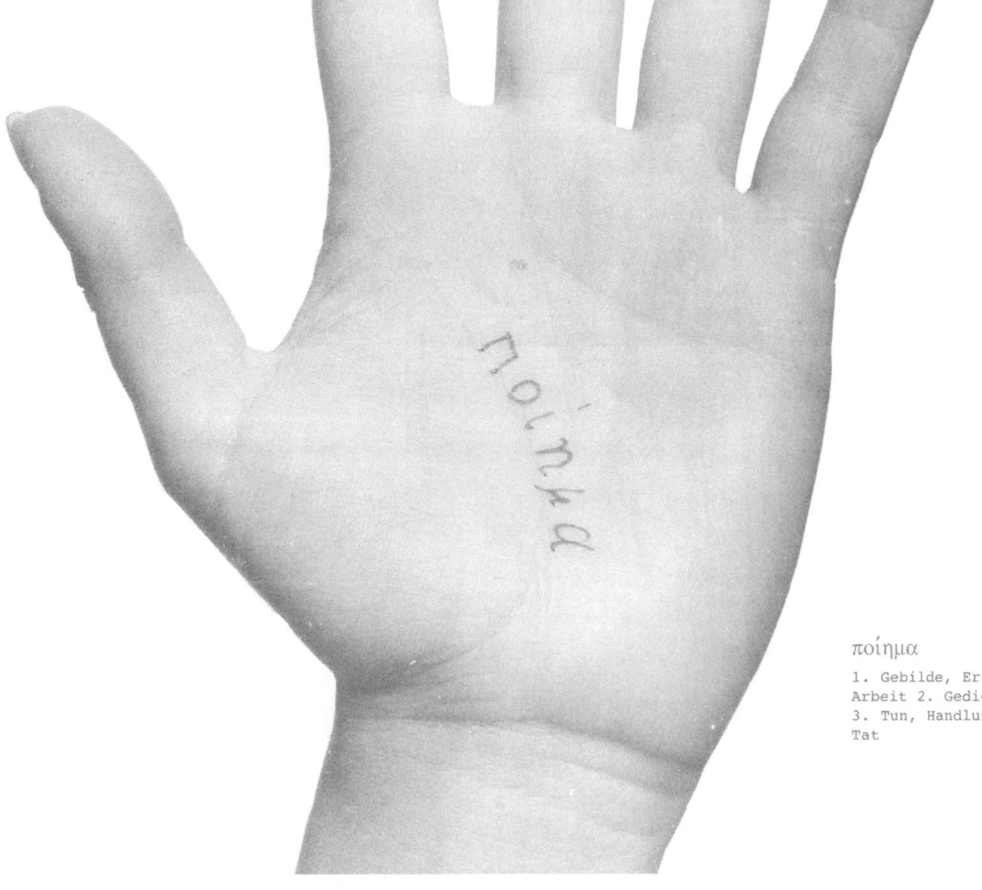

ποίημα

1. Gebilde, Erzeugnis, Wert, Arbeit 2. Gedicht, Dichtung 3. Tun, Handlung, Tätigkeit, Tat

soti triantafillou

biography

Soti Triantafillou was born in Athens in 1957. After studying pharmacology in the Greek capital, she did her doctoral work in Paris at the École des Hautes Études en Sciences Sociales in the fields of history and history of civilization. She wrote a Ph.D. in urban studies at the University of New York and then studied Romance languages and literatures at the University of Athens. Triantafillou works as a lecturer, translator, editor and journalist. Not only has she edited six monographs on the cinema, but since 1990 she has also produced an extensive literary oeuvre with bestseller qualities.

In Greece, the cosmopolitan Triantafillou is perhaps the most successful writer of her generation. She embodies precisely the self-ironic city neurotic that one has to date sought in vain in Greek literature. What also distinguishes her from her contemporaries is that she not only writes about the Greeks in Greece, but she immediately situated three of her novels in the U.S. In her first novel »Sávvato vrády stin ákri tis polis« (1996) as well as in »Poor Margo« (2001) that was written in English, with great narrative lightness Triantafillou thematises the subversive dreams of fortune of the young generation in the big cities of the 80s; she tells of long, intoxicated nights, of a passion for cinema and music, of friendship and love, and of course always about failure. On the other hand, »O ipójios uranos« (1998) is about the radical sense of being uprooted and the lack of orientation experienced by second-generation emigrants in the American hinterland.

Triantafillou's historical studies focused in particular on the beginnings of socialist politics – this finds expression in two controversial historical novels, which juxtapose the collective history of progress with individual microcosms; fictive figures are placed next to historical characters like Lenin and Rosa Luxemburg. Carefully researched and masterfully staged in a whole host of settings »To ergostásio ton molivión« (2000) – scheduled for publication in German translation in 2004 under the title »Die Bleistiftfabrik« – follows the meandering destiny of an unconventional Greek family, which from the end of the 19th century until the beginning of the Second World War attempts to actively involve itself in the revolutionary processes in technology, politics and art. In contrast, in her current work »Albatros« (2003), Triantafillou uses a couple in which the two partners are very different from one another to outline the history of the suffragettes.

Meres pou emiasan me mantarini
Ägokeros, Athen, 1990
To enaerio treno sto Sitwell
Delfini, Athen, 1994
Savato vradi stin akri tis polis
Polis, Athen, 1996
Avrio, mia alli chora
Polis, Athen, 1997
Der unterirdische Himmel
Zsolnay, Wien, 2001
[Ü: Birgit Hildebrand]
Ftochi Margo
Patakis, Athen, 2003
Albatros
Patakis, Athen, 2003

Soti Triantafillou wurde 1957 in Athen geboren. Nach einem Pharmakologiestudium in der griechischen Hauptstadt promovierte sie an der Pariser École des Hautes Études en Sciences Sociales in den Fächern Geschichte und Kulturgeschichte. An der University of New York machte sie einen Doktor in Urban Studies, anschließend absolvierte sie ein Romanistikstudium an der Universität von Athen. Triantafillou ist als Dozentin, Übersetzerin, Lektorin und Journalistin tätig. Sie hat nicht nur sechs Monographien zum Thema Kino herausgebracht, sondern seit 1990 auch ein umfangreiches literarisches Oeuvre mit Bestsellerqualitäten geschaffen.

In ihrer Heimat ist die kosmopolite Triantafillou die vielleicht erfolgreichste Schriftstellerin ihrer Generation. Sie verkörpert genau den Typ selbstironischer Stadtneurotiker, den man in der griechischen Literatur bislang vergeblich suchte. Darüber hinaus schreibt sie – auch das unterscheidet sie von ihren Zeitgenossen – nicht nur über Griechen in Griechenland, sondern hat gleich drei ihrer Romane in den USA angesiedelt. In ihrem Erstling aus dem Jahr 1996, »Sávvato vrády stin ákri tis pólis« (Ü: Samstagabend am Rande der Stadt), sowie dem in englischer Sprache verfassten »Poor Margo« (2001) thematisiert Triantafillou mit großer erzählerischer Leichtigkeit die subversiven Glücksträume der jungen Generation in den Metropolen der achtziger Jahre, berichtet von langen, berauschten Nächten, von der Leidenschaft für Kino und Musik, von Freundschaft und Liebe und natürlich immer wieder auch vom Scheitern. In »O ipójios uranos« (1998; dt. »Der unterirdische Himmel«, 2001) hingegen erzählt sie von der radikalen Entwurzelung und Orientierungslosigkeit der zweiten Emigrantengeneration im amerikanischen Hinterland.

Die geschichtlichen Studien der Autorin, deren spezielles Interesse den Anfängen sozialistischer Politik galt, haben sich in zwei umstrittenen historischen Romanen niedergeschlagen, die der kollektiven Geschichte des Fortschritts einen individuellen Mikrokosmos gegenüberstellen, in dem fiktive Gestalten neben historischen Persönlichkeiten wie Lenin und Rosa Luxemburg stehen. Sorgfältig recherchiert und an einer Fülle von Schauplätzen souverän in Szene gesetzt, folgt »To ergostásio ton molivión« (2000) – für 2004 zur deutschsprachigen Veröffentlichung unter dem Titel »Die Bleistiftfabrik« vorgesehen – dem mäandernden Schicksal einer unkonventionellen griechischen Familie, die sich aktiv in die revolutionären Prozesse in Technik, Politik und Kunst vom Ende des neunzehnten Jahrhunderts bis zum Beginn des Zweiten Weltkriegs einzubringen versucht. »Albatros« (2003) hingegen, Triantafillous aktuelles Werk, zeichnet anhand eines ungleichen Paares die Geschichte der Suffragetten nach.

charis vlavianos

biography

Charis Vlavianos was born in Rome in 1957. He studied economics, political science and philosophy at the Universities of Bristol and Oxford. Today Vlavianos lives in Athens, where he teaches history and history of ideology at the American College, and literature at the European Centre for Translation (EKEMEL). He is the publisher of the renowned literary magazine »Poiisi« (t: »Poetry«).

His language, heritage, and present home make Charis Vlavianos a Greek author. Readers with an interest in the field cannot miss his interest in the poetry of classic contemporary Greek writers like Konstantinos Kavafis, Takis Sinopoulos and Nikos Karousos. Parallels between his verse and the work of English language writers like Wallace Stevens and John Ashbery are just as evident, if not more so. Like the works of these writers, Vlavianos's verse is also engaging at an intellectual level. In his poems he is always able to maintain a balance between abstraction and sensuality, between rational reflection and the creation of a suggestive atmosphere. Another defining characteristic of Vlavianos's poetry is his adherence to certain thematic constellations, the most important of these being history (both as concept and as a string of events). Vlavianos's poems are also frequently about the twists and turns in his family's fortunes, which he consciously treats as archetypical examples of emotional dependency, loss and betrayal. Eroticism and love, on the other hand, appear in his work both in their ambivalence and as the root of a basic feeling of happiness. Poetry itself, and its endangered status, is also a source of inspiration for Vlavianos. Indeed some of his poems refer directly to current philosophical discourse. Charis Vlavianos expresses himself with a rare elegance of language, which combines a basic commitment to formal transparency with a few selectively used syntactical and lexical violations. It is the individual tone of this language that, despite the structural variety in Vlavianos's verse, gives one the impression of reading a stylistically uniform work. Perhaps it is this individuality of tone that best attests to the view that Vlavianos qualitatively enriches European verse.

To date Vlavianos has written eight books of poetry, most recently »Meta to telos tis omorphias« (2003; t: After the End of Beauty). He has also published translations, most noteably of American poets and essayists. In 1998 he received Greece's state translation prize.

Ipnovassies
Plethron, Athen, 1983
Politis thavmaton
Plethron; Nefeli, Athen, 1985
Tropos tou lejin
Hyakinthos, Athen, 1986
Aspondos anäressis
Roptron, Athen, 1989
I nostalgia ton uranon
Nefeli, Athen, 1994
Der Engel der Geschichte
Romiosini, Köln, 2001
[Ü: Dadi Sider
Dimitra Visaitou]
Meta to telos tis omorphias
Nefeli, Athen, 2003

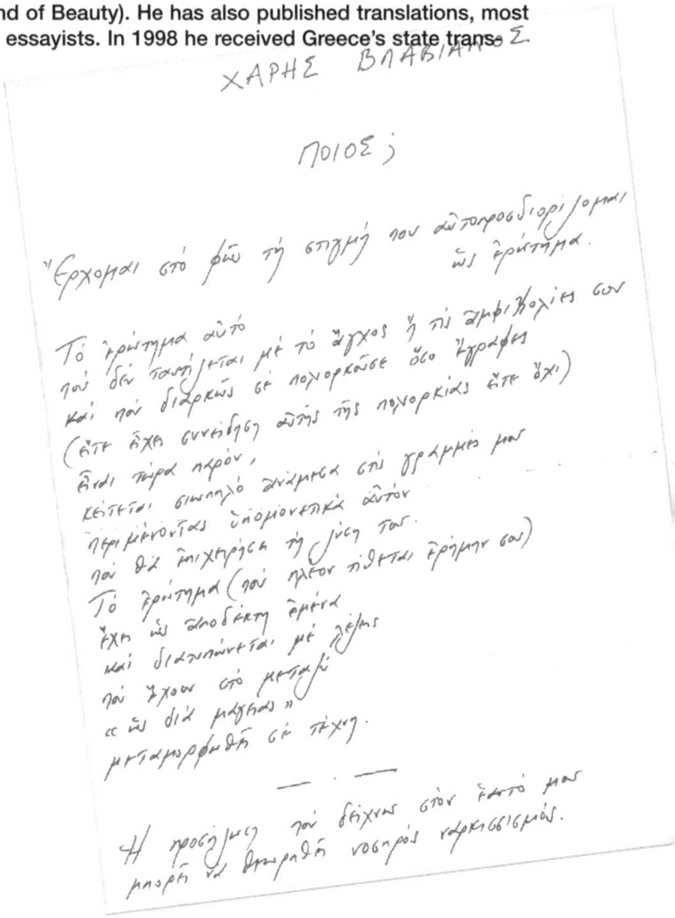

ΧΑΡΗΣ ΒΛΑΒΙΑΝΟΣ

ΠΟΙΟΣ;

Ἔρχομαι στό φῶς τή στιγμή που αὐτοπροσδιορίζομαι
ὡς ἐρώτημα.

Τό ἐρώτημα αὐτό
πού δέν ταυτίζεται μέ τό ἄγχος ἤ τίς ἀμφιβολίες σου
καί πού διαρκῶς σέ πολιορκοῦσε ὅσο ἔγραφες
(εἴτε εἶχες συνείδηση αὐτῆς τῆς πολιορκίας εἴτε ὄχι)
εἶναι τώρα παρόν,
κείτεται σιωπηλό ἀνάμεσα στίς γραμμές μου
περιμένοντας ὑπομονετικά αὐτόν
πού θά ἐπιχειρήσει τή λύση του.
Τό ἐρώτημα (πού πλέον τίθεται ἐρήμην σου)
ἔχει ὡς ἀποδέκτη ἐμένα
καί διατυπώνεται μέ λέξεις
πού ἔχουν στό μεταξύ
«ὡς διά μαγείας»
μεταμορφωθεῖ σέ τέχνη.

— · —

Η προσήλωση πού δείχνεις στόν ἑαυτό μου
μπορεῖ νά θεωρηθεῖ νοσηρός ναρκισσισμός.

Charis Vlavianos wurde 1957 in Rom geboren. Er studierte Wirtschaftswissenschaften, Politologie und Philosophie an den Universitäten von Bristol und Oxford. Heute lebt Vlavianos in Athen, wo er am American College Geschichte und Ideologiegeschichte sowie am Europäischen Übersetzerzentrum Literatur (EKEMEL) lehrt. Er ist Herausgeber der renommierten Literaturzeitschrift »Poiisi« (Ü: Dichtung).
Charis Vlavianos ist durch Sprache, Geburt und Wohnort ein griechischer Autor. Lesern mit relevanter Vorbelastung kann sein Interesse an der Dichtung neugriechischer Klassiker wie Konstantinos Kavafis, Takis Sinopoulos oder Nikos Karousos auch nicht entgehen. Mindestens ebenso deutlich sind aber die Korrespondenzen zwischen seiner Lyrik und den Werken angelsächsischer Autoren, etwa jenen von Wallace Stevens oder John Ashbery. Mit diesen verbindet Vlavianos zudem der intellektuelle Anspruch seiner Lyrik. Dabei gelingt es ihm stets, in seinen Gedichten ein Gleichgewicht zwischen Abstraktion und Sinnlichkeit, zwischen von Rationalität geprägter Reflexion und der Schaffung einer suggestiven Atmosphäre zu wahren. Ein weiteres konstitutives Merkmal der Poetik von Vlavianos ist sein Festhalten an bestimmten Themenkomplexen. Der wichtigste darunter ist Geschichte (als Begriff wie als Folge von Ereignissen). Häufig gehen die Gedichte von Vlavianos auch auf Wechselfälle im Leben seiner Familie zurück, die er jedoch als gleichsam archetypische Beispiele von emotionaler Abhängigkeit, Verlust oder Verrat zu behandeln versteht. Dagegen erscheinen Erotik und Liebe in seinem Werk sowohl in ihrer Ambivalenz als auch als Ursprung eines elementaren Glücksgefühls. Eine Inspirationsquelle für Vlavianos ist auch die Dichtung selbst und ihr gefährdeter Status. Schließlich nehmen einige seiner Gedichte direkt auf aktuelle philosophische Diskurse Bezug. Charis Vlavianos bedient sich einer äußerst eleganten Sprache, die eine grundsätzliche Festlegung auf formale Transparenz mit wenigen, aber gezielt eingesetzten syntaktischen und lexikalischen Normverstößen verbindet. Es ist der besondere Klang dieser Sprache, der beim Leser ungeachtet der strukturellen Vielfalt von Vlavianos' Lyrik den Eindruck erweckt, einem stilistisch einheitlichen Werk zu begegnen. Und es mag dieser besondere Klang sein, der dazu berechtigen könnte, von einer qualitativen Bereicherung der europäischen Lyrik durch Vlavianos zu sprechen.
Vlavianos legte bisher acht Gedichtbände vor, zuletzt »Meta to telos tis omorphias« (2003; Ü: Nach dem Ende der Schönheit). Daneben veröffentlichte er Übersetzungen insbesondere amerikanischer Lyriker und Essayisten. 1998 erhielt er den Staatlichen Übersetzerpreis Griechenlands.

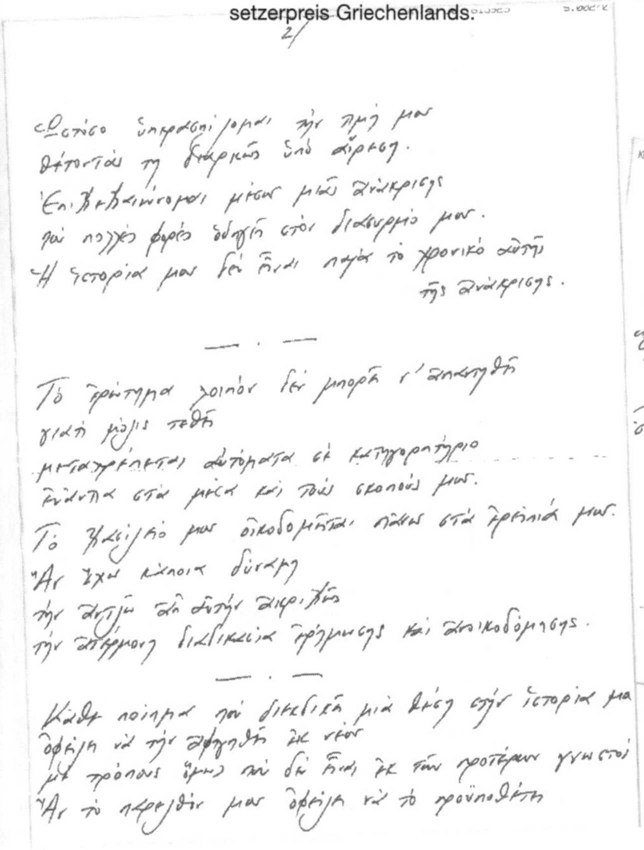
2/

Ωστόσο υπερασπίζομαι τήν τιμή μου
θέτοντάς τη διαρκώς υπό αίρεση.
Επιβεβαιώνομαι μέσω μιάς ανάκρισης
πού πολλές φορές οδηγεί στόν διασυρμό μου.
Η ιστορία μου δέν είναι παρά τό χρονικό αυτής
της ανάκρισης.

— · —

Τό ερώτημα λοιπόν δέν μπορεί ν' απαντηθεί
γιατί μόλις τεθεί
μεταμορφώνεται αυτόματα σέ κατηγορητήριο
ενάντια στά μέσα καί τούς σκοπούς μου.
Τό βασίλειό μου οικοδομείται πάντα στά ερείπιά μου.
Άν έχω κάποια δύναμη
τήν αντλώ από αυτήν ακριβώς
τήν αέναη διαδικασία ερήμωσης καί ανοικοδόμησης.

— · —

Κάθε ποίημα πού διεκδικεί μιά θέση στήν ιστορία μα
οφείλει νά τήν αφηγηθεί εκ νέου
μέ τρόπους όμως πού δέ θά είναι εκ τών προτέρων γνωστοί
Άν τό παρελθόν μου οφείλει νά τό προϋποθέτει

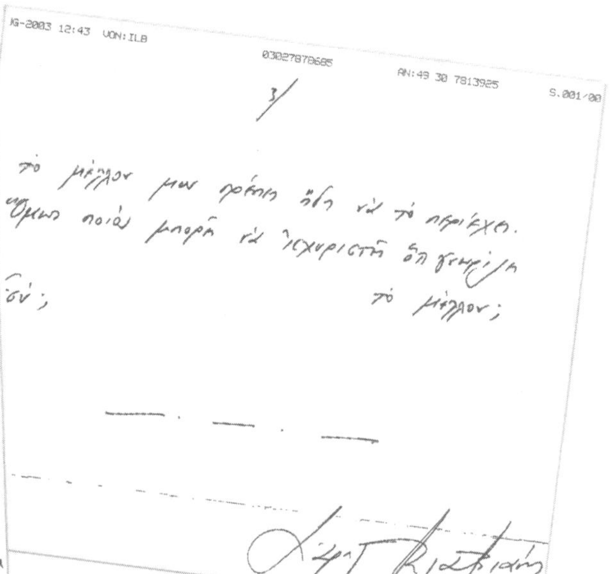
G-2003 12:43 VON:ILB 03027870685 AN:49 30 7813925 S.001/00

3/

τό μέλλον μου πρέπει όλο νά τό περιέχει.
Όμως ποιός μπορεί νά ισχυριστεί ότι γνωρίζει
σύ; τό μέλλον;

— · — · —

gäste des DAAD berlin

jorge luis arzola
oscar van den boogard
nedim gürsel
paulo lins
tomaž šalamun
ferenc szijj
david toscana

jorge luis arzola

biography

Jorge Luis Arzola was born in 1966 in Jatibonico, Cuba. Unlike those authors who have up until now shaped the image of Cuban literature, Guillermo Cabrera Infante, Miguel Barnet, Jesús Díaz and Reinaldo Arenas, Arzola belongs to a new generation of writers, the so-called »novísimos«. This generation is on the one hand influenced more than the preceeding one by the new awareness of national identity rooted in the Cuban revolution, while on the other hand questioning these reflexive ideals following the political and economic crisis facing the country since the fall of the Iron Curtain.
In 1993, when rationing, shortage of paper and the »special period in peacetime« declared by Fidel Castro were at a height, Salvador Redonet initiated a new critical debate in Cuban literature with an anthology of work exclusively by writers of the new generation, among them Arzola. In the introduction to »Los últimos serán los primeros« one reads the unusual statement: »The social and aesthetic purpose of these texts is a radical one: they are topical, they go beyond rusty conventions, examine our weaknesses and strengths, they deal with the here and now. They gloss over and hide nothing and call a spade a spade, even if it does (not) concern roses.«
About the same time as Redonet's anthology Arzola's first stories were published. With »Pájaro sin cabeza« in 1991 and »Prisionero en el Círculo del Horizonte« in 1994 he was able for the first time to reach a wider public. Other works of his, including »Fábula de ángeles« (1997) and the anthology »Cubanísimo! Junge Erzähler aus Kuba«, edited by Michi Strausfeld, now available in German and Spanish, have been published in Cuban and international anthologies. Arzola's most recent work, »La Bandada Infinita«, for which he was honoured with the Iberio-American Alejo Carpentier Prize, was published in 2000. This particular volume contains the short story entitled »Cosas esenciales« in which the author, in an unusually dense language, weaves together the varied combination of erotic desires with themes of fleeing and freedom. The narrative voice, in a constantly agitated way, loosens firmly established patterns of identity and attempts to define in language new contexts of sexual behaviour. »But I could also have been the girl. [...] and I felt the boy's hand around my waist. It was a tender hand, almost like that of a young girl.«
Jorge Luis Arzola lives and works in Berlin.

Prisionero en el circulo del horizonte
Ed. Lectras Cubanas
Havanna, 1994
La Bandada Infinita
Ed. Lectras Cubanas
Havanna, 2000

Jorge Luis Arzola wurde 1966 in Jatibonico, Kuba, geboren. Anders als die bis heute das Bild der kubanischen Literatur bestimmenden Autoren Guillermo Cabrera Infante, Miguel Barnet, Jesús Díaz oder auch Reinaldo Arenas gehört Jorge Luis Arzola einer neuen Schriftstellergeneration an, den sogenannten »novísimos«. Diese Generation ist auf der einen Seite stärker als die vorhergehende von dem neuen Bewusstsein nationaler Identität geprägt, das von der kubanischen Revolution ausging, auf der anderen Seite werden durch die politische und wirtschaftliche Krise, in der sich das Land nach dem Verschwinden des Eisernen Vorhangs befindet, diese verinnerlichten Ideale in Frage gestellt.
1993, auf dem Höhepunkt von Rationierung, Papierknappheit und der von Fidel Castro ausgerufenen »Spezialperiode in Friedenszeiten«, eröffnete Salvador Redonet mit einer Anthologie, in der ausschließlich Vertreter der jüngsten Schriftstellergeneration publiziert wurden, darunter auch Arzola, einen neuen, kritischen Diskurs in der kubanischen Literatur.
Im Vorwort zu »Los últimos serán los primeros« (Ü: Die letzten werden die ersten sein) heißt es ungewohnt offen: »Die gesellschaftlich-ästhetische Funktion dieser Texte ist radikal: sie sind aktuell, überschreiten alle verrosteten Konventionen, richten die Lupe auf unsere Schwächen und Stärken, das Hier und Heute. Sie beschönigen und verschweigen nichts und nennen die Dinge bei ihrem Namen, auch wenn es sich (nicht) um Rosen handelt.«
Ungefähr zeitgleich mit Redonets Anthologie erschienen die ersten Erzählbände von Jorge Luis Arzola. Mit »Pájaro sin cabeza« (Ü: Kopfloser Vogel) von 1991 und »Prisionero en el círculo del horizonte« (Ü: Gefangener im Kreis der Horizonts) von 1994 konnte er seine Arbeit erstmals einem größeren Publikum präsentieren. Es folgten weitere Veröffentlichungen seiner Texte in kubanischen und internationalen Anthologien, darunter »Fábula de ángeles« (1997) und der von Michi Strausfeld herausgegebene Band »Cubanísimo! Junge Erzähler aus Kuba«, der sowohl auf Deutsch wie auf Spanisch vorliegt. Im Jahr 2000 erschien sein bisher jüngster Band »La Bandada Infinita« (Ü: Die unendliche Schar), für den Arzola mit dem iberoamerikanischen Alejo Carpentier-Preis ausgezeichnet wurde. Aus diesem Band stammt auch das kurze Prosastück »Cosas esenciales« (Ü: Wesentliche Dinge), in dem der Autor in ungewöhnlich dichter Weise die vielfältigen Konstellationen erotischen Begehrens mit den Motiven der Flucht und Befreiung verwebt. Eine ständig in Bewegung gehaltene Erzählerstimme löst festgelegte Identitätskategorien auf und sucht so auch nach neuen Freiräumen in der Sprache. »Aber ich hätte auch das Mädchen sein können. [...] und um meine Taille fühlte ich auf einmal die Hand eines Jünglings. Es war eine zarte Hand, fast die eines jungen Mädchens.«
Jorge Luis Arzola lebt und arbeitet in Berlin.

oscar van den boogaard

biography

Oscar van den Boogaard was born in Harderwijk, in the Netherlands, in 1964. He grew up in the former Dutch colony of Surinam and in the Netherlands. After studying French and Law in Montpellier, Amsterdam and Brussels, he embarked on a career as a lawyer at an international law firm in Brussels. On his 25th birthday he suddenly gave up his secure life as a lawyer and became a writer. A telling decision for van den Boogaard, for whom the only thing that now mattered was »living life« so that in the end »life's bookkeeping: reality on the left, fantasy on the right« was balanced. He came into contact with the international art world as founder of the Mot & van den Boogaard Gallery for Contemporary Art in Brussels. The artist Douglas Gordon tattooed the word »Guilty«, written back to front and readable in a mirror, on van den Boogaard's left shoulder blade. A photo of the writer's back is part of the collection of the Guggenheim museum in New York.

Since the publication of his debut novel »Dentz« in 1990, Oscar van den Boogaard has been regarded as one of the most important young authors in the Netherlands. In a powerful yet sensitive way, van den Boogaard writes of how obscure compulsions cause people to deny their basic essence. The trials of everyday life, where there is no room to live out one's feelings and desires, are of central importance to the main figure in his novel »De heerlijkheid van Julia«, which has won two renowned prizes, the Dutch Libris-Literatuurprijs and the Belgian De gouden Uil. His novel »Liefdesdood« (»Love's Death«, 2001) is about complicated family situations, fantasies of escape and alienation; the novel also received the De gouden Uil. A reduced, almost sober language characterises »Liefdesdood«, which reads in a way that is both lyrical and full of feeling. The critic Hans Warren called it »a book which continuously assumes another colour.« Recently Oscar van den Boogaard has been interested in the connection between relationships and identity, more precisely in the role that the other plays as a mirror. »We need someone to ourselves be someone. But how can I be, if the other does not have the ability, the experience, and the vocabulary to perceive me.« In a creative dialogue with the Tg Stan, Antwerp, the Ro-Theatre Rotterdam, and the Toneelgroep Amsterdam, he has written five theatre pieces, including »Lucia smelt«, which will be performed this year in the German language for the first time by the State Theatre Hanover. Following stopovers in Rio de Janeiro, Los Angeles, Vienna and Paris, Oscar van den Boogaard currently lives and works in Berlin as a DAAD scholarship holder.

Julias Herrlichkeit
S. Fischer
Frankfurt a. M., 1997
[Ü: Ira Wilhelm]]
Liebestod
S. Fischer
Frankfurt a. M., 2001
[Ü: Ira Wilhelm]]

Oscar van den Boogaard wurde 1964 in Harderwijk, Niederlande, geboren. Er wuchs in der ehemaligen holländischen Kolonie Surinam und in den Niederlanden auf. Nach dem Romanistik- und Jurastudium in Montpellier, Amsterdam und Brüssel begann er eine typische Laufbahn als Anwalt in einer internationalen Kanzlei in Brüssel. An seinem 25. Geburtstag gab er überraschend das sichere Anwaltsdasein auf – und wurde Schriftsteller. Ein bezeichnender Entschluss, denn für van den Boogaard zählt nichts mehr als »das Leben zu leben«, damit am Ende »die Buchhaltung des Lebens: links die Wirklichkeit, rechts die Phantasie«, ausgeglichen ist. Als Gründer der Mot & van den Boogaard Galerie für zeitgenössische Kunst Brüssel trat er in Kontakt mit der internationalen Kunstwelt. Der Künstler Douglas Gordon tätowierte das Wort »Guilty« in Spiegelschrift auf van den Boogaards linkes Schulterblatt. Das Foto seines Rückens ist Teil der Sammlung des New Yorker Guggenheim-Museums.
Seit 1990 sein Debütroman »Dentz« erschien, gehört Oscar van den Boogaard zu den wichtigsten jungen Autoren der Niederlande. Van den Boogaard schreibt so kraftvoll wie sensibel dagegen an, dass Menschen aufgrund von obskuren Zwängen ihre vitale Essenz negieren. Das Leiden am Alltag, in dem kein Raum ist für das Ausleben von Gefühlen und Sehnsüchten, ist zentral für die Hauptfigur seines Romans »De heerlijkheid van Julia« (1995; dt. »Julias Herrlichkeit«, 1997), für den er mit dem niederländischen Libris-Literatuurprijs und der belgischen Auszeichnung De gouden Uil gleich zwei renommierte Preise erhielt. Um komplizierte Familienverhältnisse, Ausbruchsphantasien und Entfremdung geht es auch in seinem Roman »Liefdesdood« (1999; dt. »Liebestod«, 2001), der ebenfalls mit De gouden Uil ausgezeichnet wurde. »Liebestod« ist von einer reduzierten, fast nüchternen Sprache geprägt, die lyrisch und gefühlvoll zugleich daherkommt. Der Kritiker Hans Warren nannte es »ein Buch, das fortwährend eine andere Farbe annimmt«. In jüngster Zeit zeigt sich Oscar van den Boogaard fasziniert von der Frage nach Beziehung und Identität, genauer: von der Rolle eines Gegenübers als Spiegel. »Wir brauchen jemanden, um selbst jemand zu sein. Aber wie kann ich sein, wenn der andere nicht die Fähigkeiten, die Erfahrung, das Vokabular hat, um mich zu erkennen.« Im kreativen Dialog mit dem Tg Stan, Antwerpen, dem Ro-Theater Rotterdam und der Toneelgroep Amsterdam verfasste er fünf Theaterstücke, darunter »Lucia smelt« (2001; dt. »Lucia schmilzt«, 2003), das in diesem Jahr vom Staatstheater Hannover erstmalig in deutscher Sprache aufgeführt wurde. Nach Stationen in Rio de Janeiro, Los Angeles, Wien und Paris lebt und arbeitet Oscar van den Boogaard derzeit als DAAD-Stipendiat in Berlin.

nedim gürsel

biography

Nedim Gürsel was born in Gaziantep, Turkey in 1951. He had already published his first novellas and essays in Turkish literary magazines by the late 60's. After the coup d'état in 1971, he had to testify in court in defence of one of his articles. This led to his decision to temporarily reside in France. He studied Comparative Literature at the Sorbonne in Paris and completed his dissertation in 1979 on Nâzim Hikmet and Louis Aragon. Gürsel then returned to Turkey, before the military putsch of 1980 sent him back into exile in France. He first wrote articles and travel reports which were published in »Le Monde« as well as in the Turkish newspapers »Cumhuriyet« and »Milliyet« Today he teaches at the Sorbonne and directs the Centre National de la Recherche Scientifique, where he is also a lecturer in Turkish literature.

Gürsel's first book of stories »Uzun Sürmüş Bir Yaz« (t: A Long Summer) was published in 1976 and in the same year received Turkey's most prestigious award for literature, the prize of the Turkish Academy. Eleven years later, his first novel followed, »Boğazkesen« (t: The Conqueror), which was also highly regarded internationally; it is available in German under the title »Der Eroberer« (1998). It is about a writer in Istanbul in the late summer of 1980, who gets so involved in his novel's historical hero, the cruel yet equally charismatic Sultan Mehmet II, that the past and the present become one and he follows in the murderous footsteps of his conqueror. What starts out a gloriously colourful novel about passion, life and death, soon also shows itself to be a critical exa-mination of the military dictatorship of the early 80's. In his country Gürsel was accused of being a traitor for his realistic portrait of the conqueror Mehmet, who fundamentalists perceive as a saint.

In »Resimli Dünya« (t: Turbans in Venice), which was published in 1999, the author has his Turkish protagonist study his homeland from the point of view of Italian Renaissance painting. A dialogue develops between Ottoman and the European culture, which is characteristic of Gürsel's literature.

Gürsel's most recent book »Balcon sur la Méditerranée« (2003) has just been published in France. Along with Yaşar Kemal and Orhan Pamuk, he is considered one of Turkey's most important writers.

Die erste Frau
Dagyeli
Frankfurt a. M., 1986
[Ü: Eva Warth-Karabulut]
Ein Sommer ohne Ende
Dagyeli
Frankfurt a. M., 1988
[Ü: Eva Warth-Karabulut]
Paysage littéraire de la Turquie contemporaine
L'Harmattan, Paris, 1993
Der Eroberer
btb, München, 2000
[Ü: Ute Birgi-Knellessen]
Turbane in Venedig
Ammann, Zürich, 2002
[Ü: Monika Carbe]
Balcon sur la Méditerranée
Ed. du Seuil, Paris, 2003
[Ü: Esther Heboyan-DeVries und Timor Muhiddin]

Mes Sources d'Inspiration.

Nedim Gürsel

je dois parler de plusieurs
sources d'inspiration et non d'une
seule à propos de mes livres
– vingt cinq à ce jour – dont quatre
ont été traduits en Allemand.
l'errance, l'exil et l'amour érotique,
pour ne pas dire « les femmes » !
Tels sont, je crois, les thèmes recteurs
dans mes romans et nouvelles
mais je publie également des récits
de voyage dans lesquels une géographie
très affective, la Méditerranée,
occupe une place importante.
S'il est une source d'inspi-
ration majeure, presque « obsessionnelle »
dirais-je, c'est bien Istanbul,

Nedim Gürsel wurde 1951 in Gaziantep, Türkei, geboren. Erste Novellen und Essays veröffentlichte er schon Ende der sechziger Jahre in türkischen Literaturzeitschriften. Nach dem Staatsstreich von 1971 musste er sich für einen seiner Artikel vor Gericht verantworten, was ihn dazu veranlasste, vorübergehend nach Frankreich auszuwandern. An der Pariser Sorbonne studierte er Vergleichende Literaturwissenschaften und reichte 1979 seine Dissertation über Nâzim Hikmet und Louis Aragon ein. Anschließend kehrte Gürsel in die Türkei zurück, bis ihn der Militärputsch von 1980 erneut ins französische Exil trieb. Dort schrieb er zunächst Artikel und Reiseberichte, die in »Le Monde«, aber auch in den türkischen Zeitungen »Cumhuriyet« und »Milliyet« erschienen. Heute lehrt er an der Sorbonne und leitet das Centre National de la Recherche Scientifique, an dem er außerdem als Lektor für Türkische Literatur tätig ist.
Gürsels erster Erzählband »Uzun Sürmüş Bir Yaz« (Ü: Ein Sommer ohne Ende) erschien 1976 und erhielt noch im selben Jahr die höchsten Auszeichnung für Literatur in der Türkei, den Preis der Türkischen Akademie. Elf Jahre später folgte sein erster auch international vielbeachteter Roman »Boğazkesen«, der unter dem Titel »Der Eroberer« seit 1998 auf Deutsch vorliegt. Er erzählt die Geschichte eines Schriftstellers im Istanbul des Spätsommers 1980, der sich von seinem historischen Romanhelden, dem ebenso grausamen wie charismatischen Sultan Mehmet II., so sehr einnehmen lässt, dass ihm Vergangenheit und Gegenwart eins werden und er in die mörderischen Fußstapfen seines Eroberers steigt. Was sich wie ein farbenprächtiger historischer Roman über Leidenschaft, Leben und Tod anlässt, erweist sich bald auch als kritische Auseinandersetzung mit der Militärdiktatur zu Anfang der achtziger Jahre. Für sein realistisches Bild des Eroberers Mehmet, der für die Fundamentalisten ein Heiliger ist, wurde Gürsel in seiner Heimat Vaterlandsverrat vorgeworfen.
In seinem 1999 erschienenen Roman »Resimli Dünya« (dt. »Turbane in Venedig«, 2002) lässt der Autor seinen türkischen Protagonisten die Heimat aus dem Blickwinkel der italienischen Renaissancemalerei erforschen. Es entspinnt sich ein Dialog zwischen der osmanischen und der europäischen Kultur, der für Gürsels Literatur charakteristisch ist.
Gürsel, dessen neuestes Buch »Balcon sur la Méditerranée« (2003) soeben in Frankreich erschien, zählt neben Yaşar Kemal und Orhan Pamuk zu den bedeutendsten Schriftstellern der Türkei.

ville par excellence, capitale de deux grands empires – Byzantin et Ottoman – "veuve encore pucelle après mille épousailles" comme a dit un grand poète turc.

Cette première phrase de mon roman "Der Eroberer", traduit dans une vingtaine de langues, illustre parfaitement mon attachement à la ville d'Istanbul, et à travers elle, à ma langue maternelle, le Turc.

"Longtemps je me suis levé de bonne heure! C'était là-bas, sur la rive asiatique du Bosphore, dans ma ville bien-aimée qui m'a suivi partout et dont le souvenir, tel un fer rouge, est à jamais planté dans ma mémoire"

Le Roman du Conquérant, Ed. du Seuil, 1996

paulo lins
biography

Paulo Lins was born in Rio de Janeiro, Brazil, in 1958 and grew up in Brazil's most notorious favela, known to its residents as Cidade de Deus, the City of God. The writer, anthropologist and teacher used his personal experiences as the basis of his 1997 novel »Cidade de Deus«. The book, which he worked on for over eight years, took its impulse from an academic study of the favelas that Lins was involved in. It describes the development of the City of God in three parts, from a social housing project in the 60's to the ghetto it deteriorated into in the course of the late 70's. The angry young hero's life is ruled by violence and drugs. Yet at the same time the author opens our eyes to the other side of life in the ghetto, to the very individual culture it has produced and which is manifested in its own language, fashion and music. Celebrated by critics and readers in Brazil, the book has so far also been published in Portugal, Italy, France, Sweden, Spain and in Catalan. The novel was made into a film in 2002, which was also a resounding international success. The Brazilian director Fernando Mereilles, originally a very successful director of television commercials, quotes Victor Hugo by way of ironic explanation for the worldwide response to the film: »Talk about your village, and you'll be universal.«
Lins was co-founder of the Cooperativa de Poetas, a group set up in the 70's to give young authors the chance to publish their work. His poetry collection »Sob o Sol« (1986, t: Under the Sun) was a result of this cooperation. He is a member of the jury of the renowned Premio Casa de las Américas. He is currently working on a book about slavery in Brazil since the 15th century, in which he intends to carry out a fictional reconstruction of the history of a Brazilian family descended from slaves, right back to their African forefathers. Lins lives in Rio de Janeiro.

Cidade de Deus
Companhia das Letras
Sao Paulo, 2002

Paulo Lins wurde 1958 in Rio de Janeiro, Brasilien, geboren und ist in Rios berüchtigter Favela aufgewachsen, die unter den Bewohnern »Cidade de Deus«, die »Stadt Gottes«, genannt wird. Der Schriftsteller, Anthropologe und Lehrer hat seine persönlichen Erfahrungen im Roman »Cidade de Deus« von 1997 verarbeitet. Das Buch, an dem Lins über acht Jahre gearbeitet hat, ging von einer wissenschaftlichen Studie über die Favelas aus, an der er beteiligt war. Es schildert in drei Abschnitten die Entwicklung der »Stadt Gottes« von einem Sozialbau-Projekt in den sechziger Jahren zu dem Ghetto, zu dem es im Laufe der späten siebziger Jahre verkommen ist. Das Leben der jungen und zornigen Helden wird von Gewalt und Drogen bestimmt. Zugleich eröffnet sich jedoch auch der Blick auf die andere Seite des Lebens im Ghetto, auf die ganz eigene Kultur, die es hervorgebracht hat und die sich in einer eigenen Sprache, eigener Mode und Musik niederschlägt. In Brasilien von Kritikern und Publikum gefeiert, liegen bisher auch Buchausgaben in Portugal, Italien, Frankreich, Spanien, Katalonien und Schweden vor. 2002 wurde der Roman verfilmt und traf auch international auf ein großes Echo. Der brasilianische Regisseur Fernando Meirelles, ursprünglich ein sehr erfolgreicher Filmer von TV-Werbespots, erklärt die weltweite Resonanz des Films ironisch mit einer Wendung Victor Hugos: »Sprich über dein Dorf, und alle werden sich wiedererkennen.«

Lins ist Mitbegründer der Cooperativa de Poetas, einer Gruppe, die in den siebziger Jahren gegründet wurde, um jungen Autoren Möglichkeiten der Publikation zu eröffnen. Aus dieser Zusammenarbeit ging sein Gedichtband »Sob o Sol« (1986: Ü; Unter der Sonne) hervor.

Er ist Mitglied der Jury des renommierten Premio Casa de las Américas. Derzeit arbeitet er an einem Buch über die Sklaverei in Brasilien seit dem 15. Jahrhundert, in dem er die Geschichte einer brasilianischen Familie, Nachfahren von Sklaven, bis zu ihren afrikanischen Ahnen fiktiv rekonstruieren möchte. Lins lebt in Rio de Janeiro.

tomaž šalamun

biography

Tomaž Šalamun was born in Zagreb, Yugoslavia, in 1941 and grew up in Koper, Slovenia. He studied history and art history at the university of Ljubljana. In the years that followed, he continued his studies in Italy and France and celebrated his first success not only as a poet but also as a conceptual artist. Before his first poetry publications, he participated in the International Writing Program in Iowa (1971 to 1973) and was able to take an extensive look at American verse. In 1986 a Fulbright scholarship brought him to Columbia University in New York, where he returned from 1996 to 1999 as a cultural attaché with the Slovenian consulate. Today Šalamun lives with his wife, the artist Metka Krašovec, in Ljubljana. Since July 2003 he has been living in Berlin as a guest of the DAAD.
Starting in his student days, Šalamun worked for Slovenia's most important literary magazine »Perspektive«. When in 1964 the magazine published the young editor's first subversive poems, the authorities stepped in. But, according to Šalumun, it was his five-day imprisonment that first sowed the seeds for the popular success of his experimental works. The private publication of his first collection of verse »Poker« (1966) sparked the development of a Slovenian avant-garde. Since »Poker«, Tomaž Šalamun has published 32 books of poetry, won his country's most important literature prize, and made a name for himself internationally with translations into numerous European languages.
Over the years his poetry – as evident in the 1997 US retrospective »The Four Questions of Melancholy« – has matured stylistically and come to address a wider variety of themes without losing its provocative energy. From the perspective of a first-person narrator, Šalamun looks at the surreal aspects of everyday life and love, yet always remains the »bugbear«, delving into the abyss of the human soul and laying bare the borders and rules of the Slovenian language.
Šalamun's verse is characterised by the strife-torn history of the Balkans yet has a far wider relevance. The influence of contemporary American poetry, familiar to him through his translation work, cannot be missed and in the United States earned him a reputation as the »unknown force« behind a new generation of American writers. In German-speaking countries, where there are only three translations to date, he is far from receiving the attention he deserves.

Ein Stengel Petersilie im Smoking
S. Fischer
Frankfurt a. M., 1972
[Ü: Peter Urban]
Wal
Droschl, Graz, 1990
[Ü: Fabjan Hafner]
Morje
Nova revija, Ljubljana 1999
Amerika
Mondena, Grosuplje 2000
A Ballad for Metka Krašovec
Twisted Spoon Press
Prag, 2001
[Ü: Michael Biggins]
Vier Fragen der Melancholie
Edition Korrespondenzen
Wien, 2003
[Ü: Peter Urban]

Tomaž Šalamun wurde 1941 im jugoslawischen Zagreb geboren und wuchs im slowenischen Koper auf. Er studierte Geschichte und Kunstgeschichte an der Universität Ljubljana. In den Folgejahren setzte er seine Studien in Italien und Frankreich fort und feierte nicht nur als Dichter, sondern auch als Konzeptkünstler erste Erfolge. Durch die Teilnahme am International Writing Program in Iowa (1971 bis 1973), dem erste Gedichtpublikationen vorausgingen, erhielt Šalamun einen folgenreichen Einblick in die amerikanische Lyrik. 1986 führte ihn ein Fulbright-Stipendium an die Columbia University in New York, wohin er von 1996 bis 1999 als Kulturattaché des Slowenischen Konsulats zurückkehrte. Mit seiner Ehefrau, der Künstlerin Metka Krašovec, lebt Šalamun heute in Ljubljana. Seit Juli 2003 lebt er auf Einladung des DAAD in Berlin.
Schon zu Studienzeiten war Šalamun bei Sloweniens bedeutendster Literaturzeitschrift »Perspektive« tätig. Als dort 1964 erste subversive Gedichte des jungen Redakteurs erschienen, griffen die Behörden ein. Seine fünftägige Inhaftierung aber – so Šalumun – schuf in der Öffentlichkeit erst den rechten Nährboden für den Erfolg seiner experimentellen Werke. Die Publikation seiner ersten Lyriksammlung »Poker« (1966) im Samisdat war das Initial für die Entwicklung einer slowenischen Avantgarde. Seit »Poker« hat Tomaž Šalamun 32 Gedichtbände veröffentlicht, die bedeutendsten Literaturpreise seines Landes gewonnen und sich mit Übersetzungen in zahlreiche europäische Sprachen international einen Namen gemacht.
Über die Jahre ist seine Dichtung – so zeigt es der 1997 in den USA zusammengestellte Rückblick »The Four Questions of Melancholy« (dt. »Vier Fragen der Melancholie«, 2003) – stilistisch reifer geworden und hat sich eine größere thematische Bandbreite zu eigen gemacht, ohne ihre provokative Energie zu verlieren. Šalamun erzählt aus der Perspektive eines lyrischen Ich vom Surrealen im alltäglichen Leben und in der Liebe, bleibt dabei aber stets das »Scheusal«, das im Schreiben die Abgründe der menschlichen Seele erkundet und die Grenzen und Regeln der slowenischen Sprache aufsprengt.
Šalamuns Lyrik ist geprägt von der zerrissenen Geschichte des Balkans und weist doch weit über dessen Grenzen hinaus. Der Einfluss der zeitgenössischen amerikanischen Dichtung, die er durch Übersetzungsarbeiten kennenlernte, ist unübersehbar und hat ihm in den Vereinigten Staaten den Ruhm des »heimlichen Paten« einer neuen Generation von amerikanischen Dichtern eingetragen, während er im deutschsprachigen Raum mit nur drei vorliegenden Übersetzungen noch lange nicht angemessen gewürdigt worden ist.

AN:49 30 7813925
03027878685
06-AUG-2003 12:12 VON:ILB

"WHAT MAKES THE POET TICK?"
THAT'S THE FORBIDDEN QUESTION.
I'M A LION STANDING AT MY DOOR,
ROARING TO MAKE PEOPLE WITH SUCH
QUESTIONS STEP BACK AND RUN AWAY.

ferenc szijj
biography

Ferenc Szijj was born in Szombathely, Hungary, in 1958. From 1978 to 1984 he studied Hungarian studies and German language and literature at the József Attila University in Szeged. After concluding his studies, he taught German at high-school level, worked as a librarian at the university library in Budapest, and in 1989 became editor of the literary magazine »Nappali Ház«. After the magazine was discontinued in 1999, Szijj edited an internet magazine. In 1990 he published his first book of poetry »A lassú élet titka« in Budapest, later followed by his collection of short stories »A futás napja« (1992), which attained cult status in Hungary. His two collections of poetry »A nagy salakmező« (1997) and »Kéregtorony« (1999) will soon be available in German. In an interview Szijj says that he would have liked to have become an engine driver or a soccer player – but his weak eyes forced him to earn his living under bad lighting conditions: by writing. He adds: »I do not feel like a real poet, one who writes poem after poem and can only think in terms of poetry. I was never particularly interested in the perfect stylistic form. I would even go as far as to say grammatical correctness doesn't really interest me today – although, if it doesn't sound too immodest, I now know a lot about grammar and language usage – as a user.« In 2001 he published the fairytale book »Szuromberek királyfi« (t: Prince Szuromberek), which was humorously illustrated by Gabór Roskó, the cartoonist from the weekly literary magazine »Élet és Irodalom«. Szijj has also translated German writers such as Kafka, Gregor von Rezzori, and W. G. Sebald into Hungarian. He has received many awards for his literary work, including various scholarships, the Tibor Déry Prize in 2000 as well as the Attila József Prize in 2001. The author lives as a freelance writer in Budapest and since August 2003 has resided as a guest in Berlin, where he holds a scholarship from the DAAD artist's programme.

Das Geheimnis des langsamen Lebens
Droschl, Graz, 1992
[Ü: Andrea Seidler]
Der Tag des Rennens
Droschl, Graz, 1993
[Ü: Andrea Seidler]
A nagy salakmező
Jelenkor Kiadó, Pécs, 1997
Kéregtorony
Jelenkor Kiadó, Pécs, 1999

Ferenc Szijj wurde 1958 in Szombathely, Ungarn, geboren. Zwischen 1978 und 1984 studierte er in Szeged an der József-Attila-Universität Hungarologie und Germanistik. Nach Abschluss seines Studiums lehrte er an einem Gymnasium Deutsch, arbeitete als Bibliothekar an der Budapester Universitätsbibliothek und wurde 1989 Redakteur der Literaturzeitschrift »Nappali Ház«. Nach der Einstellung der Zeitschrift 1999 redigierte Szijj eine Internet-Zeitschrift. Der erste Gedichtband »A lassú élet titka« erschien 1990 in Budapest (dt. »Das Geheimnis des langsamen Lebens«, 1992). Sein Kurzgeschichtenband »A futás napja« (1992; dt. »Der Tag des Rennens« 1993) erlangte in Ungarn Kultstatus. Seine beiden Gedichtsammlungen »A nagy salakmező« (1997; Ü: Die große Schlackenwiese) und »Kéregtorony« (1999; Ü: Krustenturm) erscheinen demnächst in deutscher Übersetzung. In einem Interview erzählt Szijj, er wäre gern Lokführer oder Fußballspieler geworden – aber wegen seiner schwachen Augen ist er am Ende dazu gezwungen worden, seine Brötchen unter schlechten Lichtverhältnissen zu verdienen: mit dem Schreiben. Weiter sagt er von sich: »Ich fühle mich nicht als echter Dichter, der ein Gedicht nach dem anderen schreibt und nur in Gedichten denken kann. Die perfekte stilistische Form hat mich nie besonders gereizt. Ich würde sogar noch weiter gehen: heutzutage interessiert mich auch die grammatikalische Korrektheit nicht besonders – obwohl ich, wenn das jetzt auch nicht allzu unbescheiden klingt, viel Ahnung von Grammatik und Sprachgebrauch habe – als Anwender.« 2001 veröffentlichte er das Märchenbuch »Szuromberek királyfi« (Ü: Prinz Szuromberek), das vom Cartoonisten der wöchentlich erscheinenden Literaturzeitung »Élet és Irodalom« Gabór Roskó humorvoll illustriert wurde. Szijj übersetzte außerdem deutsche Schriftsteller wie Kafka, Gregor von Rezzori und W. G. Sebald ins Ungarische. Seine literarische Tätigkeit wurde mehrfach ausgezeichnet, so erhielt er verschiedene Stipendien und im Jahr 2000 den Tibor-Déry-Preis sowie 2001 den Attila-József-Preis. Der Autor lebt als freischaffender Schriftsteller in Budapest und ist seit August 2003 als Stipendiat des Künstlerprogramms des DAAD in Berlin zu Gast.

david toscana

biography

David Toscana was born in Monterrey in the northern Mexican state of Nuevo León in 1961. After leaving school, he qualified as an engineer and worked in Ciudad Juárez. He started to write at the age of 29. His literary influences, in terms of reading for enjoyment's sake, were classic Spanish writers like Cervantes and Calderón as well as classic Russian writers, but in terms of the obsession with writing itself, he was influenced by the new Latin American writers Juan Carlos Onetti and José Donoso. David Toscana describes his narrative aesthetics as »realismo desquiciado« (t: unrestrained realism) which breaks with magic realism. Neither rhyme nor reason determine his protagonists' actions – what goes on in their world takes place in the imagination alone, albeit as an exchange between life and fiction unfolding on more than one level. »When writing, what is important for me is keeping an eye on the concrete experience of life,« states the author, who puts himself in the place of his protagonists and strives to understand what is personally at risk for them so as to bring the situation back into the very uncertain realm of everyday life.
He developed his literary sense for atmosphere through Onetti and Juan Rulfo, and for the lavishly strange through Donoso. Toscana's first novel »Las bicicletas« (t: The Bicycles) was published in 1992 and opened with the laconic sentence: »The path to the cemetery was long.« He thereby immediately placed himself in the Mexican literary tradition that incorporates the death motif, which, as a regional writer, he sees as situated in the barren north. This was followed in 1995 by »Estación Tula« (»Tula Station«, 2000), which was also translated into Arabic, English, Greek and Serbian. In 1997 he published the short-story volume »Historias de Lontananza« (t: Stories of Distance), followed in 1998 by his third novel »Santa María del Circo« (»Our Lady of the Circus«, 2001). His fourth and most recent novel »Duelo por Miguel Pruneda« (t: Lament for Miguel Pruneda) appeared in 2002. International literary critics have praised his works of prose for the at times biting irony that gives authentic depth to the failure and solitude of his protagonists: »There is a very rich source in my region which no one else has really tapped, which is why I feel so good about working in my own storehouse, bringing forth lots of untold stories.« Since July 2003 David Toscana has lived in Berlin, where he holds a guest scholarship from the DAAD.

Historias del Lontananza
J. Mortiz, Mexiko, 1997
Endstation Tula
Krüger, Frankfurt a. M., 1998
[Ü: Willi Zurbrüggen]
Santa Maria del Circo
Plaza y Janés, Mexiko, 1998
Duelo por Miguel Pruneda
Plaza y Janés, Mexiko, 2002

David Toscana wurde 1961 in Monterrey im nordmexikanischen Bundesstaat Nuevo León geboren. Nach seiner Schulzeit ließ er sich zum Diplomingenieur ausbilden und arbeitete in Ciudad Juárez. Mit 29 Jahren begann er zu schreiben. Einerseits prägten ihn spanische Klassiker wie Cervantes und Calderón sowie die klassischen Erzähler Russlands, wenn es um das Lesevergnügen ging, andererseits die neuen lateinamerikanischen Erzähler Juan Carlos Onetti und José Donoso, wenn es um die Obsessionen des Schreibens selbst ging. Seine Erzählästhetik bezeichnet David Toscana als »realismo desquiciado« (Ü: »haltlosen Realismus«), der sich vom magischen Realismus lossagt. Seine Protagonisten handeln weder mit Logik noch Vernunft; ihre Welt spielt sich allein in der Vorstellung ab, wenngleich ein mehrschichtiger Austausch zwischen Leben und Fiktion stattfindet. »Es ist mir beim Schreiben wichtig, die konkrete Lebenserfahrung im Bewusstsein zu behalten«, bekräftigt der Autor, der sich in seine Protagonisten versetzt und ihre persönlichen Risiken nachvollziehen möchte, um aus den jeweiligen Situationen heraus in die ganz alltägliche Haltlosigkeit der Welt zu geraten.
Onetti, aber auch Juan Rulfo schulten seinen literarischen Sinn für die Atmosphäre, Donoso für das opulent Absonderliche. Toscanas Romanerstling »Las bicicletas« (Ü: Die Fahrräder) erschien 1992 und begann mit dem lakonischen Satz: »Der Weg zum Friedhof war lang.« Damit stellte er sich unmittelbar in die mexikanische Tradition der literarischen Gestaltung des Todesmotivs, die er als regionaler Schriftsteller in den kargen Norden verortet. 1995 folgte »Estación Tula« (dt. »Endstation Tula«, 1998), das auch ins Arabische, Englische, Griechische und Serbische übersetzt wurde. 1997 veröffentlichte er den Erzählungsband »Historias de Lontananza« (Ü: Geschichten der Ferne), dem 1998 sein dritter Roman »Santa María del Circo« (Ü: Die heilige Maria vom Zirkus) folgte. Sein jüngster, vierter Roman »Duelo por Miguel Pruneda« (Ü: Klage um Miguel Pruneda) erschien 2002.
Die internationale Literaturkritik lobte seine Prosawerke für die bisweilen beißende Ironie, die das Scheitern und die Einsamkeit seiner Protagonisten authentisch gestaltet: »Ich finde in meiner Region eine sehr reiche Ader, die eigentlich niemand geschürft hat, deshalb fühle ich mich sehr wohl, in meinem eigenen Bergwerk zu arbeiten und viele unerzählte Geschichten hervorzubringen.« Seit Juli 2003 lebt David Toscana als Gaststipendiat des DAAD in Berlin.

bjarte breiteig
richard john evans
angharad price
tilman rammstedt
flavio soriga

bjarte breiteig

biography | biographie

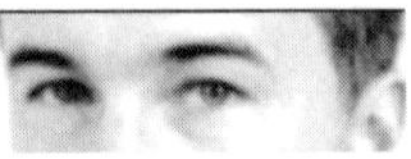

Fantomsmerter
Aschehoug, Oslo, 2000
Surrogater
Aschehoug, Oslo, 2000

Bjarte Breiteig was born in Kristiansand, Norway, in 1974. He studied Physics in Trondheim and Literature at the University of Bergen. In 1998 he published his first stories under the title »Fantomsmerter« (t: Phantom Pains); the book won the debut prize of the Aschehoug Publishing House. His second book »Surrogater« (t: Surrogate) was published in 2000 and was enthusiastically received by both the public and the critics. Breiteig lives in Oslo where he works as a freelance writer.

Bjarte Breiteig wurde 1974 in Kristiansand, Norwegen, geboren. Er studierte Physik in Trondheim und Literaturwissenschaft an der Universität Bergen. 1998 veröffentlichte er seine ersten Erzählungen unter dem Titel »Fantomsmerter« (Ü: Phantomschmerzen), für die er den Debütantenpreis des Verlags Aschehoug erhielt. 2000 erschien sein zweiter Band, »Surrogater« (Ü: Surrogate), der von Publikum und Kritik ebenfalls begeistert augenommen wurde. Breiteig lebt als freier Schriftsteller in Oslo.

richard john evans

biography | biographie

Entertainment
Seren, Bridgend, 2000

Richard John Evans was born in South Wales, Great Britain. He studied Creative Writing at the University of Glamorgan. His first novel »Entertainment« was published in 2000 and is set in his hometown of Treorchy in the Rhondda Valley. After having worked for various Welsh newspapers, including »Wales on Sunday«, he is now concentrating on his second novel. Evans lives in Cardiff.

Richard John Evans wurde in Südwales, Großbritannien, geboren. Er besuchte den Studiengang Kreatives Schreiben an der Universität Glamorgan. Sein erster Roman »Entertainment« erschien 2000 und spielt in seiner Heimatstadt Treorchy im Rhondda Valley. Nachdem Evans fünf Jahre für verschiedene walisische Zeitungen, u. a. »Wales on Sunday«, arbeitete, schreibt er nun hauptsächlich an seinem zweiten Roman. Evans lebt in Cardiff.

Monday morning. She murmurs in her sleep, I write it down. She wakes, yawns, goes to work. Clouds come from the east, stacking up over the park. Cars approach the junction, flickering through the roundabout's shrubs. Some memory – a wooden bench speckled with bottle green moss, on stout iron legs, distant trains clattering – expands mysteriously. Impossibly high birds, swallows, specks against the cloud stacks. A shout in the street; I write it down.

Richard John Evans,
Cardiff, 2003.

»What makes the poet tick?«
Richard John Evans (left)
Tilman Rammstedt (right)

angharad price

biography | biographie

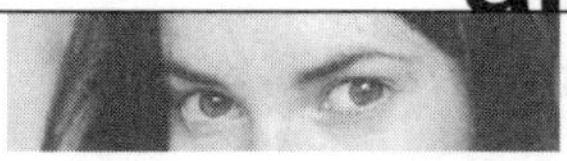

Tee mit der Königin (Hg.)
Cambria, Hildesheim, 1996
[Ü: Frank Meyer
Angharad Price]
Tania'r Tacsi
Gwasg Gomer
Llandysul, 1999
O! Tyn y Gorchudd
Gwasg Gomer
Llandysul, 2002
Rhwng gwyn a du
University of Wales Press
Cardiff, 2002

Angharad Price was born in the vicinity of Caernarfon in North Wales, Great Britain, in 1972. She studied Modern Languages at Jesus College, Oxford. She has published numerous books and articles on contemporary Welsh literature as well as several stories and two shorter novels: »Tania'r Tacsi« (t: Tania's Taxi) in 1999 and »O! Tyn y Gorchudd« (t: Oh, Pull Away the Veil), which won the prize for best prose piece at the National Eisteddfod in 2002. She is a lecturer in Welsh Literature at Cardiff University.

Angharad Price wurde 1972 in der Nähe von Caernarfon in Nordwales, Großbritannien, geboren. Sie studierte Moderne Sprachen am Jesus College, Oxford. Sie veröffentlichte zahlreiche Bücher und Artikel über zeitgenössische walisische Literatur sowie mehrere Geschichten und zwei kürzere Romane; 1999 »Tania'r Tacsi« (Ü: Tanias Taxi) und »O! Tyn y Gorchudd« (Ü: O! Lüfte den Schleier), der beim National Eisteddfod 2002 den Preis für das beste Prosastück gewonnen hat. Sie arbeitet als Dozentin für Walisische Literatur an der Cardiff University.

tilman rammstedt

biography | biographie

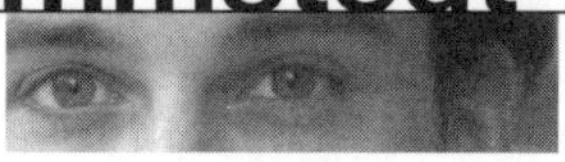

Erledigungen vor der Feier
DuMont, Köln, 2003

Tilman Rammstedt was born in Bielefeld, Germany, in 1975. He studied Philosophy and Literature in Edinburgh, Tübingen, and Berlin. He is a songwriter and musician for the group Fön as well as a member of the literary troop Visch&Ferse. In 2001 he won the ninth open-mike competition. His debut »Erledigungen vor der Feier« was published in 2003. Rammstedt lives in Berlin.

Tilman Rammstedt wurde 1975 in Bielefeld, Deutschland, geboren. Er studierte Philosophie und Literaturwissenschaft in Edinburgh, Tübingen und Berlin. Er ist Texter und Musiker der Gruppe Fön sowie Mitglied der Lesebühne Visch&Ferse. 2001 war er Preisträger des 9. Open Mike-Wettbewerbs. Sein Debüt »Erledigungen vor der Feier« erschien 2003. Rammstedt lebt in Berlin.

flavio soriga

biography | biographie

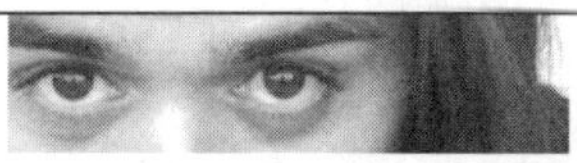

Diavoli di Nuraiò
Il Maestrale, Nuoro, 2000
Zente virtudosa
Soter
Villanova Monteleone, 2001
Neropioggia
Garzanti, Mailand, 2002

Flavio Soriga was born in Uta, a small village in Sardinia, Italy, in 1975. He studied Journalism and Media Technology in Rome and Madrid and directed television programmes for regional Sardinian channels. He received the Italo Calvino Prize in 2000 for his novel »Diavoli di Nuraiò« (t: The Devil from Nuraiò). In 2002 he published his second novel »Neropioggia« (t: Black Rain). Soriga works for the newspaper »La Nuova Sardegna« and also for various magazines. Soriga lives in Cagliari, Bologna and London.

Flavio Soriga wurde 1975 in Uta, einem kleinen Dorf auf Sardinien, Italien, geboren. Er studierte Journalistik und Medientechnik in Rom und Madrid und leitete Fernsehprogramme für regionale sardinische Sender. Für den Roman »Diavoli di Nuraiò« (Ü: Die Teufel von Nuraiò) erhielt er 2000 den Italo-Calvino-Preis. 2002 veröffentlichte er seinen zweiten Roman »Neropioggia« (Ü: Schwarzer Regen). Soriga arbeitet für die Tageszeitung »La Nuova Sardegna« sowie für verschiedene Zeitschriften. Soriga lebt in Cagliari, Bologna und London.

tariq ali
amal al-jubouri
giovanni bachelet
hans christoph buch
edoardo ferrario
paolo flores d'arcais
ralf fücks
paul ginsborg
walter haubrich
richard herzinger
reinhard hesse
laennec hurbon
huber matos
herfried münkler
adolf muschg
iván de la nuez
rüdiger safranski
karl schlögel
gianni vattimo
richard wagner
uwe wesel
arno widmann
jean ziegler

Born in Lahore, India (today Pakistan) in 1943. He studied politics and philosophy at Oxford. He opposed the military dictatorship in Pakistan, which made returning to his homeland impossible. He chose England as his place of exile. The co-editor of the »New Left Review« has written books on political topics, i.e. »The Clash of Fun damentalisms« (2002) and also novels and theatre pieces. He lives in London.

Tariq Ali

Geb. 1943 in Lahore, Indien (heute Pakistan). Er studierte Politik und Philosophie in Oxford. Sein Widerstand gegen die Militärdiktatur in Pakistan machte die Rückkehr in die Heimat unmöglich; England wurde zum Exil. Der Mitherausgeber der »New Left Review« schrieb Bücher zu politischen Themen, z. B. »Fundamentalismus im Kampf um die Weltordnung« (2002) sowie Romane und Theaterstücke. Er lebt in London.

Born in Baghdad, Iraq in 1967. After studying English language and literature she worked for Iraqi television. She left Iraq in 1997. Today she lives in Berlin and is editor of the literary magazine for Arabian and German poetry »diwan«. Many of her poems have been translated and published in German.

Amal al-Jubouri

Geb. 1967 in Bagdad, Irak Nach dem Studium der Anglistik arbeitete sie beim irakischen Fernsehen. 1997 verließ sie den Irak. Sie lebt heute in Berlin und gibt »diwan« heraus, eine Zeitschrift für arabische und deutsche Poesie. Zahlreiche ihrer Gedichte sind ins Deutsche übersetzt und veröffentlicht worden.

Tariq Ali

Hans Christoph Buch

Born in Rome, Italy in 1955. He lectures in physics at La Sapienza University in Rome. He has previously worked in the USA and in Germany. Bachelet is the co-founder of Libertà e Giustizia (Liberty and Justice), Italy's most prominent protest movement against the Berlusconi government.

Giovanni Bachelet

Geb. 1955 in Rom, Italien. Lehrt als Physiker an der La Sapienza Universität in Rom. Er hat zuvor in den USA und in Deutschland gearbeitet. Bachelet ist Mitbegründer von Libertà e Giustizia (Freiheit und Recht), der prominentesten Protestbewegung Italiens gegen die Regierung Berlusconi.

Born in Wetzlar, Germany in 1944. He studied German language and literature and Slavonic studies in Berlin. Buch has accepted numerous guest lectureships from universities worldwide. In 2001 he published a collection of articles about the various fronts in the world's civil wars under the title »Blut im Schuh«. His most recent publication was »Wie Karl May Adolf Hitler traf und andere wahre Geschichten« (2003). The literary theorist, essayist, publicist and narrative writer lives in Berlin.

Hans Christoph Buch

Geb. 1944 in Wetzlar, Deutschland. Er studierte in Berlin Germanistik und Slawistik. Buch nahm weltweit zahlreiche Universitäts-Gastdozenturen wahr. 2001 veröffentlichte er unter dem Titel »Blut im Schuh« gesammelte Reportagen von den verschiedenen Fronten des »Weltbürgerkriegs«. Zuletzt erschien »Wie Karl May Adolf Hitler traf und andere wahre Geschichten« (2003). Der Literaturtheoretiker, Essayist, Publizist und Erzähler lebt in Berlin.

Born in Luino, Italy in 1946. He is a lecturer in philosophy at La Sapienza University in Rome. He is co-founder of Italy's extremely popular Girotondi per la democrazia movement, whose members include Nanni Moretti. Last May the initiative organised the largest demonstration against the Berlusconi government to date.

Edoardo Ferrario

Geb. 1946 in Luino, Italien. Er lehrt Philosophie an der La Sapienza Universität in Rom. Er ist Mitbegründer der in Italien äußerst populären Bewegung Girotondi per la democrazia, der u. a. auch Nanni Moretti angehört. Im vergangenen Mai konnte die Initiative in Rom die bis dahin größte Demonstration gegen die Regierung Berlusconi mobilisieren.

Born in Cervignano del Friuli, Italy in 1944. He wrote his doctoral thesis on Adam Smith and Karl Marx, and is now a researcher in the philosophical faculty of La Sapienza University in Rome. He is editor of the magazine »MicroMega« and has also written for various newspapers, including »El País« and the »FAZ«. Several of his texts have been published in German, including »Die Linke und das Individuum« (1997)

Paolo Flores D'Arcais

Geb. 1944 in Cervignano del Friuli, Italien. Er promovierte über Adam Smith und Karl Marx und forscht heute an der philosophischen Fakultät der La Sapienza Universität in Rom. Er ist Herausgeber der Zeitschrift »MicroMega« und war auch für verschiedene Zeitungen, darunter für »El País« und die »FAZ« tätig. Auf Deutsch erschien von ihm unter anderem »Die Linke und das Individuum« (1997).

Ralf Fücks

Born in Edenkoben, Germany in 1951. He studied sociology, politics and economics and was active in the student movement. Fücks joined the Green Party in 1982 and was party spokesperson from 1989-90. He was deputy mayor of Bremen and responsible for urban development and environmental protection from 1991-95. He has been chair of the Heinrich Böll Foundation since 1996. He writes for various newspapers and is the editor of the book »Sind die Grünen noch zu retten?« (1991)

Ralf Fücks

Geb. 1951 in Edenkoben, Deutschland. Er studierte Soziologie, Politik und Wirtschaft und war in der Studentenbewegung aktiv. 1982 trat Fücks den Grünen bei, deren Sprecher er 1989-90 war. 1991-95 war er Senator für Stadtentwicklung und Umweltschutz sowie stellvertretender Bürgermeister von Bremen. Seit 1996 ist er Vorsitzender der Heinrich-Böll-Stiftung. Er schreibt für verschiedene Zeitschriften und ist Herausgeber des Buches »Sind die Grünen noch zu retten?« (1991).

Born in London in 1945. He was a professor at Churchill College, Cambridge, and now holds a professorship for European history at the University of Florence. He is co-founder of the protest movement Laboratorio per la democrazia. His most recent publication is »Italy and its Discontents: Family, Civil Society, State 1980-2001«.

Paul Ginsborg

Geb. 1945 in London. Er war Professor am Churchill College in Cambridge und hat jetzt eine Professur für Europäische Geschichte an der Universität von Florenz inne. Er ist Mitbegründer der Protestbewegung Laboratorio per la democrazia. Zuletzt veröffentlichte er »Italy and its Discontents: Family, Civil Society, State 1980-2001«.

Born in the Rhineland in 1935 and studied philology in Germany, France and Spain. After his degree he worked at the Universities of Mainz, Santiago de Compostela and Valladolid. Haubrich, one of the most acknowledged experts on Spain and Latin America, has been Madrid correspondent to the »FAZ« for over thirty years.

Walter Haubrich

Geb. 1935 im Rheinland. Studierte in Deutschland, Frankreich und Spanien Philologie. Nach dem Studium arbeitete an den Universitäten Mainz, Santiago de Compostela und Valladolid. Haubrich, einer der profundesten Kenner Spaniens und Lateinamerikas, ist seit über dreißig Jahren Korrespondent der »FAZ« in Madrid.

Born in Frankfurt a. M. in 1955. He has a Ph.D. in literature and is political editor of the newspaper »Die Zeit«. He has written numerous essays on literature, culture and politics in Germany, the theory of liberalism and international human rights policy. In his most recent book »Republik ohne Mitte« he argues in favour of an open society.

Richard Herzinger

Geb. 1955 in Frankfurt a. M. Der Literaturwissenschaftler ist politischer Redakteur der Wochenzeitung »Die Zeit«. Er schrieb zahlreiche Essays und Aufsätze zur Literatur, Kultur und Politik in Deutschland, über die Theorie des Liberalismus und die internationale Menschenrechtspolitik. In seinem jüngsten Buch »Republik ohne Mitte« plädiert er für eine offene Gesellschaft.

Richard Herzinger

Walter Haubrich

Reinhard Hesse

Laennec Hurbon

Born in 1956 and grew up in Cairo as the son of German parents. After university he worked as a reporter for many years, including in Beirut, Cairo, Bonn, Paris and the USA. Hesse lives in Berlin, Munich and Beirut. He has been writing speeches for Gerhard Schröder and political essays since 1998. His current book is entitled »Ground Zero«.

Reinhard Hesse

Geb. 1956. Wuchs als Kind deutscher Eltern in Kairo auf. Nach seinem Studium war er viele Jahre als Reporter tätig, unter anderem in Beirut, Kairo, Bonn, Paris und in den USA. Hesse lebt in Berlin, München und Beirut. Seit 1998 ist er Redenschreiber für Gerhard Schröder und Verfasser politischer Aufsätze. Der Titel seines aktuellen Buches lautet »Ground Zero«.

Born in Jacmel, Haiti. He studied theology and sociology in Paris and is a founding member and professor of Quisqueya University in Port-au-Prince, as well as a scientist at the Paris CNRS. He has written several socio-anthropological works on subjects including Haitian voodoo and slavery, among them »Le Barbare imaginaire« (1988) and »Pour une sociologie d'Haiti au XXIe siècle« (2001).

Laennec Hurbon

Geb. in Jacmel, Haiti. Er studierte Theologie und Soziologie in Paris und ist Gründungsmitglied und Professor der Quisqueya Universität in Port-au-Prince sowie Wissenschaftler am Pariser CNRS. Er hat mehrere sozio-anthropologische Werke, u. a. über den haitianischen Voodoo und die Sklaverei verfasst, darunter »Le Barbare imaginaire« (1988) und »Pour une sociologie d'Haiti au XXIe siècle« (2001).

Born in Yara, Cuba in 1918. He completed his Ph.D. at the University of Havana in 1944 and was a founding member of the Cuban People's Party. He gave up his position as Comandante in 1959 in protest against the radicalisation of his former comrades. Fidel Castro had him condemned to twenty years' imprisonment in a show trial in December 1959, a sentence which Matos served to the very last day. He now lives in Miami.

Huber Matos

Geb. 1918 in Yara, Kuba. Er promovierte 1944 an der Universität von Havanna und war Gründungsmitglied der Kubanischen Volkspartei. Aus Protest gegen die Radikalisierung seiner ehemaligen Mitstreiter gab er 1959 seine Stellung als Comandante auf. Fidel Castro ließ ihn im Dezember 1959 in einem Schauprozess zu zwanzig Jahren Gefängnis verurteilen, die Matos bis auf den letzten Tag absitzen musste. Heute lebt er in Miami.

Born in Friedberg, Germany in 1951. He studied German literature and language, politics and philosophy. He has been a lecturer in political theory at the Humboldt University in Berlin since 1992. He is editor of the series »Politische Ideen«. His book »Die neuen Kriege« was published in 2002 and aroused much media attention.

Herfried Münkler

Geb. 1951 in Friedberg, Deutschland. Er studierte Germanistik, Politikwissenschaft und Philosophie. Seit 1992 lehrt er Theorie der Politik an der Humboldt-Universität zu Berlin. Er ist Herausgeber der Reihe »Politische Ideen«. 2002 erschien sein vielbeachtetes Buch »Die neuen Kriege«.

Huber Matos

Herfried Münkler

Adolf Muschg

Born in Zollikon, Switzerland in 1934. He studied at the University of Zurich and Cambridge. After guest lectureships in Japan and the USA he taught German language and literature at the ETH Zurich from 1970 to 1999. His first novel »Im Sommer des Hasen" (t: In the Summer of the Hare) was published in 1965, followed by numerous novels, short stories and plays for theatre, radio and television. He became president of the Berlin Akademie der Künste in 2003.

Adolf Muschg

Geb. 1934 in Zollikon, Schweiz. Er studierte an der Universität Zürich und in Cambridge. Nach Gastdozenturen in Japan und den USA lehrte er zwischen 1970 und 1999 Deutsche Sprache und Literatur an der ETH Zürich. 1965 erschien sein erster Roman »Im Sommer des Hasen«, dem zahlreiche Romane, Erzählungen, Theaterstücke, Hörspiele und Drehbücher folgten. 2003 trat er sein Amt als Präsident der Berliner Akademie der Künste an.

Born in Havana, Cuba in 1964. He is an essayist and art critic and now lives and works as a university lecturer in Barcelona. »Das treibende Floß: Kubanische Kulturpassagen« (1998; t: The Floating Raft: Cuban Cultural Passages) has been published in Germany, an analysis of the cultural development in Cuba.

Iván de la Nuez

Geb. 1964 in Havanna, Kuba. Er ist Essayist und Kunstkritiker und lebt heute in Barcelona, wo er an der Universität lehrt. Auf Deutsch liegt »Das treibende Floß: Kubanische Kulturpassagen« (1998) vor, in dem er die kulturelle Entwicklung Kubas analysiert.

Born in Rottweil, Germany in 1945. He studied philosophy, German and history in Frankfurt a. M. and Berlin. He worked as editor and co-publisher of the »Berliner Hefte« from 1977-81. He gained recognition chiefly through his biographies of Schopenhauer, Heidegger and Nietzsche. He has presented ZDF television's »Philosophisches Quartett« along with Peter Sloterdijk since 2002. He lives in Berlin.

Rüdiger Safranski

Geb. 1945 in Rottweil, Deutschland. Er studierte Philosophie, Germanistik und Geschichte in Frankfurt a. M. und in Berlin. 1977-81 arbeitete er als Redakteur und Mitherausgeber der »Berliner Hefte«. Bekannt wurde er vor allem mit seinen Biographien über Schopenhauer, Heidegger und Nietzsche. Gemeinsam mit Peter Sloterdijk und Gästen bestreitet er seit 2002 im ZDF das »Philosophische Quartett«. Er lebt in Berlin.

Born in Hawangen in the Allgäu in 1948. He studied philosophy, sociology, Eastern European history and Slavonic studies at the Free University Berlin, in Moscow and St. Petersburg, and is a professor of Eastern European history at the Europa University Viadrina in Frankfurt/Oder. Recently he published »Die Mitte liegt ostwärts« (t: The Centre is to the East).

Karl Schlögel

Geb. 1948 in Hawangen im Allgäu. Er studierte Philosophie, Soziologie, Osteuropäische Geschichte und Slawistik an der FU Berlin, in Moskau und St. Petersburg und ist Professor für Osteuropäische Geschichte an der Europa Universität Viadrina in Frankfurt/Oder. Zuletzt veröffentlichte er »Die Mitte liegt ostwärts«.

Rüdiger Safranski

Karl Schlögel

Gianni Vattimo

Richard Wagner

Born in Turin, Italy in 1936. He is a professor of theoretical philosophy at the University of Turin. Among his numerous published works are »Das Ende der Moderne« (t: The End of Modernism), »Die transparente Gesellschaft« (t: The Transparent Society) and »Die Religion« (along with Jacques Derrida). He has translated Heidegger and Gadamer and specialises in German philosophy of the 19th and 20th centuries.

Gianni Vattimo

Geb. 1936 in Turin, Italien. Er ist Professor für theoretische Philosophie an der Universität Turin. Zu seinen zahlreichen Veröffentlichungen zählen »Das Ende der Moderne«, »Die transparente Gesellschaft« und »Die Religion« (zusammen mit Jacques Derrida). Der Übersetzer von Heidegger und Gadamer ist auf die Postmoderne und die deutsche Philosophie des 19. und 20. Jahrhunderts spezialisiert.

Born in Banat, Rumania in 1952. He studied German and Rumanian language and literature and worked as a German teacher and journalist. He has published poetry and prose in the German language. Having been banned from working and publishing in Rumania, he left the country in 1987 and has since lived as a writer in Berlin. He has received numerous awards and grants, including the Neuer deutscher Literaturpreis, first awarded in 2000.

Richard Wagner

Geb. 1952 in Banat, Rumänien. Er studierte Germanistik und Rumänistik in Temeswar und arbeitete als Deutschlehrer und Journalist. Er veröffentlichte Lyrik und Prosa in deutscher Sprache. Nach Arbeits- und Publikationsverbot verließ er 1987 Rumänien und lebt seitdem als Schriftsteller in Berlin. Er erhielt zahlreiche Preise und Stipendien, u. a. den 2000 erstmals verliehenen Neuen deutschen Literaturpreis.

Born in Hamburg in 1933. He studied law, was a professor of Roman and civil-law at the Free University Berlin and in 1969 vice president of the university. A member of the SPD since 1960, he was expelled from the party in 1974 as critics judged his views to be too extreme left. Among his numerous studies are the »Geschichte des Rechts« (1997) and most recently »Die verspielte Revolution« (2002).

Uwe Wesel

Geb. 1933 in Hamburg. Er studierte Jura, war Professor für Römisches und Bürgerliches Recht an der FU Berlin und 1969 Vizepräsident der FU. Seit 1960 SPD-Mitglied, wurde er 1974 aus der Partei ausgeschlossen, da seine Position von Kritikern als linksextrem bewertet wurde. Zu seinen zahlreichen Studien gehörten die »Geschichte des Rechts« (1997) sowie zuletzt »Die verspielte Revolution« (2002).

Born in 1948 and studied philosophy under Adorno in Frankfurt a. M. He was co-founder and editor-in-chief of the »tageszeitung« and feuilleton editor of »Die Zeit«. He now heads the »Opinion« section of the »Berliner Zeitung«. Widmann has translated Umberto Eco and other writers, and made his own literary début with the novel »Sprenger« in 2002.

Arno Widmann

Geb. 1948. Studierte bei Adorno Philosophie in Frankfurt a. M. Er war Mitbegründer und Chefredakteur der »tageszeitung« und Feuilletonchef der »Zeit«. Heute leitet er das Ressort »Meinung« bei der »Berliner Zeitung«. Als Literat debütierte Widmann, der u. a. Umberto Eco ins Deutsche übersetzt hat, 2002 mit dem Roman »Sprenger«.

Uwe Wesel

Arno Widmann

Born in Bern, Switzerland in 1934. He studied law, sociology and political sciences and lectured in sociology at the University of Geneva. His numerous publications are commonly dedicated to the economic and political situation of third world (»Wie kommt der Hunger in die Welt?«, 2002), but also that of his native country (»Die Schweiz wäscht weißer«, 1992). In 2002 he became a UN Special Correspondent on food and nutrition. His analysis »Die neuen Herrscher der Welt und ihre globalen Widersacher« (t: The New Rulers of the World and their Global Opponents) was published in 2003.

Jean Ziegler

Geb. 1934 in Bern, Schweiz. Er studierte Jura, Soziologie und Politische Wissenschaften und unterrichtete Soziologie an der Universität Genf. Seine zahlreichen Publikationen widmen sich oft der ökonomischen und politischen Situation in der Dritten Welt (»Wie kommt der Hunger in die Welt?«, 2002), aber auch der seines Heimatlandes (»Die Schweiz wäscht weißer«, 1992). 2000 wurde er UNO-Sonderberichterstatter für Nahrung. 2003 veröffentlichte er seine Analyse »Die neuen Herrscher der Welt und ihre globalen Widersacher«.

rebecca horn
hartwig klappert
jakob mattner
wolfgang weigel
péter zilahy

rebecca horn

biography | biographie

Born in 1944. Teaching since 1989 at the HdK (UdK) Berlin. Performance, installation, film, drawing and painting on photographs. In 1992 Kaiserring from the town Goslar and Medienkunstpreis Karlsruhe. Solo exhibitions e.g., in the Guggenheim Museum New York, the Neue Nationalgalerie Berlin, the Tate Gallery London and in 2001 at the Irish Museum of Modern Art, Dublin. The artist lives in Berlin and Paris.

Geb. 1944. Seit 1989 Lehrtätigkeit an der HdK (UdK) Berlin. Performances, Installationen, Filme, Zeichnungen und Fotoübermalungen. 1992 Kaiserring der Stadt Goslar und Medienkunstpreis Karlsruhe. Einzelausstellungen unter anderem im Guggenheim Museum New York, in der Neuen Nationalgalerie Berlin, in der Tate Gallery London, 2001 im Irish Museum of Modern Art, Dublin. Die Künstlerin lebt in Berlin and Paris.

hartwig klappert

biography | biographie

Born in Siegen, Germany in 1947 and studied graphic design at the HdK (UdK) Berlin. After working as art director for the advertising agency Gruppe 96, he became a freelance photo designer in 1975. He held a guest professorship at the Hochschule für Bildende Künste in Braunschweig from 1994-97. He lives in Berlin.

Geb. 1947 in Siegen. Nach dem Abitur Grafik-Design-Studium an der HdK (UdK) Berlin. Nach Tätigkeit als Art-Director in der Werbeagentur Gruppe 96 machte er sich 1975 als Foto-Designer selbstständig. 1994-97 hatte er eine Gastprofessur an der Hochschule für Bildende Künste in Braunschweig inne. Er wohnt in Berlin.

jakob mattner

Jakob Mattner, born 1946 in Lübeck, studied at the Hochschule der Künste in Berlin until 1972. A scholarship awarded by the Berliner Akademie der Künste took him to the Villa Serpentara in Olevano. He spent 1973 to 1974 in Rome on a DAAD scholarship. Assisted by the German Interior Ministry, he spent the next year in the Cité des Arts in Paris. In 1981 he was awarded an arts scholarship by the Kunstfonds in Bonn. He received the Villa Romana Prize from Florence in 1977 and the arts award of the Heitland Foundation, Celle in 1994.
Jakob Mattner's image compositions and installations have already been exhibited in numerous cities at home and abroad, including Munich, Berlin, Geneva, Paris, Barcelona, Moscow and New York. In 1996 the artist designed a »light curtain« for the Hebbel Theater in Berlin. Other »curtains« have been on display since 1999 at the Hessische Landesbank, Frankfurt/Main. He has exhibited works from his series »Zwielicht« (Twilight), compositions of light and shadow, at the Hamburger Bahnhof in Berlin. At EXPO 2000 in Hanover he arranged the stage for »Wörter:Welt« and »Lied:Strahl« at the theatre in the German pavilion. 2001 Mattner was stage designer at the Berlin Literature Festival in the Sophiensæle. This year the Moritzburg, Halle/Saale, presented his exhibition »Camera Lucida«. At the Salzburg Festival Mattner was stage and costume designer for the performance of »Musiquette Poétique« which was directed by Robert Gernhardt and Martin Mosebach. Mattner lives in Berlin.

Jakob Mattner wurde 1946 in Lübeck geboren. Er studierte bis 1972 an der Hochschule der Künste in Berlin. Danach führte ihn ein Stipendium der Berliner Akademie der Künste in die Villa Serpentara nach Olevano. 1973/74 hielt er sich als DAAD-Stipendiat in Rom auf. Unterstützt vom Bundesministerium des Inneren, residierte er im Jahr darauf in der Cité des Arts, Paris. 1981 war er Stipendiat des Kunstfond, Bonn. Er erhielt 1977 den Villa-Romana-Preis, Florenz, und 1994 den Kunstpreis der Heitland Foundation, Celle.
Jakob Mattners Bildkompositionen und Installationen wurden bereits in zahlreichen Städten des In- und Auslands ausgestellt, unter anderem in München, Berlin, Genf, Paris, Barcelona, Moskau und New York. 1996 gestaltete der Künstler einen »Lichtvorhang« für das Hebbel-Theater Berlin. Weitere »Vorhänge« sind seit 1999 in der Hessischen Landesbank, Frankfurt a. M., zu sehen. Mit Werken aus der Reihe »Zwielicht«, Kompositionen aus Licht und Schatten, trat er im Hamburger Bahnhof, Berlin auf. Für die EXPO 2000 in Hannover stattete er die Bühne für »Wörter:Welt« und »Lied:Strahl« im Theater des Deutschen Pavillons aus. Für das internationale literaturfestival berlin gestaltete er 2001 die Bühne in den Sophiensælen. In diesem Jahr präsentierte die Moritzburg, Halle/Saale, seine Ausstellung »Camera Lucida«. Für die Aufführung »Musiquette Poétique« bei den Salzburger Festspielen, die Robert Gernhardt und Martin Mosebach ausrichteten, gestaltete Mattner die Bühne und die Kostüme. Jakob Mattner lebt in Berlin.

wolfgang weigel

biography I biographie

Within his international career, which has taken him across Europe, the United States, Canada, and South America, Wolfgang Weigel's work has concentrated more and more on producing contemporary music. In the last ten years he has become one of the most successful interpreters of modern guitar music which means for him, first and foremost, Spanish music as it developed after the Franco dictatorship. This is music written by those composers who were the most played at that time and who attempted to direct Spanish culture away from Iberian clichés and folkloric overtones. Both in Spain and abroad Weigel opened an awareness of the richness of expression in modern Mediterranean music and became one of the most acknowledged artists of the musical scene in Spain. Weigel appears as both a solist and as a performer with orchestra in live performances, at festivals and on the radio.
He also emphasises the repertoire of the guitar-orchestra. He has given numerous concerts from Moscow to Madrid with leading orchestras conducted by, for example, José Ramon Enicar, Peter Schmelzer, Hilary Griffiths and Carel Coll. Composers from Italy, Spain, Russia, Chechnya and France have dedicated to him several concertos for guitar-orchestra. His recordings constitute a collection of orchestral and chamber music as well as an extensive solo programme. They also contain a number of recordings with Reinbert Evers, a substantial composition for two guitars.

Im Verlauf der internationalen Karriere, die Wolfgang Weigel quer durch Europa, die Vereinigten Staaten, Kanada und Südamerika führte, hat sich sein Schaffen immer mehr auf die Produktion zeitgenössischer Musik konzentriert. In den letzten zehn Jahren ist er zu einem der erfolgreichsten Interpreten moderner Gitarrenmusik avanciert. Dabei steht für ihn vor allem die Spanische Musik, wie sie sich nach Ende der Franco-Diktatur entwickelte, im Vordergrund – Musik, die von den meistgespielten Komponisten jener Zeit geschrieben wurde, die die spanische Kultur von »iberischen« Klischees und folkloristischen Beiklängen wegzulenken versuchten. Inner- und außerhalb Spaniens öffnete Weigel das Bewusstsein für den Ausdrucksreichtum jener modernen mediterranen Musik und wurde einer der anerkanntesten Künstler der spanischen Musikszene. Weigel tritt sowohl als Solist als auch von Orchestern begleitet in Live-Performances, auf Festivals und im Rundfunk auf.
Ein anderer Schwerpunkt seines Schaffens liegt auf dem Repertoire des Gitarrenorchesters. Von Moskau bis Madrid hat er mit führenden Orchestern unter der Leitung von Dirigenten wie José Ramon Encinar, Peter Schmelzer, Hilary Griffiths und Carel Coll zahlreiche Konzerte gegeben. Komponisten aus Italien, Spanien, Russland, Tschechien und Frankreich haben ihm viele Konzerte für Gitarrenorchester gewidmet. Seine Aufnahmen umfassen sowohl eine Sammlung von Orchester- und Kammermusik als auch ein unfangreiches Soloprogramm. Zudem ist eine Reihe von Aufnahmen mit Reinbert Evers entstanden, einer umfangreichen Komposition für zwei Gitarren.

péter zilahy

Péter Zilahy was born in 1970 in Budapest. He is a many sided author, whose prose and poetry are widely translated and who has often used photography, interactive media and performance art in his work. He is editor-in-chief of JAK BOOKS since 1998, where among others he published Victor Pelevin, Ian McEwan and Ingo Schulze. His dictionary novel »The Last Window Giraffe« was published in 1998 and has since been translated into 14 languages. He had over a hundred performances with his interactive literary movie all over the world. He was a visiting scholar at New York University in 2001 and he received several prizes and scholarships, among them Stiftung Preußische Seehandlung and the grant of the German Foreign Ministry. His selected works were exhibited in Ludwig Museum Budapest in 2002. His latest collection of prose has been published in German with the title »Drei«. This year he is a fellow of Akademie Schloss Solitude. More info at www.zilahy.net

Péter Zilahy wurde 1970 in Budapest geboren. Der vielseitige Autor, dessen Prosa und Lyrik in viele Sprachen übersetzt wurde, arbeitet oft mit interaktiven Medien, Fotografie und Performance. Bei JAK BOOKS publiziert er seit 1998 Autoren wie z. B. Viktor Pelewin, Ian McEwan und Ingo Schulze. Sein wie ein Lexikon aufgebauter Roman »Die letzte Fenstergiraffe« wurde 1998 publiziert und ist in 14 Sprachen übersetzt. Dessen interaktive Umsetzung hat er inzwischen in über einhundert Performances weltweit aufgeführt. 2001 war er Gastdozent an der New York University. Er erhielt zahlreiche Auszeichnungen und Stipendien, u. a. von der Stiftung Preußische Seehandlung und dem Deutschen Außenministerium. 2002 wurden ausgewählte Werke im Museum Ludwig in Budapest ausgestellt. Sein letzter Erzählband wurde in deutscher Übersetzung unter dem Titel »Drei« veröffentlicht. In diesem Jahr ist er Stipendiat der Akademie Schloss Solitude. Mehr Informationen unter: www.zilahy.net

What makes me tick?
Reading the footsteps of your striptease.

ancient mesopotamian

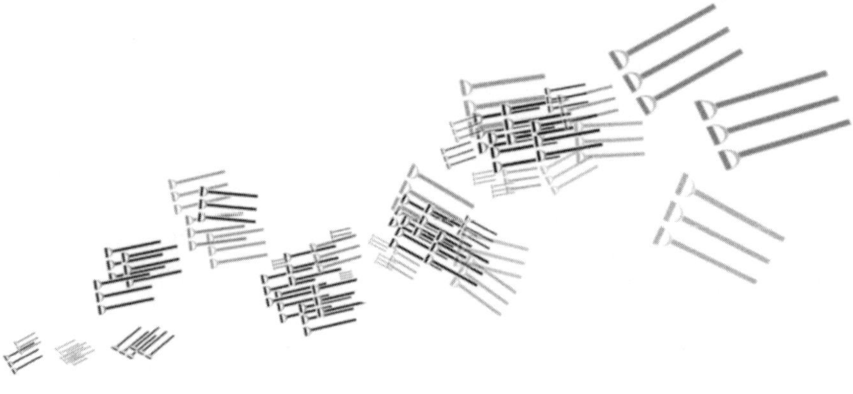

modern times

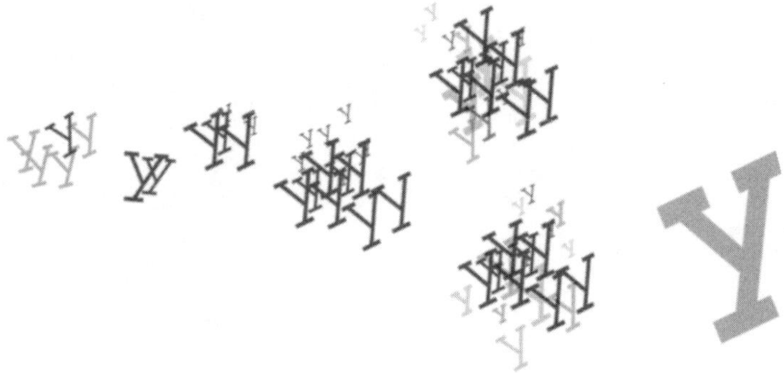

das russisch-deutsche literaturfest

tag der türkisch-deutschen literatur

Nunc Barsegyan
Vera Block
Natalja Bondar
Alexander Delphinov
Sergej Gladkich
Natalia Hantke
Igor Jedlin
Michail Kononow
Nina Madlen Korn
Manana Menabde
Sasha Puschkin
Alexej Schipenko
Trio Scho

Gönül Hürriyet Aydin
Zehra Çırak
Güney Dal
Feridun Zaimoğlu

Born in Armenia. Lives in Berlin where she works as a psychologist. The novel »Poverkh Barierov« (2001; t: After the Comma) was her literary debut.

Nune Barsegyan

Geb. in Armenien. Wohnt und arbeitet als Psychologin in Berlin. Literarisches Debüt mit dem Roman »Poverch Barierov« (2001; Ü: Nach dem Komma).

Born in Tbilisi, Georgia. Lives and works in Berlin as a journalist for Russian and German media.

Vera Block

Geb. in Tbilisi. Lebt und arbeitet in Berlin als Journalistin für deutsche und russische Medien.

Born in St. Petersburg in 1962. Actress, singer, performer of Russian rites and customs. Starred in the documentary »Russenbus – Fremde Brüder« (2003; t: »Russian Bus – Foreign Brothers«).

Natalja Bondar

Geb. 1962 in St. Petersburg. Schauspielerin, Sängerin, Darstellerin russischer Rituale und Bräuche. Hauptrolle in dem Dokumentarfilm »Russenbus – Fremde Brüder« (2003).

Nune Barsegyan

Vera Block

Natalja Bondar

Alexander Delphinov

Natalia Hantke

Igor Jedlin

Journalist, poet, musician. Published literary criticism and feature stories in major magazines and newspapers (»Ptuch«, »Ex-Libris NG«).

Alexander Delphinov

Journalist, Poet, Musiker. Veröffentlichte Literaturkritiken und Artikel in bedeutenden Zeitschriften und Zeitungen (»Ptuch«, »Ex-Libris NG«).

Born in Kalatch, Russia, in 1952. Moved to Berlin in 1976 and has worked as a free-lance translator since.

Sergej Gladkich

Geb. 1952 in Kalatsch, Russland. 1976 kam er nach Berlin und arbeitet seitdem als freier Übersetzer.

Born in Kazakhstan in 1967. Writer and essayist. Founding member of the literary stage »Erfolgsschriftsteller im Schacht« (formerly »Blauer Drache«).

Natalia Hantke

Geb. 1967 in Kasachstan. Schriftstellerin und Essayistin. Gründungsmitglied der Lesebühne »Erfolgsschriftsteller im Schacht« (ehemals »Blauer Drache«).

Grew up in Moscow. Founder of the only permanent magic theatre in Europe – the Zaubertheater Igor Jedlin in Berlin. Recipient of the Order of Merit of the Federal Republic of Germany.

Igor Jedlin

In Moskau aufgewachsen. Gründete das einzige ständige Zaubertheater Europas – das Zaubertheater Igor Jedlin. Ausgezeichnet mit dem Bundesverdienstkreuz.

Born in St. Petersburg in 1948. Published numerous short stories and essays. His last novel »Golaya Pionerka« (2001; t: The Naked Pioneer Girl) was nominated for the Russian Booker Prize 2001.

Michail Kononow

Geb. 1948 in St. Petersburg. Veröffentlichte zahlreiche Kurzgeschichten und Essays. Sein letzter Roman »Golaja Pionerka« (2001; dt. »Die nackte Pionierin«, 2003) wurde für den Russian Booker Prize 2001 nominiert.

Dramaturgue. Created the radio programme »Ole Bole erzählt Märchen aus aller Welt« (t: »Ole Bole tells fairy tales from around the world«) in 1966. Professional fairytale teller for the »Berliner Märchentage« festival.

Nina Madlen Korn

Dramaturgin. 1966 konzipierte sie die Radiosendung »Ole Bole erzählt Märchen aus aller Welt«. Märchenerzählerin bei den »Berliner Märchentagen«.

Born in Tbilisi, Georgia, in 1948. Painter, singer, writer. Concerts and exhibitions in Russia, Germany and Georgia.

Manana Menabde

Geb. 1948 in Tbilisi, Georgien. Malerin, Sängerin, Schriftstellerin. Konzerte und Ausstellungen in Russland, Deutschland, Georgien.

Michail Kononow

Nina Madlen Korn

Manana Menabde

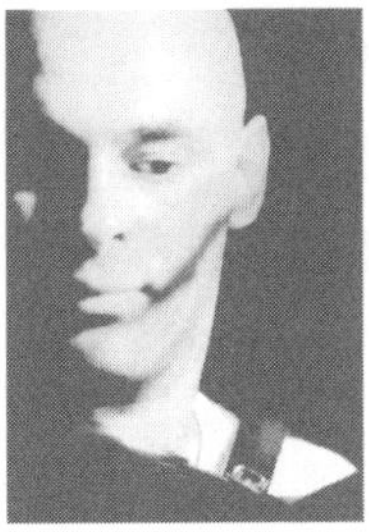

Sasha Puschkin

Alexej Schipenko

Trio Scho

Originally from St. Petersburg. Writer, performance artist, singer, pianist, band-leader. Has lived in Berlin since 1989.

Sasha Puschkin

Stammt aus St. Petersburg. Schriftsteller, Performance-Künstler, Sänger, Pianist und Bandleader. Wohnt seit 1989 in Berlin.

Born in Stavropol in 1961. Composer, musician, art director. Directed plays at the Berlin Volksbühne theatre and the Bremen theatre, etc. Composes prose, poetry, film scripts, theatre and radio plays.

Alexej Schipenko

Geb. 1961 in Stawropol. Komponist, Musiker und Regisseur. Hat u. a. an der Volksbühne Berlin und am Bremer Theater inszeniert. Schreibt Lyrik, Prosa, Drehbücher, Theaterstücke und Hörspiele.

Formed in Poltava in 1992. Since 1994 they have performed mainly in Berlin. The trio won the Berlin Senate Music Contest in summer 2000. Russian Coffeehouse music.

Trio Scho

Entstand 1992 in Poltawa. Seit 1994 treten sie vorwiegend in Berlin auf. Im Sommer 2000 gewann das Trio den Musik-Wettbewerb des Berliner Senats. Russische Kaffeehausmusik.

Born 1960 in Gümüshane/Turkey, has lived in Berlin since 1988. Writes in turkish language. Her first Book with short stories »Adsız« published in 1992, composes also poetry and plays in Turkish.

Gönül Hürriyet Aydin

Geb. 1960 in Gümüshane/Türkei, lebt seit 1988 in Berlin, 1983 erste Veröffentlichung in türkischer Sprache. Ihr erster Kurzgeschichten-Band »Adsız« erschien 1992. Sie schreibt auch Theaterstücke und Kurzgeschichten.

Born 1960 in Istanbul, has lived in Germany since 1963 and in Berlin since 1982. German language poet. 1994 Hölderlin–Promote Prize for poetry; 2001 Adalbert von Chamisso Prize. First poetry »Flugfänger« published in 1987 and than two books with poetry and short stories. Her fourth volume »Leibesübungen« (t: »Calisthenics«) came out in 2000.

Zehra Çirak

Geb. 1960 in Istanbul, lebt seit 1963 in Deutschland und seit 1982 in Berlin. Deutschsprachige Lyrikerin. 1994 gewann Zehra Çırak den Hölderlin-Förderpreis für Lyrik; 2001 erhielt sie den Adalbert-von-Chamisso-Preis. Erster Gedichtband »Flugfänger« 1987, danach zwei Bände mit Lyrik und Kurzprosa. 2000 erschien ihr vierter Gedichtband »Leibesübungen«.

Gönül Hürriyet Aydin

Zehra Çirak

Güney Dal

Born 1944 in Çanakkale/Turkey, has lived in Berlin since 1972. Turkish language novelist. Won the novel prize of the Milliyat publishing house in 1976. Received literature scholarships of the Berlin senate in 1980, 1983, and 1985. Was awarded the Adalbert von Chamisso Prize. His latest novel »Janitscharenmusik« (t: »Yanichar Music«) was published in 1999.

Güney Dal

Geb. 1944 in Çanakkale/Türkei. Lebt seit 1972 in Berlin. Romane in türkischer Sprache. 1976 erhielt er den Romanpreis des Verlages Milliyat in Istanbul; 1980, 1983 und 1985 Literaturstipendien des Berliner Senats; 1997 zusammen mit José Oliver den Adalbert-von-Chamisso-Preis. Zuletzt erschien »Janitscharenmusik« bei Piper 1999.

Born 1964 in Bolu/Turkey, has lived in Germany since 1968. Numerous books in German. Cult author, whose 1995 debut novel »Kanak Sprak« was made into a motion picture. Regular contributor to newspapers such as »Die Zeit«, »Spiegel Reporter« and »Süddeutsche Zeitung«. His latest novel »Leinwand« (t: »Canvas«) was published in 2003.

Feridun Zaimoğlu

Geb. 1964 in Bolu/Türkei, lebt seit 1968 in Deutschland und seit 1985 in Kiel. Zahlreiche Buchpublikationen in deutscher Sprache. Seit seinem Debüt 1995 mit »Kanak Sprak«, das auch verfilmt wurde, ist er zum Kultautor avanciert. Er schreibt regelmäßig für »Die Zeit«, »Spiegel Reporter« und die »Frankfurter Rundschau«. Sein bisher letzter Roman »Leinwand« ist 2003 erschienen.

Feridun Zaimoğlu

Martin Auer
Viktoria Barkova
Heinrich Gartentor
Jürg Halter
Jaromir Konecny
Sebastian Krämer
Björn Kuhligk
Hagar Peeters
Olumide Popoola
Monika Rinck
Mara Schneider

Ehrengast | Honorary Guest
Oskar Pastior

Born in Vienna in 1951. Actor, singer-songwriter, guitar instructor and magician. Published some 40 books. Considers himself an underground poet and is a celebrated artist of the Viennese poetry-slam scene.

Martin Auer

Geb. 1951 in Wien. Schauspieler, Liedermacher, Gitarrenlehrer und Zauberer. Ca. 40 Buchpublikationen. Bezeichnet sich als Underground-Dichter und ist ein gefeierter Künstler der Wiener Poetry-Slam-Szene.

Born in the USSR. Engineering degree. Published her first volume of poetry »Humor zwischen den Beinen« (t: Humour between the legs) in 1999. Commutes between Moscow and Berlin, and performs in Russian and accentuated German.

Viktoria Barkova

Geb. in der Sowjetunion. Nach ihrem Ingenieursstudium machte sie 1999 mit ihrem ersten Gedichtband »Humor zwischen den Beinen« auf sich aufmerksam. Sie pendelt zwischen Moskau und Berlin und performt auf Russisch sowie in klangvollem Deutsch.

Born in Schafmatt/Switzerland in 1965. The web activist, video and action artist, and written and spoken word poet is drifting through Europe, staging »friendly assaults« and composing autobiographical fiction. His peculiar performances tend to cause a stir.

Heinrich Gartentor

Geb. 1965 in Schafmatt/Schweiz. Der Internetaktivist, Video-, Aktions- und Written and Spoken Word-Künstler nomadisiert durch Europa, verübt »nette Attentate«, schreibt autobiographische Fiktionen und realisiert skurrile Performances, an denen sich die Gemüter erhitzen.

Born in 1980, he hails from Berne (Switzerland). The versatile lyric poet, performance-poet, MC, and arts student has made a name for himself at numerous international literature festivals and poetry slams. His latest projects combine text with electronic music.

Jürg Halter

Geb. 1980 und ansässig in Bern/Schweiz. Der umtriebige Lyriker, Performance-Poet, MC und Kunststudent hat sich bereits auf zahlreichen internationalen Literarturfestivals und Poetry-Slams einen Namen gemacht. Neuerdings kombiniert er seine Texte mit elektronischer Musik.

Born in Prague in 1956. Immigrated to Germany in 1982. The former steel worker studied chemistry in Munich, where he also earned his doctorate. Since his literary debut in 1996 he has become the King of the Southern German slam scene: his absurd Eastern European/Bavarian »Intimitäten« (t: Intimacies) have won more than 50 poetry slams accross Germany.

Jaromir Konecny

Geb. 1956 in Prag. Nach seiner Emigration nach Deutschland 1982 studierte der ehemalige Stahlarbeiter Chemie und promovierte in München. Seit dem literarischen Debüt 1996 avancierte er zum König der süddeutschen Slam-Szene: Mit seinen absurden osteuropäisch-bayerischen »Intimitäten« gewann er über 50 bundesweite Poetry-Slams.

Born in Bad Oeynhausen in 1975, has lived in Berlin since 1996. The singer, composer and moderator (Guinness record for longest moderation) has performed his musical cabaret shows in numerous venues. Took the national slam scene by storm in 2001. In 2002 he founded his own monthly poetry slam in the Berlin vaudeville theater »Scheinbar«.

Sebastian Krämer

Geb. 1975 in Bad Oeynhausen, lebt seit 1996 in Berlin. Der Sänger, Komponist und Moderator (Guinness-Rekord für Langzeitmoderation) präsentiert seine musikalischen Kabarettprogramme auf diversen Bühnen und eroberte 2001 die nationale Slam-Szene im Sturm. 2002 gründete er seinen eigenen monatlichen Poetry-Slam im Berliner Scheinbar-Varieté.

Born in Berlin in 1975, where he lives and sells books. He has won various literature competitions and open mike performances. Has published his »urban verses« in literary magazines and poetry collections: »Am Ende kommen Touristen« (2002; t: Eventually tourists come); co-edited the anthology »Lyrik von JETZT« (2003; t: Poetry from NOW) together with Jan Wagner.

Björn Kuhligk

Geb. 1975 in Berlin, lebt und arbeitet dort als Buchhändler. Er gewann diverse Literatur- und Open Mike-Wettbewerbe und veröffentlichte seine urbanen Verse in zahlreichen Literaturzeitschriften und Lyrik-Anthologien: »Am Ende kommen Touristen« (2002); mit Jan Wagner Herausgeber der Anthologie »Lyrik von JETZT« (2003).

Born in Amsterdam in 1972. Lives and studies in Utrecht. Prized protagonist of the young Dutch poetry scene. Gave some legendary performances at numerous international literature festivals. Her rhythmic poetry combines tenderness with intensity.

Hagar Peeters

Geb. 1972 in Amsterdam. Lebt und studiert in Utrecht. Preisgekrönte Ausnahmeerscheinung der jungen niederländischen Lyrik, absolvierte mit ihren rhythmischen Gedichten, in denen sich Zärtlichkeit und Intensität mischen, bei zahlreichen internationalen Literaturfestivals einige legendäre Auftritte.

The Nigerian-German poetess weaves her different voices into complex moments of politically committed speech performances. Well-known in the Berlin spoken-word-scene she has performed in different countries, drawing on a variety of styles such as hip hop, jazz poetry, slam poetry and African story telling.

Olumide Popoola

Die nigerianisch-deutsche Poetin webt ihre verschiedenen Stimmen zu komplexen Momenten politisch engagierter Sprach-Performance. Über die Berliner Spoken-Word-Szene hinaus trat sie in verschiedenen Ländern auf, inspiriert von unterschiedlichen Ausdrucksmöglichkeiten wie z. B. Hip Hop, Jazz Poetry und afrikanischer Erzähltradition.

Born in Zweibrücken in 1969. Studied religion, history and comparative literature in Bochum, Berlin and at Yale. Her volume »BEGRIFFSSTUDIO 1996-2001« (t: CONCEPT STUDIO 1996-2001) was singled out by Stiftung Buchkunst as one of the most beautiful books of the general literature in 2001.

Monika Rinck

Geb. 1969 in Zweibrücken. Studium der Religionswissenschaft, Geschichte und Vergleichenden Literaturwissenschaft in Bochum, Berlin und Yale. Ihre Buchveröffentlichung »BEGRIFFSSTUDIO 1996-2001« wurde 2001 von der Stiftung Buchkunst als eines der schönsten Bücher im Bereich Allgemeine Literatur prämiert.

Lives in Leipzig, has been writing since her melancholy puberty, has become less melancholy meanwhile. Has participated in a number of poetry slams, where she has chalked up as many wins and losses. Three of her stories will be published in the anthology »Geschichten die die Welt verändern« (Trans: »Stories that change the world«).

Mara Schneider

Lebt in Leipzig, schreibt seit ihrer schwermütigen Pubertät, ist mittlerweile nicht mehr schwermütig, hat an diversen Slams teilgenommen, dabei genauso oft gewonnen wie verloren. Demnächst erscheinen drei ihrer Geschichten in der Anthologie »Geschichten die die Welt verändern«.

what makes the poet tick?

übersetzungen

Gennadij Ajgi
Das, was Gedichte ins Leben ruft, liegt offenbar zwischen »Klage« und »Gebet«.
Es wäre aber wünschenswert, wenn es von ersterem weniger gäbe und das zweite mehr ein dankendes als ein bittendes wäre.
[Übersetzt von Viola Winokan]

Jeanne Benameur
Das Gefühl veranlasst mich zum Schreiben. Ein starkes Gefühl, entsprungen aus meinem Leben wie auch dem anderer Menschen auf der Welt. Es muss mich lange Zeit durchdringen. Oft kann ich es nicht klar benennen. Ich erkenne nicht seine exakte Form. Ich kann nur seine Intensität spüren. Ausreichend, um mich zum Schreiben anzuregen. Während des Schreibens bildet der Text seine Form aus. Sie erschließt sich mir vollkommen, wenn ich das Schreiben beendet habe. Jeder Text ist für mich diese neuerliche Erfahrung. Mit jedem Text nähere ich mich ein wenig mehr Territorien, die ich noch nicht in meinem Inneren kannte. Vor allem menschlich sein, denn wir sind alle gleich. Die Wörter sind dazu geschaffen, um das zu umschreiben, was sich nicht nennen lässt.
Dazu ist viel Ruhe nötig.
Und, natürlich, der Atem.
Dies ist das Abenteuer, das mich schreiben lässt.
[Übersetzt von Birgit Thülig]

Eduardo Chirinos
Eine langsame und vage Musik
Was veranlasst mich, Gedichte zu schreiben? Jahrelang habe ich mir die Frage gestellt, die, vom logischen Standpunkt aus gesehen, einfach zu beantworten sein sollte, denn sie beinhaltet auch das Handwerk, dem ich wohl oder übel die Hälfte meines Lebens gewidmet habe. Sie nicht beantworten zu können, halte ich für einen erfreulichen Hinweis darauf, dass ich ihr die andere Hälfte, die mir verbleibt, widmen werde. Wie auch immer, diese Unfähigkeit (der ich mehrere Bücher, Gedichte, Essays, Anthologien, Übersetzungen und meine alte Leidenschaft für den Literaturunterricht verdanke) befreit mich nicht von der Annäherung an gewisse Überzeugungen, die unbedeutenderweise auf mich als Verfasser von Gedichten verweisen. Eine davon hat mit der Musik zu tun, die wir manchmal vernehmen können. Dinge, gewisse Personen, einige Erinnerungen, die aus dem Leben oder den Büchern stammen, verströmen eine langsame und vage Musik, die sich meines Gehörs bemächtigt und, ich bitte um Verständnis für dieses Oxymoron, die sich in eine Vision verwandelt, die in Worte gefasst werden möchte. Es handelt sich um eine Herausforderung, die nur im schöpferischen Tun aufgearbeitet werden kann, also (und verstehen Sie auch bitte dieses Oxymoron) im sozialen Zusammenhang, was ja letztendlich das einsame Schreiben von Gedichten ist. Ich spreche hier nicht über »poetische« und »unpoetische« Erfahrungen; das Poetische (falls es existieren sollte) befindet sich in der Aufgeschlossenheit für diese Musik, durch die die Welt mit uns und durch uns kommunizieren will. Vielleicht vermag es dieses Gedicht besser auszudrücken als ich:

Die Stille
lädt ein zur Stille.
Zur Betrachtung der Berge,
die nichts als Berge sind,
zu den Flüssen,
die sich blau schlängeln wie irgendein Fluss.

Ich konnte nie mit der Stille. Nie
lernte ich, ihr zuzuhören:
hinter einer weißen
Wand höre ich immer Musik.

Eine langsame und vage Musik,
die dann verklingt, ohne etwas zu sagen.
[Übersetzt von Juana und Tobias Burghardt]

Lorand Gaspar
What makes the poet tick?
Das Leben. Mein Leben.
Bewusstwerden über das Ende meines Lebens.
Von der immanenten unendlichen Unendlichkeit der Welt.
Von der Relativität des gesamten humanen Wissens.
Von der Freude und dem Verdruss, manchmal humane und inhumane
Dinge zu sehen, zu hören, zu verstehen, zu denken und zu fühlen,
die Unscheinbarkeit und das Licht.
Worte finden und versuchen es zu sagen.
Etwas schreiben, das man ein Gedicht nennt,
wissend, dass man nicht das sagt, was man sagt.
[Übersetzt von Birgit Thülig]

Nedim Gürsel
Die Quellen meiner Inspiration.
Ich spreche nicht von einer einzigen, sondern von verschiedenen Quellen der Inspiration. Die Heimatlosigkeit, das Exil und die erotische Liebe, um nicht zu sagen »die Frauen«! Das sind, denke ich, die wiederkehrenden Themen meiner Romane und Novellen. Aber ich schreibe ebenfalls Reiseberichte, in denen meine seelische Landkarte, die mediterrane Welt, einen wichtigen Platz einnimmt.
Wenn es eine wichtige, um nicht zu sagen »zwanghafte« Inspirationsquelle gibt, dann ist dies Istanbul, die Stadt par excellence, Hauptstadt zweier großer Reiche – das Byzantinische und das Osmanische –, Istanbul, »tausendmal geehelichte Witwe und noch immer Jungfrau«, wie ein großer türkischer Poet sagte.
Mir scheint, dass die erste Passage meines Romans »Der Eroberer« perfekt meine Bindung an die Stadt Istanbul und an meine Muttersprache wiedergibt: »Seit längerem schon stand ich morgens früh auf. Dort, am asiatischen Ufer des Bosporus, in meiner geliebten Heimatstadt, die mich überallhin verfolgte und nie in Ruhe ließ, erhob ich mich jeden Morgen mit dem Ruf zum Frühgebet, um zu schreiben.«
[Übersetzt von Birgit Thülig]

Zbyněk Hejda
W. B. Yeats schrieb, wir würden aus dem Widerstreit mit uns selbst Gedichte schreiben. Es gäbe auch welche, die aus dem Konflikt mit der Welt heraus dichten. Meiner Meinung nach handelt es sich dabei eher um Journalisten und Chronisten. Nach meiner persönlichen Erfahrung ist es folgendermaßen: Dichter zu sein passiert einem, es stößt einem einfach zu. Mir war der Grund, warum ich Gedichte mache, anfangs verborgen. Und auch heute noch würde ich am liebsten sagen: Es ist mir passiert.
[Übersetzt von Christa Rothmeier]

Jabbar Yassin Hussin
Der in seiner Eierschale eingeschlossene Embryo verzerrt den Blick des künftigen Kükens. Die Poesie kann den Blick korrigieren, denn die außergewöhnliche Welt, die Welt des Wesentlichen, kann nicht durch die Lupe hindurch gesehen werden, sondern durch Worte, die auf wundersame Weise zusammenklingen. Wir wissen nicht, warum wir mit dieser Krankheit geschlagen sind. Doch wir wissen, die sichtbare Welt ist nicht die wirkliche Welt, die wir sehen wollten, als wir noch Embryos waren. Das Wort »Vers« hat im Arabischen den gleichen Sinn und die gleiche Schreibweise wie das Wort »Haus«. Und da die wirkliche Welt uns vertreibt, kehren wir in das Haus zurück, das uns an die Schalenhülle des Embryos erinnert, der wir waren. Das ist wieder der Mythos des Ursprungs.
[Übersetzt von Claudia Kalscheuer]

Fatou Keïta
Wenn ich mich schlecht fühle...
Wenn ich Lust habe, das Leben zu teilen
So stark, das ich es spüre
Wenn alles schlecht läuft
Wenn das Glück blass ist
Oder wenn man fühlt, wie man zu neuem Leben erwacht
Wenn das Leben seufzt
Muss ich es sagen!
Also meine Schreibfeder
Aus diesem Verlangen heraus es zu sagen
Macht es beschwingt
[Übersetzt von Birgit Thülig]

Leïla Marouane
What makes the poet tick?
Was treibt mich dazu – mich, Leïla Marouane, in der Blüte meiner vierzig Jahre –, die Worte zu kneten, zu kauen, zu malmen und wieder auszuspucken, um sie dann in Geschichten anzuordnen, für die ich Personen erfinde, die nicht allzu viel fordern? Welch ein Gebilde!
Warum, im Namen der Feder, trage ich hartnäckig mein Gedächtnis mit mir herum, von hier nach da? Um im Schlamm zu stecken, um im Morast zu rühren, bis ich damit die Dämonen und Engel geweckt habe? (Übrigens, der Titel meines nächsten Romans lautet »Der Mittagsschlaf der Engel«!)
Warum, im Namen des Buchs, dieser Eigensinn? Ich könnte mich schließlich Arbeiten widmen, die mich nicht an den Rand des Abgrunds bringen, so wie der Akt des Schreibens mich an den Rand des Abgrunds bringt.
Ich könnte mir einen Spaziergang im Jardin du Luxembourg gönnen, der nur zwei Blocks von meiner Wohnung entfernt liegt und den ich noch nie betreten habe. Ich könnte mich von den Wellen des Atlantiks tragen lassen, nur eine Stunde von Paris entfernt. Vor kurzem erst hätte ich im Massif Central herumklettern können, wohin mich Freunde netterweise eingeladen hatten. Und – sehr viel prosaischer – ich hätte mich fortpflanzen und so zum Fortbestehen der Menschheit beitragen können und zugleich das Bedürfnis nach Mutterschaft stillen, das jede »normal veranlagte« Frau in sich trägt.
Wie auch immer: Tag für Tag, Seite für Seite, Kapitel für Kapitel, Buch für Buch, im Ausbreiten der Wörter wie im Tumult der Figuren erfahre ich, wie der Akt des Schreibens, dieses eigensinnige Bedürfnis, mir erlaubt zu »sprechen«. Zu sagen, was ich nicht »schreien« kann. Diese ganze Tinte, das ganze Papier, diese ganze Energie und diese ganze Zeit! Nur um zu versuchen zu verstehen, was in mir lebt und mich beherrscht! Um meine Stimme, meinen Weg, zu finden in diesem Labyrinth meiner verdrängten Erinnerungen. Um diese Geister zu vertreiben, sanft oder heftig, und sie für alle hörbar zu machen?
Egal! Am Ende habe ich das Gefühl, meinen Emotionen das nackte Dasein gegeben zu haben. Ich brauche sie: sei es um dem Wahnsinn zu entfliehen, sei es um (für immer) den Verstand zu verlieren, oder sei es ganz einfach, um meine Rechnungen zu begleichen. Sag es mit Poesie!
Und vielleicht bin ich sogar dabei, über meine persönlichen Angelegenheiten hinaus, mich der Belange der Menschheit anzunehmen. In aller Bescheidenheit.
Paris, Juli 2003
[Übersetzt von Dagmar Seidel]

Ljudmila Petruschewskaja
Der Anstoß kann ganz unterschiedlicher Natur sein: jemandes Worte, ein Text, Musik, ein Geschmack (die berühmten »Epiphanien« von Marcel Proust, der Geschmack von Madeleine-Törtchen), ein bekanntes, aber fremdes Gesicht, ein Bild, ein Filmausschnitt, ein Bühnenstück. Es kam vor, dass ich direkt im Saal schreiben oder ihn verlassen musste, um einen Text zu notieren, den ich wie diktiert bekommen habe. Oder es geschah auf der Straße, in der Menge in der U-Bahn oder bei Dämmerung auf dem Dorf, wenn eine Herde am Fenster vorbeigetrieben wurde und die Sonne aufging, wie der Dotter im rohen Eiweiß. Der Text kam stets als Ganzes, man musste nur am Faden ziehen, damit das Knäuel sich auflöste. Später hörte ich auf, diese Texte aufzuschreiben, denn es lief schon leicht, wie am Fließband. Japanische Aquarellmaler wechselten, sobald ihnen das Malen leicht fiel, den Namen, ihren Stil und sogar die Hand – die rechte gegen die linke. Ich habe auch die »Hand« gewechselt, ging von der Prosa zum Drama über. Sobald mir dieser leicht fiel, ging ich über zur Poesie, zum Märchen, wechselte dann wieder zur Prosa. Jetzt ist meine Inspiration ihre Frage nach der Inspiration. Ich habe bereits elf Seiten geschrieben und schicke Ihnen ein kleines Stück davon ...
Ein Gruß! Ihre L. Petruschewskaja
[Übersetzt von Viola Winokan]

Notaila Rashed
What makes the poet tick?
Oh Great God...
What a nice question?!!
It is a very simple one, which makes it very difficult to answer.
So, Notaila, why not give it a try...

Oh Gott...
Was für eine schöne Frage... leicht und einfach..., und darin liegt gerade die Schwierigkeit, sie zu beantworten...
Wo beginnen, oh Gott?!
Was ist die Quelle der Inspiration, oh Herr?!
Kommt sie aus der Betrachtung der Schönheit im Universum? Aus dem Schrei des Lebens im Augenblick der Geburt des kleinen Wesens: eines Kindes, eines Kükens, einer Katze... eines Affen... eines Löwen... einer Seidenraupe?!
Sonnenaufgang... Sonnenuntergang... der Anblick eines Baumes, Königin der Nacht, wenn er sich nach Sonnenuntergang unter einem leichten Windhauch neigt und die Luft parfümiert..., es wächst, und seinem Schaffen ist Unsterblichkeit bestimmt.
Die Musik des Laubs in den Bäumen... und das Plätschern des Wassers im Fluss... die Kraft der Winde... das Tosen der riesigen Meereswogen... die Stille des Wüstensandes... das Musizieren der Schläge des Regens auf der Fensterscheibe... die Farben des Traumbilds... das Zwitschern der Vögel... das Gesicht des Kleinen, das ein Lächeln ziert, trotz der Perle auf seiner Wange und einer weiteren Träne, die nicht vergossen wurde...
Alle Visionen, die lebenden Dinge, das Wetter und der Himmel mit seinen Laternen, die Bilder und die Schatten, das zarte Geflüster, die vielen Ereignisse in einer Welt, die die Phantasie entfesselt, die mit uns in unseren Tiefen geboren wird, grenzenlos frei, und die den Pulsschlag der normalen Bewohner der Welt anregt... jedes Flüstern und jede Berührung ist eine Quelle der Inspiration, der Schöpfung und der Kreation und bringt die künstlerischen Energien, die Entdeckungslust und das Gute bei einem intelligenten, sensiblen Menschen zum Ausbruch, der eine Erzählung, einen Roman oder ein Gedicht schreibt, ein Bild malt, mit seinen Fingerspitzen den Stein bricht und eine Skulptur meißelt..., der ein Heilmittel entdeckt, ein Musikstück komponiert, musiziert, summt, singt, wie der Schmetterling mit seinen Flügeln tanzt, mit ihnen hoch oben in der Luft kreist und bis zu den Sternen hinter den siebten Himmel gelangt...
Das große Herz, Heimat der Kreation, öffnet sich, um ohne Ketten die Inspiration zu empfangen, und dank eines Lächelns der Bewunderung und Worten der Ermutigung wächst es und wächst, und seinem Schaffen ist Unsterblichkeit bestimmt.
[Übersetzt von Barbara Winckler]

Alberto Ruy Sánchez
Neun schlangenhafte Antworten,
die sich in den Schwanz beißen,
um herauszufinden, was beim Dichter Klick macht.

1. Spüren, dass der Körper ein Haus voller Gespenster ist.
2. Feststellen, dass der Kuss niemals aufhört, der die Welt in Brand setzt.
3. Aber auch auf einmal den Kuss des Todes empfinden.
2. Innerhalb des Traumes erwachen.
3. Mit anderen Augen andere Leben sehen.
4. Von der geliebten Person mit geschlossenen Augen gesehen werden.
5. Zwischen der Wut und dem Erstaunen den angehaltenen Atem unerträglich finden.
6. Wenigstens für einen Augenblick sicher sein, dass die Magie der Wörter etwas in der Welt ändert.
7. Das Fieber im Schatten kennen, wenn es Stimme und Wind wird.
8. Einen Strudel oder die stechende Anwesenheit des Nichts im Mund fühlen.
9. Sich vom Verlangen lenken lassen wie ein im Blut treibendes Piratenschiff.
[Übersetzt von Juana und Tobias Burghardt]

Boualem Sansal
Nicht auf alle Fragen gibt es Antworten, und das ist gut so, das Leben ist vor allem ein Geheimnis, das gewahrt werden muss. Endgültige Antworten lassen, unwiderruflichen Urteilen gleich, die Einbildungskraft versiegen, die Intelligenz austrocknen. Doch warum kehren wir dann immer wieder an die Grenzen des Bekannten zurück, um im Leeren herumzutasten, das Unauslotbare auszuloten, das Unsichtbare zu schauen, das Unhörbare zu hören, das Unsagbare zu sagen? Die Antworten kommen nie, und soweit unsere Hände reichen, bilden die Leere und die Stille uneinnehmbare Bollwerke.
Sollten wir wie jene Alchimisten aus früheren Zeiten sein, alte Narren oder gefährliche Raffsüchtige in ihrem Fieber nach Reichtum oder Weisheit, die in dem, was die Natur an Nichtigstem erzeugt hat, dem schwarzen, ungestalten, leblosen Urgestein, den Stein der Weisen suchten, die Wahrheit aller Wahrheiten? Ohne Zweifel. Sind sie fündig geworden? Man weiß es nicht, wohl eher nicht, denn wir, ihre fernen Erben, sind in Sachen Wahrheit arm wie Hiob. Von ihrer Geschichte, die sich ganz in der Marginalität und in der Maßlosigkeit abgespielt hat, bleiben uns hermetische Schriften, wirkungslose Axiome, aufsehenerregende Katastrophen, unergründliche Träume.
Und was ist im übrigen die Poesie? Ist es jener Drang des Herzens, der uns treibt, die Leere auszufüllen, die uns in ihren Schrecken einzwängt, oder ein Akt der Vernunft, der uns zum Aufstellen besänftigender Theorien führt? Wir werden nie aufhören danach zu suchen, was von beidem uns zum Träumen bringt.
Neben den großen Geheimnissen treiben, wie vom Packeis losgelöste Eisberge, unendlich viele Geheimnisse umher, die scheinbar harmlos sind. Ihr Körper ist unter Wasser, man sieht nur ihre Spitze, und so gewahrt man sie gelassenen Auges. Zu diesen Geheimnissen gehört die Sprache, doch sie ist das trügerischste von allen; völlig frei verfügbar, beugt sie sich allen Wünschen, sie gibt den Reichen ebensoviel wie den Armen, den Tyrannen wie den Weisen, den Visionären wie den Blinden; in allen Idiomen der Welt spricht sie mit der gleichen Leichtigkeit von Bekanntem und Unbekanntem, von Gut und Böse, vom Schönen und vom Scheußlichen, und mit einem einzigen Wort vermag sie, wie ein Gott, Zeit und Raum zu transzendieren. Und es ward Licht, doch sind wir noch immer blind! In ihr liegen all unsere Niederlagen und all unsere Sehnsüchte, die unserer Ahnen und unsere eigensten, die zerbrechlicher, weil weniger durch die Zeit gehärtet sind, und dazu ein paar, die niemandem gehören, aus den Zeiten vor der Genesis oder aus dem Weltraum gekommen, auf Meteoriten oder fliegenden Untertassen. Sie hat ihre Magie, die nicht die unsere ist. Und wenn wir schweigen, spricht sie in uns, sanft, drängend, dann immer schneller bis zum Delirium. Zu ihrem Vokabular gehören die Geräusche der Welt, wir haben ihre Phonetik übernommen, doch ihren Sinn kennen wir nicht. Jenseits allen Scheins spricht die Sprache zu sich selbst. Sie erfindet sich und erschafft sich ohne unser Wissen. Wer außer den Kindern, die in ihrer weich gepolsterten Wiege drauflos plappern und außerhalb aller gültigen Sprache mit den Engeln reden, kann sich je rühmen, ein einziges Wort erfunden zu haben? Und doch sind sie da, und wir tun so, als gehörten sie uns seit jeher. Der Nießbraucher hält sich am Ende unweigerlich für den rechtmäßigen Erben, wenn niemand ihn vor Gericht zerrt.
Wovon also spricht der Dichter, und woher nimmt er seine Inspiration? Dieser widersprüchliche, etwas verrückte Mensch sagt mit Worten, Musik und Emphase das Schweigen. Wie ihn verstehen? Baudelaire, der marginalste unter ihnen, sagte in einem jener Delirien, wie nur er sie schreiben konnte:

Boualem Sansal (continued)
»Wen liebst du am meisten, o Fremder? Deinen Vater, deine Mutter, deine Brüder oder deine Schwestern? Ich habe weder Vater noch Mutter noch Brüder noch Schwestern. Dein Land? Ich weiß nicht, in welchen Breiten es liegt. Gold? Ich hasse es so, wie Sie Gott hassen. Doch was liebst du denn, o rätselhafter Fremder? Ich liebe die Wolken... die wunderbaren Wolken, die vorüberziehen... dort draußen... am Himmel.«
What makes the poet tick? Natürlich wissen wir das nicht. Solange es Dichter gibt, werden wir nie wissen, woher die Poesie kommt. Diese Leute leben nicht wie wir, sie leben in den Tag hinein, in ewiger Erwartung. Gedichte werden im Morgengrauen gepflückt, nach einer mit Fragen oder im Gebet durchwachten Nacht.
Doch nicht alle Nächte gehen mit dem Morgen zu Ende. Es gibt solche, auf die nie ein Tag folgt.
Wir haben den 10. Juni 2003, 21 Tage nach dem Erdbeben, das um 20 Uhr, zur Stunde des Abendessens, ein freundliches Seebad, Boumerdès, meine Stadt, meine Zuflucht, in ein riesiges Trümmerfeld verwandelt hat. Das ist die Poesie des Lebens, roh, blutig, unbegreiflich, endgültig.
[Übersetzt von Claudia Kalscheuer]

Olga Schamborant
Scheinbar ist die Frage »What does not make the poet tick?« leichter zu beantworten. Tick... Ein Fremdwort, das lediglich Assoziationen zu Überzügen für Möbel, zu nervösen Muskelzuckungen weckt. Und außerdem scheint es, als ob mir jemandes Hand, undeutlich, aus irgendeinem fremden Nebel, entweder einen entwerteten Straßenbahnfahrschein oder den Zahlungsabschnitt für die Überquerung der Gewässer des Styx überreicht... Geben Sie zu, wenn Ihnen dieses Wort weiter nichts bedeutet, ist es schwierig, seine freien Gedanken in die richtige Richtung zu lenken.
Also wenn ich die Frage richtig verstehe, geht es um einen gewissen Impuls, dessen Effekt Puschkin 1833 im Gedicht »Der Herbst« so ausführlich beschrieben hat. Hier die letzten Strophen:

10
Vergessen ist die Welt. Und meine Phantasie
Entzündet sich und lässt mich schwärmen süß im stillen.
Erwachend tönt in mir die holde Poesie.
Bis ganz der Lyrik Gluten meinen Sinn erfüllen.
So hebt, so klingt und sucht, gleichwie im Traume, sie
Des Dichters freien Geist nun endlich zu enthüllen.
Von alten Freunden werd aufs neue ich besucht –
Aufs neu' genieße ich der goldnen Träume Frucht.

11
Gedanken wirbeln mir im Kopf – nichts kann sie zäumen!
Entgegen ihnen läuft der Reime leichte Reih.
Rasch Feder und Papier, um nur nicht zu versäumen
Den Augenblick... und sieh: – die Verse fließen frei.
So schlummert still das Schiff in stillen Wasserräumen,
Doch das Kommando schallt, die Mannschaft eilt herbei,
Auf, ab – vom Winde schon sieht man die Segel schwellen,
Es regt sich der Koloss, bald schneidet er die Wellen.

12
Er schwimmt... Wohin die Fahrt?...

Was also erzeugt diesen Funken und verursacht den Kurzschluss? Das Wort? Ist am Anfang immer das Wort? Wo kommt es her?
Es gibt so schrille, sehr bedeutende und gleichzeitig erstaunlich leichte Momente des Seins, in denen man plötzlich ganz deutlich die VERBINDUNG des jeweiligen Augenblicks mit der Ewigkeit wahrnehmen kann. Die VERBINDUNG zwischen der in der Hand zusammengepressten und einschneidenden Scherbe des Seins und dem Ganzen.
Eben diese Wahrnehmung einer Verbindung, antreibend und blendend, gibt der Seele den Anstoß. Und auf einmal entflammt daraus das Wort, beginnt damit der Tonfall. »Rasch Feder und Papier, um nur nicht zu versäumen/Den Augenblick... und sieh: – die Verse fließen frei.«
Sicher, mag sein, dass das viel zu hoch ist. Wer erinnert sich nicht an das Achmatowsche »Aus welchem Kehricht wachsen die Gedichte«. Nun ja. Es gibt hier keinen Widerspruch.
Wenn Ihnen ein riesengroßes, bizarr zerknülltes Blatt Papier auf der Fahrspur wie ein überfahrener Hund vorkommt, kann Ihnen die enorme Erleichterung, die Sie erfahren werden, wenn Sie näher kommen, eben jene ENERGIE, jenen Impuls geben, der Sie die Welt ad hoc aus einer anderen Perspektive sehen lässt.
Plötzlich, im Bruch der Typenbauten aus Beton, erschallt gleich einem Chor von undenkbarem Schein und Farbe der frühabendliche vielschichtige Himmel. Und mit der gerade erlebten zeitweiligen Aufhebung des »Auf-das-Schlimmste-gefaßt-Seins« führt er mit einem Mal jenen Windstoß herbei, der die Segel bläht. Und es entsteht die Illusion, dass das schmutzige Papier, das sich nicht als toter Hund erwiesen hat (Kehricht!), auch keiner ist unter der Einwirkung derselben Kräfte, die die Himmelsschichten zwischen den Häusern aufgerissen haben, und dass auch Sie ebenso zufällig zwischen diesen wunderbaren Erscheinungen umhergehen.
Und wenn man den Moment nicht versäumt, wenn man innerlich nicht träge ist, kann man in dem, was geschieht, einen höheren, durchscheinenden Sinn – das Geschehene überhaupt – erfassen. Das Leben erhält augenblicklich einen Sinn. Und der Sinn des Lebens ist uns fast wichtiger als das Leben selbst, denn er verleiht Energie. Die Energie, um das Unsagbare und alles, wovon Sie gelebt und wonach Sie sich gesehnt haben, auszudrücken und um den Charakter des Moments zu reflektieren.
[Übersetzt von Viola Winokan, Alexander Puschkins Gedicht »Der Herbst« von Franz Leschnitzer, aus: Alexander Puschkin. Poetische Werke, Aufbau-Verlag Berlin, 1962]

Charis Vlavianos
Wer?
Ich trete in dem Moment ans Licht in dem ich mich selbst als Frage definiere.
Diese Frage
die sich nicht mit deiner Angst oder deinen Zweifeln deckt
und die dich ununterbrochen belagerte während du schriebst
(mag dir diese Belagerung bewusst gewesen sein oder nicht)
ist jetzt präsent,
liegt schweigend zwischen deinen Zeilen
und wartet geduldig auf den
der versuchen wird sie zu beantworten.

(Charis Vlavianos continued)
Die Frage
(die sich nunmehr in deiner Abwesenheit stellt)
hat mich zum Adressaten
und wird in Worten formuliert
die sich in der Zwischenzeit
»wie durch Zauber«
in Kunst verwandelt haben.

Die Hingabe an mich selbst die ich erkennen lasse
könnte als krankhafter Narzissmuss betrachtet werden.
Doch ich verteidige meine Ehre
indem ich sie ständig Zweifeln aussetze.
Ich erfahre Bestätigung durch eine Ermittlung
die oftmals zu meiner Schmähung führt.
Meine Geschichte ist nichts anderes als die Chronik dieser Ermittlung.

Die Frage kann also nicht beantwortet werden
denn sobald sie gestellt wird
verkehrt sie sich von selbst in eine Anklage
gegen meine Mittel und Absichten.
Mein Reich wird erbaut über meinen Ruinen.
Wenn ich eine gewisse Macht besitze
schöpfe ich sie aus genau
diesem endlosen Prozess von Verheerung und Wiederaufbau.

Jedes Gedicht das nach einem Platz in meiner Geschichte strebt
ist dazu verpflichtet sie von neuem zu erzählen
aber mit Methoden die nicht schon zuvor bekannt sind.
Wenn meine Vergangenheit verpflichtet ist es vorauszusetzen
muss meine Zukunft es bereits enthalten.
Doch wer vermag zu behaupten dass er die Zukunft kennt?
Du?
[Übersetzt von Torsten Israel]

Zhang Jie
Mir ist klar, was du sagen willst

Wenn Gott dich nicht mag,
lässt er dich wohl andren unsichtbare Farben schauen.
Wenn Gott dich mag,
lässt er dich wohl andren unsichtbare Farben schauen.

Wenn Gott dich nicht mag,
lässt er dich wohl andren unhörbare Stimmen hören.
Wenn Gott dich mag,
lässt er dich wohl andren unhörbare Stimmen hören.

Wenn Gott dich nicht mag,
schenkt er dir vielleicht ein Herz mehr.
Wenn Gott dich mag,
schenkt er dir vielleicht ein Herz mehr.

Wenn Gott dich nicht mag,
gibt er dir nur eine Wahl zu leben,
wenn Gott dich mag,
gibt er dir nur eine Wahl zu leben –
Literatur ist für mich der Weg des Lebendigen,
selbst wenn mir nichts mehr bliebe.
[Übersetzt von Wolfgang Kubin]

Fotografen
Arditti/Denoel I S. 162
Jerry **Bauer**/Suhrkamp I S. 60, 72, 138, 142
Cleo **Campert** I S. 16
Basso **Cannarsa**/Hanser I S. 178
Barbara **Cole** I S. 68
Jane **Dufaqar** I S. 237
Michael **Dyer** Associates Ltd. I S. 164
Ellen Ane **Eggen** I S. 228
Constantin **Falk** I S. 248
Marianne **Fleitmann** I S. 214
John **Foley**/Opale I S. 56
Linden J. **Fraser** I S. 80
Prof. Dr. R. **Freiburg** I S. 30
Melanie **Grande** I S. 249
Souad **Guenoun** I S. 14
Ysabel **Halpin** I S. 150
Roswitha **Hecke** I S. 234
Steven **Holt** I S. 166
Douglas **Kirkland**/Agentur Focus/Suhrkamp I S. 130
Roberto **Koch** I S. 82
Morten **Krogvold** I S. 170
Daniel de **La Fuente** I S. 224
Lihi **Lapid** I S. 110
Cato **Lein** I S. 94, 184
M. Michel **Liannet** I S. 54
Salvatore **Ligios** I S. 229
Veronica **Macias** I S. 58
Renate von **Mangoldt** I S. 24, 42, 247
Marcandrea I S. 174
Greg **Martin** I S. 96
mcgómez I S. 86
Markus **Mex** I S. 247
Louis **Monier** I S. 28
Isolde **Ohlbaum** I S. 70, 148, 194, 235, 248
Ordolis/National Book Center of Greece I S. 196
Peter **Peitsch** - www.peitschphoto.com I S. 46, 76, 88, 92, 106, 108, 114, 122, 126, 134, 204, 232, 236
Ute **Perrey** I S. 240
Berislava **Picek** I S. 168
Wladimir **Pika** I S. 12
Günter **Prust** I S. 236
Jorgos **Pupis** I S. 202
Clara **Rojas** I S. 176
Angel Lázaro **Sánches** I S. 212
J. **Sassier** I S. 132
Sabine **Sauer** I S. 128, 136
Bernd O. **Schmidt** I S. 26
Barbara **Schindler** I S. 100
Ekko von **Schwichow** I S. 50
S. B. **Skopelitis** I S. 192
Monique **Soesman** I S. 140
Nigel **Spalding** I S. 118
Nina **Subin** I S. 144
Gerhard **Steidl** I S. 98
Horst **Tappe** I S. 216
Fotostudio Horst **Urbschat** I S. 246
Monica **Villa** I S. 18
Yann **Vimard** / Souil I S. 160
V. **Vrettos** I S. 186
Jürgen **Walter** I S. 248
Bernd **Weisbrod** I S. 52
Rolf **Zöllner** I S. 112
Verlage/Stiftungen/Zeitungen etc.
Editorial **Alfaguara** I S. 62
BHX LOHMER I S. 102
Bloomsbury I S. 182
citylights I S. 48
DuMont Verlag I S. 229
Econ Verlag I S. 234
Europa Universität Viadrina Frankfurt I S. 236
Frankfurter Allgemeine Zeitung I S. 234
Frederking & Thaler Verlag I S. 40, 90
Graywolf Press I S. 152
Heinrich-Böll-Stiftung I S. 233
Verlag **Herder** I S. 236
J. W. Cappelens Forlag A/S I S. 84
Jelenkor Editors I S. 222
Limbus Press I S. 247
Pendragon Verlag I S. 116, S. 120
Prager Kulturministerium I S. 104
Editorial **Pre-Textos** I S. 20, 38
Verlag **Verso** I S. 232
privat I S. 22, 34, 36, 44, 64, 66, 72, 74, 124, 146, 158, 180, 190, 198, 208, 218, 220, 229, 234, 235, 243, 246, 247
ohne Angabe I S. 32, 154, 200, 206, 228, 237

Wir haben bei der Rechteermittlung der Fotos größtmögliche Sorgfalt walten lassen. Sollten dennoch Fehler aufgetreten sein, bitten wir dies zu entschuldigen. Die Rechteinhaber werden gebeten, sich zu melden.

Biographen
Dominic Angeloch
Walter Kempowski
Katja Baigger
Raymond Federman, Aris Fioretos, Imre Kertész, Dimosthenis Kourtovik, Martin Walser
Barbara von Bechtolsheim
Nuruddin Farah, Etgar Keret, Semezdin Mehmedinović, Nuala Ní Dhomhnaill, Tomaž Šalamun, Lee Siegel, Susan Swan
Nico Bleutge
Alessandro Baricco, Peter Schneider
Tobias Burghardt
Adolfo Castañón, Eduardo Chirinos, Juan Gustavo Cobo Borda, Dario Jaramillo Agudelo, José Manuel Prieto, Alberto Ruy Sánchez, David Toscana
Beatrice Faßbender
Clara Janés, Ryszard Krynicki, Eliot Weinberger
Rosalind Hammer
Anita Desai
Birgit Hildebrand
Nikos Panajotopoulos, Jorgos Skambardonis, Soti Triantafillou
Torsten Israel
Charis Vlavianos
Babette Jonas
Lee Hochol, Ayu Utami
Alexandra Kleihues
Bora Ćosić, Lars Gustafsson
Dimosthenis Kourtovik
Katerina Angelaki-Rooke
Wolfgang Kubin
Zhang Jie
Lim Jong-Dae
Ko Un
Torben Lohmüller
Jorge Luis Arzola, Fatou Keïta, Carlos Ruiz Zafón
Andrea Mayer
Jorgi Jatromanolakis, Menis Koumandareas, Ljudmila Petruschewskaja, Viktorija Tokarjewa
Miriam Gabriela Möllers, Hendrik Peeters, Julia Schmidt-Wellenburg
sämtliche Kinder- und Jugendbiographien
Martin Mooij
Remco Campert
Dirk Naguschewski
Mohammed Bennis, Achmat Dangor, Hanif Kureishi, Leïla Marouane, Abdelwahab Meddeb, Lewis Nkosi
Friederike Pannewick
Saadi Youssef
Ina Pfitzner
Michèle Métail
Michaela Prinzinger
Ioanna Karystiani
Christa Rothmeier
Zbyněk Hejda
Dagmar Seidel
Oscar van den Boogaard, Lars Saabye Christensen, Lorand Gaspar, Jabbar Yassin Hussin, Navid Kermani, Yôko Ogawa, Oskar Pastior, Tilman Spengler, Tatjana Tolstaja, Dieter Wellershoff, Stefan Ludmilla Wieszner, Leon de Winter
Julia Schmidt-Wellenburg
László Darvasi, Lee Siegel
Ute Stollreiter
Günter Grass, Nedim Gürsel, Witi Ihimaera, Reinhard Jirgl, Boualem Sansal, Ersi Sotiropoulos, Shashi Tharoor, O. V. Vijayan, Jeanette Winterson
Jana Thiele
Lajos Parti Nagy, Olga Schamborant, Ferenc Szijj
Anouschka Urrejola
Gennadij Ajgi, Biyi Bandele, Jonathan Franzen, Romesh Gunesekera, Mila Haugová, Paulo Lins, László Márton, José Maria Ridao

Ein ganz besonderer Dank gilt den Praktikanten des Lektorats:
Babette Jonas, Vera Milde, Kathleen Noreisch, Hendrik Peeters, Manos Perrakis, Julia Schmidt-Wellenburg, Cathrin Wirtz

Das internationale literaturfestival berlin wird finanziert aus Mitteln von

STIFTUNG PREUSSISCHE SEEHANDLUNG

Förderer

Medienpartner

Unterstützer

Folgende Botschaften und Kulturinstitute: Goethe-Institut; Ägypten: Botschaft der Arabischen Republik Ägypten - Kulturabteilung und Studienmission der Arabischen Republik Ägypten; China: Botschaft der Volksrepublik China in der Bundesrepublik Deutschland, Chinese Writers' Association; Frankreich: Französische Botschaft in Berlin, Institut Français de Berlin; Großbritannien: British Council; Haiti: Botschaft von Haiti in Berlin; Iberoamerkanisches Institut; Indien: Indische Botschaft in Berlin, Indian Council for Cultural Relations; Irland: Botschaft von Irland in Berlin, Cultural Relations Committee of Ireland; Israel: Botschaft des Staates Israel - Berlin; Japan: Japanisches Kulturinstitut Köln – The Japan Foundation; Kanada: Canada Council; Kolumbien: Botschaft der Republik Kolumbien; Korea: Botschaft der Republik Korea, Korea Literature Translation Institute; Kroatien: Botschaft der Republik Kroatien, Kulturministerium der Republik Kroatien, Stadt Zagreb; Mexiko: Botschaft von Mexiko; Neuseeland: Botschaft von Neuseeland, Creative New Zealand – Arts Council of New Zealand; Niederlande: Ambassade van het Koninkrijk der Nederlanden, Stiftung für die Produktion und Übersetzung niederländischer Literatur; Norwegen: Königlich Norwegische Botschaft, NORLA – Norwegian Literature Abroad; Polen: Polnisches Institut in Berlin; Russland: Botschaft der Russischen Föderation in der Bundesrepublik Deutschland; Schweden: Schwedische Botschaft, Schwedisches Institut; Schweiz: Pro Helvetia Schweizer Kulturstiftung; Slowakei: Slowakisches Institut, Literatur- und Informationszentrum Bratislava; Slowenien: Botschaft der Republik Slowenien; Spanien: Botschaft von Spanien, Instituto Cervantes Berlin; Tschechien: Tschechisches Zentrum Berlin; Ungarn: Collegium Hungaricum Berlin - Ungarisches Kulturinstitut, Ungarischer Schriftstellerverband; USA: Botschaft der Vereinigten Staaten von Amerika

Sowie: Deutsche Medienbeobachtungs Agentur GmbH, Berliner S-Bahn Werbung, Copy Clara, ELBA Bürosysteme GmbH & Co. KG, Schwan STABILO Schwanhäußer GmbH & Co. KG, TBWA, Museumspädagogischer Dienst Berlin, Henkel und Söhnlein Sektkellerei AG, Kia/Bouchon, Underberg AG, Wodka Gorbatschow, Weinhandlung Weinberg, ENOTECA Werner Blanck, Les Rouges du Midi, Weinert 17, Weinhandlung Hardy, ALLES KLAR Veranstaltungsservice GmbH, Das süße Leben-Pralinen & Geschenke, Berliner Flower Service,

Kooperationspartner in Berlin

Sophiensaele; Berliner Ensemble; Deutsches Theater; Schaubühne am Lehniner Platz; Maxim-Gorki-Theater; Theater unterm Dach; Goethe-Institut Berlin; Zentrum für Literaturforschung; Künstlerhaus Bethanien; Partner für Berlin, Martin Gropius Bau; Deutsche Guggenheim, Tacheles e.V., BÜCHERGILDE Buchhandlung am Wittenbergplatz; Dorotheenstädtischer und Friedrichwerderscher Kirchhof; Galerie Paula Böttcher; quicksilver Galerie für Gegenwartskunst/kulturbüro city west; Frauenjustizvollzugsanstalt Lichtenberg; Kulturhaus Mitte; Justizvollzugsanstalt Tegel; The Pegasus Hostel; The Circus Hostel; Sergej-Mawrizki-Stiftung; Berlin türk müzik konservatuari; Aziz Nesin Grundschule; Weinkeller Mahzen; Gülsah Braut- und Festmoden; Yanki.info. Kültüt; Sanat; Edebiyat ve Düsün Dergisi; Zaubertheater Igor Jedlin, Hitit Verlag Ibrahim Aslan; *EggersLandwehr; DGB Berlin-Brandenburg; Kurvenstar; Evas Arche; Café Littéraire TU des Frankreich-Zentrums Technische Universität; breitengraser room for contemporary sculpture; Haus der Sinne, Joseph-Roth-Diele; Kalkscheune; Q 205; Kulturring in Berlin e.V. / Kulturbund Treptow; Künstlerheim Luise; KunstRaum; Landesvertretung Hessen; Mori-Ôgai-Gedenkstätte; unsicht-Bar; Weißer Elefant Café Restaurant; Werkstatt der Kulturen; Zentral- und Landesbibliothek Berlin; Centrum Judaicum; Museum für Kommunikation

Kooperationspartner Kinder- und Jugendliteratur

Alphabet; Kinderbuchfonds Baobab; Berliner Märchentage; Berliner Öffentliche Bibliotheken/Kinder- und Jugendbibliotheken; Besucher-Dienste der Staatlichen Museen zu Berlin PK; Cabuwazi e.V.; carrousel Theater an der Parkaue; Druckhaus Dresden GmbH; Friedrich-Bödecker-Kreis in Brandenburg e.V.; GRIPS Theater; iBbY International Board on Books for Young People; JugendKulturService; kiekmal - Die Berliner Kinderzeitung; Le Matou; LesArt Berliner Zentrum für Kinder- und Jugendliteratur; mono - das jugendmagazin; Senatsverwaltung für Bildung, Jugend und Sport; unesco-projekt-schulen; Weinmeisterhaus; Senatsverwaltung für Bildung, Jugend und Sport

Kooperationspartner Filmprogramm
Masterschool Drehbuch Schreibstudio; Berliner Filmkunsthaus Babylon; Greek Film Centre; Yorck-Kino; Stiftung Deutsches Rundfunkarchiv Frankfurt am Main - Potsdam-Babelsberg; Humboldt-Universität Berlin, Dr. Thomas Beutelschmidt/DFG-Projekt »Programmgeschichte DDR-Fernsehen-komparativ«; Kinderkanal ARD/ZDF, Freunde der Deutschen Kinemathek e.V., ERT, Filia e.V., Institut Francais - Bureau de cinéma; dffb; ConceptAV; fxfactory; das werk; Geyer Kopierwerke; Schieffer & Schieffer; KODAK; cine plus - Media Service GmbH & Co KG

Kooperierende Hotels
Hotel Alameda; Hotel Berlin; Hotel Brandenburger Hof; Dietrich-Bonhoeffer-Haus; Hotel Gendarm; Hotel Hansablick Garni; Hecker's Hotel; Hotel Heidelberg Garni; Künstlerheim Luise; Hotel Kurfürstendamm; Hotel Morgenland; Hotel München; Hotel Park Consul; Park Plaza Hotel; relaxa Hotel Stuttgarter Hof; Hotel Seehof; Sorat Spree-Bogen; Hotel Sylter Hof; Hotel Villa Kastania; Hotel Augustinerhof; Hotel Albrechtshof; Hotel Allegra; Hotel Hackescher Markt; Apart Hotel Citadines

Kooperierende Restaurants
Brasserie am Gendarmenmarkt; Paris Bar; VAU Restaurant; Margaux; Blue Band Berlin Plaza Hotels; Restaurant Kese; Cassambalis; Gambrinus; Schwarzenraben; Theaterrestaurant Schlicht; Oxymoron; Sarah Wiener; Café-Restaurant Dressler; Hackescher Hof Restaurant; Rosmini Pastamanufaktur; TV - Turm GmbH; Südostasien; Café Einstein

Kooperationspartner in Deutschland
Ernst Klett Verlag, Heinrich Hugendubel Verlag, Merlin Verlag, Alpha Übersetzungen, Deutsches Nationaltheater Weimar; Literaturprojekt Bella triste Hildesheim; Literaturzentrum Vorpommern im Wolfgang-Koeppen-Haus Greifswald; Mitteldeutsche Sanierungs- und Entsorgungsgesellschaft mbH (MDSE) Bitterfeld; Stadtbibliothek Kassel; Stadtbibliothek Reutlingen; Evangelische Kirchengemeinde Am Falkenhagener Feld, Ev. Kirchenkreis Spandau, Kunstamt Spandau, St.-Marien-Kirche, Kleisthaus, Zitadelle Spandau

Internationale Kooperationspartner
The Guardian Hay Festival, Festivaletteratura Mantova; Bjornsonfestivalen Molde; Sarajevo Rencontres Européens du Livre – Centre André Malraux; Schweizerisches Kulturinstitut Rom; Stiftung für griechische Kultur Athen; Thomas-Bernhard-Privatstiftung Wien; Activiteitenorganisatie Elzenveld Antwerpen; Foundation Poets of all Nations, Capelle/Niederlande

Besonderen Dank an:
Günter Piening, Céline und Heiner Bastian, Lilian-Astrid Geese, Giokhiang Gornik, Omar Hamdan und Hans Hütt